ISLAM RE-EXAMINED

Christian Questions – Muslim Answers

ISLAM RE-EXAMINED

PASTOR MICHAEL MAHOMED

First Edition – No ISBN number – First print June 2002 – 500 copies – out of print

Revised Edition: ISBN 978-0-6398402-7-7: Second print June 2020 – 100 copies – out of print

Revised (2nd) Edition: ISBN 978-0-6398402-7-7: Third print October 2021 available from Amazon

COPYRIGHT RESERVED © 2020 Pastor Michael Mahomed

No part of this publication may be reproduced,

Stored in a retrieval system, transmitted in any form:

Electronic – mechanical – photocopying – recording or otherwise without **WRITTEN** permission from the author, except in accordance with the provisions of the

Copyright Act, 98 of 1978

If you find **"ANY MISTAKES"** whether factual, spelling, grammar, misprints or a misrepresentation of Islamic doctrines or things that are worded, according to you, in an offensive way in this book,

PLEASE contact me at **cfmpastormahomed1@gmail.com**

I would like, if necessary, to correct that.

Holy Bible

King James Version: New Testament - St. John 8:32

"Know the Truth and the Truth shall set you free."

Quran

Translation by Abdullah Yusuf Ali – Surah 2:256

"Let there be no compulsion in religion: Truth stands out clear from Error…"

YOUR SUPPORT

If you are blessed by this humble book and you would like more people to read it:

1. **YOU MAY PURCHASE COPIES AS GIFTS FOR YOUR FAMILIES, FRIENDS, ETC.**

2. **YOU MAY DONATE GENEROUSLY** to help the growth and spreading of the truth: Email me **cfmpastormahomed1@gmail.com** and I will get in contact with you.

3. **YOUR PRAYERS ARE WELCOMED.** God still answers prayers. O*nly believe all things are possible.*

YOUR EXPERIENCE:

If the Book is a blessing to you,

please send me an email **cfmpastormahomed1@gmail.com**,

I would like to share in your joyous experience.

FOREWORD

I am acquainted with Pastor Michael Mahomed since 1983 and on a personal level since 1987. He has shown great commitment to Biblical studies, as well the study of the Islam religion. Apart from his commitment to studies, he lives an exemplary life of a true Christian believer in his private and public life, and is a gift to the Body of Christ. Over the years, Pastor Mahomed has been inspired to research and studies the religion of Islam in conjunction with the Quran, related literature and the Christian Bible. He wrote his first unpublished book on Islam in early 2003.

As a Christian and scholar of Biblical principles, I highly recommend this book to any religious sector and leader, to understand the doctrine of Islam in relationship to the Quran. Different views are exposed and gaps being identified in the religious system. The book introduces the practical fundamental doctrines of Islam.

The information captured in the book offers invaluable insight and highlight different variables of the Islam religion. This book serves as a concise guide for religious scholars leaders and the Christian community for research and evangelistic purposes.

Any religious organisation could benefit from his knowledge and personal experience. As you read and study this book, may you find great revelatory insight and knowledge, in your walk with God.

Reverend Marlon Steyn Director: Centre of Wisdom Senior Pastor of Perfecting Centre

Revised Edition

Table of Content

Introduction 1
   What is the purpose of this book?.. 1
   References 1
   A short message to the reader.. 2
   Bible and Quran: English translations... 2
   The Muslim's challenge and my acceptance 3

Section 1: The Quran 4
   1. How the Quran was revealed to Muhammad?.. 4
      Muhammad claimed the Quran was inspired to him 4
      Muhammad could not read initial Quranic verses 5
      Muhammad could not recite initial Quranic verses 5
      Muhammad informed that Gabriel revealed the Quran to him 6
   2. Did Muslims always recite only ONE Arabic Quran?............................... 7
      Islam's most sacred books second to the Quran 7
      Muhammad recited different Arabic Quran Versions 8
      More recitations evolved after Muhammad's death 10
   3 Does the Qurans only differ in pronunciation or texts also? 12
      Leaving out what Ubayy received from Muhammad 13
      Scholars admit variant Qurans has variant texts................................... 14
      Different readings for Surah 1:4.. 14
      Different readings for Surah 2:119 15
      Different readings for Surah 2:184 16
      Different readings for Surah 3:7.. 16
      Different readings for Surah 3:146 17
      Different readings for Surah 9:49.. 17
      Different readings for Surah 21:4.. 19
      Different readings for Surah 25:61 20
      Different readings for Surah 33:6.. 20
      Different readings for Surah 38:45 21

Different readings for Surah 43:19	22
Different readings for Surah 46:15	22
Different readings for Surah 47:4	22
Different readings for Surah 92:3	22
Different readings for Surah 98:6	24

4 Is today's Quran the same as that which Muhammad recited? 25

Muslims claim: "Not a single word was changed!"	25
Missing Quran verses: Stoning of the adulterer	26
Missing Quran verses: Don't claim to be the offspring	28
Missing Quran verses: Valleys full of riches	28
Missing Quran verses: Suckling grow-up men	29
Ibn Masud's Quran version had 111 chapters	30
Muhammad said Surah Fatiha is not part of Quran	31
Surah Fatiha now added to modern-day Qurans	31
Surah 9:128-129 added to Hafs Version, omitted from Dr. R. Khalifah's Version	32

5 When was the Quran compiled into a standardized text? 33

No complete written Quran in Muhammad's day	33
Quran passages were lost during the battle of Yamama	33
Bakr collected the first unofficial text in book-form	34
Muslims in Uthman's day recited variant readings	35
Uthman's challenge to standardize the Quran	35

6 What happened to the variant Quranic texts? 37

The order for non-Uthmanic texts to be destroyed	39
The reason non-Uthmanic texts were destroyed	40
Abu Bakr's first manuscript is also destroyed	41
Some Muslims' hidden variant copies survived	42

7 When was the Uthmanic Quran canon established? 43

8 Is the Quran verses in the order Muhammad recited it? 45

9 Is today's Quran the same as Uthman's Quran? 46

Uthman's text had no vowels and diacritical points	48
These additions were added after Uthman's death	49
Time-line chart and Quran Manuscripts	50

The Sana'a Quran Manuscript 51

The Topkapi Quran Manuscript 51

The Birmingham Quran Manuscript 52

The Tubingen Quran Manuscript 53

The Samakant Kufic Quran Manuscript 54

The Parisino-Petropolitanus Quran Manuscript 54

The AlHusseini Cairo Quran Manuscript 55

The Mail Quran Manuscript 55

The Blue Quran Manuscript 56

The Earliest Complete Kufi Quran Manuscript 56

Hafs Qira'at became Egypt's standard text in 1924 56

Egypt destroyed Qurans contrary to the 1924 text 57

Egypt's Edition became the popular Qira'at and Text 57

10 Why was the Quran revealed in Arabic? 59

11 Was the Quran copied from the Holy Bible? 60

Islamic sources verify the Bible was available in 600AD in Arabic 61

Muslims admit Muhammad was influenced by Jews 61

Was Noah's flood universal or local? 62

12 Is the Quran 100% God's Words? 64

Words of God, prophets and historians in the Bible 64

Words of God in the Quran 65

Words of prophets in the Quran 65

Words of angels in the Quran 66

Words of transgressors in the Quran 66

Words of Satan in the Quran 66

Words of unknown beings in the Quran 67

13 Does the Quran have contradictions in it? 68

a) What is the size of "the garden"? 69

b) How long did Allah take to create the universe? 71

c) Which was created first: earth or stars? 75

d) Is the earth: egg-shaped or sphere or flat? 78

Dr. Rashad Khalifah's Version - the earth is egg-shaped 78

Dr. Zakir Naik says the earth is egg-shaped 78

Muslim scholar Mr. Ayoob Karim says earth is egg-shaped 78
Muslim council of Britain says earth is egg-shaped 78
Some Quran Translators have the earth as flat 79
e) Which is closer to the Islamic-egg-shaped-earth or flat earth: stars or moon? 79
f) Does the sun set in a spring of water? 80
g) Are the stars as guards against evil spirits? 82
h) Does the moon follow the sun? 82
i) The creation of man: which version is correct? 82
j) Sperm proceed from: testicles or kidney area? 85
k) How long does ejaculated sperm survive in a womb? 86
l) Bones and flesh: which develops first? 86
m) Freedom of religion or must it be by force? 87
n) Does Allah forgive all sins? 88
o) Does Allah forgive idolatry? 88
p) Who bowed first in Islam: Abraham or Muhammad? 89
q) The genealogy of Jacob 89
r) The genealogy of Jesus 90
s) Killing which prophets? 90
t) Which book was taught to Jesus Christ? 91
u) Who were the prophets among Moses' people? 91
v) The Gospel in Moses day 92
w) What did the Voice really say? 92
x) Did Allah say "dwell" or "enter" into the land? 96
y) Did Allah say "get ye down" in the dual or plural? 99
z) Two hearts or more than two hearts? 99
aa) Breathed into "him" or into "her" 100
bb) Are all beings devoutly obedient to God? 102
cc) The purpose of the angels' visitation to Lot? 103
dd) "Lot's people gave no answer but this…" 104
ee) Does Satan have offspring? 104
ff) How many creators are there? 104
gg) Did God speak directly to Pharaoh? 104
hh) Did Pharaoh drown or not? 105

ii) Is it Allah's or men's own will to disbelief?.. 106
jj) Misfortunes: is it men's doing or Allah's will?.. 106
kk) Good and evil: is it all from Allah? 107
ll) Did Noah's seed survive the flood or not?.. 107
mm) The impossible dialogue between Noah and son!.. 107
nn) Was Jonah cast on the shore or not? 108

oo) Did Allah raise warners among all nations or not? 108

pp) Do all the spoils or a fifth belong to Muhammad?... 109
qq) Normal gestation: nine or six months? 109
rr) Did the Arabs before Muhammad receive guidance? 109
ss) Did Allah forbid every animal with a claw? 110
tt) Did Allah send His Spirit or angels to Mary? 111
uu) Was Mary (mother of Jesus) an idol-worshipper? 112
vv) How can painful torture be good news? 112
ww) Can a sinner bear the sins of another sinner?.. 112
xx) What food is available in hell: pus or bitter plants?... 113
yy) Is the Quran a fully detailed book? 113
Where did Quran Translators get the name Samuel from?.. 114
Prophet Samuel is a Biblical character... 114
What is Adam's wife's name according to the Quran? 114
According to the Quran, what is Abraham's wife's name? 114
Muslim scholars admit the Quran is not detailed?.. 115
Quran not clear and not easy to understand!... 115
zz) Is Allah the only "wali"? 117

14 Does the Quran have true prophecies?... 117

Romans conquering the Persians... 117
False prediction that Qurash will never be Muslims... 119
Prediction about hell-fire is no prophecy 119
Non-Quranic predictions of Muhammad, some came true and some failed 120

15 Why were certain verses in the Quran revealed?... 121

Surah 2:144 to fulfil Muhammed's qibla preference... 121
Surah 2:158 to continue with pagan practice 122
Surah 3:161 to clear Muhammad from theft... 123

Surah 4:24 allow Muslims to have sex with slave-married-women 124
Surah 4:34 allow Muslims to beat their wives 124
Surah 4:95 to dismiss the disable from partaking in war 125
Surah 5:87 to make contractual prostitution legal 125
Surah 6:108 to stop Muslims from mocking idols 127
Surah 22:52 confirms all "Islamic Prophets" had Satanic verses 128
Surah 24:33 slaves, on conditions, may not be forced into prostitution 129
Surah 33:69 naked Moses to verify no skin defect 130
Allah in Surah 66:5 threatens Muhammad's wives with divorce 132

Section 2: Muslims Is Changing The "Meaning" Of The Quran 133

16 Jesus Christ: begotten son or only son? 133

Not different Bibles, different Translations 133
Even Islam is faced with the same challenges 135
According to the Quran, is Jesus Lord? 135

17 Is there pornographic language in the Bible? 136

Pornographic language in the Quran 137
The Quran's language regarding Jesus' conception? 137
Who breathed into Mary's private part, i.e. vagina? 139

18 Do the Gospels have light or did it once have light? 139

19 Was the Torah given to Moses? 140

20 Does Allah pray? 141

Surah 33:56 - Translation of Abdullah Yusuf Ali 142
Surah 33:56 - Translation of Drs. Hilali and Khan 143
Surah 33:56 - Translation of Dr. Rashad Khalifah 144
Surah 33:56 - Translation of Mustafa Khattab 144
Surah 33:56 Tafsir - Ibn Al Kathir 145
Translation of the word salat by Maulana M. Ali and Hammudah Abdalati 145
Muslim scholar Mohammad Hijab and Allah praying 145
More examples showing Allah praying and interceding 146
Most Muslims, unawares, pray daily to Muhammad 146
Do Muslims worship Muhammad and Muslim scholars 147

Section 3: Muslims Disregard The Quran 149

- Christians and deadly poison ... 149
- Muslims, the Quran and Ahadith ... 150

21 According to Quran: what is Halaal and Haraam food? ... 151
- Who decides what food is Halaal or Haraam? ... 151
- According to Quran, what's unlawful for Jews to eat? ... 152
- According to Quran, what is un/lawful for Muslims? ... 153
- Is food cooked in Christian homes Halaal? ... 155
- Muhammad receive no additional revelations ... 155
- According to Quran, when can Muslims eat pork? ... 156

22 Must Muslim women wear scarfs as a religious dress code? ... 156
- Umar, original messenger of the hijab ... 156
- The word "hijab" in the Quran ... 156
- Understanding the word "Jilbab" in Surah 33:59 ... 157
- Cover your breasts not your heads ... 157
- Women abused because of head-covering ... 158
- Is Purdah Islamic? ... 158

Section 4: What The Quran Say About The Bible ... 160

24 Does the Arabic Quran mention the English word "Bible"? ... 160

25 Did God reveal the Bible? ... 161

26 Can the Words of God be changed? ... 161

27 Did "TODAY'S" Bible exist in Muhammad's day? ... 161
- Quran mistranslations can be deceiving ... 161
- Quran verify today's Bible is uncorrupted ... 163

28 Did Muhammad have a preserved Biblical text in mind? ... 164

29 Does the Quran teach Biblical textual corruption? ... 167
- Muslims misquote the Quran to prove Bible corruption ... 168

30 Bible tampering before Quran came or after Quran came ... 171
- Who did the tampering? ... 172
- What part of the Biblical text was changed? ... 172

31 Is the message of the Bible universal? ... 173
- Jesus earthly ministry undoubtedly to Jews only ... 174

  Jesus charged His disciples to preach the Gospel to all 174

  Quran teach that the Gospel is a universal message 174

  According to Allah must Christians uphold the Bible? 175

  According to Quran must Muslims follow the Bible? 175

Section 5: Muhammad, A Muslim Prophet 178

32 Historical background about Muhammad 178

33 Was Ishmael the progenitor of the Arabs? 178

34 Was Muhammad illiterate? 179

35 Did Muhammad worship idols before he was a prophet? 182

36 Did Prophet Muhammad sin during his prophethood? 183

37 Did Muhammad know the future? 185

38 Did Muhammad have a perfect memory? 185

39 Did Muhammad fear people more than Allah? 185

40 Was it Muhammad's duty to explain the Quran? 188

41 Could Muhammad benefit anyone through guiding them? 189

43 Is obeying Muhammad conditional? 189

44 Did Muhammad cause the moon to split? 189

  Allah deny sending miracles to Muhammad 190

  Muhammad says Quran is given to him as miracle 191

  Muslim scholars admit Muhammad had no miracles 191

  Quran Translators and their commentaries 191

45 Was Muhammad a prophet like unto Moses? 191

  Muslims believe Deut. 18:15-18 refers to Muhammad 192

  Muslims comparing Moses to Muhammad and Jesus. 192

  Deedat's examples why Jesus isn't like Moses. 192

  Christians ask. 193

  The Word of God in all true prophets' mouths 193

  A prophet unto WHO?. 194

  A prophet from among THEIR BRETHREN 195

  God spoke to Moses FACE TO FACE 196

Muhammad unrecognized as a prophet like Moses 197
Considering Jesus as the prophet like unto Moses 197

46 Was Muhammad the promised Comforter? 198

The Muslim objection that John 14:16 is corrupted 198
Manuscript corruption before or after Muhammad? 199
Why the Comforter cannot be Muhammad 199
The Comforter that Jesus prophesied would come 200
Advantage of the Comforter sent to Jesus' disciples 201

47 Is Muhammad mentioned in the Old Testament Books? 201

48 What the "Bible says" about Muhammad? 204

Muhammad committed adultery 204
Muhammad will confess Jesus Christ is Lord 204
Muhammad was a transgressor of the law 204
49 Was Muhammad a universal or local messenger? 205
Muhammad's last duty will be of a local witness 209

50 Did Muhammad gain personal profit? 209

Muhammad got paid by Muslims for his prayers to purify them 209

51 Did Muhammad show mercy to his enemies? 211

Did Muhammad promote lies? 212

52 Wine in the Bible and Quran 214

Does Christendom winks at drunkenness? 214
Bible forbid wine as a pleasure beverage 214
Why did Paul advise Timothy to drink a little wine? 214
Allah say there is benefit in wine 215
Wine not totally forbidden in the Quran 216
Muhammad drank wine 217
Allah and Muhammad only forbid strong drinks 217
Alcoholic beverages in the Muslim heaven 218
Islam's and Christianity's responds to alcohol users 218

53 Did Muhammad believe in superstitions? 219

The dead are tortured when relatives cry 219
Drinking urine as medicine 219

Muhammad believed a black dog is a devil 220

Yawning is from Satan 220

Perform wudu because Satan sleeps in your nose.. 220

Muhammed did wudu with water wherein was excrement, period-blood, dead dogs............ 220

Muhammad said dip the house fly into your drinks.. 221

Did Muhammad allow men to kiss his naked belly? 221

Angels don't enter where there are pictures 221

Why a child looks like his father or mother?... 221

Muhammad vs silk, music, false hair, etc. 222

Muhammad said, after eating, don't wipe your hands, lick each others' hands 222

54 Was Muhammad a white man who owned black slaves?....................................222

Muhammad used slaves for sexual satisfaction.. 223

Bilal, Muhammed's black slave that became Abu Bakr' slave...................................... 224

Muhammad traded with black slaves 224

Black slaves were displayed in mosques 225

Islam and the word "kaffir" 225

Black people will go to hell and white people goes to heaven..................................... 225

Allah's worse creation was a black man... 225

56 Does Quran teach Muhammad is the last messenger? 227

How did Muhammad die? 228

Muhammad received Quran wearing woman clothes 229

Section 6: Allah 230

56 Has the word "Allah" been omitted from the Holy Bible? 230

57 What is God's name? 231

The Bible and God's Name... 232

58 Characteristics of Allah in the Quran..232

Does Allah know all things?.. 233

One Muslim will vanquish 10 unbelievers 234

Allah prescribing and altering fasting to satisfy Muslim lust 235

Allah decree adultery 236

Allah brings misfortune into existence 236

Allah deceives, misleads and sends people astray 237

Allah spreads hatred ... 239
Allah and hate speech towards non-Muslims ... 239
Allah's messenger kills the innocent ... 239
According to Quran, Allah was, not, Allah is ... 240
Allah will inherit the earth ... 241
Allah's image ... 241
Can Allah write? ... 243
Does Allah promote incest? ... 243
Allah promote lip services (lies) ... 243
Allah inspired making of images (images in heaven) ... 245

60 Is the word "Trinity" in the Bible text? ... 246
The word Trinity not found in the Arabic Quran ... 246
Quran mistranslated to reflect the word Trinity ... 246

61 Does the word "Tawhid" appear in the Quran? ... 248

62 What did Muhammad mean by: "say not three…"? ... 250

63 Does Allah have a Spirit? ... 252
Some Muslims object that Allah have a Spirit ... 253
Characteristics of Allah's Spirit in the Quran ... 255
Allah also moves from one place to another ... 257

64 Does the Quran state that Jesus is created like Adam? ... 257

Section 7: Family Life In Islam ... 263

66 Does Allah promote domestic violence? ... 263
Did Muhammed taught wives to retaliate against violent husbands? ... 263
Allah sent Gabriel to Muhammed to support wife beating ... 263
➢ Muslim scholars agree, Muhammed wanted retaliation, but Allah supported wife ... 264
Did Allah say beat (tap) them (lightly)? ... 264
Abdullah Yusuf Ali's commentary on wife beating ... 266
After Muhammad received Surah 4:34 he gave men permission to beat wives ... 266
Husbands will not be asked about wife beating ... 266
Even Muhammad, also, beat his wife ... 267
Umar also beat his wife and daughter ... 267
Muslim women in the 7TH century suffered much abuse ... 268

- Muhammad disapproved severely beating your wives before sex 268
- Did Job, famous for his patience, also beat his wife? 268
- Muhammed said beat your non-praying teen-ager 269

67 Are women allowed to attend mosques? 269

68 Were Muhammad's wives' examples to the community? 270

69 Marriage, divorce and remarriage in Islam 271
- When can a divorced couple remarry? 271
- Conditions for divorce in Islam 272
- Sodomized boy's mother is unlawful to sodomizer 272

70 Monogamy in Christianity 273

71 Polygamy (definition) 274

72 Polygamy in Islam 274
- Does the Quran allow for polygamy relationships? 274
- What was the first Quranic condition for polygyny? 275
- Limited number of women Muslims could marry 278
- What was the next Quranic condition for polygyny? 279
- Did Allah say no-man can treat his wives equal? 280
- How do Muslim Translators understand Surah 4:129? 280
- Did Muhammad treat his wives fair and equal? 281
- Why do Muslims continue to practice polygyny? 281
- Are there more women than men in the world? 282
- Muhammad said men's penis will be erected 24/7 in heaven 284

74 Islam and the status of women? 285
- One male witness equals two female witnesses 285
- Women's minds are deficient 285
- Women made from a man's rib 285
- Women are most harmful affliction 285
- Angels curse women who desert their husbands' beds 285
- Women are the majority in hell 286

75 Are Muslims who have Christian friends, true Muslims? 286
- Muslims with Christian parents as friends are wrong 287
- Muslims are instructed not to greet Christians first 287

Section 8: Islam And The Sword 288

76 How is Christianity and Islam spread: peace or violence? 288

Muslims can fight against fraudulant Muslims 290

Islam teach apostates must be killed 291

Modern-day Muslim scholars agree, kill apostates 293

Islam teach that disbelievers must be killed 294

Muslims not to live in peace with non-Muslims? 295

Muslims ordered to fight Christians until they join Islam or pay jizyah 296

Muslims admit Islam threatens with the sword 299

Section 9: Islam And The Cross 301

77 Crucifixion and resurrection of Jesus Christ: fact or fiction? 301

Christian view: crucifixion and resurrection is a fact 301

Muslim view: crucifixion and resurrection is a fiction 301

79 Were the disciples' witnesses of the crucifixion of Jesus? 303

Quran mistranslated to support *"The Substitution Theory"* 307

"The Substitution Theory" reveals the two-face hypocrisy of Sunni Muslims 309

"The Substitution Theory" portrays the Islamic Jesus as a coward 309

"The Substitution Theory" shows Allah allowed the innocent to die for another 309

"The Substitution Theory" confirms the Quranic view that Allah is a deceiver 310

"The Substitution Theory" contradicts Jesus life events 311

"The Substitution Theory" contradicts secular history 312

Quran negate that the Jews crucified and killed Jesus Christ 313

Who then crucified and killed Jesus Christ? 315

81 Does the Bible teach that Jesus was put on the cross? 316

Muslim scholars admit Jesus Christ, son of Mary, was put on the cross 317

82 Do the Quran and Bible teach that Jesus fainted on the cross? 319

83 Does the Quran and Bible teach Christ would not die? 321

Jesus' bones, while on the cross, was not broken 324

84 Does the Quran teach Jesus survived the cross? 324

Quranic verses show that Jesus Christ died 325

85 Does Surah 4:157 have historical errors? 326

- The first historical error 327
- The second historical error 327
- The third historical error 327

86 What does "…so it was made to appear to them…" mean? 328

87 Who differ in the crucifixion and death of Jesus Christ? 330

88 Did Jesus rise from the dead and ascended into heaven? 332
- Deedat's double hypocracy standards 333
- Did Jesus believe he would be alive in the tomb? 333
- Did Jesus say he would be dead for literal 72 hours? 335

90 Who moved the tombstone? 337

91 Why did the apostles think they saw a spirit? 338

92 Did Jesus teach all resurrections results into immortality? 339
- Deedat misunderstood the resurrection 339
- Lazarus resurrected, but not immortalized 339

Section 10: Salvation 341

93 Did Allah, before people were born and sinned, ordained them to burn in hell-fire? 341
- Adam, Abrahan, Moses, Jesus, Muhammad, we will all end up in hell-fire 341
- Even sinless Jesus, who is in heaven now, is promised hell-fire 342
- Men will burn in hell and some will later be rescued from hell to enter heaven 344
- Quranic Abraham worshipped idols, perhaps the reason he will be hell-fire 346
- Muhammed even believed that his own father is in hell-fire 347

94 Does Allah prefer people to sin instead of being sinless? 348
- Allah predetermined for people to sin and do evil 348
- Allah's will, is for some people to disbelieve 349

95 Do Christianity offer salvation without first going to hell? 349

96 Are Christians free to sin, since Jesus paid for their sins? 350

97 What is righteousness? 350

98 Will our good works save us from hell? 351
- Allah could not get the shahadah – testimony right 354

99 What is the original sin? 354

Did Satan really disobey Allah or was Allah unjust against Satan? 354

Adam was the first to disobey Allah and caused his offspring to fall into sin 356

Bibliography 361

Recommended Webpages 376

Introduction

What is the purpose of this book?

At first I wanted to present a booklet that would address the alleged claims of deceased Muslim Apologist and Founder of the Islamic Propagation Centre International (IPCI), Mr. Ahmad Deedat [South Africa - Durban] that the Bible is not the pure unadulterated Word of God. Instead of adopting a defense approach, I decided to ask Muslims the same questions that they have been asking Christians for centuries, hopefully, Muslims will see that their double standards towards the Bible is bias, since their book, the Quran, are faced with similar or greater challenges and that it [the Quran], according to Muslim criteria set against the Bible, fails to be considered as the pure unadulterated Word of God.

Of course, since the Holy Bible and Quran presents conflicting messages, both can't be the Word of God, one of the two books is false and ONLY one book can be considered to be the True Word of God or both books can be false scripture. If the Bible cannot be regarded as the unchanged and incorruptible Word of God, because of certain reasons, then the Quran, if guilty of the same reasons, must be rejected, just like the Bible, as the unchanged and incorruptible Word of God. This Book outlines the difficulties in the Muslim belief that the Quran is the Word of God and that Islam is God's True religion. I studied Islam for about 30 years and done adequate research in order to produce this book. I do not claim to be an authoritative figure on the subject of *"Islam"*, but feel that my findings need close and honest attention.

Finally, this book is a Revised (2nd) Edition and part of my third print in 2021.

References

All information (answers) will be directly quoted from ISLAMIC SOURCES (books, magazines, pamphlets, web-sites, debate, etc.). ***Hence, before a Muslim addresses his responds to me, where he/she disagrees with the answers quoted from the*** *referenced sources and provided in this book, I suggest you FIRST take it up with the authors (publishers) of the referenced sources.*

You are welcome to email me, if you disagree with the Islamic sources, but please note that I am not responsible for the existence of those sources.

A BIBLIOGRAPHY will be provided at the back of this book and recommended website-pages on future reading of Islamic literature.

I WILL BE QUOTING FROM:

- SOURCES THAT USES ROUND (...) INTERPOLATION BRACKETS.
- INTERPOLATIONS IN SQUARE [...] BRACKETS IS MY OWN EMPHASIS.
- ALL OTHER EMPHASIS IS MINE.

A short message to the reader

Both Christians and Muslims are encouraged to read this book and to follow up on all provided references. This is important to be able to honestly evaluate the contents within this book or to make sound criticism to this book. This book is for those who appreciate researching the truth, it is not meant for emotional people who ignore the facts.

Bible and Quran: English translations

Bible quotations are taken from the King James Version [KJV], unless otherwise indicated. All Quranic translations were taken from Muslim scholars' work, unless otherwise indicated.

- Quran Translation and Commentary by Abudullah Yusuf Ali: First Edith
- Quran Translation and Commentary by Abudullah Yusuf Ali: Revised & Edited Version
- Quran Translation and Commentary by Abudullah Yusuf Ali: With Roman Transliteration

- The Noble Quran and Commentary by Drs. Khan and Hilali
- Authorized English Version and Commentary by Dr. Rashad Khalifah
- Message of the Quran and Commentary by Dr. Muhammad Asad
- The Holy Qur'an and Commentary by Maulana Muhammad Ali
- Meaning of the Glorious Quran & Footnotes by M. Pickthall
- The Koran and Commentary by NJ Dawood
- Quran Translation by Professor Arthur J Arberry
- Quran Translation by Shakir
- Saheeh International Quran, English meanings revised
- Die Heilge Quran vertaal in Afrikaans deur Imam MA Baker

The Muslim's challenge and my acceptance

Mr. Ahmad Deedat: AL-Quran - The Miracle of Miracles. Page 11 "The Book? Yes, the "BOOK" [Quran] itself, carries its own evidence proving its Divine Authorship. **STUDY THE BOOK FROM ANY ANGLE. SCRUTINIZE IT**. Why not take up the Author's challenge if your doubts are genuine?"

I accepted the above challenge from Deedat and studied the book, Al-Quran, from all possible angles. I scrutinized it as fair and honest as possible and I presented my unbiased findings herein, reflecting various verifiable evidences of inconsistencies concerning the Quranic message.

SECTION 1

THE QURAN

1. How the Quran was revealed to Muhammad?

It needs to be explained that when Christians claim that the Holy Bible is God's Word, we are not saying that every word in the Bible was spoken by God. We do **NOT** claim that God dictated to the Bible-scribes word-for-word what they must write, we believe God inspired specific men to record specific religious history, doctrines, the actions and sayings (good or bad) of certain people, angels, etc. into the pages of the Holy Bible.

<u>*2 Timothy 3:16*</u> "All scripture is given *by inspiration* of God…"

<u>*2 Peter 1:21*</u> "Holy men of God spoke as they were *moved by the Holy Ghost*."

Muhammad claimed the Quran was inspired to him

<u>*Quran Translation by Abdullah Yusuf Ali – Surah 6:19*</u> "This Quran hath been ***revealed to me by inspiration***."

Like the Bible, the whole Quran also did **NOT** come all at once in a complete compiled physical book from heaven to Muhammad. The Quran, according to Islam, was revealed to Muhammad over a period of 23 years, i.e. 610-632AD. As Muhammad received the Quran, he recited it to his followers.

The Quran, *ACCORDING TO ISLAM*, was **ORALLY** transmitted from Allah to the Archangel Gabriel to Muhammad to Muslims. The first official and universally accepted Quranic **TEXT** was produced about 20 years after Muhammad's death, in 652AD by the Third Caliph, Uthman. Since Muhammad died in 632AD, it is evident that Muhammed didn't approve the 652AD Uthmanic Quran Version as accurate.

Muhammad could not read initial Quranic verses

The first Quranic chapter and verses, according to Islam, received by Muhammad is Surah 96:1-18 (see the table presented in Q8).

<u>Tafsir - Ibn Al Kathir S. 96:1-5</u> "The **BEGINNING** of the Prophethood of Muhammad and the **FIRST** of the Qur'an revealed: Imam Ahmad recorded that *AISHAH SAID*: ...The Messenger of Allah ... used to go to the cave of Hira and devote himself to worship there... The angel came to him... and said: Read! - The Messenger of Allah said: I am not one who reads ... he [Muhammad] said: So the angel seized me and pressed me ... Then he released me and said: Read! So I replied: I am not one who reads. So, he [the angel] pressed me a second time... [and] released me and said: Read in the Name of your Lord who has created." https://quranx.com/Tafsir/Kathir/96.1 [Last accessed 24 April 2021]

Please note carefully, the above event, according to Islamic sources, have Aisha reporting the events what she was told. Aisha was not born at the time Muhammad at age 40 went into the cave. Muhammad was married to Khadijah for about 10 years and after her death, he at age 50 got married to Aisha. Did Allah and Gabriel (who was seemingly send to Muhammad) not know that Muhammad can't read? The context **seems to assume** that the angel showed Muhammad a text to read from and thereafter told him to read from it or why would the angel say read? Muhammad who seemingly can't read, was seemingly squeezed a few times by the angel who told him thrice to read, yet still Muhammad could seemingly still not read. I find it strange that **Allah and Gabriel was unaware** Muhammad could not read.

Muhammad could not recite initial Quranic verses

Some Muslims claim that the Arabic word "**iqra**" here means to "**recite – repeat from memory**". That, however, in the Hira Cave context, also doesn't make any sense at all. Since this is the first time that Muhammad is going to receive Quranic revelation, how could Gabriel request Muhammed to recite the Quran or part of it, if Muhammad did not previously receive the Quran?

If Gabriel meant to say recite, instead of read (from a text), did Allah and Gabriel forgot this was Muhammad's first Quranic revelation to be received and then to be recited later by him? Here we see that the beginning of Islam started-out with discrepencies in Muhammad's supposed angelic visitation.

Muhammad informed that Gabriel revealed the Quran to him

Notice how **the reporters have Aisha say that an angel appeared to Muhammad** in the cave (see above quote from Tafsir Ibn Kathir S. 96:1). When Muhammad reported this event to his first wife, Khadijah (about 10 years before Aisha came on the scene) Muhammad made no mention of an angel that came to him. In fact, Muhammad was in fear, because of the Cave experience and his wife, Khadijah, comforted him that nothing bad will happen to him. Let's continue to read where we ended.

Tafsir - Ibn Al Kathir S. 96:1-5 "(I fear that something may happen to me.) Khadijah replied: Never! By Allah, Allah will never disgrace you… Khadijah then accompanied him to her cousin Waraqah bin Nawfal … Waraqah asked [Muhammad]: What have you seen? Allah's Messenger described what he saw. Waraqah said: This is *An-Namus* whom Allah had sent to Musa."

How did Khadijah know about Allah when Muhammad returned from the Cave of Hira to her? Did she have the Christian God in mind? Remember, the Arabs were stone worshippers before the advent of Muhammad's Islamic prophethood. According to Quran, the Arabs had no guidance before Muhammed.

Quran Translation by Abdullah Yusuf Ali: Page 1752 Commentary 6183 "**The holy prophet was born in the midst of the idolatry and polytheism of Mecca**, in a family, which was the custodian of false worship. He wandered in quest of unity and found it by the guidance of God…"

The Arabs had **NO** guidance (Surah 36:06), even Muhammad, according to the Quran (Surah 93:7) had no inspired revelatory guidance before the Hira Cave experience. In fact, Muhammad did not even know that the recitation of Surah 96:1-18 were to be part of a Book to be called *"Quran"*. Not Muhammad, nor Khadijah, nor Waraqah, knew that this was to be the Quran being piece-meal revealed to Muhammad.

In the Quran, after about 10 years of supposed prophethood, Surah 2:97 was seemingly revealed to Muhammad in Medina, wherein we read that the Quran is revealed through Gabriel to Muhammad's heart.

2. Did Muslims always recite only ONE Arabic Quran?

Every Muslim whom I ever asked this question, instantly, like a tape-recorder or in similar words, replied: "There always was and is only ONE ARABIC VERSION of the Holy Quran *anywhere in the world*"

Dr. Dawid Wood: Preservation Debate – Snipped by Sheik Yasir Qadi: Time line 1:12 – 1:46 "There is only ONE Quran, no variant versions of the Quran, ONLY ONE STANDARD copy of the Quran across the Muslim World." https://www.youtube.com/watch?v=Wa8ulxgJ8Rc [Last accessed 24 April 2021]

Of course, I expect no different answer from a Muslim, whose response is based on an emotional defense of the Quran. However, when we look at Islamic literature available to us, we notice that the said Muslim response is hopelessly false and misleading. Such an emotional response is based on two factors: [i] These Muslims are ignorant of their most authentic sources, which confirms differently, e.g. **Muslims across the world do recite more than one Arabic Quran Version** or [ii] these Muslims are aware of their documented Islamic history about the different Arabic Versions of the Quran, but chooses to suppress their historical information about the different Arabic Quran Versions. [see heading below: Muhammed recited different Arabic Quran Versions]

Islam's most sacred books second to the Quran

An Introduction to Islam Page 41 "**Rigorously authenticated (Sahih). That is, it is a hadith which has very strong evidence for its authenticity.** Well-authenticated (Hasan): While not as strong as a Sahih hadith, this grade has enough evidence to convince one of its authenticities. *Weak (Da'if): This is a hadith that is weakly supported by the evidence, but this does not mean it is necessarily false.* Fabricated (Mawdu'): This is an alleged hadith whose purport contradicts clear teachings of Islam, or has someone who is a known liar in its chain of transmission."

Sahih Bukhari: Vol. 1, Page xvi, Introduction "It has been unanimously agreed that *Imam Bukhari's work is the most authentic of all the other books in Hadith literature put together.* **The authenticity of Al-Bukhari's work is such that the religious learned scholars of Islam said concerning him: The most authentic book, after the Book of Allah (e.g. The Quran) is Sahih-Al-Bukhari.**"

The Muslim Digest: Vol. 29 Nos. 3&4 Oct./Nov. 1978 Page 37 "Bukhari's celebrated Sahih – the most authentic of all the books after the Quran."

Dr. Maurice Bucaille: The Bible, The Quran & Science – Page 243 "Al Bukhari's work is generally regarded as the most authentic after the Quran…"

IA Ibrahim: A Brief illustrated guide to understanding Islam – Page 49 "Is there any **sacred source** other than the Quran? *Yes!* The Sunnah (what the Prophet Muhammad said, did or approved) is the second source in Islam. The Sunnah is comprised of Hadeeths, which are reliable transmitted reports by the Prophet Muhammad's companions of what he said, did or approved. Belief in Sunnah is a basic Islamic belief."

Let's turn to Bukhari to see if the Muslims' response, that **only** one Arabic Quran exist, holds any water.

Muhammad recited different Arabic Quran Versions

Sahih Bukhari Vol. 6, Page 482, Hadith 514 "Narrated Umar bin Al-Khattab: I heard Hisham bin Hakim reciting Surat Al-Furqan *DURING THE LIFETIME OF ALLAH'S APOSTLE.* I listen to his recitation and noticed he recited it in *SEVERAL DIFFERENT WAYS,* which Allah's Apostle had not taught me… When he completed his prayer, I said: Who taught you this Surat, which I heard you reciting? He replied: Allah's Apostle taught it to me. I said: You lied, for *ALLAH'S APOSTLE HAS TAUGHT IT TO ME IN A*

DIFFERENT WAY TO YOURS. So I dragged him to Allah's Apostle and said: I heard this person reciting Surat Al-Furqan in a way, which you haven't taught me… Allah's Apostle said: Release him (Umar), recite O Hisham! Then he recited in the same way I heard him reciting. *Then Allah's apostle said it was revealed in this way* and added, recite, O Umar, I recited it as he [Muhammad] has taught me. Allah's apostle said: It was [also] revealed in this way. **THIS QURAN HAS BEEN REVEALED TO BE RECITED IN SEVEN DIFFERENT WAYS**…"

According to Islam, in Sahih Bukhari the most authentic recording after the Quran, Allah revealed to Muhammad, not ONE, but SEVEN different ways of reciting the Quran and Muhammad taught those SEVEN DIFFERENT WAYS to his contemporaries. Muslims are faced with the unbearable challenge of whether to uphold their emotional response that only *One Arabic Version of the Quran recitation ever existed* or whether Bukhari's collection is genuine and authentic and if yes, *more* than one Arabic Quran recitation were in existence in the lifetime of Muhammad. If Muslims accept their opinion and rejects Bukhari's literature, then Islam's history falls flat to the ground, as the Muslim's religious actions (dress code, manner of prayers, burials, beard-growing, etc.) are based on Muhammad's Sunnah, found in the Book of Bukhari, according to Islam, the second sacred and most authentic book after the Quran.

In the light of what YOU as a Muslim just read, before you continue to read on, ask yourself this life-changing question: Do you believe your elders' opinions that only "ONE" Arabic Quran Version always existed or do you believe Islam's most authentic history that confirms that the Quran was revealed in "SEVEN DIFFERENT" Arabic recitations? You are welcome to email me your honest and well documented researched responds after you read this book.

When Muhammad died, the Quran was still recited in its seven different recitations. Allah and Muhammad, NOWHERE, ever instructed any Muslim to stop reciting any of the "seemingly" seven different REVEALED RECITATIONS of the Quran. Muslims took it upon themselves to stop reciting these recitations. Why? These seven recitations soon evolved into more variant ways to be recited by Muslims.

More recitations evolved after Muhammad's death

Muslims are facing the embarrassment of having, not only seven different Arabic Quran Versions, but according to Muslim Scholars, there are at least fourteen different Arabic Quran Transmitted Versions.

Cyril Glassé, The Concise Encyclopedia of Islam: Page 324 "There resulted from this **SEVEN BASIC TEXTS, EACH HAVING TWO TRANSMITTED VERSIONS WITH MINOR VARIATIONS**..." *(Taken from: The Different Arabic Versions of the Quran by Samuel Green)*

Islamic Awareness: Versions of the Quran? "The Quran continued to be read according to the 7 ahruf **until midway through Caliph Uthman's rule**... *Abu Ameenah Bilal Philips, Tafseer Soorah Al-Hujuraat, 1990, Tawheed Publications, Riyadh, pages 28-29*... The seven sets of readings accepted by Ibn-Mujahid represent the systems prevailing in different districts. There was one each from Medina, Mecca, Damascus and Basra and three from Kufa. For each set of readings (Qira'at) there was **two slightly different versions.** *"WM Watt & R Bell, Intro. to the Quran, 1994, Edinburgh at University Press P. 49."*

District	Reader	First Rawi	Second Rawi
Medina	Nafi	Warsh	Qalun
Mecca	Ibn Kathir	Al-Bazzi	Qunbul
Damascus	Ibn Amir	Hisham	Ibn Dhakwan
Basra	Abu Amr	Ad-Duri	Al-Susi
Kufa	Asim	Hafs	Shuba
Kufa	Hamza	Khalaf	Khallad
Kufa	Al-Kisa'i	Ad-Duri	Abul Harith

Public debate: 27 September 2014 "Which is the Word of God: Bible or Quran?" Christian speaker, Dr. Jay Smith and Muslim speaker, Dr. Shabir Ally [quoting Ally:] "Now, I am not speaking about the other readings. MUSLIMS DO HOLD, AS JAY HAS POINTED OUT, THAT THERE ARE SEVEN AUTHENTIC READINGS. **I HOLD TO THE**

IDEA THERE ARE TEN AND THERE ARE ANOTHER FOUR THAT ARE NOT SO AUTHENTIC** that can be used in commentary." [https://www.youtube.com/watch?v=fWHV9VnOJtc Time line 00:59:14 – 00:59:40 - Last accessed 24 April 2021]

Youtube presentation by Dr. Jay Smith: Shabir Ally finally admits the Quran has indeed changed! [Ally admits that...] "Most Muslims read the Quran in a text that is referred too as the Egyptian Edition of 1924 [Hafs], but **THIS IS NOT THE ONLY TEXT OF THE QURAN THAT IS READ THROUGHOUT THE WORLD. IN NORTH-AFRICA, THERE IS A SLIGHTLY DIFFERENT TEXT** that is based on a slightly different reading, MOSTLY corresponding to what we read in the rest of the world, but with some slight variations that do not effect anything that Muslims believe and do not have any major impact on Muslim practices. **IN SOME PARTS OF AFRICA THERE IS ANOTHER READING OF THE QURAN WITH A MATCH MANUSCRIPT** that is prevalent with some slight variations…" [https://www.youtube.com/watch?v=F6agQmo5OTc Time line 00:03:37 – 00:04:34 - Last accessed 24 April 2021].

Youtube presentation by Dr. Jay Smit: Why dates of the different Qurans are so damaging? [Dr. Shabir Ally admits…] "Amongst the **VARIOUS RECITATIONS** and even in the manuscripts that we are finding, certainly there are variations and let's stay with the RECITATIONS for a moment. So we have **TEN DIFFERENT RECITATIONS, WHICH ARE APPROVED BY MUSLIM SCHOLARS.** They say these are fine to be recited in your prayers and are valid. There are further four which could be used as tafsir, but you wouldn't recite them in your prayers." https://www.youtube.com/watch?v=X4vC4rDl8UU [Time line 00:01:54 – 00:02:50 - Last accessed 24 April 2021]

Youtube presentation by Dr. Jay Smit: Why dates of the different Qurans are so damaging? [Muslim scholar, Dr. Yasir Qadhi agrees with Dr. Shabir Ally that…] "The other recitations **AND THERE ARE TEN RECITATIONS**…" [https://www.youtube.com/watch?v=X4vC4rDl8UU Time line 00:04:29 – 00:04:33 Last accessed 24 April 2021]

Dr. Dawid Wood: Preservation Debate – Snipped by Sheik Yasir Qadi: [Yasir admitted that] "If you were to compare **TWO PRINTED QURANS**, you will see **DIFFERENCES IN THEM**."

https://www.youtube.com/watch?v=Wa8ulxgJ8Rc Time line 3:42 – 6:23 - Last accessed 24 April 2021

See Q3, heading: "Different readings for Surah 1:4" where Muslim Attorney, Yusuf Ismail, admitted that there are **DIFFERENT QURAN READINGS IN SOUTH AFRICA AND MOROCCO**.

CONCLUSION: Islam's most authentic historical records substantiate the fact that the Quran was revealed, not in one Arabic recitation, as uninformed Muslims wants us to believe, but the Quran were originally recited by Muhammad in 7 different Arabic versions. From each of the 7 different seemingly revealed versions, developed a further 2 different transmitted versions, leaving the embarrassed Muslims, not with 7 versions, but with 14 differently recited Quran versions. Dr. Ally may only accept 10 versions and claim the other four are doubtful, but he can never again boast that only one Arabic Quran Version always existed in the world. **No honest Muslim scholar or Islamic-layperson today, after reading the above, can ever again, with a clear conscience, boast that the Quran in their possession, is the one and only Arabic Quran Version that ever existed**. In order to do so, Muslims will have to deny their authentic Islamic literature published and sold at Muslim bookstores for a lovely profit.

3 Does the Qurans only differ in pronunciation or texts also?

Public Debate 1986: "Is the Bible the Word of God?" Christian Speaker, Evangelist Jimmy Swaggart and Muslim Speaker, Sheik Ahmad Deedat: Q&A "[Question to Deedat:] Does the glorious Quran exist in its original and pure form and was the originals in fact burned? [Deedat's response] … THE ARABIC SCRIPTURE WERE WRITTEN originally without vowel points … Vowels were added to make the proper pronunciations … *SO THE VARIANT READINGS, WAS OF THE VARIANT PRONUNCIATIONS*. The revelation was given in the dialect of the Quraysh, the family of the tribe of Muhammad and that pronunciation was preserved..." https://www.youtube.com/watch?v=genex9BqlmI Time line 01:32:10 – 01:36:14 - Last accessed 24 April 2021

Emotional Muslims, like Deedat, tries to tell us that the original Quran is preserved and variant Quran readings (that came into existence as a result of pronunciation difficulties) were destroy, but as we now know (see the heading: Muhammed recited different Arabic Quran Versions) the Quran was seemingly **REVEALED** in seven different ways. Angel Gabriel seemingly gave the Quran to Muhammad in **7 VARIANT RECITATIONS**, not as mispronunciations, but as text variants, as we will see below. The recitation of the different Arabic Quran Versions has nothing to do with non-Arabs mispronouncing Arabic words. The problem here was that of **DIFFERENT TEXT BECAUSE OF DIFFERENT REVEALED RECITATIONS**, proving that Muhammad and his companions didn't recite only one universal Arabic Quran Version, as deceptive Muslims, like Deedat, wants us to believe, but they recited 7 different Arabic Quran Versions.

Leaving out what Ubayy received from Muhammad

<u>Sahih Bukhari, Vol. 6, Page 489, Hadith 527</u> "Narrated Ibn Abbas: Umar said **UBAYY WAS THE BEST OF US IN THE RECITATION (OF THE QURAN) - YET WE LEAVE SOME OF WHAT HE RECITES. UBAYY SAYS, I HAVE TAKEN IT FROM THE MOUTH OF ALLAH'S APOSTLE (SAW) AND WILL NOT LEAVE IT FOR ANYTHING WHATEVER.**"

Umar clearly acknowledged that Ubayy was the best in reciting the Quran and yet Umar and some Muslims refused to follow the Quranic recitation by Ubayy. They said: *"...yet we leave **some** of what he recites..."* They NEVER said: *"...we pronounce it differently from him..."* They disregarded some verses and wordings as recited by Ubayy, which he learnt directly from Muhammad, not what he pronounced differently. Ubayy continued with his version as authentic, since he got it **DIRECTLY** from Muhammad. [also see below heading: Different readings for Surah 33:6 where another variant is listed].

Scholars admit variant Qurans has variant texts

Youtube presentation by Dr. Jay Smit: Why dates of the different Qurans are so damaging? [Dr. Yasir Qadhi confirms…] "The **number of verses in the Quran depends upon the recitation**, the qira'at that you are reciting. The most common qira'at that people are reciting that are living in English speaking countries is **Hafs. It has 6236 verses** that we recite. The other recitations, they have different number of verses, **i.e. 6210, a difference of 20 or 30 verses**…"

https://www.youtube.com/watch?v=X4vC4rDI8UU Time line 03:55 – 04:44 - Last accessed 24 April 2021

THE HAFS QIRA'AT QURAN VERSION IS THE 1924 EGYPTIAN CAIROO EDITION, THE PREDOMINANTLY ARABIC VERSION USED IN SOUTH AFRICA, FROM WHICH ABDULLAH YUSUF ALI TRANSLATED HIS ENGLISH VERSION OF THE QURAN. NOTICE, NOT MISPRONUNCIATIONS OF WORDS, BUT A DIFFERENCE OF ABOUT 30 VERSES.

Different readings for Surah 1:4

Contemporary Muslim scholar, Attorney Mr. Yusuf Ismail from Durban [South Africa - IPCI], in a debate with Christian speaker, Dr. James White, tried to explain that the DIFFERENT RECITATIONS OF THE QURAN does not contradict each other and simultaneously admitted that **textual variations of two Quran recitations exists in Surah1:4**.

Notice how Yusuf verified two facts Muslims generally *WON'T* admit:

(i) Muslims *don't* recite the same one and only Arabic Quran Version,

(ii) Variant readings are *not* based on mispronunciations only, but textual variants.

Public debate: 01 October 2013 "Has the Quran been accurately transmitted?" Christian speaker, Dr. James White and Muslim speaker, Attorney Yusuf Ismail: [Quoting Yusuf in his explanation about Quranic variants] … **SO FOR EXAMPLE,**

WHERE YOU FIND EVEN POSSIBLE VARIATIONS IN RECITATIONS, that in Islamic Law, terminology would be described as [Arabic words] ... *the seven authentic readings in terms of which you can recite the Quran* ... for example today, in the HAFS [Egyptian 1924 Standard Version predominantly used in SA] if I would recite ... [unquote: Arabic words - **maaliki – Master** of the day of judgment] and *IF I WERE TO GO TO MOROCCO THEY WOULD RECITE IT LIKE* [Unquote... WARSH version - Arabic words – **mâlikaa – King** of the day of judgment]." One reading is "master" and the other is "king". https://youtu.be/RNB7GHmk7uE Time line 00:06:15 – 00:07:00 Last accessed 24 April 2021

Clearly, every time Yususf Ismail tells his uninformed audience that there is only ONE Arabic Quran recitation in the world, he is blatantly lying to them and deceiving them.

Youtube presentation by Dr. Jay Smith: Dr. Shabir Ally finally admits the Quran has indeed changed! [Jay presents...] "Hafs Quran reads: "The **maaliki (only owner)** of the day of recompense." Warsh Quran reads: "The **malikaa (king)** of the day of recompense."

[https://www.youtube.com/watch?v=F6agQmo5OTc Time line 08:17 – 09:00 Last accessed 24 April 2021

Different readings for Surah 2:119

Apostate Prophet [Ex-Muslim] with Abdullah Gondal [Ex-Muslim]: The proof of the corruption of the Quran – Dated 28 June 2020 [Presentation by Gondal] "Hafs Quran reads: "Verily We have sent thee in truth as a bearer of glad tidings and a warner: **But of thee no question shall be asked [tusal]** of the Companions of the Blazing Fire." Warsh reads: "... **and do not ask [tasal]** of the Companions of the Blazing Fire." [https://www.youtube.com/watch?v=aYwwX5lc_ww Time line 00:31:19 Last accessed 24 April 2021]

Hafs states that Muhammad shall not be questioned, but Warsh states that Muhammad must not do the questioning.

Different readings for Surah 2:184

Apostate Prophet [Ex-Muslim] with Abdullah Gondal [Ex-Muslim]: The proof of the corruption of the Quran – Dated 28 June 2020 [Presentation by Gondal] "Hafs Quran reads: "(Fasting) for a fixed number of days; but if any of you is ill, or on a journey, the prescribed number (should be made up) from days later. For those who can do it (with hardship), is a ransom, the feeding of **one that is indigent [a poor man – taamu miskeen]** …" Warsh Quran reads: "…feeding **poor people [taami masaakeen]** …" Must you feed one poor person or poor people? https://www.youtube.com/watch?v=aYwwX5lc_ww Time line 00:15:40 Last accessed 24 April 2021

> Different readings for Surah 2:238

Quran Translation by Abdullah Yusuf Ali: "Guard strictly your (habit of) prayers, especially the Middle Prayer and stand before Allah in a devout (frame of mind)."

The Quran that Muhammad recited … **Sahih Muslim:** "Abu Yunus, the freed slave of 'A'isha said: 'A'isha ordered me to transcribe a copy of the Qur'an for her and said: When you reach this verse: "Guard the prayers and the middle prayer" (ii. 238), inform me; so when I reached it, I informed her and she gave me dictation (like this): Guard the prayers and the middle prayer **AND THE AFTERNOON PRAYER** and stand up truly obedient to Allah. 'A'ISHA SAID: THIS IS HOW I HAVE HEARD FROM THE MESSENGER OF ALLAH (ﷺ) [https://quranx.com/Hadith/Muslim/USC-MSA/Book-4/Hadith-1316 Last accessed 24 April 2021]

Different readings for Surah 3:7

Quran Translation by Abdullah Yusuf Ali: "…But no one knows its hidden meaning **EXCEPT GOD.** And those who are firmly grounded in knowledge say…"

In the above version, **ONLY** God knows the hidden meanings, but there is another recitation wherein **BOTH** God and certain people (those who are firmly grounded in knowledge) knows the hidden knowledge. Both readings can't be right and that's why some Muslims vehemently rejects the second reading as we will see below.

Quran Translation by Abdullah Yusuf Ali: Page 123 – Commentary 348 "One reading, **REJECTED** by the majority of Commentators, but accepted by Mujahid and others, would not make a break at the point here marked *Waqfa Lazim*, but would run the two sentences together. In that case the construction would run: *"No one knows its hidden meanings* **EXCEPT GOD AND THOSE** *who are firm in knowledge. They say…"*

Authorized English Version of the Quran – Surah 3:7 "…None knows the true meaning thereof **EXCEPT GOD AND THOSE** well founded in knowledge. They say…"

Here Ali's and Khalifah's versions emphasize the fact that at least two variants of Surah 3:7 are in existence; recited by different schools of Muslims. Therefore, the different Quranic recitations are not based on different dialects or non-Arabian Muslims mispronouncing the original Arabic Quran, but it is based on variant content acceptable to Muslims.

Different readings for Surah 3:146

Youtube presentation by Dr. Jay Smith: Shabir Ally finally admits the Quran has indeed changed! [Jay presents…] "Hafs Quran reads: "And how many *a prophet* **qaatala (fought)**, with whom were many worshippers of the Lord." Warsh Quran reads: "And how many *prophets* **qutila (were killed),** with whom were many worshippers of the Lord." Did the prophets *also* fight or were they *just* killed? [https://www.youtube.com/watch?v=F6agQmo5OTc Time line 00:09:30 – 00:09:40

Last accessed 24 April 2021.

Also see below heading: Different readings for Surah 47:4.

Different readings for Surah 9:49

Muhammad was preparing to attack in Jihad the Romans. In doing so, to entice a Muslim Chief to be part of the fighting, Muhammad told this man that the Romans have beautiful women that will become their booty. The man responded to Muhammad that Muhammad must not tempt him with these beautiful women, as he, this man, have a weakness for beautiful women, however, the man asked Muhammad for exemption from this Jihad and then this verse was revealed to address this man.

Tafsir - Ibn Al Kathir S. 9:49 "The Messenger of Allah said to **AL-JADD BIN QAYS** from Bani Salimah: Would you like to fight the yellow ones (Romans) this year. **HE** said: O Allah's Messenger! Give **ME** permission (to remain behind) and do not cause Fitnah for **ME**. By Allah! **MY** people know that there is not a man, who, is fonder of women than **I**. **I** fear that if **I** see the women of the yellow ones, **I** would not be patient. The Messenger of Allah turned away from **HIM** and said: I give you permission…"

[https://quranx.com/Tafsir/Kathir/9.49 Last accessed 24 April 2021]

Quran Translation by Shakir "Among them there is **HE** who says: allow **ME** and do not try **ME**…"

The verse is clear – a man "**HE**" said unto Muhammad "Allow **ME** and do not try **ME**. But then we see that in the second part of the verse, Allah made a grammatical error by responding as if it is not one man, but more than one man who have fallen by asking Muhammad to stay at home while others will go to war. Notice Allah's responds…

Quran Translation by Shakir "Among them there is he who says: allow me and do not try me. Surely into trial have **THEY** already tumbled down, and most surely, hell encompasses the unbelievers."

Allah was supposed to have said: "Surely into trial have **HE** already tumbled down…" to be consistent to the previous text. Ali is aware of the grammatical error and added an interpolation to make his readers think the text states that more than one man requested leave from going into Jihad against the Romans.

Quran Translation by Abdullah Yusuf Ali: "Among them is (**MANY**) a man who says: Grant me exemption and draw me not into trial. - Have they not fallen into trial already? …"

Ali added the word "many" into interpolation brackets to make the responds of Allah "they have fallen" to be consistent with "(many) a man asked" instead of only "a man" asked. Even so, Ali forgot to change the singular pronoun "me" into "us" to make the whole verse consistent. This is how Ali should have changed it: "Among them is (**MANY**) a man who says: Grant **US** exemption and draw **US** not into trial. - Have **THEY** not fallen into trial already? Indeed, Hell surrounds the Unbelievers…" The error, is therefore clearly made in the responds of Allah: "Have **THEY** not fallen into trial already…" or is "they" a scribal error made by Uthman's scribes? **In fact, muslim scholars admit that there is a variant reading that is actually using the correct singular pronoun.**

Tafsir Al-Jalalayn S. 9:49 "…He, says: Surely they have [already] fallen into temptation! By staying behind - **a variant reading for saqatū**, **THEY** have fallen' has the singular form **saqat**, '**HE** has fallen'."

[https://quranx.com/Tafsir/Jalal/9.49 Last accessed 24 April 2021]

Different readings for Surah 21:4

Apostate Prophet [Ex-Muslim] with Abdullah Gondal [Ex-Muslim]: The proof of the corruption of the Quran – Dated 28 June 2020 [Presentation by Gondal] "Hafs Quran reads: "**He said [Qaala]**: "My Lord knoweth (every) word (spoken) in the heavens and on earth: He is the One that heareth and knoweth (all things)." Warsh Quran reads: "**Say [Qul]**: …" Hafs version reflects that Allah is reporting what Muhammad said and in the Warsh version the verse reflects Allah commanding Muhammad to say something. Abdullah Yusuf Ali is well aware of the variant and that the Hafs version seems to show that the Quran contains Muhammad's words. Ali therefore mistranslated **Qaala** as "say" instead of "He said" – Ali is aware that **Qaala** must be translated as "He said" as he got it right in the same Surah in verse 52 "Iz **qaala** li-abiihi… Behold **he said** to his father…" [https://www.youtube.com/watch?v=aYwwX5lc_ww Time line 00:25:55 – Last accessed 24 April 2021]

Different readings for Surah 25:61

Christian Rob: Hijab busted for deceiving Muslims – Apostate Prophet vs Mohammed Hijab [Hijab quoting from the Khalaf Quran Version said:] "…It says in chapter 25 [vs. 61] buroojan wajaAAala feeha **surujan** wamuneer<u>an</u>… the Quran say there are many **suns**…" Unquote: Hafs Quran Version 25:61 reads: "…buroojan wajaAAala feeh<u>a</u> **sirajan** [lamp – sun] _waqamaran_ muneer<u>an</u>." [Hijab omitted the word _waqamaran_] [https://www.youtube.com/watch?v=5d-Y4JpbUwI Time line 03:35 – 05:50 Last accessed 24 April 2021]

Tafsir Al-Jalalayn S. 25:61 "…A lamp, namely, the sun and a shining moon - a variant reading for sirājan, 'sun' has the plural surujan…] [https://quranx.com/Tafsir/Jalal/25.61 Last accessed 24 April 2021]

> Different readings for Surah 28:48

Apostate Prophet [Ex-Muslim] with Abdullah Gondal [Ex-Muslim]: The proof of the corruption of the Quran – Dated 28 June 2020 [Presentation by Gondal] "Hafs Quran reads: "…They say: "**Two kinds of sorcery [sahraan]** each assisting the other… Warsh Quran reads: "…**two magicians [saahiraan]**…"

[https://www.youtube.com/watch?v=aYwwX5lc_ww Time line 00:24:16 Last accessed 24 April 2021]

Different readings for Surah 33:6

Ali informed us of at least two variant readings in relation to this verse.

Quran Translation by Abdullah Yusuf Ali: "The prophet is closer to the believers than their own selves and his wives are their mothers…"

Ali's Version is a popular translation distributed by IPCI. In his commentary to the above verse, Ali documented another variant reading of Surah 33:6, which was recited by Obay ibn Ka'b (the best Quran reader – see above heading: _Leaving out what Ubayy received from Muhammed_]

Quran Translation by Abdullah Yusuf Ali: Page 1104 – Commentary 3674: "In **SOME QIRAATS** like that of Ubai ibn Ka'b occur also the words: *"and he is a father to them"*, which imply his spiritual relationship and connect on with the words: *"and his wives are their mothers"*.

Muslims always brag how they can memorise the Quran. Here we see them acknowledge that Ubay was the best reciter of the Quran and yet they reject his recitation.

Muslim translator of the Quran, Dr. Muhammad Asad is so assured of Ubai ibn Kab's version, he even added the words: *"and he is a father to them"* into interpolation brackets (…) in his translation.

Message of the Quran – Surah 33:6 "The prophet has a higher claim on the believers than (they have on) their selves ***(seeing that he is as a father to them)*** and his wives their mothers…"

How can you crown a man to be the best Quran reciter and then reject his Quran recitation? Ubay's recitation makes more sense, if the wives of Muhammad are the spiritual mothers of the Muslim believers, then it is obvious that Muhammad is the spiritual father of the Muslim Believers.

Different readings for Surah 38:45

Youtube presentation by Dr. Jay Smith: Shabir Ally finally admits the Quran has indeed changed! [Jay presents…] "Hafs Quran reads: "And remember our **ibaa**danaa **(slaves)**, Ibrahim, Isaac and Jacob, owners…" Al Bazzi Quran reads: "And remember our **ab**danaa **(slave)**, Ibrahim, Isaac and Jacob, owners…" [https://www.youtube.com/watch?v=F6agQmo5OTc [Time line 10:37 – 11:00 Last accessed 24 April 2021]

The second version is obviously in error since more than one person, who are the slaves, are mentioned. The correct reading in this case would be "slaves" and not "slave".

Different readings for Surah 43:19

<u>*Youtube: by Dr. Jay Smith: Shabir Ally finally admits the Quran has indeed changed!*</u> [Jay presents...] "Hafs Quran reads: "And they make the angels, which are **ibaadu (slaves)** of the Beneficient, females." Rawh Quran reads: "And they make the angels, which are **inda (in the presence)** of the Beneficient, females." [Hafs says that the angels that are slaves are being made females, Rawh doesn't say that the angels are slaves, but that they are being made females. Are the angels' slaves or not? The answer you give will indicate which reading is right for you.

[https://www.youtube.com/watch?v=F6agQmo5OTc Time line 12:30 Last accessed 24 April 2021]

Different readings for Surah 46:15

<u>*Youtube presentation by Dr. Jay Smith: Shabir Ally finally admits the Quran has indeed changed!*</u> [Jay presents...] "Hafs Quran reads: "And We have enjoined on man **ihsaanan (doing good)** to his parents." Al Doori Quran reads: "And We have enjoined on man **husna (beauty)** to his parents." I agree with Jay, I would rather my child be good to me, than being beautiful.

https://www.youtube.com/watch?v=F6agQmo5OTc Time line 14:31 – 15:25 Last accessed 24 April 2021

Different readings for Surah 47:4

<u>*Quran Trans. by A. Yusuf Ali: Page 1379 – Commentary 4824*</u> "There are **TWO ALTERNATIVE READINGS**, (i) *qatalu – those who fight* and (ii) *qutilu – those who are slain*." Here we see in the Quran Surah 47:4, the reading according to Hafs "qatala" isn't just a different (mis) pronunciation from the Quran reading of Warsh. It is two different words with different meanings. (See 2:9,10,58,259, 3:81, 4:152, 26:217, 42:30).

Different readings for Surah 92:3

<u>*Quran Translation by Abdullah Yusuf Ali:*</u> "**By the creation** of male and female."

Message of the Quran "**Consider the creation** of the male and female."

While Muslim scholar, Ali's Version is based on a vow: "***BY THE CREATION OF*** *male and female*", Muslim scholar, Dr. Asad's Version is based on something to ponder over: "***CONSIDER THE CREATION*** of the male and female." Clearly, these different Quranic recitations are not mispronunciations or different word choice during translations, but that of "textual" variants. It is Muslim scholar, Mr. Pickthall, who in his Version made us aware of a third variant reading, changing the emphasis from a vow and something to ponder over to the Creator himself.

Meaning of Glorious Quran "**And Him Who hath created** male and female."

When we looked at Islam's authentic traditions, we see that a fourth variant reading, comes to light.

Sahih Bukhari Vol. 6 Pages 441-442, Hadith 468 "Narrated Ibrahim. The companions of Abdullah (bin Masud) came to Abi Darda', (and before they arrived at his home), he looked for them and found them. Then he asked them, who among you can recite (Quran) as 'Abdullah recites it? They replied all of us. He asked: Who amongst you knows it by heart? They pointed at 'Alqama. Then he asked Alqama: **HOW DID YOU HEAR ABDULLAH BIN MASUD RECITING SURAT AL-LAIL (THE NIGHT)? ALQAMA RECITED: "BY THE MALE AND THE FEMALE." ABU AD-DARDA SAID: I TESTIFY THAT I HEARD THE PROPHET RECITING IT LIKEWISE, BUT THESE PEOPLE WANT ME TO RECITE: "AND BY HIM WHO CREATED MALE AND FEMALE" BUT BY ALLAH, I WILL NOT FOLLOW THEM.**"

According to Islam's most authentic literature, Surah 92:3 "By the male and the female" recited 1400 years ago by Muhammad and Masud, don't agree to any of the modern day versions in our hands today. Just with this simple verse alone Muslims have four different recitations.

WHICH QURAN VERSION IS CORRECT: THAT WHICH IS RECORDED IN...

- ✓ Bukhari's Version: "**By the** male and female"?

- ✓ Pickthall's Version: "**By Him who created** male and female"?
- ✓ Abdullah Yusuf Ali's version: "**By the creation of** male and female"?
- ✓ Asad's Version: "**Consider the creation of the** male and female"?

Bring me a Quran recitation like the one Muhammad recited: *"By the male and female."*

Different readings for Surah 98:6

<u>***Youtube presentation by Dr. Jay Smith: Shabir Ally finally admits the Quran has indeed changed!***</u> [Jay presents...] "Hafs Quran reads: "Indeed, they who disbelieve among the people of the scripture and the polytheists, will be in the fire of hell, abiding eternally therein. Those are the worst of **al bareiyyati (creatures)**." Warsh Quran reads the same until the end of the verse: "...**al bare'ati (innocent)**." Are Christians and polytheists the worst of God's creatures or actually innocent? If innocent, why are they in hell according to the Warsh Quran? [https://www.youtube.com/watch?v=F6agQmo5OTc Time line 00:15:36 – 00:16:55 Last accessed 24 April 2021]

It was dishonest of Deedat to claim that the different recitations of the Quran were only differences of mispronunciation and not textual differences. **NEVER AGAIN WILL DECEPTIVE MUSLIMS BE ABLE TO LIE** to informed non-Muslims that all Muslims around the world recite only one Arabic Version of the Quran, word for word, exactly the same. Never again!

All Muslims' who tries to tell us there is only one Arabic Quran being recited in the world, *they are either ignorant of their Islamic sources or they are well aware of these damning sources, but suppresses these embarrassing historical Islamic facts and are trying hard to deceive us*, hoping we are not aware of these Islamic Quran crippling sources. Authentic Islamic records attest to the fact that there were/are more than one Arabic recitation of the Quran in existence today and that more than one Quran recitation are being recited in different parts of the world today. The deceptive Muslim response that Muslims recite only one Quran Version around the world, fell flat to the ground.

4 Is today's Quran the same as that which Muhammad recited?

Muslims claim: "Not a single word was changed!"

The Noble Quran – Surah 15:9 "Verily, we [Allah], it is we who sent down the Dhikr (e.g. the Quran) and surely, we will guard it (from corruption)."

The Noble Quran: Page 339 – Footnote (1) "This verse (15:9) is a challenge to mankind and everyone is obliged to believe in the miracles of this Quran. It is a fact that more than 1400 years have elapsed and **NOT A SINGLE WORD OF THIS QURAN HAS BEEN CHANGED**, although the disbelievers tried their utmost to change it in every way, but they failed miserably in their efforts. As it is mentioned in this holy verse – *We will guard it* – by Allah, He has guarded it…"

Dr. Dawid Wood: Preservation Debate – Snipped by Sheik Yasir Qadi: [Yasir states that:] "There have never been two copies of the Quran that are different even in one letter or one word…"

[https://www.youtube.com/watch?v=Wa8uIxgJ8Rc Time line 2:02 – 2:47 Last accessed 24 April 2021]

Attorney Mohammed Coovadia: Basic Islamic Principles for Christians & those of other Faiths – Page 8 "The Quran remains **untampered** since God revealed it to Prophet Mohammed over 1400 years ago."

Ahmad Deedat: "Is all of the Bible God's Word?" Page 10 "We already know that the Holy Quran is the infallible Word of God, revealed to our Holy Prophet Hazrat Muhammad Mustapha [Arabic phrase] word for word, through the agency of the Archangel Jibraeel (known as Gabriel in English) and **perfectly preserved and protected from human tampering** for the past fourteen hundred years!"

We already informed by Islamic authentic records that Allah seemingly revealed seven different Arabic Quran recitations to Muhammad, which caused uneasiness and rejection of recitations between early Muslims. Also, we have already noted

above that certain verses recited by Muhammad as per the best Quranic reader, Ubayy ibn Ka'b (see heading: Leaving out what Ubayy received from Muhammed) were rejected by Muslims and those rejected verses are not part of today's Quran, i.e. Hafs Qira'at. As we have seen, based on Islamic resources, the Quran is **not** preserved. Muslims will have to decide whether they will continue to follow emotional blind-belief or historical authentic Islamic documents.

Remember:

- If they acknowledge the authentic Ahadith, they have to objectively reject the notion of a pre-served Quran and poor Allah failed to do his job or,
- If they reject the authentic Ahadith, meaning it is no more authentic, then Islam falls anyhow as majority of the religious beliefs is based on the Ahadith. Both ways Islam crumbles.

Missing Quran verses: Stoning of the adulterer

Below is a tradition where Muhammad practiced stoning of the adulterer.

Muwatta Malik "Malik related to me from Yaqub ibn Zayd ibn Talha from his father Zayd ibn Talha that Abdullah ibn Abi Mulayka informed him that a woman came to the Messenger of Allah… and informed him that she had committed adultery… **The Messenger of Allah gave the order and she was stoned** …"

https://quranx.com/Hadith/Malik/USC-MSA/Book-41/Hadith-5 Last accessed 27 April 2021

Why did Muhammed practice, stoning of the adultery? Because it was part of the original Quran.

Sahih Bukhari Vol. 8, Page 539, Hadith 817 "[Umar said:] Allah sent Muhammad with the Truth and revealed the holy book to him and **AMONG WHAT ALLAH REVEALED**, was the verse of Rajam (the stoning of married persons) … who commit adultery and **WE DID RECITE THIS VERSE, UNDERSTOOD AND MEMORIZED IT.** Allah's Apostle did carry out the punishment of stoning and so did we after him. I am afraid that after a long time has passed, somebody will say: **BY ALLAH, WE DO NOT FIND THE VERSE OF RAJAM IN ALLAH'S BOOK AND THUS THEY WILL GO ASTRAY BY LEAVING AN OBLIGATION WHICH ALLAH HAS REVEALED."**

Umar, who became the second Calipha of Islam, clearly stated that Allah **revealed** to Muhammad in al-Quran the stoning verse to punish the adulterer and that they memorized, recited and also practiced it.

Muwatta Malik "Malik related to me from Yahya ibn Said from Sulayman ibn Yasar from Abu Waqid al-Laythi that a man came to Umar ibn al-Khattab while he was in ash-Sham. He mentioned to him that he had found a man with his wife… **Umar gave the order and she was stoned**."

https://quranx.com/Hadith/Malik/USC-MSA/Book-41/Hadith-9 Last accessed 27 April 2021

This is not a matter of mispronunciation of Quranic words, but a strong example of actual verses expunged from the Quran that Muhammad recited in comparison to the variant Qurans that Muslims recites today. The variant Qurans recited by Muslims today, is therefore not the same as the Quran that Muhammad and his contemporaries recited and practiced 1400 years ago. Modern day Muslims still believe and practice this obliterated Quranic verse as God's revealed Word.

Drum Magazine: The voice of Africa. 14 March 2002 No: 497 - Pages 18-21 "Last June [2001], an Islamic court, in Sokoto [Northern Nigeria], the regional capital, **SENTENCED HER [SUFIYAHU HUSEINI] TO DEATH BY STONING FOR COMMITTING ALDULTERY** … Aliyu Abubakar Sanyinna, *the attorney general* of Sokoto state, says that: "He would be happy to cast the first stone if asked to by the court." Mansur Ibrahim Sa'id, *a member of the committee who drafted Sokoto's new legal code and dean of the law faculty at Dan Fodio University* in Sokoto, says that he, too, would take part in the stoning if asked to do so by the court. **GOD HAS SAID THAT IS THE WAY SHE SHOULD GO, BECAUSE SHE HAS BROKEN THE LAW AND THOSE**

STONING HER WILL BE HAPPY, BECAUSE THEY ARE CARRYING OUT GOD'S WILL."

No Muslim will ever have the privilege again to recite the original Quran according to how Muhammad and his contemporaries recited it *with the stoning verse in it*. Never again! They must be content with what is left of the surviving remnant of the Hafs Quran. Only Muslims ignorant of their fundamental traditions or those dishonest Muslims who cover their history up will argue that the Quran is unchanged for the past 1400 years since Muhammad received it.

If you are a Muslim that accepts Bukhari's literature as authentic recordings of early Muslim days, then you must admit that the Quran without the stoning verse in your hands today, is a different Quranic Version of that which was recited by Muhammad.

Missing Quran verses: Don't claim to be the offspring

Sahih Bukhari, Vol. 8 Page 540 Hadith 817 "Umar said: ... **WE USED TO RECITE AMONG THE VERSES IN ALLAH'S BOOK**: "O people! Do not claim to be the offspring of other than your fathers, as it is disbelief on your part that you claim to be the offspring of other than your real father."

This verse is annihilated from all current variant Quran readings. No Muslim will ever have the privilege to recite the Quran with it as Muhammad and his contemporaries recited it.

Missing Quran verses: Valleys full of riches

Sahih Muslim, Vol. 2 Page 501 "Abu Musa al-Ash'ari... is reported to have said to the Reciters of Basra: "**WE USED TO RECITE A SURAH, WHICH RESEMBLED IN LENGTH AND SEVERITY TO (SURAH) BARA'AT. I HAVE, HOWEVER, FORGOTTEN IT WITH THE EXCEPTION OF THIS, WHICH I REMEMBER OUT OF IT**: "If there were two valleys full of riches, for the son of Adam, he would long for a third valley and nothing would fill the stomach of the son of Adam, but dust ..."

Unquote: Sahih Muslim is considered to be the second most authentic Ahadith after Sahih Bukhari. Here we see this Surah about 286 verses if compared to Surah Bara'at in the Hafs version that Muslims used to recite during the time of Muhammad, is missing from all variant recitations.

Missing Quran verses: Suckling grow-up men

Sahih Muslim "Aisha (Allah be pleased with her) reported that it had been revealed in the Quran that ten clear suckling make the marriage unlawful, then it was abrogated by five suckling and **ALLAH'S APOSTLE (SAW) DIED AND BEFORE THAT TIME [BEFORE THE DEATH OF MUHAMMAD] IT WAS FOUND IN THE QURAN**" [https://quranx.com/Hadith/Muslim/USC-MSA/Book-8/Hadith-3421 Last accessed 24 April 2021

Notice: double abrogation took place here:

1. The first abrogation – the ten suckling verse was changed to five suckling verse and …
2. The second abrogation - the five suckling verse was removed from all Qurans.

Can you imagine, Allah in the original Quran that Muhammad recited used to tell Muslim women to suckle men, other than their husbands, to ensure that these ADULT-men will not lust after them or so that the jealousy of their husbands can disappear. To "suckle" means to "suck on a woman's breasts".

Sahih Muslim "A'isha (Allah be pleased with her) reported that Sahla bint Suhail came to Allah's Apostle (may peace be upon him) and said: Messenger of Allah, I see on the face of Abu Hudhaifa (signs of disgust) on entering of Salim (who is an ally) into (our house), whereupon **Allah's Apostle said: Suckle him. She said: How can I suckle him as he is a <u>grown-up</u> man? Allah's Messenger smiled** …"

https://quranx.com/Hadith/Muslim/USC-MSA/Book-8/Hadith-3424 Last accessed 24 April 2021

https://quranx.com/Hadith/Muslim/USC-MSA/Book-8/Hadith-3425 Last accessed 24 April 2021

The husband is already jealous and now his wife must still take out her breasts and make a grown-up-man suck on it so that the husband's disgust can disappear. Thank God we are not Muslims! I would never obey Muhammad's instruction that another man must suck my wife's breasts. [Surah 33:36]

https://www.youtube.com/watch?v=AasZIP2UxwM&t=1441s Time line 25:20 Last accessed 24 April 2021

Muslims say: "We have **ONE** Arabic Quran Version recited around the world!" I say: Bring me the Quran:

- ✓ With the "stoning verse" in it that Muhammad used to recite.
- ✓ With the "suckling verse" in it that Muhammad used to recite.

These examples demonstrate how today's Hafs Quran Version in our hands is a changed product and different from the Quran which were recited by Muhammad and his companions. Not only are verses **that were** in Muhammad's Quran left-out from the Hafs Quran in our hands, but verses that were **not in the Quran** recited by Muhammad were later added to the Hafs Quran, which is in our hands.

Ibn Masud's Quran version had 111 chapters

Later, I'll be quoting from Mr. Farug Sherif's book wherein he mentioned that Ibn Mas'ud had a copy of the Quran, which he (Mas'ud) considered to be an Authentic Version. However, the Hafs Version in our hands today **has a different canon** from the Quran Version that Mas'ud (one of Islam's then best Quran reciters) had. Note, Muslims disregard the Quran recitations by Islam's best reciters.

Muslim Scholar Mr. Ahmad Von Denffer wrote: ***"Ulum al Quran: An Introduction to the Science of the Quran." Chapter 2 Page 2 & 9*** "Sahih Bukhari Vol. 6, Page 486, Hadith 521 - Narrated Masruq: Abdullah bin Amr mentioned Abdullah bin Masud and said: I shall forever love that man for I heard the prophet saying: <u>LEARN THE QURAN FROM FOUR</u> [1] Abdullah bin Masud, [2] Salim, [3] Muiadh and [4] Ubayy bin Ka'b … **THE MUSHAF OF IBN MASUD (D. 33/653) in which Surahs 1, 113 and 114 were NOT included.**" [Sahih Bukhari Vol. 5, Page 95, Hadith 150-3]

Here we see the number one person, mentioned by Muhammad, from whom the Quran must be learned, Masud, his canon **ex**cluded 3 whole surahs, including Surah Fatiha – Chapter 1.

Muhammad said Surah Fatiha is not part of Quran

<u>Malik's Muwatta Book 3, Hadith 39</u> "…The Messenger of Allah called to Ubayy ibn Kab while he was praying. When Ubayy had finished his prayer he joined the Messenger of Allah and he was intending to leave by the door of the Mosque, so the Messenger of Allah said: I hope that you won't leave the mosque until you know **A SURAH WHOSE LIKE ALLAH HAS NOT SENT DOWN IN THE TAWRAH, NOR IN THE INJIL, NOR IN THE QURAN**. Ubayy said: I began to slow down my paste in hope of that. Then I said: Messenger of Allah, the Surah you promised me! He said: What do you recite when you begin the prayer? **I RECITED THE FATIHA (SURAH 1) UNTIL I CAME TO THE END OF IT AND THE MESSENGER OF ALLAH SAID: IT IS THIS SURA, IT IS THE SEVEN OFT-REPEATED…**"

Here we see the Quran recited by Muhammad, Mas'ud and Ubayy did *<u>not</u>* include Surah 1 as part of the ORIGINAL Quran. Again, these differences are more than just mispronunciations, but that of textual substance, proving that the Quran recited by Muhammad in the 7TH century, is different from the Qurans recited by modern Muslims in the 21ST century.

Surah Fatiha now added to modern-day Qurans

When *we* consider the Hafs and Warsh Qurans and other versions *today*, it makes sense why Muhammed and Ibn Mas'ud didn't include Fatiha as part of the 7TH century Quran. **Surah 15:87 distinguish** Surah Fatiha as something separate from the Quran.

(https://www.youtube.com/watch?v=-NIO3mAKlzl time line 23:45 to hear how Surah Fatiha was revealed to Muhammad.) Last accessed 24 April 2021

Quran Transl. by Abdullah Yusuf Ali: **Surah 15:87** "We bestowed upon thee the 7 oft-repeated (verses) **AND** the grand Quran."	*The Noble Quran: Surah 15:87* "...We bestowed upon you seven of Al-Mathani (Surat Al-Fatihah) **AND** the grand Quran."

If Surah Fatiha was part of the original 7TH century Quran revealed to Muhammad, the verse would have read: *"And We bestowed upon thee the grand Quran."* Or it would have read: *"And We bestowed upon thee the grand Quran with Surah Al-Fatihah in it."* Surah 15:87 distinguished the Quran to be **SOMETHING DIFFERENT** from Surat Al-Fatihah. *Bring me the Quran that Muhammad said I must learn from Masud.* Today's variant Quran Versions have Surah 1 added into it, proving the current Quran Versions are different to the 7th century Version. Muslims can never again brag the Quran is unchanged.

Surah 9:128-129 added to Hafs Version, omitted from Dr. R. Khalifah's Version

AFTER MUHAMMAD DIED, HIS CONTEMPORARIES (COMPANIONS) ATTESTED TO THE FACT THAT VERSES THAT WAS NOT RECITED BY MUHAMMAD AS PART OF THE QURAN, WERE ADDED TO THE QURAN.

<u>Authorized English Version of the Quran – Appendix 24 "Tampering with the Word of God" Page 444</u> "Ali was asked: *Why are you staying home?* He said: "SOMETHING has been added to the Quran." Nine years after the prophet's death, **SOME SCRIBES INJECTED TWO FALSE VERSES AT THE END OF SURAH 9**."

Surah 9:128-129 is now removed from Dr. Rashid Khalifah's Authorized English Version of the Quran.

CONCLUSION: As we have seen, the Hafs Quran is not the same as the Quran recited by Muhammad and his companions. Verses were removed and verses were added to the Quran recited by Muhammad, which resulted in the Hafs Quran recitation. As I have clearly dedmonstrated, these differences are not mispronunciations, but actual Quranic text variants. No honest Muslim can say that what they have **in their hands today** is the one and only true preserved Arabic Quran Version that Muhammad recited.

5 When was the Quran compiled into a standardized text?

No complete written Quran in Muhammad's day

<u>Sahih Bukhari: Vol. 6, Page 477, Hadith 509</u> "Narrated Zaid bin Thabit. Abu Bakr said: You should search for (the fragmentary scripts of) the Qur'an and collect it (in one book) … I said to Abu Bakr: How will you do something which **ALLAH'S APOSTLE (SAW) DID NOT DO?**"

<u>Mr. Faruq Sherif: A Guide to the Contents of the Quran: Page 13</u> "Thus **AT THE PROPHET'S DEATH** no authoritative compilation of the Quran was in existence…"

The above proves that no complete Quranic manuscript text can date back directly to Muhammad. Parcements (animal skin) may date back to the 7th century or even earlier, but not the Quranic text (**ink**). The original complete Quranic text never existed in Muhammad's day and it will never exist. What exist today are the remnant of variant texts of Quran recitations of what Muhammad used to recite.

Quran passages were lost during the battle of Yamama

<u>Christian writer Mr. John Gilchrist: "Jam Al-Quran: The Initial Collection of the Quran Text</u> "Many (of the passages) of the Qur'an that were sent down were known by those who died on the day of Yamama, but *they were not known (by those who) survived them, nor were they written down, nor had Abu Bakr, Umar or Uthman (that time) collected the Qur'an, nor were they found with even one after them.*" <u>(Abi Dawood, Ki tab al-Mashie, p. 23)</u>

Notice, early Muslims admitted what modern-day Muslims refuse to accept, that is, passages of the Quran that Muhammad recited, is gone forever.

Bakr collected the first unofficial text in book-form

Sahih Bukhari: Vol. 6, Page 477, Hadith 509 "Narrated Zaid bin Habit. Abu Bakr As-Siddiqi sent for me when the people of Yama-ma had been killed (e.g. a number of the prophet's companions who fought against Musailama) (I went to him) and found Umar bin Al-Khattab sitting with him. Abu Bakr then said: Casualties were heavy amongst the Qurra of the Quran (e.g. those who knew the Quran by heart) on the day of the Battle of Yama-ma and I am afraid that more casualties may take place among the Qurra on other battlefields, *WHEREBY A LARGE PART OF THE QURAN MAY BE LOST*. I suggest that you (Abu Bakr) order that the Quran be collected ... So I [Zaid] started looking for the Quran and collected it from (what was written on) palm-leaf stalks, thin white stones and *also from the men who knew it by heart* ... Then the complete manuscripts (copy) of the Quran remained with Abu Bakr till he died, then with Umar till the end of his life and then with Hafsa, the daughter of Umar."

After many passages of the Quran went lost, Bakr, before more casualties (who knew the remains of the Quran) would die, arranged for the remnant Quran to be written down. Note, the verses of stoning, valleys of riches and suckling, etc. were leftout of the Quran as early as Abu Bakr's remnant Quran Version. If they were included in Abu Bakr's Quran Version, it would have appeared in Uthman's Recension when the scribes used Bakr's Quran Version as a guide to reconstruct Uthman's Recension.

Christian writer Mr. John Gilchrist: "Jam Al-Quran: The Initial Collection of the Quran Text "It is reported... from Ali who said: May the mercy of Allah be upon Abu Bakr, the foremost of men to be rewarded with the collection of the manuscripts, for he was *THE FIRST TO COLLECT THE TEXT BETWEEN TWO COVERS. **(Ibn Abi Dawud, Kitab al-Masahif, p. 5)***"

Other Muslims also began to collect the surviving parts of the remnant Quran for their private use. These manuscripts were different from eachother, hence we will later see that Uthman was forced to unite the Muslims on an official standardized Quran and to destroy competing contrary versions.

Mr. Faruq Sherif: A Guide to the Contents of the Quran: Page 14 "Side by side with it [1. Abu Bakr's unofficial Quran compilation] EXISTED OTHER COLLECTIONS which belong to private individuals, notably that of [2] Ali, [3] Abdullah ibn Abbas, [4] Ibn Mas'ud, [5] Abu Musa Ash'ari and [6] Obay ibn Ka'b… **EACH POSSESSOR OF A PRIVATE COPY NATURALLY HELD HIS VERSION TO BE AUTHENTIC…**"

After Muhammad died and later, when some of the Qurra at the battle of Yamama died, thereafter, <u>since the first Caliphate Abu Bakr, until the third Caliphate Uthman</u>, readers collected the surviving parts of the remnant Quran in book-form for their private versions, **NOT** as universal authoritative and official versions accepted by the Muslim population.

Muslims in Uthman's day recited variant readings

Sahih Bukhari: Vol. 6, Page 478, Hadith 510 "Narrated Anas bin Malik: Hudhaifa bin Al-Yaman came to Uthman at the time when the people of Sham and the people of Iraq were waging war to conquer Arminya and Adhar-bijan, Hudhaifa was afraid of their (the people of Sham and Iraq) **DIFFERENCES IN THE RECITATION OF THE QURAN**, so he said to Uthman: O Chief of the Believers! Save this nation before they differ about the Book (Quran) as Jews and Christians did before…"

Since different Quran recitations exist from the 7th century, it shows how desparate some modern-day Muslims are to ignorantly or deceptively state that ONLY ONE Arabic version of the Quran always existed.

Uthman's challenge to standardize the Quran

Sahih Bukhari: Vol. 6, Page 478, Hadith 510 "[Above quote continues…] Save this nation before they differ about the Quran as Jews and Christians did before. So Uthman sent a message to Hafsa saying: Send us the manuscripts of the Quran so that we may compile the Quranic materials in perfect copies and return the manuscripts to you. Hafsa sent it to Uthman. Uthman ordered Zaid bin Thabit, Abdullah bin Az-Zubair, Sa'id bin Al-As and Abdur-Rahman bin Harith bin Hisham to rewrite the manuscripts in perfect copies and returned the original to Hafsa."

But the Uthmanic Quran compilers soon realized that Abu Bakr's **REMNANT** Quran was incomplete and found more verses that they added to their current compilation (see below examples).

Christian writer: Mr. John Gilchrist: "Jam Al-Quran, The Uthmanic Recension of the Quran" Page 9 "Khuzaimah ibn Thabit said: I see you have **OVERLOOKED VERSES AND HAVE NOT WRITTEN THEM**. They said: Which are they? He replied: I had it directly from the Messenger of Allah (saw) (Surah 9:128-129) – There has come to you a messenger from yourselves. It grieves him that you should perish, he is very concerned about you and to the believers he is kind and merciful – to the end of the Surah. Uthman said: I bear witness that these verses are from Allah." *(Ibn Abi Dawu, Kitab al-Masahif – Page 11)*

Jami' at-Tirmidhi: "…**ZAID BIN THABIT SAID: I MISSED AN AYAH OF SURAT AL-AHZAB** that I heard the Messenger of Allah (ﷺ) reciting: Among the believers are men who have been true to their covenant with Allah, of them some have fulfilled their obligations, and some of them are still waiting (33:23) - so I searched for it and found it with Khuzaimah bin Thabit, or Abu Khuzaimah, so I put it in its Surah."

https://quranx.com/Hadith/Tirmidhi/DarusSalam/Volume-5/Book-44/Hadith-3104

Last accessed 24 April 2021

Carefully notice, Abu Bakr's remnant Quran was handed down from him to Umar to Hafsah to Uthman and only at **THIS TIME** was it said that the aboved mentioned verses were also recited by Muhammad and then it became part of *"UTHMAN'S RECENSION of the Quran"*, proving that these Caliphates and Muslims responsible for the Quranic Text, did not know the Quran Recitation by heart.

Faruq Sheriff: A guide to the contents of the Quran Pages 14-15 "Uthman called upon Hafsah to entrust him with the "leaves" prepared for Abu Bakr and thereupon the commission of four embarked on a *REVISION* of the "suhuf", taking into account, *additions and alterations, new fragments, which has come to light, as well as the memory* *of persons who had not been consulted on the first occasion.* **THE RESULT WAS A COMPLETE RECENSION ... THUS CAME INTO BEING THE OFFICIAL VERSION OF THE QURAN."**

No Muslim can deny the fact that Abu Bakr's unofficial collected Quranic Version were incomplete and now revised, hence the official written Quran Version is not named after him, but after Uthman.

T.P. Hughes: Dictionary of Islam Page 487 "...**THIS RECENSION OF THE QURAN** *produced by Khalifah Usman has been handed down...*"

What does the word *"recension"* mean? **Oxford Dictionary:** "A revised edition of a text."

N.J. Dawood, an Arabic graduate during 1945 from the London University and also a Quranic translator and founder of an Arabic Advertising & Publishing Co Ltd., publicly admitted that ...

The Koran – Introduction Pages 3 "**AN AUTHORIZED VERSION WAS ESTABLISHED DURING THE CALIPHATE OF UTHMAN.** BELIEVERS REGARD THIS VERSION AS THE AUTHORITATIVE WORD OF GOD."

The Qur'an (Saheeh International) Page 661 "The **STANDARDIZATION** of one authentic volume (mushaf) took place during the caliphate of Uthman bin Affan."

6 What happened to the variant Quranic texts?

Public Debate 1986: "Is the Bible the Word of God?" Christian Speaker, Evangelist Jimmy Swaggart and Muslim Speaker, Sheik Ahmad Deedat: Q&A Session: "Does the glorious Quran exist in its original and pure form and was the originals in fact burned? ... [Deedat's response] ... Brother Swaggart mentioned something about variant readings and that Uthman had those variant readings burned ... The Arabic scripture were written originally without vowel points ... Vowels were added to make the proper pronunciations ... So the variant readings were of the variant pronunciations ... The revelation was given in the dialect of the Quraysh, the family of the tribe of Muhammad and that pronunciation was preserved and **EVERY OTHER PRONUNCIATION WITH DIFFERENT VOWEL POINTS, THEY SAID ELIMINATE THEM…**" https://www.youtube.com/watch?v=genex9Bqlml Time line 01:32:10–01:36:14 Last accessed 24 April 2021

FIRSTLY, DEEDAT <u>**CORRECTLY**</u> SAID THAT THE ORIGINAL MANUSCRIPTS HAD NO VOWEL POINTS, BUT <u>**ERRONEOUSLY**</u> SAID PRONUNCIATIONS WITH DIFFERENT VOWEL POINTS WERE ELIMINATED (BURNED). How can you eliminate (burn) pronunciations without eliminating or burning people's tongues? What was destroyed were manuscripts, written variant texts, not pronunciations. Muslim-laymen I spoke to were unaware of the fact that Allah seemingly revealed seven different Arabic Quran recitations to Muhammad.

They, like Deedat, believed and explained that the different readings were a result of non-Arab Muslim converts, who mispronounced the words of the Arabic Quran, but as we have seen, that was not the case. The differences in variant recitations were based on the idea that Allah directly revealed to Muhammad seven different ways to recite the Quran and after he died, verses were removed and added to the Quran. Truth seekers must note that Christians openly admit that **BIBLICAL TRANSLATIONS ARE REGULARLY REVISED - NOT ITS ORIGINAL HEBREW AND GREEK MANUSCRIPTS**. It is necessary to produce *revised translations* for both the Bible and Quran as all-living languages change over the years and fresh translations are required as new words developed and the meaning of words changes.

<u>***Quran Translation by Abdullah Yusuf Ali: Page iii – Preface to First Edition, 1934***</u> "It may be asked: Is there any need for a fresh English Translation? To those who ask this question I commend a careful consideration of the facts which I have set out in my *Note on Translations…*"

<u>***Quran Translation by Abdullah Yusuf Ali: Page xii – Translation of the Quran***</u> "The ambition of Muslims is to read the sounds of the Arabic Text. I wish his or her ambition were to understand the Quran, in Arabic or in their mother tongue or some well-developed

tongue which, he or she understands, **HENCE THE NEED FOR GOOD AND ACCURATE TRANSLATIONS."**

Quran Translation by Abdullah Yusuf Ali: Page viii – Commentary on the Quran "(1) Arabic words in the Text have acquired other meanings than those, which were understood by the Apostle and his Companions. **ALL LIVING LANGUAGES UNDERGO SUCH TRANSFORMATIONS."**

We agree with Ali that fresh translations from the original text of books are absolutely important and necessary. We agree with Ali that these translations need to be revised as languages undergo change and words take on new meanings, hence the different Bible Translations, called Versions.

WHAT WE DISAGREE WITH ISLAM, IS FOR CONFLICTING MANUSCRIPT TEXTS OF HOLY BOOKS, TO BE DESTROYED AND ONLY FOR A REVISED MANUSCRIPT TEXT TO BE KEPT IN CIRCULATION, LIKE IS THE CASE WITH THE QURAN.

The order for non-Uthmanic texts to be destroyed

Sahih Bukhari: Vol.6, Page 478, Hadith 510 "Uthman returned the original manuscripts [first unofficial written collection of the remnant Quran] to Hafsa and sent to every Muslim province one copy of what they had copied and ordered **ALL THE OTHER QURANIC MATERIALS, WHETHER WRITTEN IN FRAGMENTARY MANUSCRIPTS OR WHOLE COPIES BE BURNT…"**

T.P. Hughes - Dictionary of Islam: Page 487 "… Usman sent a copy to every quarter of the countries of Islam **ORDERING ALL OTHER LEAVES TO BE BURNED…"**

Muslim Professor Masudul Hasan: History of Islam, Vol. 1, Page 605 "Zaid … under the directions of the Caliph Hadrat Abu Bakr collected the verses from copies written on flat stones, pieces of leather, palm leaves, from the breasts of men and *from this collection he compiled a fair copy*. This transcript passed from Hadrat Abu Bakr to Hadrat Umar, who bequeathed it to his daughter Hafsa, one of the wives of the holy prophet. When Hadrat Othman became the Caliph, **ZAID REVISED THE COMPILATION. WHEN THE**

REVISION WAS COMPLETED, THE STANDARD TEXT WAS PRESCRIBED AND ALL UNAUTHORIZED TEXTS WERE COLLECTED AND DESTROYED."

It is not Allah nor Muhammad that authorized the 652AD revised Quran compilation as the official written standardized text, nor did they order the burning of variant texts, it was Uthman's decision.

The reason non-Uthmanic texts were destroyed

<u>*Mufti Muhammad Taqi Usmani – The Preservation of the Quran:*</u> "These folios… of Abu Bakr… remained with him during his lifetime… Then with 'Umar… [then with] Hafsah… After the death of Hafsah, Marwan ibn al-Hakam had them burnt since the copies of Quran ordered by Uthman were ready at that time and a consensus of the Ummah had already been reached that following Uthmanic copies of the Quran was obligatory. **MARWAN IBN AL-HAKAM THOUGHT IT INADVISABLE TO LET ANY COPY, WHICH WAS CONTRARY TO REMAIN IN EXISTENCE**."

There you have it! The competing written versions of the remnant Quran were destroyed and burned, not by the enemies of Islam, not because it was old manuscripts, but it was destroyed by practicing Muslims who tried to get rid of unauthorized text and contradictory Quranic material. Some contemporary Muslim scholars today admit that the Quranic material were burnt and destroyed by Muslims, but they want to make us believe it was done because Muslims burn and destroy old manuscripts out of honor and respect. Of course, this reason is nothing, but wishful thinking, not supported in any form by ancient Islamic sources.

Below is an example of a contemporary Muslim saying they burn old Qurans out of respect.

FROM: MOHAMMED COOVADIA [email address removed] Sent: 13 August 2012 01:12 PM To: Michael Mahomed; 'Buxson'; 'rehan ali'; 'Brian Marrian'; 'Yusuf Ismail'; 'Asad Mohamed'; 'Gian Luca'; 'Fadeel Hassen'; 'ahmed pandor'; 'Strydom, Piet'; 'P.J.Strydom'; Ayoob Karim; Snowy Smith' Subject: Quran according to Uthman … So the references are just companions compiling the Quran in the sequence, form and manner and standardizing it so many parchments in remotes areas would now be replaced and previous copies burnt. **In Islam we burn old copies of the Quran or bury them. For us that is the due respect we show to our scripture."**

ALLAH AND MUHAMMAD DIDN'T INSTRUCT MUSLIMS TO BURN QURANIC MANUSCRIPTS, AS IT WERE NOT IN EXISTENCE IN MUHAMMAD'S DAY. I WONDER WHO GAVE THE INSTRUCTION THAT OLD QURANIC MANUSCRIPTS MUST BE BURNED OUT OF RESPECT?

Please note that the Quranic material that was burned in Uthman's day were not old, but contrary to the Uthmanic Recension. I responded (asked) Mr. Coovadia in a followed-up email, how many old Qurans he burnt and buried out of respect. To date, none of the above Muslims responded.

Any Muslim reading this Book, please email me if you already burnt old Quranic copies out of respect or, even better, if you are going to burn old Qurans, please email me. I would like to both witness your respect for old Quranic copies and video record it.

Myself as a Christian, I think it is utter disrespect to burn Quranic manuscripts, irrespective whether it's contradictory or old, I think all religious manuscripts must be kept to prove authenticity and accuracy.

Abu Bakr's first manuscript is also destroyed

<u>*Faruq Sheriff - A guide to the contents of the Quran: Pages 14-15*</u> "The suhuf [Abu Bakr's unofficial script of the Quran] were then returned to Hafsah, **ON WHOSE DEATH SOME THIRTY YEARS LATER THEY WERE DESTROYED."**

<u>*Christian writer: Mr. John Gilchrist – "Jam Al-Quran, The Uthmanic Recension of the Quran" Page 9*</u> "...The **DESTRUCTION** of Hafsah's codex during the time when Marvan ibn al-Hakam was governor of Medinah..." *(Ibn Abi Dawud, Kitab al-Masahif Page 24)*

Some Muslims' hidden variant copies survived

***Jami' at-Tirmidhi: Surah* 33.23** "Az-Zuhri said: Ubaidullah bin 'Abdullah bin 'Utbah informed me that *'Abdullah bin Mas'ud disliked Zaid bin Thabit copying the Musahif and he said: O you Muslim people! Avoid copying the Mushaf and the recitation of this man*. By Allah! When I accepted Islam, he was but in the loins of a disbelieving man – meaning Zaid bin Thabit – and it was regarding this that **'Abdullah bin Mas'ud said: O people of Al-'Iraq! Keep the Musahif that are with you, and conceal them.** For indeed Allah said: And whoever conceals something, he shall come with what he concealed on the Day of Judgement (3:161). *So meet Allah with the Musahif.*"

https://quranx.com/Hadith/Tirmidhi/DarusSalam/Volume-5/Book-44/Hadith-3104

Last accessed 24 April 2021

Sahih Muslim: "'Abdullah (b. Mas'ud) reported that he (said to his companions to conceal their copies of the Qur'an) ..." https://quranx.com/hadith/Muslim/USC-MSA/Book-31/Hadith-6022/

Last accessed 24 April 2021

The Koran: Intro. Page 3 "...Variant readings are recognized by Muslims, as equal authority."

T.P. Huges: Dictionary of Islam: Page 487 "The various readings are wonderfully few..."

CONCLUSION: Nowhere did Muhammad ever tell Muslims to standardize the different Qurans as one recitation. After his death and later when some of the Qurras died, parts of the Quran went missing. Abu Bakr collected the surviving parts of the Quran into an **UN**official Book. Other Muslims also made unofficial written copies for their private use. Of the surviving versions of the seven different ways to recite the Quran, each had at least two additional readings that developed later. Uthman used the collection of the remnant Quran by Abu Bakr and revised it and produced a standard copy that was universally accepted in Islam, by the majority of Muslims, as the official version of the collected Quran. Uthman ordered that all other conflicting Quranic material be destroyed and burnt. Variant readings survived. No Muslim will ever be privileged again to recite the Seven Quranic revelations that Muhammad seemingly received from Allah and taught to earlier Muslims, NOR will they ever be privileged to hold in their hands the first unofficial written Quran compiled by Caliph Abu Bakr. **THEY MUST BE CONTENT WITH THE QURANIC REVISED VERSION ACCORDING TO HAFS.** Never in history did the Jews and Christians ever come together *to produce an edited universal accepted version* of the Holy Bible as the authoritative Word of God and destroyed or burnt any CONFLICTING MANUSCRIPTS no matter how incomplete it was, to ensure the prevalence of a uniform version. Although we envision fresh translations of the Holy Bible as is necessary, there is simply no evidence that we did to the Holy Bible what devout Muslims UNASHAMEDLY DONE TO THE QURAN.

7 When was the Uthmanic Quran canon established?

The Muslim statement: *"The fact that Jesus did not personally collect the Gospel into book form is a clear sign that the Gospels were for a certain time period only and what is now recorded is men's fabrication, as Jesus did not verify what is truth or false nor did the writers of the Gospels sign their names to it"* is a weak Muslim argument to discredit the Bible, since this is exactly the case much worst with the current Qurans.

THERE IS NO QURAN IN EXISTENCE SIGNED-OFF BY MUHAMMAD OR ABU BAKR OR UTHMAN AS AUTHORITATIVE AND ACCURATE. THE CURRENT QURANS IN OUR HANDS IS NOT THE QURAN COLLECTED BY MUHAMMAD, ABU BAKR NOR UTHMAN.

<u>Public Debate 1986 "Is the Bible the Word of God?" Christian Speaker, Evang. Jimmy Swaggart & Muslim Speaker, Sheik Ahmad Deedat: Q&A Session</u> ""Does the glorious Quran exist in its original, pure form and was the originals in fact burned? [Deedat's response] **THERE IS AN UTHMANIC QURAN**..."

https://www.youtube.com/watch?v=genex9BqlmI Time line 01:32:10–01:32:38

Last accessed 24 April 2021

See what I mean? It isn't a Quran collected by Muhammad. He didn't collect it into bookform. The official Quranic text wasn't collected by Muhammad, nor Abu Bakr, but it was compiled by Uthman.

Quran Translation by Prof. Arthur J. Arberry – Introduction on back-cover page
"The definite canon was established **SOME 20 YEARS AFTER MUHAMMAD'S DEATH**…"

This is confirmed by Attorney and 21st century contemporary Muslim debater, Yusuf Ismail: **FROM: YUSUF ISMAIL** [email address removed] Sent: 10 August 2012 11:11 AM To: Michael Mahomed … Subject: Quran according to Uthman … Michael your question is silly and smacks of mischief-making. I say this with no ill-feeling. Principally the Qur'an is fundamentally a recitation and was thus memorized as such during the time of the Prophet by his companions. The question of preservation shouldn't even arise. **Nevertheless, it was written down by various individuals on parchments, but not as a codified book. The process of being compiled in the form of a completed book (codex) occurred 20 years after the prophet's death**… If we can produce a carbon-dated Qur'an to the 6th century and autographed are you now willing to accept it as the word of God? Otherwise your question is purely semantic gymnastics! Sent from my BlackBerry® smartphone."

Apart from Yusuf's insults towards me, he confirmed that the Quran was initially recorded in writing by various individuals and that the standardized Quran, in its written form was established in 652AD, about 20 years after Muhammad's death in 632AD. It will be welcomed from Muslims to present carbon-dated and ***autographed*** manuscripts with the complete rasm (no vowel and diacritical points – see below heading: Uthman's text had no vowel and diacritical points) Quran from the 6th – 7th century for thorough analyses and for comparison with the current Hafs Quran in our hands. It is strange that Yusuf asked that, if they can produce a 6th century carbon-dated Quran, will I accept it as the Word of God, knowing such complete Quran manuscripts doesn't exist (see heading: Oldest complete Quranic manuscript with sub-heading: Earliest complete Kufi Quran Manuscript).

8 Is the Quran verses in the order Muhammad recited it?

The Koran: Introduction Page 3 "In preparing the contents of the Koran for book-form, ITS EDITOR OR EDITORS, FOLLOWED **NO** CHRONOLOGICAL SEQUENCE."

Message of the Quran: Page I, FOREWORD: Footnote 1 "It is to be borne in mind that, in its final compilation, the Quran is … **NOT** IN THE CHRONOLOGICAL ORDER…"

Attorney Mohammed Coovadia: Basic Islamic Principles… Page 9 "(The Quran) does **NOT** follow a chronological sequence…"

Dr. Maurice Bucaille: The Bible, the Quran and Science – Page 132 "Authencity of the Quran – How it came to be written – The 114 Surahs were arranged in decreasing order of length, there were nevertheless exceptions. THE CHRONOLOGICAL SEQUENCE OF THE REVELATIONS WAS **NOT** FOLLOWED."

The chronological order of the Surahs (Chapters) and Ayats (Verses) as Muhammad received and recited it, can be seen here: http://tanzil.net/docs/revelation_order Last accessed 24 April 2021

Below is a table, ***provided by Dr. Rashad Khalifah***, showing the sequence order of Quran verses as Muhammad seemingly received it.

- ***1ˢᵀ column is the original sequence*** in which the chapters were seemingly received by Muhammed.

- ***2ᴺᴰ column is the current order*** in which the Muslim scholars decided to re-arrange the Quran.

Authorized English Version of the Quran: Page 442 – Appendix 23

Order	Surah	Surah Order	Order	Surah	Order	Surah	Order	Surah

9 Is today's Quran the same as Uthman's Quran?

1	96	24	80	47	26	70	16	93	99
2	68	25	97	48	27	71	71	94	57
3	73	26	91	49	28	72	14	95	47
4	74	27	85	50	17	73	21	96	13
5	1	28	95	51	10	74	23	97	55
6	111	29	106	52	11	75	32	98	76
7	81	30	101	53	12	76	52	99	65
8	87	31	75	54	15	77	67	100	98
9	92	32	104	55	6	78	69	101	59
10	89	33	77	56	37	79	70	102	24
11	93	34	50	57	31	80	78	103	22
12	94	35	90	58	34	81	79	104	63
13	103	36	86	59	39	82	82	105	58
14	100	37	54	60	40	83	84	106	49
15	108	38	38	61	41	84	30	107	66
16	102	39	7	62	42	85	29	108	64
17	107	40	72	63	43	86	83	109	61
18	109	41	36	64	44	87	2	110	62
19	105	42	25	65	45	88	8	111	48
20	113	43	35	66	46	89	3	112	5
21	114	44	19	67	51	90	33	113	9
22	112	45	20	68	88	91	60	114	110
23	53	46	56	69	18	92	4		

Muslims mistranslated the Quran to reflect the idea of a preserved book.

Surah 56:77-78

Quran Translation by Shakir: "Most surely it is an honored Quran in a book that is **PROTECTED**."

Quran Trans. by Abdullah Yusuf Ali: "This is indeed a Qur'an most honorable in a Book **WELL-GUARDED**."

Let's see what the Quran really says:

Christian writer, Mr. John Gilchrist "Jam Al-Quran: The Compilation of the Quran in Perspective" Pages 2-3 "Mr. Abdul Kader concludes by claiming that the Quran, in the following verse, actually testifies to a "master copy" of its text that was being preserved that THIS IS INDEED A NOBLE QURAN, IN A BOOK PRESERVED, Surah 56:77-78. **WHAT'S THE ORIGINAL ARABIC WORD IN THE TEXT**, which Abdul Kader translates as "preserved"? It is *mahnuun*, which comes from the root word *kanna*, meaning: "to hide". From this word comes the following words used in the Quran: *aknaan,* meaning: "a refuge" or "hiding-place" in the mountains (Surah 16:81), *akkinah,* meaning "veils" or coverings upon men's hearts (Surah 6:25) and *akanna,* meaning "to hide" something in the heart (Surah 2:235) ... The clear underlying meaning of any form of this word is to conceal / hide."

This is precisely why other Translators rendered Surah 56:78 as below:

<u>Meaning of Glorious Quran</u> "In a book kept **HIDDEN**."

<u>Quran Translation by Prof. Arthur J. Arberry</u> "...Koran in a **HIDDEN** book..."

We already presented **undeniable** evidence from the most Authentic Islamic literature that the seven Arabic Versions of the Quran were not preserved as received and recited by Muhammad and his companions. We have seen that chapters and verses were removed from and added to the Quran. Variant readings survived and are still in print today. These examples of the corruption of the original Quran are to silence the proud-blinded Muslims once and for all, **invalidating their emotional claim** that the Quran is preserved, since Muhammad received it.

Let's look again at Surah 15:9

<u>The Noble Quran</u> "Verily, we, it is we who have SENT down the Dhikr (e.g. the Quran) [Reminder] and surely, we will guard it (from corruption)."

This Surah, according to Islamic literature [see the table presented in Q8.] is actually the 54th revealed Surah in its chronological order. Please notice that verse 9 is in the past tense: "SENT", meaning that this verse referred to all the Surahs and its respective verses, preceding it. By implication, it excludes all the Surahs not yet revealed after Surah 15:9. How-else could Surah 15:10 [Chap. 54] to Surahs 114 in chronological order, be guarded in the minds of Muhammad and his people, if it were not yet revealed at the time Surah 15:9 was first recited?

Christian writer - Mr. John Gilchrist: Facing the Muslim Challenge: Page 30 "**AS-SUYUTI AL ITQAN FII ULUM AL-QURAN, PAGE 524** "ABDULLAH IBN UMAR [SAID]: Let no one of you say: I have acquired the whole of the Qur'an. HOW DOES HE KNOW WHAT ALL OF IT IS WHEN MUCH OF THE QURAN HAS DISAPPEARED? *Rather let him say: I have acquired what has survived.*"

Behind The Veil: "Those who adopt the notion of the perversion of the Qur'an are present among all different Islamic groups… (*Dr. M. E. Mosawy: El-Sheaa and Correction: Page 131)*"

Apart from the fact that Muhammad's 7 Quran versions were not preserved, I will present evidence that Uthman's Quran Recension was also **NOT** preserved. In other words, the Quran Version of today, is not the same as the Quran produced by Uthman. Remember the boast of Muslims: *"Not a single dot or word in the Quran was changed."*

Uthman's text had no vowels and diacritical points

Public Debate 1986: "Is the Bible the Word of God?" Christian Speaker, Evangelist Jimmy Swaggart and Muslim Speaker, Sheik Ahmad Deedat: Q&A Session: "Does the glorious Quran exist in its original and pure form and was the originals in fact burned? [Deedat's response] … **THE ARABIC SCRIPTURE WERE WRITTEN ORIGINALLY WITHOUT VOWEL POINTS**…" https://www.youtube.com/watch?v=genex9BqlmI Time line 01:32:10–01:34:09 Last accessed 24 April 2021

Ahmed Von Denffer: Ulum al Quran: Introduction to the Science of the Quran. Chap 3 Page 2 – Chap 4 Page 1 "All old Quranic scripts are completely **WITHOUT ANY DIACRITICAL POINTS AND VOWEL SIGNS**. There are **NO** headings and separations between the Surahs, nor any kind of division nor even any formal indication of the end of a verse… All 114 Suras in the Quran have names, which serve as a sort of heading. **THE NAMES ARE OFTEN DERIVED FROM AN IMPORTANT OR DISTINGUISHING WORD IN THE TEXT ITSELF**…"

The Koran: Introduction Pages 3 "The Kufic script, in which the Koran was originally written, **CONTAINED NO INDICATION OF VOWELS OR DIACRITICAL POINTS**…"

The Qur'an: Saheeh International, Page 661 "The mushaf of Uthman had **NO** dots or vowel marks…"

These additions were added after Uthman's death

TP Huges: Dictionary of Islam – Page 487 "…The vowel points and diacritical signs, these marks **WERE INVENTED AT A LATER DATE**."

Quran Translation by Abdullah Yusuf Ali: Page xx: Punctuation Marks in the Arabic Text: "The punctuation marks in the Arabic Text have been **WORKED OUT BY OUR ULAMA** [learned men]."

The Qur'an (Saheeh International) Page 662 "Short vowel sounds were first represented by dots positioned above, below and left to the letter. **THIS SYSTEM WAS INTRODUCED DURING THE CALIPHATE OF MUAWIYAH** bin Abi Sufyan by Abdul-Aswad ad-Duli, after he had heard errors in recitation of the Quran. Similarly, written letters were differentiated by **ANOTHER SYSTEM OF DOTS ABOVE AND BELOW THEM DURING THE CALIPHATE OF ABDUL-MALIK BIN MARVAN**. At the caliphate's order, his governor, al-Hajjaj, appointed scholars Nasr bin Asim and Hayy bin Yamur to implement this improvement. **THE PRESENTLY USED SYSTEM OF SHORT VOWEL SYMBOLS WAS DEVISED BY AL-KHALEEL BIN AHMAD AL-FARAHEEDI DURING THE ABBASINE PERIOD**."

Brief History of the Compilation of the Quran: "Three stages of dotting and diacritization: 1. Abu Al-Aswad Al Doaly put dots as syntactical marks, during the time of Muawiya Ibn Abi Sufian (661-680 CE). 2. The letters were marked with different dotting by Nasr Ibn Asem and Hayy ibn Yaamor, during the time of Abd Al-Malek Ibn Marawan (685-705CE) **3. A COMPLETE SYSTEM OF DIACRITICAL MARKS (DAMMA, FATAHA, KARA) INVENTED BY AL KHALEEL IBN AHMAD AL FARAHEEDY (786CE)**."

It's vital to know that the unofficial Quran by Abu Bakr and the official Revised Quran by Uthman had no vowels and diacritical marks, *which were worked out by Muslim Scholars who added it to Uthman's Version*. The reader will now realize that the modern-day Qurans with vowels and diacritical points in his hands, is not the same as the Quranic text written down in Muhammad's day, nor is it the same as Caliphates Abu Bakr, Umar and Uthman's. Except for vowels and diacritical marks invented and added by Muslim Scholars <u>134 YEARS LATER AFTER UTHMAN'S DEATH,</u> **Muslims in 786CE also took it upon themselves to correct some grammar errors that were made in the official Revised Uthmanic Quran**.

➢ Grammar errors were edited 134 years post-Uthman

<u>Muslim writer, Mr. Ahmed Von Denffer: Ulum al Quran: Introduction to the Science of the Quran. Chap 2 Page 16</u> "According to Ibn Abi Dawud, **11 changes were made under al-Hajjaj**, among them e.g. 5:48 *"shari atan wa minhajan"* into *"shir atan wa minhajan"* 12:45 *"ana atikum bi-ta wilihi"* into *"unabbi ukum bi ta wilihi"*.

<u>Muslim Dr. MSM Saifullah said in an email discussion:</u> "That leads us to the conclusion that Al-Hajjaj did not tamper with the text of the Quran or **RATHER HE MADE CORRECTIONS OF THE ERRORS, WHICH THE SCRIBES MADE IN THE UTHMANIC TEXT."**

CAN YOU IMAGINE HOW THE MUSLIM-WORLD WOULD HAVE CONDEMNED JEWS AND CHRISTIANS, IF THIS WERE THE CASE WITH THE BIBLE? SO WHAT WE HAVE IN OUR HANDS TODAY IS THE MUSLIMS SCHOLARS' REVISED VERSION OF THE UTHMANIC REVISED QURAN.

Time-line chart and Quran Manuscripts

DATES: AD = Anno Domini "the year of our Lord" / CE = Common Era (none Christian)				
ROMAN YEARS	ROMAN CENTURY	ISLAMIC CALENDER STARTS WITH MUHAMMAD'S MIGRATION TO MEDINAH IN 622 CE	ISLAMIC YEARS	ISLAMIC CENTURY

000 – 100 AD	1ST	Pre- Islamic		Pre-Islamic
100 – 200 AD	2ND	Pre- Islamic		Pre-Islamic
200 – 300 AD	3RD	Pre- Islamic		Pre-Islamic
300 – 400 AD	4TH	Pre- Islamic		Pre-Islamic
400 – 500 AD	5TH	Pre- Islamic		Pre-Islamic
500 – 600 AD	6TH	Muhammad born in 570 CE		Pre-Islamic
600 – 700 AD	7TH	622 – 722 CE	000 – 100 AH	1ST
700 – 800 AD	8TH	722 – 822 CE	100 – 200 AH	2ND
800 – 900 AD	9TH	822 – 922 CE	200 – 300 AH	3RD
900 – 1000 AD	10TH	922 – 1022 CE	300 – 400 AH	4TH
1000 – 1100 AD	11TH	1022 – 1122 CE	400 – 500 AH	5TH

The Sana'a Quran Manuscript

Presentation by Dr. Jay Smit and Al Kadi: The Quran's many problems 07 – Early Quran Manuscripts – San'a Pamlipsest: "The manuscript was discovered in 1975 and it contain 26% of the Quran. It is dated 705AD [early 8TH century]. It is different from the 1924 Edition."

https://www.youtube.com/watch?v=EnkFp9IZWHY Last accessed 24 April 2021

The Topkapi Quran Manuscript

Presentation by Dr. Jay Smit and Al Kadi: The Quran's many problems: 04 – Early Quran Manuscripts – Topkapi: "Muslim Scholar - Prof. Dr. Ekmeleddin Ihsanoglu – We have none of Uthman's mushaf, nor do we have any copies of those mushafs. THESE MUSHAFS DATE FROM THE LATE UMMAYYAD PERIOD." https://www.youtube.com/watch?v=2lJe3XOpnto Timeline 06:16 – 06:47 **Muslim Scholar – Dr. Tayyar Altikulaç** – No serious scholarly work has been done on them. These mushafs date from early to mid 8th century [722AD – 752AD] due to the vowelling and dotting. They are not Uthmanic, nor copies sent by him. https://www.youtube.com/watch?v=2lJe3XOpnto Timeline 07:33 – 11: 52 **Dr. Tayyar Altikulaç** concludes that the Topkapi have 2270 variants in comparison with the Fahd Mushaf [Hafs]." https://www.youtube.com/watch?v=2lJe3XOpnto Timeline 12:35 – 13:18 Last accessed 24 April 2021

https://www.youtube.com/watch?v=2lJe3XOpnto Timeline 13:19 – 14:14 Last accessed 26 April 2021

Topkapi mid 8th Century reads:	Cairene Text (1924 Canon) reads:
Surah 14:38 "You know what we conceal and what HE revealed"	Surah 14:38 "You know what we conceal and what WE revealed"
Surah 3:158 "If you should die or be slain, you shall NOT be gathered."	Surah 3:158 "If you should die or be slain, BEFORE HIM YOU SHALL UNDOUBTEDLY BE GATHERED."

This manuscript is located at the Topkapi Palace Museum, Istanbul, Turkey.

It is neither Uthmanic, nor Hafs Quran. The Topkapi and the Hafs contain variants proving it is not the same Quran.

The Birmingham Quran Manuscript

https://www.bbc.com/news/business-33436021

https://www.youtube.com/watch?v=jowQond7_UE

https://www.youtube.com/watch?v=z0Q19RT6LYc

Last accessed 26 April 2021

MOST IMPORTANT, THIS MANUSCRIPT IS NOT A COMPLETE QURAN, IT HAVE 3 CHAPTERS (NAMELY 18,19,20) in comparison to today's Hafs Quranic Version that have *114* Chapters. SURAHS 1-17, 21-114 IS MISSING in this manuscript. **EQUALLY WORSE**, today's Hafs Quran, chapters 18,19,20, have 343 verses, this manuscript only has about 33 verses (about one page), which is about (33/343 = 0.096) **0.1%** of the Hafs verses in relation to chapters 18-20. The Hafs Quran have 6236 verses in total, which means, this manuscript consists out of (33/6236 = 0.00529) **0.005% verses** in comparison to Hafs Version.

Dr. Jay Smit: On the state of the Quran – the hole story: [Jay talks about the two folios with its 33 verses for Surahs 18-20 and how radiocarbondating works.]

https://www.youtube.com/watch?v=fDuLG4IJG20 Time line 55:00 – 58:00 Last accessed 26 April 2021

This manuscript is believed to be the oldest Quran in the world. Scientist dated this parcement with a 95.4% accurary between 568AD – 645AD. In other words, according to radiocarbon-analysis, **the animal skin** on which the Quranic text was written, was of an animal killed between 568AD – 645AD. It is the animal skin that is dated, not the ink. The text on the parcement is of a later date. If the dating, as some uninformed Muslims convince themselves to believe, refers to the text, it would mean the Quran dates **2 years prior to Muhammad's birth-date, i.e 570CE and 42 years prior to his prophethood, i.e. 610CE**. No thinking Muslim will accept this contradictory conclusion. It is critical to note that the Uthmanic Recension script of 652CE had no vowel and diacritical dottings (see heading: Uthman's text had no vowel and diacritical points). These were invented in the late 8th Century (see heading: These additions were added after Uthman's death). *Since the Birmingham Quran manuscript contain vowel and diacritical marks, it can't be Uthmanic.* therefore, it must date after 786ce when the dotting system was developed. it is also obvious today's quran of 114 surahs (chapters) and 6232 ayats (verses) isn't based on the incomplete birmingham university manuscript with only 3 chapters and 33 verses.

The Tubingen Quran Manuscript

https://www.islamic-awareness.org/quran/text/mss/tubingen.html Page last updated 8 April 2020.

Last accessed 26 April 2021

This **manuscript date from the "second half of the first Islamic century" and therefore could not be one of the original Uthmanic copies.** The parchment (**animal skin**) on which the Quranic text was written, was that of an animal that was killed **earliest 20 years after the Uthmanic Rescencion, and more accurately between 672AD – 722AD.** It contains Quranic text from Surahs 17:35 to 36:57, which is about 26.2% in comparison to the Hafs Quran Version. It means today's Hafs Quran Version cannot be based on this manuscript. Since the Tubingen Quran manuscripts contain vowel and diacritical marks, it can't be Uthmanic and therefore its <u>**TEXT MUST DATE ANY TIME AFTER 786CE**</u>.

The Samakant Kufic Quran Manuscript

Presentation by Dr. Jay Smit and Al Kadi: The Quran's many problems 05 – Early Quran Manuscripts – Samarkant – Last viewed 27 July 2020. https://www.youtube.com/watch?v=Hi__1rCS4QQ Timeline 00: 01:40 – 00:03:00 "Muslim Scholar – Dr. Tayyar Altikulaç: It is not Uthmanic as it **dates from the 8th century**... It contains later additions and has 43 Surahs. One chapter, Surah 6 is complete and 24 Surahs is incomplete." This manuscript is kept at Hast Imam Library, Tashkent, Uzbekistan.

The Parisino-Petropolitanus Quran Manuscript

Presentation by Dr. Jay Smit and Al Kadi: The Quran's many problems 05 – Early Quran Manuscripts – Parisino-Petropolitanus: "**This manuscript dates to the early 8th Century.** Muslim scholar, Franscois Deroche: There are corrections to the text. It disagrees with the 1924 Cairene Mushaf in 93 places. Later modified with erasusers and additions. Contain 26% of the Quran."

https://www.youtube.com/watch?v=Hi__1rCS4QQ Timeline 08:00 – 09:00 Last accessed 26 April 2021

https://www.youtube.com/watch?v=Hi__1rCS4QQ Timeline 09:04 – 10:45 Last accessed 26 April 2021

Petropolitanus 8th Century reads:	Cairene Text (1924 Canon) reads:
Surah 14:37 "Our Lord, I have settled some of my descendants in an uncultivated valley near your sacred house, our Lord, that they may establish prayer AND make hearts among the people incline towards them."	*Surah 14:37* "Our Lord, I have settled some of my descendants in an uncultivated valley near your sacred house, our Lord, that they may establish prayer. SO make hearts among the people incline towards them."

Research by Yassin Dutton show the manuscript may have been written in Syria as **it is written in the recitations of Ibn Amir of Damascus**.

The AlHusseini Cairo Quran Manuscript

Presentation by Dr. Jay Smit and Al Kadi: The Quran's many problems 05 – Early Quran Manuscripts – Al Husseini: "**Muslim Scholar – Dr. Tayyar Altikulaç:** This manuscript is not Uthmanic. It is dated from early to mid 8th century… Timeline 05:30 – 06:10 **Muslim scholar: Franscois Deroche:** mid 8th century." Timeline 06:17 – 06:47 https://www.youtube.com/watch?v=Hi__1rCS4QQ Last accessed 26 April 2021

The Mail Quran Manuscript

Presentation by Dr. Jay Smit and Al Kadi: The Quran's many problems 05 – Early Quran Manuscripts – Mail: "In the British Library (Ridblatt Gallery). It is written in the Hijazi script and goes up to Surah 43. It includes only 53% in comparison to the Hafs Quran. Dr. Tayyar Altikulaç dates it as early 8th Century [700AD -750AD]. Dr. Martin Lings dates it as late 8th Century [750AD – 800AD]."

https://www.youtube.com/watch?v=Hi__1rCS4QQ Timeline 03:20 – 04:50 Last accessed 26 April 2021

Nadia Idriss Mayen: London exhibition unveils ancient Quran: "The highlight of the exhibition is the Ma'il Koran… One of the earliest known from 8th Century. It was probably copied in Mecca or Medina in the Hijaz. It's in a beautiful style of script, one of the earliest forms of Arabic script called "Ma'il", which literally means *sloping*."

https://www.youtube.com/watch?v=mqyzrScyAqA Time line 01:00 – 01:54 Last accessed 26 April 2021

The Blue Quran Manuscript

Located in the National Institute of Art and Archaeology Bardo National Museum in Tunis, Tunisia. It is one of the famous and beautiful ancient Qurans in the world. The manuscript has been dated to between the late 9th to the early 10th century. The Blue Quran was created for the Great Mosque of Qairawan in Tunisia. The pages are written with gold ink on vellum colored with indigo, giving it a distinct blue color.

https://www.oldest.org/religion/qurans/ Last accessed 26 April 2021

The Earliest Complete Kufi Quran Manuscript

"Complete Kufi manuscript dated to 393 AH... This is regarded as the earliest complete, dated Quran Manuscript. **It is written in the Kufic script and dated 393AH, which is approximately 1002CE.** Scholars have not identified any other complete dated Quran manuscript written in the Kufic script. Located in the Tareq Rajab Museum in Kuweit."

https://www.usna.edu/Users/humss/bwheeler/quran/kufi_393.html Last accessed 26 April 2021

The oldest complete Quran in the Kufic script dates about 350 years (3-4 centuries after Uthman and 400 years (4 centuries) after Muhammad. There are much older Quran manuscripts, but these are in fragments of 2-3 pages, some manuscripts contain 3 out of 114 chapters, etc.

Hafs Qira'at became Egypt's standard text in 1924

Wikipedia: The free encyclopedia: "Hafs ibn Sulayman was born in 706AD in Baghdad (during the Umayyad dynasty) and died 796AD." https://en.wikipedia.org/wiki/Hafs Last accessed 26 April 2021

Wikipedia: The free encyclopedia: "The Egyptian Edition is based on the **Ḥafṣ Version (qira'at), [which is] based on ʿAsim's recitation, the 8th-century recitation**

of Kufa. IT USES A SET OF ADDITIONAL SYMBOLS AND AN ELABORATE SYSTEM OF MODIFIED VOWEL-SIGNS AND FOR MINUTE DETAILS, NOT IDENTICAL TO ANY OLDER SYSTEM… A committee of leading professors from Al-Azhar University had started work on the project in 1907, but it was not until **10 July 1924 that the "Cairo Qur'an" was first published** under the patronage of Fuad I of Egypt."

https://en.wikipedia.org/wiki/History_of_the_Quran#1924_Cairo_edition Last accessed 26 April 2021

Egypt destroyed Qurans contrary to the 1924 text

Once again, history repeated itself, just like Uthman destroyed Quranic material contrary to his REMNANT Quran recension, so did Egyptian Muslims try to destroy Qurans contrary to the Hafs REMNANT Quran published as the Cairoo 1924 Text by dumping conflicting Qurans into the Nile River.

Wikipedia: The free encyclopedia: "The goal of the government of the newly formed Kingdom of Egypt was not to delegitimize the other qir'at, **but to eliminate that, which the colophon labels as errors, found in Qur'anic texts used in state schools.** To do this they chose to preserve one of the 14 Qira'at, i.e. Hafs (d. 180/796)… Its publication has been called a "terrific success" and the edition has been described as one *"NOW WIDELY SEEN AS THE OFFICIAL TEXT OF THE QUR'AN"*. Minor amendments were made later in 1924 and 1936… **A LARGE NUMBER OF PRE-1924 QURANS WERE DESTROYED BY DUMPING THEM IN THE RIVER NILE.**"

https://en.wikipedia.org/wiki/History_of_the_Quran#1924_Cairo_edition Last accessed 26 April 2021

Egypt's Edition became the popular Qira'at and Text

Youtube presentation by Dr. Jay Smit: Why dates of the different Qurans are so damaging? [Muslim scholar, Dr. Yasir Qadhi confirms…] "**The most common qira'at that people are reciting that are living in English speaking countries is the Hafs** that has

6236 verses **that we recite**. The other recitations and there are ten recitations, they have slightly different number of verses…"

https://www.youtube.com/watch?v=X4vC4rDI8UU Time line 03:55 – 04:44 Last accessed 26 April 2021

Wikipedia: The free encyclopedia "The influential standard Quran of Cairo is the Quran that is in "general use" throughout almost all the Muslim world today… **The Cairo Edition became the standard for modern printings of the Quran** *WITH EXCEPTION OF THOSE USED IN ALL NORTH AFRICA WHERE THE WARSH VERSION IS USED.*"

https://en.wikipedia.org/wiki/History_of_the_Quran#1924_Cairo_edition Last accessed 26 April 2021

The Hafs Quran Recitation is not one of the seven ahruf (see heading: Muhammed recited different Arabic Quran versions). It is one of the fourteen variant transmitted recitations. It isn't Medinian, nor Meccan, but from the Kufa district (see heading: More recitations evolved after Muhammed's death).

CONCLUSION: None of the found Quranic manuscripts conform to the Hafs 1924 Egyptian Edition. The Hafs Quran **recitation** dates from the late 8th century, but it was **FIRST** published, printed in 1924. Todate there is no Hafs manuscript that dates from the 8th century. Also note, the Hafs Quran contains vowel and diacritical points not identical to the system invented in 786AD, which sets it apart from the oldest manuscripts. The seven versions of the recitations of the Quran that Muhammad seemingly received from Allah, were not preserved, but variants of it survived. The Uthmanic Quran Recension was also re-edited post-Uthman, about 134 years later by the learned Muslims who added vowel and diacritical points to the Uthmanic rasm (text without vowel and diacritical points). Thereafter, according to Muslim literature, 11 grammar corrections in 786AD were made to the edited Uthmanic Quran. Uthman who passed away, couldn't have approved the Revised Uthmanic Version with dots and diacritical marks worked out by learnt Muslim Scholars a century later. Muslims cannot honestly claim that the Uthmanic Quran manuscripts has been perfectly preserved as there are no complete manuscripts dating from the 7th century without vowel and diacritical points. **The earliest complete Quran manuscript date 372 years (four centuries) after Muhammad**. Please note that this complete manuscript has not been compared to Uthman's Recension since it does not exist. The trophied recitation of Hafs became the 1924 Egyptian Edition, now known as a standard text for most Muslims. It is not strange that the Hafs Quranic text was also standardized while other conflicting texts were destroyed through it being dump into the Nile River.

10 Why was the Quran revealed in Arabic?

The Noble Quran – Surah 6:156-157 "**LEST YOU (PAGAN ARABS) SHOULD SAY**: The Book was only sent down to two sects (Jews / Christians) before us and for our part, we were in fact unaware of what they studied or **LEST YOU (PAGAN ARABS) SHOULD SAY**: If only the Book had been sent down to us, we would surely have been better guided than they ... **41:44** And if we had sent this as a Qur'ân in a foreign language other than Arabic, **THEY WOULD HAVE SAID**: "Why are not its verses explained in detail (in our language)? What! (A Book) not in Arabic, (the Messenger) an Arab?" Say: "It is for those who believe, a guide and a healing ... **42:7** And thus We have inspired unto you (O Muhammad SAW) a Qur'ân **(IN ARABIC) THAT YOU MAY WARN THE MOTHER OF THE TOWNS** (Makkah) and all around it [neighboring Arabic speaking people] ... **14:4** We *sent not* a Messenger, except with the **LANGUAGE OF HIS PEOPLE**, in order that **HE MIGHT MAKE (THE MESSAGE) CLEAR FOR THEM** ..." (See Q49: Was Muhammad a universal or local messenger?)

CONCLUSION: The Arabic Quran, according to the Quran itself, was sent to an Arab to warn the Arabs, so that they were without an excuse of being unaware of the previous guidance. The Arabs could no longer claim ignorance and non-understanding of religious scriptures, since the guidance now supposedly came in their own language unto them.

There is no **other** Quranic evidence why the Quran was revealed in Arabic, but the given reasons.

11 Was the Quran copied from the Holy Bible?

It is predictable to expect Muslims to give counter explanations that the Quran was copied from the Bible, God's True Word, but for Muslims to lean towards illogical counteracts, only draw attention to the fact that the Quran was copied from the Holy Bible, God's True Word. In order to dismiss any possibilities of the Bible being available to Arabs in Arabic, from which the Quran could have been copied by Muhammad, Deedat denied that the Bible was translated into Arabic in Muhammad's day.

Mr. Ahmed Deedat: Al-Quran: The Miracle of Miracles! – Page 11 Footnote "The Bible was not translated into Arabic until the tenth century of the Christian era, **NO ARAB LIVING BEFORE THE YEAR 1000** would have had the opportunity to examine the *written text of the Bible* in his own [Arabic] language."

Deedat implied the Quran couldn't be copied by Muhammad from the Bible, because the Bible wasn't translated into Arabic until after 1000AD. That the Holy Bible was not available in the Arabic Text before the year 1000 is an unsubstantiated statement and Deedat's argument that "NO ARAB LIVING BEFORE THE YEAR 1000 would have had the opportunity to examine the *written text of the Bible* in his own language" falls flat to the ground, as my findings will vindicate the opposite.

Why would Deedat make such a blunder? Deedat was ignorant concerning his own religious sources as is accentuated in this publication:

The Muslim Digest: Vol. 31 Nos. 2 - 5 Sept. to Dec. 1980 Page 95 "It is essential to state and stress that Mr. Deedat is not a man of Islamic learning."

I will provide Islamic sources to assist us to prove the Bible was available to Muhammad in Arabic and by default prove Deedat to be wrong again, in other words, the Bible was available in Arabic for Muhammad to have accessed its text and had opportunity to copy from it.

Islamic sources verify the Bible was available in 600AD in Arabic

Muslim Prof. Fazl Ahmad: Muhammad, The Prophet of Islam: Heroes of Islam 1, Pages 45, 51 "Khadija was married to the holy prophet. She was 40 years of age at the time and he was only 25… She took her husband to Waraqa bin Naufal, a cousin of hers. **This man was a scholar of the holy books of the Christians and the Jews.**"

From his time of marriage, until his self-acclaimed prophethood, is 15 years. Muhammad had at least 15 years of opportunity to learn Bible stories from his wife's cousin, Waraqa.

Sahih Bukhari: Vol. 4, Page 395, Hadith 605 "Narrated 'Aisha: She [Khadijah] took him [Muhammad] to Waraqa who was a Christian convert and who **USED TO READ THE GOSPELS IN ARABIC**."

Sahih Bukhari: Vol. 6 Page 452 Hadith 478 "Waraqa used to write Arabic and **WRITE OF THE GOSPEL IN ARABIC** as Allah wished him to write."

According to Abdullah Yusuf Ali, Arabic Versions of the Bible, existed during the period of Jesus.

Quran Translation by Abdullah Yusuf Ali: Page 283: Appendix II "…By the time we come to the period of Jesus, most cultivated Hebrews used the Greek language and others used Aramaic, Latin or Local dialects. **THERE WERE ALSO ARABIC VERSIONS**…"

Muslims admit Muhammad was influenced by Jews

Quran Translation by Abdullah Yusuf Ali: Page 7 – Introduction: Footnote 8 "It was on such [caravan] visits that he [Muhammad] met and conversed with Nestorian Christian monks like Bahira…"

The Koran: Page 1 – Introduction to the Translation of the Quran "…[MUHAMMAD] **HAD COME UNDER THE INFLUENCE OF JEWISH AND CHRISTIAN TEACHINGS.**"

Was Noah's flood universal or local?

Dr. Shabir Ally argued that the Quran isn't copied from the Bible, because the details contained in the stories of the Quran and the Bible is different. In other words, Muhammad could have only copied the Bible if the Noah-Flood-story in the Bible and Quran were the same.

Dr. Shabir Ally on Noah's flood: "All evidence show that the Qur'an could not have been copied from the Bible... One important difference between the two accounts is that whereas the Bible describes the flood as a worldwide flood (see Genesis Ch. 7), the Qur'an mentions it as a local flood, affecting the people of Noah (see Qur'an 7:59-64)." http://answering-islam.org/Responses/Shabir-Ally/q16_copied.htm

Last accessed 26 April 2021

- Firstly, there are **NO VERSES** in the Quran informing us unquestionably that Noah's flood was a local flood and that **ONLY** Noah's people were affected by the flood.

- Secondly, the Quran **INDIRECTLY** say that Noah's flood was universal; this conclusion is reached through interpretations of certain verses in the Quran.

Quran Translation by Abdullah Yusuf Ali – Surah 71:26, 11:40 & 44 "O my Lord! Leave not of the unbelievers, a single one **ON EARTH** ... And the **FOUNTAINS OF THE EARTH** gushed forth ... The word went forth: **O EARTH**! Swallow up thy water..."

If this was a local flood, Noah would have prayed... *"O Lord, allow not of the unbelievers to escape to the neighboring cities..."* The word "earth" is used to indicate world events. As we'll see, just like in the Bible, in the Quran, Noah was also instructed to take of every species on board. If it was a local flood, the animals by instinct would have escaped to neighboring cities. This was obviously a universal flood, hence God ordered Noah to take the animals of every species on board to secure their survival after the flood.

Quran Translation by Abdullah Yusuf Ali – Surah 23:27 "…Take thou on board pairs of **EVERY SPECIES**, male and female…"

Why did God instruct Noah to take on board two species of every kind of animal before the flood? To preserve animal life on earth after the flood. If the flood was local, it would make no sense to take on board animals of every kind, animals by instinct would have fled to neighbouring lands. These verses clearly indicate a universal event affecting the earth, not a local event. The quote below is not from the Quran, but it's to illustrate that Muhammad believed Noah was sent to the world, not only his people.

The Noble Quran: Page 8 – Footnote 1 "…Noah, for he was the first messenger Allah sent to the **inhabitants of the earth**…"

Another example as prove the Quran was copied from the Bible is…

Quran Translation by Abdullah Yusuf Ali – Surah 21:105 "Before this we wrote in the Psalms, after the message (given to Moses): My servants, the righteous, shall inherit the earth."

The above Quranic verse is a direct quotation copied from ***Psalms 37:29*** "The righteous shall inherit the earth and dwell therein forever."

When the Bible records the sins of prophets, Muslims argue that God would never reveal wickedness as the actions of prophets. Yet Muhammad had no problem to copy the wickedness of Lot from the ***Bible Genesis 19*** into the ***Quran Surah 11:78***. In both Books, Lot is portrayed as a father who offered his daughters to be ravished by homosexuals, who actually wanted to sodomize Lot's angelic visitors. Lot should have defended his daughters with his own life. This however, was not necessary because his visitors were angels in human form that came to warn Lot and his family that judgment will fall on the people of that land. The angels were capable of defending themselves as the story later revealed. In the Bible, Lot is described as a just man (***2 Peter 2:7***) and in the Quran (***Surah 6:84-89***), Lot is elevated to a prophet. Why don't Muslims speak out about the cowardice act of their Allah's prophet, Lot.

CONCLUSION: Muhammad was well aware of Biblical teachings and used it to formulize his Message. Of course, it is obvious he didn't copy it word-for-word, but the events are evidently the same. The fact that Muhammad knew Biblical stories was best put in the words of Islam's giants. The Quran will always trace back to the Holy Bible, as its source.

12 Is the Quran 100% God's Words?

In his booklet: *"Is all the Bible God's Word?"* Deedat quotes biblical verses to illustrate that THE ENTIRE BIBLE IS NOT the Word of God. Again, we find Deedat's examples to be very weak as the **SAME UNRECOGNISED AND SELF-IMPOSED STANDARDS** used by him against the Bible, can be used more convincingly against the Quran.

Words of God, prophets and historians in the Bible

"Is all the Bible God's Word?" Pages 7-9 "We Muslims have no hesitation in acknowledging that in the Bible, there are three different kinds of witnessing recognizable…

- **FIRST TYPE:** Note the first person pronoun singular (in bold) "**I**, even **I**, am the Lord and beside **Me** there is no Savior… Look unto **Me** … for **I** am God, and there is non-else." (Isaiah 43:11, 45:22), namely: The Words of God.

- **SECOND TYPE:** Words attributed to prophets: "**Jesus cried** with a loud voice, saying Eli, Eli, lama sabachtani? …" (Matthew 27:46) "And **Jesus answered** him…" Mark 12:29, namely: The Words of Prophets.

- **THIRD TYPE:** The words of a third person. "And seeing a fig tree afar off having leaves, **He (JESUS)** came, if haply **He (JESUS)** might find anything thereon…" (Mark 11:13), namely: Words of Historians…

[Quote continues…] For the Muslim it is easy to distinguish the above types of evidence, because he has them in his faith. But of the followers of the different religions, they [Muslims] are the most fortunate in this that their various records are contained in

SEPARATE BOOKS! [Deedat claims that] *All of the Quran is "Type 1"* (the Word of God) and Muslims jealously keep the three grades apart in Islam, for example…

- **FIRST TYPE:** God's Word is found in a Book called the Holy Qur'an.
- **SECOND TYPE:** The Words of Prophets is recorded in the Traditions.
- **THIRD TYPE:** Words of Historians is in different volumes of Islamic history."

UNQUOTE: Let us investigate Deedat's examples in relation to the Quran and see if the Quran passes the same unrealistic criteria that Deedat prescribed for the Bible.

Words of God in the Quran

<u>*Quran Trans. by Abdullah Yusuf Ali – Surah 51:56*</u> "I… created Jinns and men that they may serve **ME**."

Based on Deedat's criteria this verse does qualify to be the Word of God as they are recorded in the first person singular pronoun.

We'll now proceed to see whether the Quran contain words of prophets. (**<u>At this stage I'm using the title "prophet" loosely as I don't believe Muhammad was God's true prophet</u>**).

Words of prophets in the Quran

<u>*Quran Trans. by Abdullah Y. Ali – Surah 69:40*</u> "That this is verily **THE WORD OF AN HONORED APOSTLE**."

<u>*Surah 27:91*</u>

<u>**Quran Translation by Abdullah Yusuf Ali:**</u> "I have been commanded to serve *THE LORD* of this city, *HIM* who has sanctified it and *TO WHOM* (belong) all things and I am commanded to be those who bow in Islam *TO GOD'S* will."

<u>The Noble Quran</u> "I **(MUHAMMAD)** have been commanded only to worship the Lord of this city … I am commanded to be from among the Muslims…"

If Muhammad is not the God of Islam, then the Quran is definitely not 100% God's Word, but it, the Quran, also contain the words of Muhammad mixed into it.

Quran Translation by Abdullah Yusuf Ali – Surah 19:33, 20:33, 60:4 "So peace is on **Me [Jesus]** the day that **I** was born ... **MOSES SAID**: O my Lord, expand me my breast ... **ABRAHAM SAID** to his father: I'll pray for forgiveness for thee..."

Even a child will be able to affirm that Jesus said: "So peace is on me". Moses said: "O my Lord" and Abraham said that he'll pray for his father's forgiveness. Based on Deedat's criteria these verses are not the Word of God, they are the words of prophets (*that belongs in the Ahadith*) mixed into the Quran.

Words of angels in the Quran

Quran Translation by Abdullah Yusuf Ali – Surah 19:64 "(THE ANGELS SAY:) "**WE** descend not, but by command of thy Lord. TO HIM belong what is before **US** and what is behind **US**..."

The Koran: Page 218 – Footnote 1 "Commentators say that **THESE ARE THE WORDS OF THE ANGEL GABRIEL**, in reply to Muhammad's complaint of long intervals elapsing between periods of revelation."

Based on Deedat's criteria, these are not God's Word, but that of angels.

Words of transgressors in the Quran

Quran Trans. by Abdullah Y. Ali Surah 20:49 "(**PHARAOH SAID**): Who then, O Moses is the Lord of you?"

Even a child will be able to affirm that Pharaoh said... These are indubitably the words of Pharaoh and are not the Word of God.

Words of Satan in the Quran

Quran Translation by Abdullah Yusuf Ali – Surah 4:118 "**HE [SATAN] SAID**: I will take of thy servants a portion marked off..."

Even a child will be able to affirm that Satan said... Based on Deedat's criteria this verse is not the Word of God, but the words of Satan.

Words of unknown beings in the Quran

Quran Translation by Abdullah Yusuf Ali – Surah 70:40 "...I do call to witness THE LORD..."

One entity is calling another entity, The Lord (God), to be his witness. Unless Muslims confess that there are two deities' in Islam, the entity calling is definitely not God, since the "I" entity is calling "The Lord" entity, thus, not every word in the Quran is God's Word.

Quran Translation by Abdullah Yusuf Ali – Surah 1 "In the Name **OF GOD**, the most gracious, most merciful. Praise be **TO GOD**, the cherisher and sustainer of the worlds... Master of the day of judgment. Thee do **WE WORSHIP** and Thine aid **WE SEEK. SHOW US** to the straightway, the way on those whom Thou hast bestowed Thy grace..."

Surah 1 is a **PRAYER DIRECTED TO GOD,** unless a FEW ALLAHS are praising and worshipping another ALLAH [Surah 19:63-64], this is a prayer of some unknown worshippers. Based on Deedat's criteria this complete chapter does not constitute the Word of God. In fact, we have seen that Muhammad and his companions, the best of Quran reciters, Masud and Ubayy (see heading: Ibn Masud's Quran version had 111 chapters) did not recognize Surah Fatiha to be part of the Quran and the Quran distinguished itself from this Surah (see heading: Muhammed said Surah Fatiha is not part of Quran). I wonder how Deedat responded to Dr. M. Asad's below comment!

Message of the Quran: Page 498 – Footnote 77 "In this, as well as in several other passages relating to Solomon, **THE QUR'AN ALLUDES TO MANY POETIC LEGENDS**..."

According to Deedat, God's Word ALONE is found in the Quran, and as we have seen, that's not the case, ALSO, in fact, God's Word, the true Word of God, is also copied into the Muslim Tradition, attributed to Muhammad, which is supposed to contain only the words of prophets.

The Noble Quran: Page 709 – Footnote 1.b "Allah's Messenger said: **ALLAH SAID:** I have prepared for my pious slaves, things which have never been seen by an eye, nor heard by an ear or imagined by a human being." *Sahih Bukhari Vol. 4, Pages 306/7, Hadith 467)."*

These words, mentioned in the above Ahadith, seemingly spoken by the Muslim god, are NOT found in the Quran, it is found in God's True Word, the Holy Bible, in the New Testament, written by Apostle Paul, from whom Muhammad, about 500 years later copied it from.

1 Corinthians 2:9 "But as it is written: Eye hath not seen, nor ear heard, neither have entered into the heart of man, the things which God hath prepared for them that love Him."

Here we see Muhammad quoted Saint Paul's writing as God's Word, yet it is not found in the Quran, proving that the Quran is not complete and that not only is the words of prophets found in the Muslim Traditions, but it is also found in God's Word, which nullifies Deedat's claim that these three types are kept separated by Muslims. Deedat obviously made another blunder to say all of the Quran is God's Word and the entire Bible is not all God's Words.

13 Does the Quran have contradictions in it?

Quran Translation by Abdullah Yusuf Ali – Surah 4:82 "Do they not consider the Qur'an (with care)? Had it been from other than Allah, they would surely have found therein **MUCH** discrepancy."

This verse creates the idea that if the Quran is from God, we'll find **FEW** discrepancies in it and if it was from men there will be **MANY** descrepancies in it! In fact, if the Quran is from the Omniscient (All-knowing) there should be **NO** discrepancies in it. Any evidence of discrepancies is an earmark of humanity. The True God cannot at anytime contradict Himself.

Mr. Ahmad Deedat: "Al-Quran: The Miracle of Miracles!" Page 12 "Any man during the course of such a mission, would be forced by "honorable" compromises, cannot help contradicting himself. **NO MAN CAN WRITE THE SAME ALWAYS**…"

Let's look at the proven contradictions in the Quran.

a) What is the size of "the garden"?

Deedat, who always tried to find fault with the Holy Bible, wrote in his booklet:

Al-Quran: The Miracle of Miracles! Page 30 – Footnote 1 "The first verse of the Bible speaks about *"the **heaven** and the earth"* in the singular. In the Quran the word "earth" is always in the singular, WHEREAS THE WORD "HEAVENS" IS IN THE PLURAL. *Something to ponder upon*!"

It is true that the first verse in the **ENGLISH TRANSLATION** of the Bible (KJV) reads: "…the *heaven* and the earth…" Deedat, as it is obvious, did not even bother to look at the original Hebrew text, showing that his purpose was not to understand Biblical teachings, but only to discredit the Holy Bible at all possible cost.

In the Hebrew manuscripts, the word used in ***Genesis 1:1*** is "**hashamayim**" of which the correct **translation** should be "heaven**s**" in the plural. This verse was correctly translated in ***"The Interlinear Bible: Hebrew-Greek-English"***. However, we find the same Hebrew word mentioned in the manuscripts for ***Genesis 2:1*** and this time the KJV translators have it right: "Thus the heaven**s** and the earth were finish and all the host of them." The Holy Spirit inspired Moses to pen down the same Hebrew word "**hashamayim**" in ***Genesis 1:1 and 2:1***. There is no discrepancy in the manuscripts, only in the **English MIS**translation of the KJV. If Deedat was interested in understanding the Biblical Message, he would have picked it up, but unfortunately his aim was only to find fault and to discredit the Holy Bible.

It was already mentioned (see Q11), according to his Muslim brethren, that Deedat was not a learned man in Islamic matters, LET ALONE JUDAISM AND CHRISTIANITY.

Considering his footnote, it becomes obvious that Deedat was unlearned in the Quran and Bible.

A casual reading of the Quran shows that the word "heaven" in the Quran is also used in its singular form, at least twice (**Surahs 38:27 and 57:21**). How could Deedat have read the whole Quran and concluded that the word "heaven" is always in the plural form in the Quran? Did he, like most Muslims recite it in Arabic without understanding its meaning, or did Deedat conveniently overlook these Surahs where "heaven" is mentioned in the singular form? Like with the Holy Bible (**Genesis 1:1**), does **Surah 57:21** perhaps contain a *possible* mistranslation (is it supposed to be in the plural form "heaven**s**" and not in the singular form "heaven")? *Something to ponder upon!*

In fact, it is **NOT** a Quranic **MIS**translation! The transliteration-form for heaven is *"sama"* meaning that Abdullah Yusuf Ali translated it correctly into the singular and that Deedat either lied that the word heaven is always in the plural in the Quran or he never read the whole Quran in both English and Arabic with understanding. He, like many, repeated the nice sound of the Arabic, but like a donkey that carry books without knowing what it says, Deedat carried the Quran without knowing what it says.

In studying the Quran to see if "HEAVEN" is always in the plural, the result was an observation that the Quran contradicted itself in the following way:

Quran Translated by Abdullah Yusuf Ali:

Surah 3:133 "...A garden whose width is that (of the whole) of the **HEAVENS** [Samawath: PLURAL] and the earth..."	**Surah 57:21** "A garden, the width whereof is as the width of the **HEAVEN** [Sama: SINGULAR] and the earth..."

Dr. Asad is aware of the contradiction and tried to cover it up by **MIS**translating the English into the plural form: **The Message of the Quran - Surah 57:21** "...And (thus) to a paradise as vast as the heaven**S** and earth..." Who gave Dr. Asad the right to hide the contradiction?

What is the Garden's accurate size: "heaven**S** and earth" or "heaven and earth"?

Interesting to know, **IN ALLAH'S PARADISE**, <u>each Muslim man</u> will have 80 000 boy-servants, serving wine and <u>each Muslim man</u> will have 72 young wives with fully developed breasts (2 houris and 70 women rescued out of hell-fire – all wives will have desirable vaginas) and men's penis will be erected 24/7 deflowering virgins (see heading: Muhammed said men's penis will be erected 24/7 in heaven).

The Noble Quran - Surah 52:17-24 "The Muttaqun (pious) will be in Gardens (Paradise)… v20 We shall marry them to Houris… v23 There they shall pass from hand to hand a (wine) cup… (because it will be legal for them to drink). v24 There will go round boy-servants… 78:33 And grape yards and young full breasted (mature) maidens of equal age."

Jami` at-Tirmidhi: "Abu Sa'eed Al-Khudri narrated that the Messenger of Allah said: The least of the people of Paradise in position is the one with eighty thousand servants and seventy-two wives."

https://quranx.com/Hadith/Tirmidhi/DarusSalam/Volume-4/Book-36/Hadith-2562

Last accessed 26 April 2021

b) How long did Allah take to create the universe?

Quran Translation by Abdullah Yusuf Ali – Surah 2:117, 16:40, 54:50 "Of the heavens and the earth, when He decreed A MATTER, He saith to it: Be and it is … FOR TO ANYTHING WHICH WE HAVE WILLED, WE BUT SAY THE WORD: BE AND IT IS … OUR COMMAND IS BUT A SINGLE (ACT), LIKE THE TWINKLING OF AN EYE."

Quran Translation by Abdullah Yusuf Ali – Page 50 Commentary 120 "… The Amr (command, direction, design) is a single thing, UNRELATED TO TIME, LIKE THE TWINKLING OF AN EYE (liv:50) …"

Surahs 3:47,59, 6:73, 36:82, 19:35, 40:68. According to these verses, when Allah decreed a matter (anything), Allah only say: Be and it, i.e. **HEAVENS AND THE EARTH, ETC. CAME INTO EXISTENCE WITHIN A TWINKLING OF AN EYE**, much less than a millisecond (0.001 seconds), unrelated to time.

Contradicted by…

Quran Trans. by Abdullah Y. Ali Surah 9:36 "…The **DAY HE CREATED THE HEAVENS AND THE EARTH**…"

Contradicted by …

Quran Translation by Abdullah Yusuf Ali: Roman Transliteration – Surah 41:9 "Say: Is it that ye deny Him who **CREATED THE EARTH IN 2 DAYS**? …"

WAS THE EARTH CREATED IN A TWINKLE OF AN EYE – *BE AND IT WAS* **OR IN A DAY OR IN TWO DAYS?**

Contradicted by …

Quran Trans. by Abdullah Y Ali Surah 7:54 "…God who created the heavens and the earth **IN SIX DAYS**…"

Contradicted by…

Quran Translation by Abdullah Yusuf Ali: Roman Transliteration – Surah 41:

- [*V9*] "Say: Is it that ye deny Him who **created the earth in 2 Days**? …

- [*V10*] He set on earth mountains… bestowed blessings on earth… **nourishment in due proportion in 4 Days**… [Unquote: Surahs 13:3, 15:19, 16:15, 21:31, 31:10, 50:7, 77:27 – This is a scientific error, mountains are not placed on earth, mountains are formed as a result of tectonic plates (Iirregular, massive slap of solid rock) in earth's crusts pushing against each other upwards. https://www.youtube.com/watch?v=AasZlP2UxwM&t=1441s See 34:08 Last accessed 24 April 2021]

- [*V11*] THEN HE TURNED to the sky and it had been (as) smoke: He said to it [the sky] and to the earth: "Come ye together, willingly or unwillingly. They said: We do come (together)…

- **[V12]** **So He completed them as seven firmaments in 2 Days**… adorned the lower heaven with lights."

Quran Translation by Abdullah Yusuf Ali: Page 1288 – Commentary 4470 "*This is a difficult passage*… If we count the two days mentioned in this verse [9], the four days mentioned in verse 10 and the two days mentioned in verse 12, **we get a total of eight days**… The Commentators understand the "four days" in verse 10 to include the two days in verse 9, so that the total of the universe comes to six days."

Ali starts his comments with *"this is a difficult passage"* and concluded that the heavens and earth were created in 8 days. However, to get rid of the obvious contradiction, Ali alluded to … *"The Commentators understand…"* and introduced these unknown people to save the Quran from a contradiction. It is wishful thinking to say, the two days in verse 9 is included in the four days in verse 10, because that is not how the Quran reads. Any grade one child can read that Allah created the earth in 2 days, **THEN ALLAH TOOK 4 DAYS** to nourish the existing (already created) earth.

*The verse **DOESN'T** read: "…the creation of the earth and the blessings on it were altogter four days".*

Dr. Rashad Khalifah agrees that Allah took four days for the provisions on the ALREADY created earth.

Authorized English Version of the Quran: Page 2229 – Footnote: "…The calculation of provisions for all the creatures on earth, required 4 [days]."

Ali is right – Surah 41:9-12 is a difficult passage for Muslims who don't want to admit the Quran is self contradictory. It is clear, according to Surah 41, Allah took 8 days to create the earth and the heavens.

Contradicted by…

If we focus on Surah 41:11, another contradiction emerges that is left undiscussed by Ali and the unknown Commentators. We see that the Quran actually indicated Allah took more than eight days to create the heavens and the earth. Let's look at more translations of Surah 41:11.

Quran Translation by Abdullah Yusuf Ali: "…He turned **to the sky** and it had been smoke…"

Meaning of Glorious Quran "…Turned He **to the heaven** when it was smoke…"

Allah turned towards a previously creat**ed** sky (heaven) that was in a stage of smoke [Surah 51:47 We constructed the heaven **with power** [should be translated: **Tafsir - Ibn Al Kathir** ...**with our hands** … https://quranx.com/Tafsir/Kathir/51.47] [S.38:75 where it clearly says Allah made Adam with his hands.]

See https://www.quranbrowser.org/quranbrowse.php Last accessed 26 April 2021

Quran Translation by Abdullah Yusuf Ali: Page 1289 – Commentary 4475 "…It is stated here that when the sky was made into seven firmaments, *it [the sky] had existed previously as smoke or vapor or steam*. The idea I derived from a collation of the relevant Quranic passages is that *God first created primeval matter*, which was at yet without order or shape…"

Meaning of Glorious Quran – Surah 2:29 "Created for you all that is in the earth…Turned He **to the heaven and fashioned it** as seven heavens."

These verses (Surah 41:11, 2:29) and Ali's commentary confirms a pre-existing heaven, which was smoke, then Allah turned towards it and renovated it into 7 heavens. Note, nowhere are we informed how many days Allah took to create this heaven (smoke) in Surahs 41:11 and 2:29. **Since the creation period for the initial heaven is unknown, it is safe to conclude that Allah took X-days to create the initial heaven.**

Therefore, in Surah 41:9-12, Allah actually took 8+X days to create the heavens and earth:

- **X days** to create the initial heaven (sky – smoke),
- **2 days** to create the earth and

- **4 days** to nourish the created earth,
- **2 days** to renovate the heaven (sky) into seven heavens with lamps (stars) in the lower heaven.

Contradicted by…

Sahih Muslim: "Abu Huraira reported that Allah's Messenger (ﷺ) took hold of my hands and said: Allah, the Exalted and Glorious, created **[1]** the clay on Saturday and He created **[2]** the mountains on Sunday and He created **[3]** the trees on Monday and He created **[4]** the things entailing labour on Tuesday and created **[5]** light on Wednesday and He caused **[6]** the animals to spread on Thursday and created **[7]** Adam (peace be upon him) after 'Asr on Friday; the last creation… i. e. between afternoon and night. **[From Saturday to Friday = 7 days]**

https://quranx.com/Hadith/Muslim/USC-MSA/Book-39/Hadith-6707 Last accessed 26 April 2021

Was the universe created, as per Islam, in a twinkling of an eye (less than millisecond) "Be and it is" or in 1 day or in 6 days or in 6 days + X days or in 7 days or in 8 days or in 8 days + X days? We leave this confusion for Muslim Mathematians to solve since Allah and Muhammed clearly made a mess out of it.

c) Which was created first: earth or stars?

Quran Translation by Abdullah Yusuf Ali: Roman Transliteration – Surah 41:9
"…Him who created the earth in two Days … v10 … and bestowed blessings on the earth … in four Days… v11 **THEN HE TURNED TO THE SKY** … 12 SO HE COMPLETED THEM AS SEVEN FIRMAMENTS IN TWO DAYS and He assigned to each heaven its duty and command **AND WE ADORNED THE LOWER HEAVEN WITH LIGHTS [STARS]**…"

1ST Allah in X-days created a sky that existed as smoke ONLY,

2ND Allah in 6 days created the earth and bestowed blessings on the created earth,

3ʳᴰ THEN ALLAH TURNED to the existing sky and in 2 days renovated it into seven heavens and placed

created lamps (lights – stars) as decorations in the first (lower) heaven nearest to the earth.

Tafsir - Ibn Al Kathir 41:9-12 "Allah says that **HE CREATED THE EARTH FIRST**, because it is the foundation … **THEN THE ROOF** …" https://quranx.com/Tafsir/Kathir/41.9 Last accessed 26 April 2021

Meaning of Glorious Quran – Surah 2:29 "Created for you ALL THAT IS IN THE EARTH … **Turned He to the heaven and fashioned it** as seven heavens."

Tafsir - Ibn 'Abbâs "…He it is Who created for you… all that is in the earth… **Then turned He to the heaven** … and fashioned it as seven heavens…" https://quranx.com/Tafsir/Abbas/2.29

Last accessed 26 April 2021

In both Quran 41:9-12, 2:29 and Muslim scholar interpretations, it is indicated that Allah **first** created the earth and its blessings and **thereafter** the roof as he renovated the pre-existing heaven into 7 heavens and decorated the lower heaven nearest to earth with stars.

Contradicted by…

Quran Translation by Abdullah Yusuf Ali: Surah 79:27 "Are **YE** more difficult to create or the heaven (above)? (Allah) hath construct**ED** it: v28 On high hath He raised its canopy and He hath given it order and perfection. v29 Its night doth He endow with darkness and **its splendour doth He bring out (with light)**. He made dark the night thereof and He **brought forth the morn** thereof. v30 AND THE EARTH, MOREOVER, HATH HE EXTENDED…"

Tafir Al-Jalalayn S 79:29 "…He exposed the light of **ITS SUN**…" https://quranx.com/Tafsir/Jalal/79.29

Last accessed 26 April 2021

Here Allah created the light first, meaning the sun, which brought the morning. Ali tried to hide the sequence of the seven heavens with stars being created before the earth by translating it as "moreover" instead of "after that". Drs. Hilali and Khan translated it correctly, which clearly shows the heavens with stars was created first and after that Allah created the earth.

The Noble Quran - Surah 79:29-30 "Its night He covers with darkness, and its forenoon He brings out **(WITH LIGHT). AND AFTER THAT** He spread the earth."

Tafsir - Ibn Al Kathir 41:9-12 "... **79:27-33 THIS AYAH STATES THAT THE SPREADING OUT OF THE EARTH *CAME AFTER* THE CREATION OF THE HEAVENS**..." https://quranx.com/Tafsir/Kathir/41.9

Last accessed 26 April 2021

https://www.youtube.com/watch?v=AasZIP2UxwM&t=1441s See 39:00

In the Quran in Surahs 41:9-12 and 2:29 the earth was created 1ST, BUT in Surah 79:29-30 the heavens (stars) is stated as being created 1ST. Both statements can't be true, showing, the Quran can't be God's Word. Which Quranic version is correct and which is false? What does modern science confirm?

Uppsala University: Department of Physics & Astronomy, First Stars and Galaxies
"Did stars or galaxies form first? The first stars likely formed when the Universe was about 100 million years old, *prior to the formation of the first galaxies.* **As the elements that make up most of planet Earth had not yet formed.**"

https://www.google.com/search?q=which+were+created+first%2C+the+stars+or+the+earth%3F&oq=which+were+created+first%2C+the+stars+or+the+earth%3F&aqs=chrome..69i57j33.29580j0j4&sourceid=chrome&ie=UTF-8 Last accessed 26 April 2021

Science confirms the heavens (stars) were created before earth, meaning Surahs 2:29, 41:9-12 is false.

https://www.youtube.com/watch?v=VcEEdvEBG3I&t=6043s Time line 40:00 Last accessed 26 April 2021

d) Is the earth: egg-shaped or sphere or flat?

Dr. Rashad Khalifah's Version - the earth is egg-shaped

Authorized English Version of the Quran – Surah 79:30 and Page 2678 Footnote
"He made the **earth egg-shaped** … *The Arabic word "dahhaahaa" is derived from "Dahhyah" which means "egg."*

Dr. Zakir Naik says the earth is egg-shaped

"The Shape of Earth is mentioned in Quran 1400 years ago" He says: "Surah 79:30… the **earth egg-shaped**…" https://www.youtube.com/watch?v=NosGnATJE7A Time line 02:20 - Last accessed 26 April 2021

Muslim scholar Mr. Ayoob Karim says earth is egg-shaped

Public debate: "The Bible & Quran in relation to Science" - Christian speaker, Mr. Piet Strydom and Muslim speaker, Mr. Ayoob Karim: [During Q&A, a man says when he reads the Quran, it says the **earth is egg-shaped** (can you explain)? Quoting Karim:] "The Arabic word **dahaha** in this verse means the **shape of an ostrich egg**, *which is ecliptical and the earth is ecliptical.*"

https://www.youtube.com/watch?v=IMd5ynlY52I Time line 11:00 Last accessed 26 April 2021

The Quranic verse doesn't mention the Arabic word *naeama* for ostrich. Anyhow, an ostrich egg is **OVAL: 15CM LONG, 13CM WIDE,** while earth, out of space, appears to be round (sphere in shape).

Muslim council of Britain says earth is egg-shaped

Egg-shaped earth – BBC big questions: "Ameena Blake – Quran says that the **earth is egg-shaped**." https://www.youtube.com/watch?v=6UrAm7v_IZk Time line 01:35 – 01:55

Last accessed 26 April 2021

Some Quran Translators have the earth as flat

Quran Trans. by Abdullah Y. Ali – Surah 79:30, 20:53 "The earth, moreover, hath He **extended (to a wide expanse)** ... He Who has, made for you **the earth like a carpet spread out**..." [Unquote: Carpets are flat.]

Tafir Al-Jalalayn: "...He spread out the earth: **HE MADE IT FLAT** ... One Who made for you, as well as [for] all creatures, **THE EARTH A CRADLE, A BED**..." [Unquote: Beds are flat.]

https://quranx.com/Tafsir/Jalal/79.30   https://quranx.com/Tafsir/Jalal/20.53   Last accessed 26 April 2021

e) Which is closer to the Islamic-egg-shaped-earth or flat earth: stars or moon?

Quran Trans. by Abdullah Yusuf Ali – Surahs: 67:3-5, 37:6 [41:12] "He Who created the **seven heavens one above the other** ... We have indeed **decked the lower heaven with beauty (in) the stars**..." [67:3-5]

In Islam there are 7 heavens and the stars are located in the lower heaven, the heaven nearest to earth.

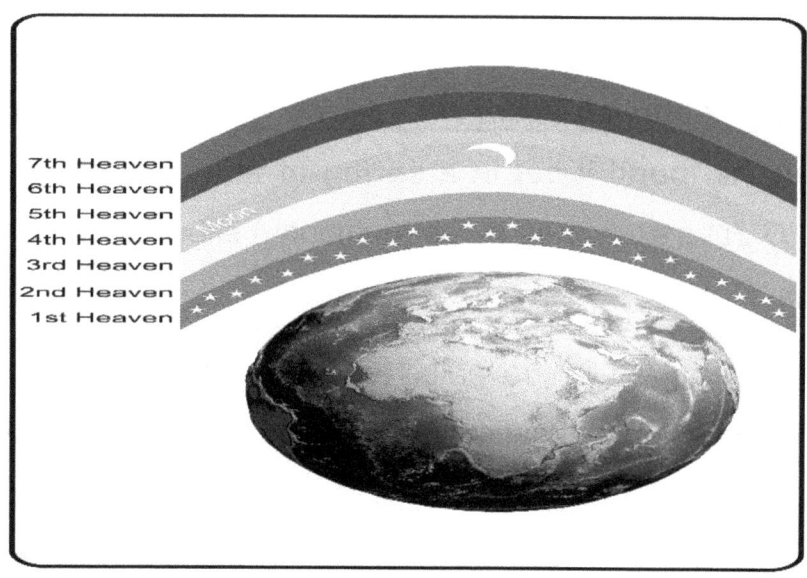

Each bow in the illustration represents a heaven, one above the other (seven heavens).

Quran Translation by Abdullah Yusuf Ali – Surah 71:15-16 "'See ye not how Allah has created the seven heavens one above another, **the moon a light in their midst**…"

The Quranic scenario depicted implied that the moon that is located in the midst of the seven heavens: e.g. "fourth" heaven is further away from the earth, then the stars that are located in the "first - lower" heaven that is nearest to the earth.

Contradicted by modern-day science…

The estimated **distance from earth to the sun** is 93 million miles [+/- 150 million km]. http://hypertextbook.com/facts/KathrynTam.shtml Last accessed 26 April 2021

On average, the **distance from earth to the moon** is about 238,855 miles (384,400 km).

https://www.google.com/search?q=The+estimated+distance+from+earth+to+the+moon&oq=The+estimated+distance+from+earth+to+the+moon&aqs=chrome..69i57j33l5.1233j0j8&sourceid=chrome&ie=UTF-8. Last accessed 26 April 2021

Here the Quran is in complete gross error with science. The moon is not further away from the earth than what the stars are, as Allah or Gabriel or Muhammad, mistakenly described the locations of the stars in the 1st heaven and the moon further away, located in the midst of the 7 heavens!

f) Does the sun set in a spring of water?

Quran Translation by Abdullah Yusuf Ali – Surah 18:86 "Until, when **he reached the setting of the sun, he found it set in a spring of murky water**: Near it he found a people: We said: "O Zul-qarnain! (thou hast authority,) either to punish them, or to treat them with kindness."

After Allah, according to the Quran, revealed to Muhammad that Zul-qarnain **REACHED THE SETTING** of the sun, Muhammad had confidence to inform his companions W-H-E-R-E the sun sets.

Sunan Abu Dawud "Narrated Abu Dharr: I was sitting behind the Messenger of Allah (ﷺ) who was riding a donkey, while the sun was setting. He asked: Do you know where this sets? I replied: Allah and his Apostle know best. **He said: It sets in a spring of warm water** (Hamiyah)."

https://quranx.com/Hadith/AbuDawud/Hasan/Hadith-3991 Last accessed 26 April 2021

The sun is 150 million km's away from the earth (see bullet E above), never did and never will the sun set on earth in a spring of water. Here the Quran and ahadith clearly demonstrated how foolish Allah and Muhammad was/is. Also, the sun is a thousand times bigger than the earth. Both Allah and Muhammad have it hopeless wrong, this is a gross scientific error, easily proven false through modern-day science. But then we read the sun's final destination is below Allah's throne, which is located above the seventh heaven, SOMEWHERE in the mythical west.

Sahih Bukhari, Volume 4, Page 283, Hadith 421 "Narrated Abu Dhar: The Prophet (ﷺ) asked me at sunset - Do you know where the sun goes (at the time of sunset)? - I replied: Allah and His Apostle know better. - He said: It *GOES (I.E. TRAVELS)* till it prostrates itself underneath the Throne and takes the permission to rise again and it is permitted and then (a time will come when) it will be about to prostrate itself but its prostration will not be accepted... it will be ordered to return whence it has come and so it will rise in the west. That's the interpretation of Allah's statement: "And the sun runs its fixed course for a term... 36.38"

Sahih Muslim: "Abdullah b. 'Amr b. al-'As reported: I heard Allah's Messenger (ﷺ) as saying: Allah ordained the measures (of quality) of the creation 50 000 years before He created the heavens and the earth, as His Throne was upon water."

https://quranx.com/Hadith/Muslim/USC-MSA/Book-33/Hadith-6416 Last accessed 26 April 2021

g) Are the stars as guards against evil spirits?

Quran Translation by Abdullah Yusuf Ali – Surah 37:6-10 "We have indeed decked the lower heaven with beauty (in) the stars, (for beauty) **AND FOR GUARD AGAINST ALL OBSTINATE REBELLIOUS EVIL SPIRITS** … they are pursued by a flaming fire of piercing brightness."

Sahih Bukhari Vol. 4, Page 282, Hadith 420 "The creation of stars is for three purposes: as decoration of the sky, **AS MISSILES TO HIT THE DEVILS** and as signs to guide the travelers."

The Muslim-science-champion, Dr. Maurice Bucaille made an unimaginary remark against the Quran in his book: *"The Bible, The Quran and Science" Page 158.* Dr. William Campbell reproduced it in his book to illustrate that the Quran contradicted science:

The Quran & the Bible in the light of history and science: Section 1 – Prologue Chap. II "[Dr. Bucaille admits] "When, however the Quran Surah 37:6-10 associates material notions intelligible to us, enlightened as we are today by modern day science, with statements of a purely spiritual nature, **THEIR MEANING BECOMES OBSCURE**."

https://www.youtube.com/watch?v=AasZIP2UxwM&t=1441s Time line 36:00 Last accessed 24 April 2021

h) Does the moon follow the sun?

Quran Trans. by A. Yusuf Ali Surah 91:2 "By the sun and his splendor, by the moon **as she follows him**."

The Quran is scientifically wrong to state that the moon **"TALAAHAA"** *follows the sun*. The sun, moon and earth, **each travels (rotates) in their own *separate* orbits**.

i) The creation of man: which version is correct?

Let's look at the Quranic verses in its chronological order [see the table presented in Q8] as received by Muhammad.

Quran Translation by Abdullah Yusuf Ali – Surah 96:1-2 "…Thy Lord and Cherisher, who created. **Created man out of a clot of congealed blood**."

Amongst the very first of the revelations Muhammad claimed to have received from Allah, informs us that Allah seemingly first created a clot of congealed blood (dead blood), then Allah used the clot of congealed blood to create our progenitor, Adam, but when Allah seemingly revealed another verse to Muhammad on the creation of the first man, Adam was not created from dead blood, this time we are told that he was created from…

Quran Translation by Abdullah Yusuf Ali – Surah 25:54 "It is He Who has created man **from water**…"

When another revelation reached Muhammad, Allah changed His mind that Allah used dead-blood or water, but now revealed to Muhammad that Adam was actually created from…

Quran Translation by Abdullah Yusuf Ali – Surah 6:2 "He it is who created you **from clay**…"

Clay is a mixed of water and dust, but then Allah again changed His mind and now we read…

Quran Translation by Abdullah Yusuf Ali – Surah 16:4 "He has created man **from a sperm-drop**…"

If this verse refers to Adam, it implies that Allah first created a sperm-drop and then Allah took the sperm-drop into His two hands (Surah 38:75) and created Adam from a sperm-drop and Adam became an open disputer against Allah. If this verse refers to reproduction of mankind, its also an error since we are **not** reproduced from a sperm-drop, but from a single sperm and egg. [See bullet J below.] It seems that Allah could not make up His mind from what man was created from, because the next revelation Muhammad seemingly received, says that Allah used…

Quran Translation by Abdullah Yusuf Ali – Surah 19:66-67 "…Does not man call to mind that We created him before **out of nothing**?"

83

Finally, Muhammad got another verse on the creation of man and this time we are told that Allah used…

Quran Trans. by Abdullah Yusuf Ali – Surah 30:20 "…He created you **from dust**…" (15:28) [*dry* sand]

Which creation information is correct: Did Allah initially use blood or water or sperm or dust or nothing? Muslims who are interested to determine which version (96:1-2 or 25:54 or 16:4 or 19:66-67 or 30:20) is correct, will do well to follow Allah's advice in Surah 10:94 quoted below.

Quran Translation by Abdullah Yusuf Ali: "If thou wert in doubt as to what we have revealed unto thee, **ASK THOSE WHO HAVE BEEN READING THE BOOK FROM BEFORE THEE**…"

Let's go to the Book, the Bible to confirm, which of the five Quranic versions is correct. In **Genesis 2:7** the Bible teach that the first man, Adam, was made out of dust. Muslims can now rejoice that Surah 30:20 is the right version, but they also have to reject Surahs 96:1-2, 25:54, 16:4 and 19:66-67 as false contradicting revelations. Perhaps, these variants are surviving parts from the 7 different ways the Quran was seemingly revealed (see heading: Muhammed recited different Arabic Quran Versions). Whatever the Muslim decide, it is still contradictions. It is true that our bodies contain dust, sexual fluids, water and blood, but the verses do not say: "We were created <u>with</u> these elements in us", which would be right, rather it states that we were initially created <u>from</u> either of them, which makes it contradictory. These things, blood-water-sperm-dust had to pre-exist Adam, for Allah to use it to create Adam from it, which is again contradicted, since we were told that Allah created man from nothing.

In addition, **Surah 21:30** "Do not the Unbelievers see the heavens and the earth were joined together (as one unit of creation), before we clove them asunder? We made <u>from water every living thing</u>…"

Contradicted by…

Surah 7:12 "...[Allah] didst create me [Satan] from fire..."

j) Sperm proceed from: testicles or kidney area?

Quran Translation by Abdullah Yusuf Ali – Surah 86:6-7 "...Created from a *DROP* emitted. **PROCEEDING FROM BETWEEN THE BACKBONE AND THE RIBS.**"

Man isn't reproduced from a sperm-***drop*** (about 100 million sperms), but from **a sperm** mixed with an egg. https://www.webmd.com/infertility-and-reproduction/guide/sperm-and-semen-faq#1

https://www.youtube.com/watch?v=oKyBdziBrEA [Last accessed 26 April 2021]

Tafsir - Ibn Al Kathir "...meaning, the backbone (or loins) of the man and the ribs of the woman, which is referring to her chest." https://quranx.com/Tafsir/Kathir/86.1 [Last accessed 26 April 2021]

Tafsir al-Jalalayn "issuing from between the loins, of the man, and the breast-bones, of the woman."

https://quranx.com/Tafsir/Jalal/86.7 [Last accessed 26 April 2021]

It is scientifically proven that sperm proceeds from a man's testicles, not from between his backbone and ribs. How could Allah get this one wrong? Or should we blame the 7th Century Arab, Muhammad? Whoever we blame, the Quran can never be divinely inspired reflecting such unscientific gross errors!

Christian writer: Dr. William Campbell: The Quran and the Bible in the light of history and science: Section four: Science and Revelation: Chapter II B Anatomy, Embryology and Genetics: "Since the verse is speaking of the movement of adult reproduction it can't be talking about the time of embryonic development. Moreover, since "sulb" is being used in conjunction with "gushing fluid", which can only be physical and "tara'ib" which is another physical word for chest or thorax or ribs, it can't be euphemistic. Therefore, we are left with the very real problem that the semen is coming from the back or kidney area and not the testicles. Dr. Bucaille, as a physician recognizes this problem only too well, so he wiggles and squirms (as he accuses the Christian commentators of doing) and finally after quoting the verse as we have seen it translated and says: This would seem more to be an interpretation than a translation. **IT'S HARDLY COMPREHENSIBLE**."

k) How long does ejaculated sperm survive in a womb?

Sahih Muslim: "Hudhaifa b. Usaid reported directly from **Allah's Messenger (ﷺ) that he said: When the drop of (semen) remains in the womb for forty or fifty (days) or forty nights**, the angel comes and says: My Lord, will he be good or evil? And both these things would be written. Then the angel says: My Lord, would he be male or female? And both these things are written. And his deeds and actions, his death, his livelihood; these are also recorded…"

https://quranx.com/Hadith/Muslim/USC-MSA/Book-33/Hadith-6392 Last accessed 26 April 2021

Contradicted by …

Science - Infertlity and reproduction: "When sperm are inside women's body, it **lives up to 5 days.** https://www.webmd.com/infertility-and-reproduction/guide/sperm-and-semen-faq#1

https://www.youtube.com/watch?v=VcEEdvEBG3I&t=6043s time ine 1:02:15

Last accessed 26 April 2021

l) Bones and flesh: which develops first?

Quran Translation by Abdullah Yusuf Ali – Surah 23:14 "…We made the sperm into a clot of congealed blood, then of that clot we made a (foetus) lump, then we made out of that lump bones **AND CLOTHED THE BONES WITH FLESH**…"

It is scientifically wrong, in the embryology stages, to say the sperm becomes blood. Also see https://www.youtube.com/watch?v=VcEEdvEBG3I&t=6043s timeline 1:00:15 Last accessed 26 April 2021

This time Allah got it right, mankind was pro-created from a sperm, not a sperm-drop (multiple sperms). However, the contradiction here remains, since mankind is not pro-created from sperm only, but from sperm and egg fused. https://www.webmd.com/infertility-and-reproduction/guide/sperm-and-semen-faq#1 Last accessed 26 April 2021

However, in the Quran, Allah made the sperm to become dead-blood and transformed the dead-blood into a fetus and changed the fetus into bones and covered the bones with flesh. This whole process is scientifically incorrect, however, just concerntrating on the last stage as per the Quran, the skeleton is clothed with flesh, again, this is gross error.

Christian writer: Dr. William Campbell: The Quran and the Bible in the light of history and science: Section four – Science and Revelation – Chapter II B Anatomy, Embryology and Genetics: "Conclusion: On bone development Dr. Sadler and Dr. Moore agree. There is no time when calcified bones have been formed AND THEN the muscles [flesh] are around them. *The muscles are there several weeks before there are calcified bones*, rather than being added around previously formed bones as the Quran states. **THE QURAN IS IN COMPLETE ERROR HERE**."

Christian Prince and Rob Christian refuting embryology stages in Quran

https://www.youtube.com/watch?v=oKyBdziBrEA&feature=em-lsp Last accessed 26 April 2021

m) Freedom of religion or must it be by force?

Quran Translation by Abdullah Yusuf Ali:

| *Surah 2:256* "Let there be NO COMPULSION in religion..." *Page 103 Commentary 300* "Compulsion is incompatible with religion: because (1) religion depends upon *faith and will,* and these would be meaningless if induced by force..." | *Surah 9:29* "FIGHT THOSE WHO BELIEVE NOT in Allah nor the Last Day, nor hold forbidden, which hath been forbidden by God and his apostle nor acknowledge the religion of truth, (even if they are) of the People of the Book..." |

Faruq Sheriff admits: **_A guide to the contents of the Quran, Page 59_** "**SEVERAL INCONSISTENCIES EXIST IN THE VERSES OF THE QURAN.** One important incompatibility is that which exists between the statements in ii.256 to the effect that there shall be no compulsion in religion and in ix.29, which commands Moslems to fight non-Moslems…"

n) Does Allah forgive all sins?

Quran Translation by Abdullah Yusuf Ali – Surah 39:53 "Allah **FORGIVES ALL** sins."

CONTRADICTED BY…

Allah does **NOT** forgive Muslims who leaves Islam, i.e. Muslims who disbelieve and who plunges deeper into disbelief, i.e. ex-Muslims who becomes Christians or idolaters or atheists, repentance will not be accepted from them.

Quran Translation by Abdullah Yusuf Ali – Surah 3:90, 4:48, 24:23 "Those who disbelieve after believing, then plunge deeper into disbelief, their **REPENTANCE WILL NOT BE ACCEPTED** from them… Allah **FORGIVETH NOT** that partners should be set up with Him … Surely those who falsely accuse married women who are pious believers, have incurred condemnation **IN THIS LIFE AND IN THE HEREAFTER.**"

Note, in its chronological order, Surah 39 was first recited, followed by Surahs 3, 4 and 24. Allah FIRST announced that He forgives **ALL** sins, but contradicted that with later verses where Allah don't forgive **certain sins**:

> [1] Allah forgives not those who change their religion from Islam,
>
> [2] who commits idolatry,
>
> [3] who falsely accuse married pious women.

o) Does Allah forgive idolatry?

Quran Translation by Abdullah Yusuf Ali:

Surah 39:53 "Allah FORGIVES ALL sins."	Surah 4:48 "Allah forgiveth NOT that partners should be set up with Him."	Surah 4:153 "They worshipped the calf [idolatry], even after clear signs had come to them, EVEN SO WE FORGAVE them."

Surah 39:53 says "YES", CONTRADICTED BY Surah 4:48 that says "NO", CONTRADICTED BY Surah 4:153 where Allah forgave willfull idolatry.

p) Who bowed first in Islam: Abraham or Muhammad?

Quran Translation by Abdullah Yusuf Ali:

Surah 39:12 "And I [Muhammad] am commanded to be the first of those who bow to God in Islam." [6:14/163] Page 1240 Commentary 4262 "The first need not necessary be chronological, it may also refer to the FIRST RANK IN ZEAL and in readiness to suffer for the cause."	Surah 2:131 "Behold! His Lord said to HIM [ABRAHAM]: Bow (thy will to Me), He said: I bow (my will) to the Lord." [28:53] Page 1204 Comm. 4097 "Halim, this title ... refers to the patient way in which father and son CHEERFULLY OFFERED to suffer self-sacrifice in order to obey God."

According to Biblical history, Abraham was a Hebrew, NOT a Muslim!

q) The genealogy of Jacob

Quran Trans. by Abdullah Yusuf Ali – Surah 2:133 "Your [Jacob's] fathers: Abraham – **ISHMAEL** – Isaac..."

Ishmael was Abraham's firstborn son through Hagar. Isaac was Abraham's second son born through Sarah. Jacob was Isaac's son. Therefore, Ishmael being Isaac's elder brother was Jacob's uncle. Genealogy **NEVER** includes uncles. Jacob's correct genealogy from himself backwards would be Isaac (his father), next is Abraham (his grandfather), etc., it can never include Ishmael, again, the Quran is in gross error here. Also see Surah 12:6, 38 where Ismail is this time correctly excluded as a forefather of Jacob.

r) The genealogy of Jesus

Muslims and Christians believe that Jesus was virgin-born, without the intervention of the male sperm, meaning Jesus can't have a natural father, hence, Muslims accuse Christians of creating a genealogy for Jesus in the Gospels.

In trying to explain that the virgin-birth, as a miracle, was not public news; hence Jesus by law had to be registered as a descent. Muslims are not willing to accept this factual scenario why Jesus had to have a genealogy, in forcing their interpretation of no genealogy under these circumstances, Muslims has proven the Quran to be self-contradictory, since Allah included Jesus in the lineage of Abraham.

Quran Translation by Abdullah Yusuf Ali – Surah 6:84 "**AMONG HIS [ABRAHAM'S] PROGENY**, David, Solomon, Job, Joseph, Moses and Aaron: thus do We reward those who do good: 85 And Zakariya and John **AND JESUS** and Elias: all in the ranks of the righteous … 29:27 and ORDAINED AMONG HIS [ABRAHAM'S] PROGENY *prophethood and revelation…*"

- ✓ Since Jesus was a virgin-born son, how is it than possible for Jesus to be mentioned amongst the **progeny-seed-offspring** of Abraham?
- ✓ Since Jesus is not from the **literal seed** of Abraham, when (Allah made Jesus a prophet and gave Jesus revelation, did Allah forget He ordained prophethood only from amongst Abraham's seed?

s) Killing which prophets?

The Noble Quran - Surah 2:91 "When it is said to **THEM (THE JEWS)**: Believe in what Allah has sent down – **THEY [THE JEWS]** say: We believe in what was sent down to us … **SAY (MUHAMMAD TO THEM)**: Why then have **YOU** killed the prophets of Allah aforetime … 33:40 Muhammed… the last of the prophets."

Sahih Muslim "Abu Huraira reported Allah's Messenger saying: No Prophet was raised between me and Jesus." https://quranx.com/Hadith/Muslim/USC-MSA/Book-30/Hadith-5835 Last accessed 21 April 2021

ACCORDING TO ISLAM, **Jesus is the 2ND last prophet** who on about 13 May 33AD ascended ALIVE into heaven without tasting death. **Muhammad is the last prophet** whose prophethood started in 610AD. In Surah 2:91 we see Muhammad addressing Jews standing in front of him in Medinah at about 622AD. Allah is instructing Muhammad to question *these Medina Jews why they have killed Allah's prophetS* (more than one prophet). According to Islam, in the period 33AD – 610AD, no true prophets existed, **ALLAH IS IN ERROR TO INSTRUCT MUHAMMAD TO ASK THESE 622AD MEDINA JEWS WHY THEY HAVE KILLED NON-EXISTING PROPHETS OF ALLAH**. Also, according to Surah 53:38, a sinner will not be responsible for the sin of another sinner, meaning, it was/is an error for Allah to keep these 622AD Medinah Jews responsible for the murder of prophets committed by their Jewish ancestors who lived more than 600 years before them. Either way, Allah is in error and the Quranic self-contradiction stands.

t) Which book was taught to Jesus Christ?

Quran Trans. by Abdullah Yusuf Ali: Surah 3:48 "God will teach Him [Jesus] **THE BOOK** and wisdom, **THE LAW AND THE GOSPEL**." Unquote: Notice, the Book is something different from the Law and Gospel!"

u) Who were the prophets among Moses' people?

Quran Translation by Abdullah Yusuf Ali – Surah 5:22 "Remember **MOSES SAID TO HIS PEOPLE**: O my people, call in remembrance the favor of God unto **YOU, WHEN HE PRODUCED PROPHETS AMONG YOU AND MADE YOU KINGS** and gave you what he had not given to any other among the peoples."

Quran Translation by Abdullah Yusuf Ali – Surah 5:22, Page 248 – Commentary 721
"There was a long line of patriarchs and prophets before Moses, e.g. Abraham, Isaac, Ismail, Jacob, etc.

The contradiction is that Saul, who lived about 400 years <u>after</u> Moses, was the first king among the Jews. **When was the Jews made kings before Moses time and during Moses time?**

v) The Gospel in Moses day

Quran Translation by Abdullah Yusuf Ali – Surah 7:155 "Moses ... prayed: "O my Lord! ... 156a Ordain for us that which is good... **156b HE [GOD] SAID [UNTO MOSES]**: With My punishment I visit whom I will, but My mercy extend to all things. That (mercy) I shall ordain for [i] those who do right and practice regular charity and [ii] those who believe in Our signs. 157 [iii] Those who follow the messenger, the unlettered Prophet, whom they find mention**ED** in their own (scriptures) in the Law **AND THE GOSPEL** ... 158 Say: "O men! I am sent unto you all, as the Messenger of Allah."

For Allah to speak to Moses and say that **THE PEOPLE OF MOSES CAN FIND** the unlettered prophet mention**ED** in the Gospel is strong evidence against Allah confusing the chronological order of revelation, since the Gospel was not available to Moses and his people to read from it about the _seemingly_ unlettered prophet who is to come about 2600 years later after their death.

w) What did the Voice really say?

Quran Translation by Abdullah Yusuf Ali:

Surah 20:11-12 "...O Moses! Verily I am **THY LORD!**"	_Surah 27:9_ "O Moses! Verily I am **GOD, THE EXALTED IN MIGTH, THE WISE!**"	_Surah 28:30_ "O Moses! Verily I am **GOD, THE LORD OF THE WORLDS.**"

Since all three verses refer to the same event, date and time, here again, we have three different versions of the seemingly seven contradictory versions of the Quran fused into the Hafs Version.

However, only one of the above three versions can be correct and two of them are false. Finally, it can also mean that the Uthmanic scribes got it wrong the second and third time. Whichever explanation, the Quran is self-contradictory. Muslims have to choose a version and reject the other two versions as false.

Quran Trans. by Abdullah Yusuf Ali: Surah 20:20 "He threw it and behold! IT WAS A SNAKE, active in motion."	_Surah 27:10 (28:31)_ "...AS IF IT HAD BEEN a snake..."

Which version must Muslims believe to be an accurate report? Muslims who are interested to determine which version is correct will do well to follow the Quranic instruction below:

Quran Translation by Abdullah Yusuf Ali – Surah 10:94 "If thou wert in doubt as to what we have revealed unto thee, **ASK THOSE WHO HAVE BEEN READING THE BOOK FROM BEFORE THEE**..."

Let's do what the Quran instructed Muslims and turn to the ***OT Exodus 4:3*** "...it became a serpent..." Surah 20:20 is correct and Surahs 27:10, 28:31 is false.

Quran Translation by Abdullah Yusuf Ali:

Surah 27:12 "...The **NINE** signs (thou will take) to Pharaoh and his people..."	***Surah 28:32*** "Those are the **TWO** credentials from thy Lord to Pharaoh..."

Did Allah say nine signs or two signs or two signs amongst the nine signs? In ***OT Exodus 4:9*** God literally said two signs, therefore Surah 27:12 is false and Surah 28:32 is correct.

Quran Translation by Abdullah Yusuf Ali – Surah 20:9 "Has the story of Moses reached thee? 10 ... He saw a fire: So he said to his family: Tarry ye; I perceive a fire; perhaps I can bring you some burning brand therefrom, or find some guidance at the fire. 11 But when **HE CAME TO THE FIRE**, a voice was heard: O Moses... 25 (Moses) said: "O my Lord! expand me my breast ... 29 and give me a minister from my family. 30 Aaron, my brother ... 36 (Allah) said: Granted is thy prayer, O Moses! 37-40 And indeed We conferred a favour on thee another time ... 41 I have prepared thee for Myself (for service) ... 42-44 Go, thou and thy brother... **45 THEY (MOSES AND AARON) SAID: "OUR LORD! WE FEAR LEST HE HASTEN WITH INSOLENCE AGAINST US**..."

SUMMARY: Allah asked Muhammad if the story of Moses have reached him (Muhammad) and then Allah begins to inform Muhammad about the event of Moses at the burning bush. Moses' attention was attracted by a strange fire. Moses then instructed his family to remain behind, while **HE ALONE** will approach the fire. When **MOSES**

ALONE arrived at the place of the fire, a voice addressed **HIM** and this voice introduced itself in three variant ways (Surahs 20-11-12, 27:9, 28:30 – see bullet W above) to be God. Then God demonstrated His power to Moses, again, in two variant ways (Surahs 20:20, 27:10 see bullet W above). Moses asked God if his brother, Aaron, who is not present at that moment, to be his (Moses') assistant when he (Moses) must go to Pharoah. God approved Moses' request and reminded Moses of a previous favor when he, Moses, was a baby and then God says to Moses that he and Aaron must go to Pharoah. **BUT THEN WE READ THAT BOTH MOSES AND AARON RESPONDED TO GOD**. This is clearly an error since Moses alone went to the burning-tree. Surah 20:45 is a clear error to include Aaron into the conversation, but the descrepancies in the story of Moses continues…

Quran Trans. by Abdullah Yusuf Ali – Surah 20:47 "So go ye both [Moses/Aaron] to **him** and say: We are messengers sent by thy **Lord**: Send forth, therefore, the Children of Israel with us **and afflict them not**…"

Contradicted by…

Quran Translation by Abdullah Yusuf Ali – Surah 26:16 "So go forth, both of you, to **Pharoah** and say: We have been sent by the **Lord and Cherisher of the worlds**. 17 Send thou with us the Children of Israel."

The contradiction is that Allah is incapable to recall the same events with the exact literal words spoken.

WHAT WAS ALLAH'S ACTUAL-LITERAL WORDS?

Surah 20:47	Surah 26:16
"…to him…"	"…to Pharoah…"
"…sent by thy Lord…"	"…sent by the Lord *and Cherisher* …"
"…and *afflict them not*…"	WORDS OMITTED

In Surah 20:47 the Arabic reads rasuul**AA** and is rightly translated as messenger**S** (more than one) since Allah is sending **BOTH** Moses and Aaron. In Surah 26:16, the same event, it reads rasuu**U** and should be translated as messenger (singular, only one), which is wrong, since Allah is sending two, not one.

ALI, IN HIS ENGLISH TRANSLATION OF SURAH 26:16 OMMITTED THE PHRASE: "MESSENGER" as if it is not mentioned in the Arabic text. Why? Ali is embarrassingly aware of the grammatical error within the Arabic Text. While the context refers to **TWO MESSENGERS (BOTH – WE – US – MOSES AND AARON)** being sent to Pharoah, in the Arabic text, it says that a singular "messenger" was sent. If Ali decided to translate it correctly, the English Version would have read: "So go forth, *both* of you, to Pharoah and say: We, <u>the messenger</u> have been sent by the Lord and Cherisher of the worlds" and even non-Arabic readers would have picked up the grammatical error in this verse.

The context of Surahs 20:47 and 26:16 is clear that Allah sent TWO (*both / we / us*) messengers, NOT one messenger! Surah 20:47 is grammatically correct, but Surah 26:16 contains an obvious grammar error.

Below are verses where the singular word "rasuu**U**" for messenger were correctly translated by Ali.

Quran Translation by Abdullah Yusuf Ali – Surahs 2:101 & 12:50 "…There came to them a **MESSENGER** [rasuu**U**] … But when the **MESSENGER** [rasuu**U**] came to him…"

Shakir in his English Version also *attempted* to render Surah 26:16, but he deceptively **MIS**translated it as messenger**S** (more than one messenger), which is contrary to the Arabic text as already demonstrated:

Quran Translation by Shakir – Surah 26:16 "…We are the messenger**S** of the Lord of the worlds…"

Shakir should've translated it <u>as "messenger" to be true to the Arabic Text,</u> but then his English Version would also have exposed the grammatical error in this verse. The Quranic grammatical error in Surah 26:16 is therefore in both the Arabic Text [rasuu<u>u</u> instead of rasuu<u>a</u>] and in the English Versions. For the mistakes in the English Versions, we'll blame Ali and Shakir, but who are we going to blame for the mistakes in the Arabic Text: Allah or Gabriel or Muhammad or the Uthmanic scribes or the Hafs reciters?

x) Did Allah say "dwell" or "enter" into the land?

Quran Translation by Abdullah Yusuf Ali:

Surah 7:161-162 "And remember it was said to them: **DWELL** in this town..." (17:104)	*Surah 2:58-59* "And remember We said: **ENTER** this town...." (5:23)

We need to emphasize that these examples do not originate from *"word choices"* during Ali's English translation, but is examples of actual text differences in the Arabic manuscript, as is admitted by Ali.

Quran Trans. by Abdullah Yusuf Ali: Page 31 Commentary 72 "There are **TWO VERBAL DIFFERENCES**..."

- ✓ Did Allah say: "DWELL or ENTER" OR did Allah say enter into the land and dwell there?
- ✓ Is Allah, Gabriel, Muhammad, the Uthmanic scribes or the Hafs reciters liable for these differences?

WHAT LAND DID GOD IN THE BIBLE AND ALLAH IN THE QURAN, GIVE UNTO THE CHILDREN OF ISRAEL?

Genesis 17:8 "I [God] will give to thee [Abraham] and **thy seed** after thee ... **ALL THE LAND OF CANAAN** ... 19 God said: Sarah thy wife shall bear thee a son ... **Isaac** and I'll establish my covenant **with him** ... and with **his seed after him**. 20 AS FOR ISHMAEL... I HAVE BLESSED HIM..." (Exodus 33:1, Amos 9:15)

NOTE: ISMAILITES ARE NOT ARABIANS (SEE Q33) ISMAIL ISN'T THE PROGENITOR OF THE ARABS.

The World Book Encyc. Vol. 15 – Page 102-103 "P" "The **LAND OF CANAAN, LATER CALLED PALESTINE**..."

The Noble Quran – Surah 5:20 "And (remember) when **(Moses) said to his people [Children of Israel]** … **21 O MY PEOPLE! ENTER THE HOLY LAND (PALESTINE), WHICH ALLAH HATH ASSIGNED UNTO YOU**…"

Tafsir - Ibn Al Kathir S.5:20 "(which Allah has *assigned to you*) meaning: *which Allah promised you*…" https://quranx.com/Tafsir/Kathir/5.20 Last accessed 26 April 2021

Tafsir - Ibn 'Abbâs S.5:21 "(Go into the holy land) … **Damascus, Palestine and parts of Jordan** (*which Allah hath ordained for you*)…" https://quranx.com/Tafsir/Abbas/5.21 Last accessed 26 April 2021

Tafsir al-Jalalayn S.5:21 "O my people, enter the Holy Land, which God has ordained for you… He commanded you to enter and **this is Syria**…"

https://quranx.com/Tafsir/Jalal/5.21 Last accessed 26 April 2021

The Noble Quran – Surah 17:104 "We said to the **Children of Israel… Dwell in the land**…"

Tafsir: Ibn Abbâs "Dwell in the land of **Jordan and Palestine**"

https://quranx.com/Tafsir/Abbas/17.104 Last accessed 26 April 2021

Quran Translation by Abdullah Yusuf Ali: Page 248 Commentary 724, Page 249 Commentary 725, Page 724 Commentary 2313, Page 954 Commentary 3169 "We now come to the events detailed in the 13th and 14th chapters of the Book of Numbers in the OT… Examine a good map of the Sinai Peninsula, showing its connection with Egypt on the West, North-west Arabia on the east and Palestine on the Northeast… We may suppose that Israel crossed from Egypt into the Peninsula somewhere near the northern extremity of the Gulf of Suez. Moses organized and numbered the people and instituted the priesthood. They went south about 200 miles to Mount Sinai where the Law was received. Then, perhaps a 150 miles north, was the desert of Paran, close to the southern borders of Canaan… From the camp there, 12 men were sent to spy the land and they penetrated as far as Hebron, say 150 miles north of their camp, about 20 miles south of the future Jerusalem… **THE PEOPLE (OF ISRAEL) WERE NOT … WILLING TO FIGHT**

FOR THEIR INHERITANCE... THE CHILDREN OF ISRAEL CERTAINLY INHERITED THE GARDENS... POSITIONS IN PALESTINE _AFTER MANY YEARS WANDERING IN THE WILDERNESS_."

Also see https://www.youtube.com/watch?v=VcEEdvEBG3I&t=6043s Last accessed 26 April 2021

It is clear that Allah [God] in the Quran and Bible gave Palestine to the Children of Israel. There is **NO** scriptural (divine) evidence where Allah [God] took it back from Israel to give it to another people. After Muhammad's death in 632AD, WITHOUT DIVINE instruction, Muslims as from 633AD acted contrary to scriptures and invaded Palestine, Jordan, Damascus and Syria, which God (Allah) promised (assigned – ordained) for Israel (Surah 2:122), conquered it by the sword and it came under Muslim rule.

The World Book Encyclopedia – Vol. 15 – Page 102-103 "P" "...*The Land of Canaan, later called Palestine, was held by the 12 Tribes of Israel*... **During the AD 600's, Muslim armies moved north from Arabia to conquer most of the Middle East, including Palestine.**"

A History of Islam – Page 62 "...Major part of Iraq and Syria came under Muslim rule (during the reign of Abu Bakr in 634AD just before his death) ... his successor was Umar who reigned for 10 years (634–644AD). **[unquote: When Islam was weak, Muhammad got asylum from Ethiopia for his followers, but when Islam's military power got strong.]** Umar during his reign captured Ethiopia and brought it under Islamic rule. He also finally conquered Damascus, thereafter, Jordan, Jerusalem, Hims and Antioch was conquered and thus the entire Syria came under Muslim rule. Later, Iraq also came under Muslim rule. In 639AD a large part of the Mediterranean area came under Muslim domination. Umar's rule, at age 61 years old, came to end in 644AD, when he was assassinated by a Persian slave. Uthman was the third caliph, he ruled for 12 years (644-656AD). By 651AD Cyprus was captured and by 655AD they ruled the Eastern Mediterranean. The Muslims by then ruled over a vast part of the known world, i.e. from Kabul to Morocco. Uthman, aged 82, was murdered by Muslims. Ali was the fourth and last Caliph (656-661AD). The first civil war in Islam was during his reign. He, aged 63, was killed with a poisoned sword."

y) Did Allah say "get ye down" in the dual or plural?

Quran Trans. by Abdullah Yusuf Ali: Surah 20:123 "He said: ihbitA Get ye down, BOTH of you..."	Surah 2:38 "We said: ihbitU Get ye down, ALL from here..."

Quran Translation by Abdullah Yusuf Ali: Page 816 Commentary 2646 "THE LITTLE VARIATION between this passage: "*ihbita* (get ye down) is in the dual number and ii:38 *ihbitu* is in the plural number."

- ✓ Is Allah or Gabriel responsible for this little variation: Surah 20:123 "IHBIT**A**" or Surah 2:38 "IHBIT**U**"?
- ✓ Or is Muhammad responsible for these verbal variations?
- ✓ Or are Uthmanic scribes responsible for these textual differences?
- ✓ Or is Hafs responsible for these verbal and textual differences?

z) Two hearts or more than two hearts?

The Noble Quran - Surah 66:4 "If you **TWO** (wives of the prophet: Aisha and Hafsah) turn in repentance to Allah, (it will be better for you), your **HEARTS** are indeed so inclined..."

"Hearts" in the English language may refer to more than 1 heart, e.g. 2 or 3 or 100 or more, but "hearts" in the context of this verse **REFERS ONLY** to two hearts, that of both Aisha's and Hafsah's.

However, in the Arabic language, there are distinct words for hearts.

- ✓ Qalb - singular (one heart):

  Quran Translation by Abdullah Yusuf Ali: Roman Transliteration – Surah 2:97 Page 970 Comm. 3225 "...He brings down the (revelation) to **thy heart** (**qalbika**) ... Qalb (heart)..."

- ✓ Qalbaan - dual (two hearts):

   Quran Translation by Abdullah Yusuf Ali: Roman Transliteration – Surah 33:4
   "Allah has not made for any man **two hearts (qalbayni)**…"

- ✓ Quloob - plural (more than two hearts):

   Quran Translation by Abdullah Yusuf Ali: Roman Transliteration – Surah 2:7
   "Allah hath set a seal on **their hearts (quluubihim)**…"

The grammar in Ali's <u>**English**</u> Translation of Surah 66:4 is correct, but the grammar error is actually found in the Arabic text of the current Hafs Quran from which Ali translated his English Version from.

Quran Translation by Abdullah Yusuf Ali: Roman Transliteration – Surah 66:4 "In-tatuubaaa 'ilallaahi fa-qad saghat **QULUUB**UKUMAA…"

Since the context demands that only Aisha's and Hafsah's **TWO** hearts are referred to, the grammatical error here is that the plural word for hearts (Quluub - more than two hearts) was incorrectly used, instead of the dual word for hearts (Qalbaan – only two hearts).

Is Allah, Gabriel, Muhammad, Uthmanic scribes or the Hafs reciters responsible for this grammar error?

aa) Breathed into "him" or into "her"

Quran Translation by Abdullah Yusuf Ali: Roman Transliteration – Surahs 15:29, 21:91 "When I have fashioned him (in due proportion) and breathed into **HIM** (fee***hi***) [Adam] of My Spirit… We breathed into **HER** (fee***ha***) [Mary] of Our Spirit…"

- The *masculine* in the Arabic is *hi*, translated as *him* and…
- The *feminine* in the Arabic is *ha*, translated as *her*.

But then we read in Surah 66:12 …

Quran Translation by Abdullah Yusuf Ali: Roman Transliteration "…Mary the daughter of Imran, who guarded her chastity and We breathed into **HER** (fee**hi**) (body) of Our spirit…"

The correct translation is: "…We breathed **INTO HIM** of Our spirit…" to be true to the Arabic text. If Ali translated it correctly, everyone would have seen that according to the Quran, Jesus already existed in the womb of Mary **PRIOR TO** Allah breathing His Spirit into the already existing Jesus in Mary's womb.

Dr. M. Asad, in his translation below, is aware that the verse doesn't say that Allah breathed into Mary.

The Message of the Quran "…Mary, the daughter of Imran, who guarded her chastity, we breathed of Our Spirit into **THAT (WHICH WAS IN HER WOMB)** …"

Dr. Asad is aware the Arabic pronoun **hi** must be translated as "him" and rendered his version as *"that (which was in her womb)"* of course, THAT which was in her womb could only be Jesus in Mary's womb. As already stated, this rendering presupposes that Jesus was already in Mary's womb, that she was already pregnant with existing Jesus in her womb. The correct rendering of this verse, as Dr. Asad has it, presuppose that Mary was already sexually touched by the time (when) Allah breathed into the existing Jesus in her womb, insinuating Jesus in the Quran 66:12 is **NOT** a virgin-birth-son and that Jesus is of the literal seed from Adam's lineage.

Maulana Muhammad Ali agreed that the correct translation is "him" not "her", here is his translation:

The Holy Qur'an – Surah 66:12, Page 1078 Comm. 2525 "Mary, Amran's daughter guarded her chastity, so we breathed into **HIM** our inspiration … EVIDENTLY, the word *him* (Arabic **hi**) *CANNOT REFER TO MARY*."

This Quranic error is clear! **The verse should have read**: "…Mary the daughter of Imran, who guarded her [**farjaha vagina**] and We breathed into (**feeha**) [**her**] of Our spirit…" to be in line with Jesus being a virgin-borned-son. In that way the Quran would have been consistent, showing Mary as a virtuous woman who guarded her chastity.

Surah 19:17, 19-20 "Then We sent to her [Mary] our angel ... 19 He said: Nay, I am only a messenger from thy Lord ... 20 **SHE SAID: How shall I have a son, *seeing no man has touched me*...**"

If Surah 66:12 is inspired, it means **the Quranic Jesus** is a premarital-sex conceived baby, contradicting Surah 19:20. If Surah 66:12 is not inspired, how many more Quranic verses are not inspired?

Is the Arabic of Surah 66:12 supposed to be (fee<u>ha</u>) instead of (fee<u>hi</u>)?

Who made this mistake - who are we going to blame for this grammar error in Surah 66:12? Is it Allah or Gabriel or the Uthman scribes or Hafs reciters? Let's patronize Allah a little bit, since he is supposed to be perfect and put the blame on Gabriel who could have recited Surah 66:12 incorrectly to Muhammad or maybe Muhammad recited it incorrectly to his companions or perhaps it is the Uthmanic scribes who made the scribal error in the Quran or perhaps, it is a variant in the Hafs reading! We leave the contradictory grammatical mystery for Muslims to resolve.

bb) Are all beings devoutly obedient to God?

Quran Translation by Abdullah Yusuf Ali – Surah 30:26 "To Him [Allah] belongs **EVERY BEING** that is in the heavens and on earth: **ALL ARE DEVOUTLY OBEDIENT TO HIM**." [13:15]

- ✓ Are all transgressors, rapists, homosexuals, murderers and idolaters devoutly obedient to Allah? No!
- ✓ Are all Christians, Hindus, atheists, agnostics and blasphemers devoutly obedient to Allah? No!
- ✓ Are all demons, devils and Satan devoutly obedient to Allah? No!

The contradiction is obvious, **NOT ALL BEINGS** in the heavens and on the earth (devils and mankind – even prophets) are devoutly obedient to God.

cc) The purpose of the angels' visitation to Lot?

Quran Translation by Abdullah Yusuf Ali:

Surah 11:77-81 "When our messengers came to Lut ... His [Lot's] people came rushing towards him [towards Lot] and they [Lot's people] had been long in the habit of practicing abominations [homosexuality]. He [Lut] said: O my people! Here are my daughters... They [Lut's people] said: Well dost thou know we have no need of thy daughters ... (THE MESSENGERS) SAID: O Lut, we are messengers from thy Lord! By no means shall they reach thee! Now travel with thy family while yet a part of the night remains and let not any of you look back, *but thy wife*..."	**Surah 15:61-77** "At length when the messengers arrived amongst the adherents of Lut. He [Lut] said: Ye appear to be uncommon folk. They [the messengers] said: Yea, we have come to thee to accomplish that of which they doubt. We have brought to thee the inevitable and assuredly we tell the truth. Then travel by night with thy household, when a portion of the night (yet remains) and do thou bring up the rear ... Let no one amongst you look back, but pass on whither ye are ordered ... The inhabitants of the City came in (mad) joy (at the news of the young men) ... He [Lut] said: There are my daughters..."

> According to Surah 11 ... At the time the messengers arrived, Lot's people came to Lut to sexually abuse the messengers. LOT COWARDLY OFFERED HIS DAUGHTERS TO BE RAPED BY HIS HOMOSEXUAL COUNTRY MEN, all this happened **BEFORE** the messengers revealed the purpose of their visit. *The messengers told Lot and his family not to look back, except for Lot's wife.*

> According to Surah 15 ... At the time the messengers arrived, the messengers revealed the purpose of their visit to Lot. It was at this time that the messengers told Lot and all his family not to look back. **THEN ONLY** did Lot's people come to him to sexually abuse the messengers, and **THEN ONLY** did Lot cowardly offered his daughters to be raped by his homosexual country men.

Which chronological order is correct: Surah 11 or Surah 15? Muslims who wants to determine which version is correct will do well to follow the Quranic instruction in Surah 10:94 (see bullet W above). Muslims will be amazed to know the correct order is Surah

11 according to the Bible and except for the order of events, Surah 15 correctly omitted that the messengers told Lot's wife to look back.

dd) "Lot's people gave no answer but this…"

Quran Translation by Abdullah Yusuf Ali:

Surah 7:82 "And his people gave NO ANSWER BUT THIS: *They said: Drive them out of your city: these are indeed men who want to be clean and pure.*"	_Surah 29:29_ "But his people gave NO ANSWER BUT THIS: *They said bring us the wrath of Allah if thou told the truth.*"

ee) Does Satan have offspring?

**The Noble Quran – Surah 18:50** "…So they prostrated themselves except Iblis (Satan). He was one of the Jinn; he disobeyed the command of his Lord. Will you then take **HIM (IBLIS) AND HIS OFFSPRING** as protectors and helpers rather than Me…" [Unquote: So Satan had a wife and children? Really?]

ff) How many creators are there?

**Quran Trans. by A.Y. Ali, Surah 37:125** "Will ye call upon Baal and forsake the Best of Creator**S**" [23:14]

Allah, the best of the creators! This implies God isn't the only creator. Here we are looking at the *Degree of Comparison (a positive statement:* e.g. John is a **good** swimmer - *The comparative:* e.g. Mark is a **better** swimmer than John. *The superlative:* e.g. Luke is the **best** of swimmers.) The comparative degree "better", refers to at least two groups, things or people and the superlative degree "best", refers to <u>more than two</u> groups, things or people. Is it perhaps a scribal error, was the verse supposed to read: *"Will ye call upon Baal and forsake the Creator"*?

gg) Did God speak directly to Pharaoh?

Quran Translation by Abdullah Yusuf Ali:

Surah 10:90-92 "… (IT WAS SAID TO HIM [PHAROAH]): "Ah now! But a little	_Surah 4:164_ "Of some messengers We have already told thee the story; of others We have

while before, wast thou in rebellion! Thou didst mischief..." [37:104-110]	not, **TO MOSES ALLAH SPOKE DIRECT**"

Who spoke to Pharaoh while he was busy drowning? [Who spoke to Abraham?]

Dr. Maurice Bucaille: The Bible, The Quran & Science – Page 238 "...V90 to 92, sura 10 informs us the Children of Israel crossed the sea while Pharaoh and his troops were pursuing them and it was only when Pharaoh was about to be drowned that he cried: "I believe that there is no God, except the God in which the Children of Israel believe. I'm of those who submit to Him." **GOD REPLIED:** "What? Now! Thou has rebelled and caused depravity. This day we save thee in thy body..." [Unquote: Surah 37:103-104]

hh) Did Pharaoh drown or not?

Quran Translation by Abdullah Yusuf Ali – Surah 17:103, 28:40, 43:55, Page 1013 Commentary 3373 "...We did drown him and all who were with him... So we seized him and his hosts and we flung them into the sea... We drowned them all ... [Ali's Comm.] Pharaoh and his hosts were drowned in the sea..."

CONTRADICTED BY:

Surah 10:92

Quran Translation by Abdullah Yusuf Ali: "This day shall we **SAVE THEE** in the body..."

Quran Translation by Shakir "We will this day **DELIVER YOU** with your body..."

Dr. Muhammad Asad observed the contradiction between Surahs 17:103 and 10:92 and decided to **MIS**translate the latter verse, see below:

Message of the Quran – Surah 10:92 "...But today we shall save **ONLY THY BODY**..."

Dr. Asad's English Translation here creates the idea that Pharaoh drowned, which would be consistent with Surah 17:103, but only his body was washed out by the sea, saved from being sunk to the bottom of the sea, preserved. Dr. Asad knows his version is wrong and not fair to the Arabic text and couldn't suppress his conscious enough, so he provided the correct translation in his footnote.

Message of the Quran: Page 306 Comm. 112 "Lit. We shall **SAVE THEE** in thy body... Some Egyptologists assume the evil Pharaoh of the Quran and Bible was Ramses II, about 1324-1258 BC. While others identify him with his unlucky predecessor, Tut-ankh-amen or even with Thotmes III, who lived in the 15th century BC. However, all these identifications are speculative and have no definitive historical value."

Surah 10:92, Pharaoh is saved with his body, is contradicted with the Surahs where Pharaoh drowned.

ii) Is it Allah's or men's own will to disbelief?

Quran Translation by Abdullah Yusuf Ali:

Surah 10:100 "No soul can believe EXCEPT BY THE WILL OF ALLAH."	Surah 6:12 "It is they who have lost their own souls that THEY WILL NOT BELIEVE."

How can a soul be blamed for unbelief, if it is Allah's will for that soul to disbelieve? How can Allah be just if he causes a soul to disbelief and send that soul to hell for unbelieve. (Surahs 4:88, 14:4 & 6:125 – see heading: Allah deceives, misleads and sends people astray). In other words, Allah is to be blamed for people being atheists or non-Muslims, etc.

jj) Misfortunes: is it men's doing or Allah's will?

Quran Translation by Abdullah Yusuf Ali:

Surah 42:30 "Whatever misfortunes happen to you IS BECAUSE OF THE THINGS YOUR HANDS HAVE WROUGHT."	Surah 57:22, 9:51 "No misfortune can happen on earth or in your souls BUT IS RECORDED IN A DECREE BEFORE WE BRING IT INTO EXISTENCE ... Say: Nothing will happen to us, EXCEPT WHAT GOD HAS DECREED FOR US."

If all misfortunes are recorded in a decree and brought into existence by Allah, why does Surah 42:30 attribute the misfortune that happens in the world to us (mankind), should

Allah not be held responsible? You can't be assaulted (no misfortune – nothing will afflict you) **UNLESS** it is ordained by Allah. Nothing will happen to us, **EXCEPT** what Allah has decreed to befall us:

- ✓ If a Muslim woman gets raped, did Allah decree the rape and brought it into existence?
- ✓ When a Muslim baby gets molested, did Allah decree it and brought it into existence?

kk) Good and evil: is it all from Allah?

Quran Translation by Abdullah Yusuf Ali:

> *Surah 4:78* "When they are blessed with good fortune, they say: This is from God, but when evils befall
> them, they say: It was your fault. Say to them: **ALL IS FROM GOD.**"
> *Page 497 Commentary 1439* "...Even in regard to myself, **ANY HARM** or good that befalls me **IS BY THE COMMAND AND IN THE POWER OF GOD.**"

- ✓ If you are raped, abused, etc. say: All is from Allah, **it was by His command and in the power of God.**
- ✓ If you are stabbed, say: All is from Allah, **it was by His command and in the power of God.**

ll) Did Noah's seed survive the flood or not?

Quran Translation by Abdullah Yusuf Ali:

Surah 11:43 "And THE SON [OF NOAH] was among those overwhelmed in the flood."	*Surah 37:77* "And made HIS [NOAH'S] PROGENY to endure (on the earth)."

mm) The impossible dialogue between Noah and son!

> Quran Translation by Abdullah Yusuf Ali – Surah 11:42-43 "So the Ark floated with them on the waves
> (towering) like mountains and Noah called out to his son, who had separated himself (from the rest):
> O my son! Embark with us [in the ark] and be not with the unbelievers! The son replied: I will betake

> [swim] myself to some mountain: it will save me from the water [there I will rest until the flood is over].
> Noah said: This day nothing can save, from the command of Allah, any but those on whom He hath
> mercy! And the waves came between them..."

Imagine the size of the ship containing all kinds of animals... **Quran Translation by Abdullah Yusuf Ali – Surah 23:27** "... Take thou on board pairs of **EVERY SPECIES**, male and female..." already floating, e.g. "out on the water" ON WAVES TOWERING LIKE MOUNTAINS. Imagine the strong winds that generated those waves and the noise that goes with it. Call it, "The Perfect Storm". Notice, there was NO HAVEN BUILD FOR REGULAR DOCKING OF SHIPS. Noah's son **COULD NOT HAVE BEEN STANDING ON DRY LAND** in a distance allowing conversation, because the gushing of water was everywhere on the earth and the noise generated from the winds and the gushing forth of water. The Quran teach that mountain high waves separated Noah and his son.

Quran Translation by Abdullah Yusuf Ali – Surah 54:12-12 "So we opened the gates of heaven, with water pouring forth. And we caused **THE EARTH** to gush forth with springs, so the waters met (and rose) to the extent decreed."

It is obvious that Noah's son must have been busy drowning while swimming as hard as he was tossed about by the waves, let alone having a conversation with Noah. Both the scene and conversation are unscientific and couldn't have happened the way the Quran explained it.

nn) Was Jonah cast on the shore or not?

Quran Translation by Abdullah Yusuf Ali:

Surah 68:49 "...HE WOULD INDEED HAVE BEEN cast off on the naked shore.	Surah 37:145 "But WE CAST HIM forth on the naked shore."

oo) Did Allah raise warners among all nations or not?

Quran Translation by Abdullah Yusuf Ali:

| Surah 16:36 "We HAVE RAISED AMONG EVERY PEOPLE a messenger." [S. 6:84-89, 10:47, 13:7/38, 87:18-19] | Surah 25:51 "We COULD have sent to every community a warner"[S. 27:24, 32:13] |

pp) Do all the spoils or a fifth belong to Muhammad?

| Quran Translation by Abdullah Yusuf Ali – Surah 8:1,41 "They ask Thee concerning (things taken as) spoils of war. Say: **Spoils are at the disposal of God and the apostle**... Know that out of all the booty that ye may acquire **A FIFTH** share is assigned to God and the apostle..." | Message of the Quran Surah 8:1,41 "**ALL** spoils of war belong to God and the Apostle... Whatever booty you acquire **ONE-FIFTH** thereof belongs to God and the Apostle..." |

Muhammad quickly found out that money can turn a devout supporter against a leader. They were not going to fight wars and see how all the booty goes to Muhammad, even if Allah said he must get it, it was not long and a convient revelation saved Muhammad from an uprising and the faithful warriors was offered a share in the booty.

qq) Normal gestation: nine or six months?

Quran Translation by Abdullah Yusuf Ali:

> Surah 31:14, 46:15 "...In travail upon travail did his mother bear him and IN YEARS TWAIN WAS HIS WEANING... In pain did she give him birth, the CARRYING OF THE (CHILD) TO HIS WEANING IS (A PERIOD OF) THIRTY MONTHS..."

Carrying of the child and weaning = 30 months **MINUS** weaning period 24 months **EQUALS** gestation period according to Allah = 6 months contradicted by general gestation of 9 months.

rr) Did the Arabs before Muhammad receive guidance?

Quran Translation by Abdullah Yusuf Ali:

| Surah 36:06 "In order that thou [Muhammad] may admonish a **PEOPLE [ARABS] WHOSE FATHERS HAD RECEIVED NO ADMONITION** and who | Surah 10:47, 13:7/38, 16:36, 87:18-19, 6:84-89 "To EVERY PEOPLE (was sent) an apostle... And for EVERY NATION there is a guide... For each period is a book revealed ... We have raised among EVERY PEOPLE a messenger... The books |

therefore remain heedless (of the Signs of Allah)."	**of Ebrahem... Ismail**... These were the men we gave the book."

ss) Did Allah forbid every animal with a claw?

> Quran Translation by Abdullah Yusuf Ali – Surah 6:146 "For those who followed the Jewish Law, we forbid every (animal) with undivided hoof ..."

The Arabic words for *"undivided hoof"* are not in the text. The Arabic word for hoof is "**thilif**" and is absent. The Arabic word "**zufur**" is used in the text, which is the singular for "claw." If translated correctly, the verse would read: *"For those who followed the Jewish Law, we forbid every (animal) with **A CLAW**"*. Ali is aware of the **grammatical error** in this verse, that "**zufur**" is in its singular form *claw* and that the context demands for the plural *claws*. Dr. Asad and Mr. Pickthall ignored the single form of the word as it is written in the Arabic Text and changed it into its plural form to hide the obvious grammatical error in their English versions.

Message of the Quran "Those who followed the Jewish faith, did we forbid all beasts that have **CLAWS**..."	*Meaning of Glorious Quran* "Unto those who are Jews we forbid every animal with **CLAWS**."

- Israel's iniquities that inspired God to forbid them certain food.

Quran Translation by Abdullah Yusuf Ali – Surah 4:154-161 "And for their covenant **we raised over them (the towering height) of Mount (Sinai)** and (on another occasion) we said: Enter the gate with humility and (once again) we commanded them: Transgress not in the matter of the Sabbath and we took from them a solemn covenant. (They have incurred divine displeasure): in [i] that they broke their covenant, [ii] they rejected the signs of God, [iii] **they slew the messengers** in defiance of right... [iv] They rejected faith, [v] that **they uttered against Mary** a grave false charge, [vi] **they said: (in boast) we killed Christ** ... *FOR THE INIQUITY OF THE JEWS WE MADE UNLAWFUL FOR THEM CERTAIN (FOODS)...*"

Quran Translation by Abdullah Yusuf Ali – Surah 6:146 "For **those who followed the Jewish law**, we forbid every (animal) with undivided hoof and we forbade them the fat of the ox and the sheep, except what adheres to their backs or their entrails or is mixed up with a bone: THIS IN RECOMPENSE FOR THEIR WILLFUL DISOBEDIENCE…"

Based on the context *"…we raised over them (the towering height) of Mount (Sinai)…"* of Surah 4 it is clear that the Jews referred to in verse 154 are non-other than those of Moses' day. WHICH messenger**S** did they kill during the time of Moses? According to verse 157 the context changed to the Jews in Mary's time: *"…that they uttered against Mary a grave false charge… they said: We killed Christ…"* Did Allah forbid Jews certain food in Moses' day for the future disobedience of the Jews in Jesus' day?

tt) Did Allah send His Spirit or angels to Mary?

Quran Translation by Abdullah Yusuf Ali:

Surah 19:17 "Then we sent to her our **ANGEL [RUUH] AND HE APPEARED BEFORE HER AS A MAN** in all respects … 19 He said: Nay, I am only a messenger from thy Lord (to announce) to thee the gift of a holy son. *20 SHE SAID: HOW SHALL I HAVE A SON, SEEING NO MAN HAS TOUCHED ME…"*	***Surah 3:45*** "Behold, the **ANGELS [MALAAAIKA]** said: O Mary, Allah giveth thee glad tidings of … [a] son… *47 SHE SAID: "O MY LORD! HOW SHALL I HAVE A SON WHEN NO MAN HAS TOUCHED ME?"*

Based on Islamic records [see the table presented in Q8] God seemingly revealed Surah 19 first and then Surah 3. Let's look at Surah 19:17. Ali mistranslated [**ruuh**] as **ANGEL**, it is supposed to be translated as **SPIRIT**. The Arabic word [**malaaaika**] for angels is not mentioned in Surah 19:17, like in Surah 3:45.

See Muslim scholar, Shakir's translation for Surah 19:17: ***Quran Translation by Shakir*** "…Then We sent unto her Our **SPIRIT** and the **SPIRIT SAID**: I am only a messenger…" Allah sent His Spirit to Mary and His Spirit spoke in the singular first person to Mary and announced to her that she will have a son <u>CONTRADICTED BY</u> Surah 3:45 where we are now informed that not Allah's Spirit, but at least **TWO ANGELS** came to Mary and they spoke to her … giving her glad tidings of a son that she will bear.

uu) Was Mary (mother of Jesus) an idol-worshipper?

Quran Translation by Abdullah Yusuf Ali:

> *Surah 19:17, 19-20* "Then we sent to her [Mary] our angel ... 19 He said: Nay, I am only a messenger from thy Lord... 20 SHE SAID: How shall I have a son, seeing that no man has touched me..." *Surah 3:45-47* "...The **ANGELS [MALAAAIKA]** said: O Mary, Allah giveth thee glad tidings... 47 **SHE SAID: O MY LORD!** How shall I have a son when no man hath touched me ..."

In Surah 19:19, God's Spirit – not angels (see bullet tt for accurate translations) appeared in the form of a man unto Mary, in verse 20 she asked Him: How shall I have a son? Here we see <u>MARY DIDN'T ADDRESS GOD'S SPIRIT AS HER LORD.</u> WHY? He looked like a human and she thought it was a normal man. However, in Surah 3, a later version of the same event, the details are now twisted from God's Spirit to angels that visted Mary and one of them spoke to her. In verse 47 Mary called one of the angels (the spokeperson) her "Lord".

Is Mary according to Surah 3:64 an idolater for addressing the angel as her Lord? If not, why?

vv) How can painful torture be good news?

Quran Translation by Abdullah Yusuf Ali:

> *Surah 2:25* "But give glad tidings (**"BASHIR"**) to those who believe and work righteousness..."
> *Surah 4:138* "To the hypocrites give the glad tidings (**"BASHIR"**) that there is for them (but) a grievous penalty."

The mention of torture is *certainly not good tidings,* but a horrible threat.

ww) Can a sinner bear the sins of another sinner?

Quran Translation by Abdullah Yusuf Ali:

Surah 53:38 (17:13-15) "Namely, that no bearer of burdens can bear the burden of another..."	*Surah 16:25* "Let them bear, on the Day of Judgement, their own burdens in full **AND ALSO** of the burdens of those without knowledge, whom they misled."

Sahih Bukhari Vol. 6, Page 60 Hadith 75 "…This letter is from Muhammad, Apostle of Allah, to Heraclius… I call you to embrace Islam… but if you reject this, **YOU WILL BE RESPONSIBLE FOR THE SINS OF ALL THE PEOPLE OF YOUR KINGDOM**…"

Quran Translation by Abdullah Yusuf Ali:

<u>Surah 29:12</u> "The unbelievers say to the believers: Follow our path and we will bear of your faults – Never in the least will they [unbelievers] bear their [believers] faults…"	<u>Surah 29:13</u> "They [unbelievers] will bear their own burdens **AND (OTHER) BURDENS ALONG WITH THEIR OWN**…"

xx) What food is available in hell: pus or bitter plants?

Quran Translation by Abdullah Yusuf Ali:

<u>Surah 69:31</u> "And burn ye him in the Blazing Fire … 36 Nor hath he **ANY FOOD, EXCEPT** the corruption from the washing of wounds…"	<u>Surah 88:4</u> "The while they enter the Blazing Fire … 6 **NO FOOD WILL THERE BE FOR THEM, BUT** a bitter Dhari."

yy) Is the Quran a fully detailed book?

Quran Translation by Abdullah Yusuf Ali – Surah 6:114 & 16:89 "…He it is who had sent unto you **THE BOOK [QURAN], EXPLAINED IN DETAIL** … And we have sent down to thee **THE BOOK EXPLAINING ALL THINGS**…"

If we read certain verses in the Quran, the above claim become hopelessly false, for example…

Quran Translation by Abdullah Yusuf Ali – Surah 2:246-247 "They said **TO A PROPHET** among them: Appoint for us a king … Their prophet said to them: God hath appointed Talut as king over you…"

Quran Translation by Abdullah Yusuf Ali: Page 98 – Comm. 278 "This was Samuel…"

The Noble Quran, Surah 2:247 "…Their prophet (**Samuel**) said to them…"

Please note that the Noble Quran have the name Samuel placed within interpolation (…) brackets, simply, because it is not mentioned in the Arabic Text of the Quran.

Where did Quran Translators get the name Samuel from?

NOWHERE in the Arabic Text of the Quran is the name of the prophet Samuel mentioned, as the prophet who told Israel that Saul will be their king. If the Quran is fully detailed, Muslims are challenged to provide a verse/s from the Quran where the name of the prophet "Samuel" is mentioned, until then, the Quran is not a fully detailed book and once more information is stolen from the Bible to make sense to the Quran.

Unlike the Quran, the Bible doesn't claim to be detailed, yet the Author of the Bible provides more detailed information than the Author of the Quran can ever dream of.

Prophet Samuel is a Biblical character

It is strange that Muslims say the Bible is corrupted, yet they use the Bible to make sense to their so-called uncorrupted Quran that is NOT fully detailed as the Quran falsely claimed!

What is Adam's wife's name according to the Quran?

__Quran Translation by Abdullah Yusuf Ali – Surah 2:35__ "We said: O Adam! Dwell thou and thy wife in the Garden…"

Using the Quran ALONE, since it claimed to be a fully detailed book, Muslims are challenged to provide the name of Adam's wife with Quranic references, again, Muslims will have to turn to the so-called corrupted Bible (**_Genesis 3:20_**) to show that Adam's wife's name is Eve.

According to the Quran, what is Abraham's wife's name?

Using the Quran alone, as a fully detailed Book, what were the names of the wives of Abraham? To spare Muslims the pain of an unsuccessful search in the Quran, allow me to confirm that the only woman mentioned by name in the Quran, is Mary the mother of Jesus Christ. Muslims will forever turn to the Bible, if they ever want to give detailed answers.

Muslim scholars admit the Quran is not detailed?

Sheikh Abdul Azziz bin Abdullah bin Baaz seems to reason the Quran is not complete and detailed. *__It is compulsory to act on the Sunnat and its rejection is Kufr. Page 11__* "There are numerous laws that are reliably mentioned in the Sunnat and not in the Quran."

The Quran lack vital information to make sense to its juggled stories and its claim that it's detailed or explains things in detail, falls to the ground.

Quran not clear and not easy to understand!

__Quran Translation by Abdullah Yusuf Ali – Surah 12:2, 16:103, 54:40__ "We have sent it down as an Arabic Quran, **IN ORDER THAT YE MAY LEARN WISDOM** ... While this [Quran] is Arabic, **PURE AND CLEAR** ... And we have indeed made the Quran **EASY TO UNDERSTAND**..."

The above verses are false when we realize the Quran is full of meaningless verses that not even native Arabs could / can understand. For example: the meanings of Surahs 2:1, 3:1, 7:1, 19:1, 20:1, 26:1, 28:1, 29:1, 30:1, 31:1, 32:1, 36:1, 40:1, 41:1, 42:1-2, 43:1, 44:1, 45:1 & 46:1 remains to this day a mystery unsolved even by native Arabic speakers.

__The Noble Quran – Surah 2:1__ "Alif-Lam-Mim (These letters, **NONE BUT ALLAH KNOWS THEIR MEANINGS**)."

__Message of the Quran: Pages 992-993 Appendix II__ "There is **NO EVIDENCE** of the prophet having ever referred to them in any of his recorded utterances... We must content ourselves with the finding that **A SOLUTION OF THIS PROBLEM STILL REMAINS BEYOND OUR GRASP**. This was apparently the view of the four Right-Guided Caliphs, summarized in these words of Abu Bakr: In every divine writ (Kitab) there is (an element of) mystery and the mystery of the Quran is in the openings of the Surahs."

__Quran Translation by Abdullah Yusuf Ali: Page 17 – Commentary 25__ "Much has been written about the meaning of these letters, but **MOST OF IT IS PURE CONJECTURE**."

Quran Translation by Abdullah Yusuf Ali: Page 481 Introduction to Surah X (Yunus)

"…The abbreviated letters are mystic symbols, about whose meaning there are **NO AUTHORITATIVE EXPLANATION**."

How could the Quran be pure and clear Arabic, revealed to give wisdom, if not even Arabic speaking people can understand its meanings?

WHAT DOES "LEWDNESS" MEAN IN THE QURAN?

Quran Translation by Abdullah Yusuf Ali – Surah 4:15 "If any of your women are guilty of lewdness, take the evidence of four (reliable) witnesses amongst you against them and if they [the witnesses] testify, **CONFINE THEM [THE GUILTY WOMEN] TO HOUSES UNTIL DEATH DO CLAIM THEM OR GOD ORDAIN FOR THEM SOME (OTHER) WAY**…"

Quran Translation by Abdullah Yusuf Ali: Page 183 Comm. 523 "Most Commentators understand this to refer to adultery or fornication. In that case they consider the punishment was altered to 100 stripes by verse xxiv:2…"

IF THE COMMENTATORS ARE RIGHT THAT LEWDNESS REFERS TO ADULTERY, then it means that Allah changed the punishment of adultery from stoning the adulterous to death (see heading: Missing Quran verses: Stoning of the adulterer) to house imprisonment until death (Surah 4:15) and again changed it to 100 stripes (Surah 24:2). It seems that Allah does not know how to deal with adultery.

Quran Translation by Abdullah Yusuf Ali: Page 183 Commentary 523 "**I think** it refers to unnatural crime [lesbianism] between women, analogous to unnatural crime [homosexuality] between men in iv:16…"

Quran Translation by Abdullah Yusuf Ali – Surah 4:16 "If two men among you are guilty of lewdness, punish them both. **IF THEY REPENT AND AMEND, LEAVE THEM ALONE**, for God is Oft-returning, Most Merciful…"

Regardless who is right, the Commentators who say lewdness refer to adultery/fornication or Ali who says it is lesbianism/ homosexuality…

- Since the guilty women are confined to house imprisonment until death, if found guilty, why are men given a lighter punishment for the same act of "lewdness" and even cleared from punishment if they repent – why are women not given the same mercy to repent and to be left alone?

- Is adultery or lesbianism committed by a woman an unpardonable sin and adultery or homosexuality committed by a man a pardonable sin? Why the different outcomes for guilty men and women?

zz) Is Allah the only "wali"?

Quran Translation by Abdullah Yusuf Ali – Surahs 5:55, 9:116 "**Your (wali) friends** are Allah, *HIS MESSENGER AND THE BELIEVERS*... Except for Him [Allah] ye have **no (wali) protector nor helper** ..." [Unquote: Who is your "wali": Allah, His messenger and the believers OR Allah alone?

CONCLUSION: These contradictions proof that God is not the Author of the Quran. In the words of Mr. Ahmad Deedat: *"...no man can write the same always..."* proving that God did not inspire the Quran with all these discrepancies in it. All these descrepcies are the wall-mark of a man, not an All-knowing God.

14 Does the Quran have true prophecies?

Romans conquering the Persians

IA Ibrahim: A Brief illustrated guide to understanding Islam – Pages 35-36 "**AN EXAMPLE OF THE EVENTS FORETOLD IN THE QURAN** is the victory of the Romans over the Persians within three to nine years after the Romans were defeated by the Persians... Quran 30:2-4 ... Let us see what history tells us about these wars. A book entitled: *"History of the Byzantine State"* says that the Roman army was badly defeated at Antioch in 613 and as a result, the Persians swiftly pushed forward on all fronts - At that time *it was hard to imagine that the Romans would defeat the Persians, but the Quran FORETOLD that the Romans would be victorious within three to nine years*. In 622 the two forces (Romans and Persians) met on Armenian soil and the result was the decisive victory of the Romans over the Persians, for the first time after the Romans' defeat in 613. The **PROPHECY** was fulfilled just as God has said in the Quran."

What we do know about the wars between the Romans and the Persians, *according to the above information*, is that the Romans were beaten in 613 and nine years later, they won the battle in 622. Surah 30:3-4 seemingly says the Romans, who were beaten in 613AD, will be victorious soon within 9 years, i.e. 622AD. For it to qualify as a prophecy, these verses, Surah 30:3-4, seemingly revealed to Muhammad had to be spoken before the war. When was it revealed? Surah 30, in its chronological Quranic order when initially recited by Muhammad is the 84th chapter [see the table presented in Q8], it is the third last Meccan chapter, just before Muhammad's migration to Medinah in June 622. Surah 30, according to Islamic literature quoted below, **came in 622 directly AFTER the Romans victory** over the Persians, hence it can't be regarded as a prophecy – as an event foretold.

Jami` at-Tirmidhi: "Narrated Abu Sa'eed: "On the Day of Badr, *the Romans* **had [past tense]** *a victory over the Persians. So the believers* **were pleased [past tense]** *with that,* **THEN THE FOLLOWING WAS REVEALED:** Alif Lam Mim. The Romans have been defeated..." up to His saying: '...the believers will rejoice. (30:1-4)" He said: "So the believers were happy with the victory of the Romans over the Persians.

https://quranx.com/Hadith/Tirmidhi/DarusSalam/Volume-5/Book-43/Hadith-2935

Last accessed 26 April 2021

Notice, since Mr. IA Ibrahim in his booklet quoted above, informed us that the victory took place in 622, and that Muhammad's prophecy had a possible timespan of nine years to be fulfilled, for Surah 30 to be a prophecy, it had to be initially recited by Muhammad around 613 to cover nine years, but that would mean that the Muslim sources concerning the dates when Quranic Surahs were revealed to Muhammed, is hopelessly wrong by nearly a decade. Surah 30 failed the conditions to be a prophesy.

False prediction that Qurash will never be Muslims

Quran Translation by Abdullah Yusuf Ali – Surah 109:1&5 "Say: O ye that reject Faith … Nor will ye worship that which I worship."

Tafsir - Ibn Al Kathir S.109 "(Say: "O disbelievers!") includes every disbeliever on the face of the earth, however, **this statement is particularly directed towards the disbelievers of the Quraysh**."

According to Allah, or Gabriel or Muhammad, said during the early Meccan verses that the disbelieving Qurash, would not worship Allah with Muhammad. This is a false statement by Allah or Gabriel or Muhammad, since the disbelieving Quraysh Tribe about 15 years later, accepted Islam in 630AD when Muhammad victoriously conquered Mecca, marching into it with 10 000 warrior Muslims. Islamic history shows that the **Quraysh** did staunchly oppose Muhammad, **but convered to Islam in 630AD**.

Sahih Bukhari Vol. 4, Page 464, Hadith 707 "Narrated Abu Huraira: **Allah's Messenger said: The tribe of Quraish … are my disciples** and [they] have no protectors, except Allah and His Apostle."

Not only did the Quraish Tribe later worshipped Allah, they also became the ruling Muslim tribe in Islam.

Sahih Bukhari Vol. 4, Page 463, Hadith 705 "Narrated ibn Umar: The prophet said: **Authority of ruling will remain with Quraish**…"

Prediction about hell-fire is no prophecy

Quran Translation by Abdullah Yusuf Ali – Surah 111 "Perish the hands of the father of flames! Perish he! No profit to him from all his wealth and all his gains! **Burnt soon will he be in a fire** of blazing flame! His wife shall carry the wood as fuel! A twisted rope of palm leaf fiber round her (own) neck!"

Since this relates to hell, this statement can't be verified, until after Judgement Day. It is impossible to test its accuracy of fulfillment in evidence of Muhammad's prophethood.

This rather sounds more like a curse, than a prophecy. In fact, these verses were revealed right after Muhammad was insulted, proving it to be a curse upon his uncle. Notice, the verses were spoken, AFTERWARDS, by Muhammed in retaliation of what Lahab said.

The Noble Quran – Page 853 Footnote 1 "Narrated ibn Abbas… Allah's Messenger said… I am a plain warner to you of a coming severe punishment. Abu Lahab said: May you perish! Then Abu Lahab went away. So perish the hands of Abu Lahab was revealed (v.111:1) (Bukhari Vol 6, Page 467, Hadith 495)."

In the Bible, we are taught to bless those who disagree with us: **_Matthew 5:44_** "I say unto you: Love your enemies, bless them that curse you, do good to them that hate you and pray for them which despitefully use you and persecute you." Wow, how different the preaching of Jesus was to that of Muhammad.

Non-Quranic predictions of Muhammad, some came true and some failed

Sahih Bukhari Vol. 9, Page 50, Hadith 64 "Narrated `Ali: I heard the Prophet saying: In the last days there will appear young people with foolish thoughts and ideas. They will give good talks, **they will go out of Islam as an arrow goes out of its game**… So, wherever you find them, KILL THEM, FOR THERE WILL BE A REWARD FOR THEIR KILLERS on the Day of Resurrection."

Muhammad predicted that young people will leave Islam and we see it happening today.

Mohammad Hijab: Islam is finished: Muslims acknowledging that 23% young Muslims are leaving Islam. https://www.youtube.com/watch?v=FyTWdrQRCSE Time line 01:35 Last accessed 26 April 2021

Dr. David Wood: Muslim scholar warns of avalance of apostacy: [Paraphrasing: Dr. Bilal Phillips on 25 January 2018 confirmed that in Muslim countries, because of the culture, people are forced to conform to Islam, because of the community pressure, **but in Canada young ones are educated and leaves Islam.**" https://www.youtube.com/watch?v=3LITVNGCBG4 Last accessed 26 April 2021

LET'S LOOK AT A MAJOR PROPHESY THAT FAILED. *Jami'at-Tirmidhi* "Abu Hurairah narrated the Prophet said: By the One in Whose Hand is my soul! Ibn Mariam shall soon **DESCEND AMONG YOU**, judging justly. He shall break the cross, kill the pig, remove the Jizyah and wealth will be so bountiful that there will be none to accept it." https://quranx.com/Hadith/Tirmidhi/DarusSalam/Volume-4/Book-31/Hadith-2233

https://quranx.com/Hadith/Bukhari/USC-MSA/Volume-3/Book-34/Hadith-425   Last accessed 26 April 2021

Here Muhammed prophesied that Jesus will descend amongst the people that Muhammed spoke to – DESCEND AMONG YOU – this never happened and it is now 1400 years later and Jesus still never came yet.

15 Why were certain verses in the Quran revealed?

Surah 2:144 to fulfil Muhammed's qibla preference

The Jews, as per a request from Solomon (**Holy Bible, OT, 1 Kings 8:44**) began to pray facing the direction of Jerusalem where the House of God was. Muhammed and the contemporary Muslims, thousands of years later, **COPIED** this Jewish tradition for 10 years (i.e. 610AD – 620AD) into Islam, praying in the direction of Jerusalem where the Jewish Temple was. After their migration in 622AD to Medinah, Umar told Muhammad his wish was, to have the Station of Abraham as their **NEW** praying place.

Sahih Bukhari Vol. 1, Page 240, Hadith 395 "Narrated `Umar (bin Al-Khattab): My Lord agreed with me in three things: (1). I said: O Allah's Messenger (ﷺ) wish we took the station of Abraham as our praying place. So came the Divine Inspiration: And take you (people) the station of Abraham as a place of prayer (for some of your prayers) …"

Allah honored Umar's wish and Surah 2:125 was seemingly revealed to Muhammad for Muslims to take the Station of Abraham as their new praying place. This excited Muhammed and he wished for the current qibla (praying direction) to be changed from

Jerusalem to Mecca and again, Allah honored Muhammed's wish and Surah 2:144 was subsequently revealed to Muhammed.

Sahih Bukhari Vol. 6, Page 14, Hadith 13 "Narrated Al-Bara: **The Prophet (ﷺ) prayed facing Bait-ulMaqdis (i.e. Jerusalem) … but he wished that his Qibla would be the Ka`ba (at Mecca). So Allah Revealed (2.144)** … A man from among those who had prayed with him, went out and passed by some people offering prayer in another mosque… He said: I testify that I have prayed with the Prophet (ﷺ) facing Mecca. Hearing that, they turned their faces to the Ka`ba, while they were still bowing. Some men had died before the Qibla was changed towards the Ka`ba."

While it was/is possible for Muslims in Arabia to face the Kaba or for Muslims, anywhere in the world, on a **FLAT** earth to also face in the direction of the Kaba in Mecca during their prayers, it is scientifically impossible for any Muslim on a **SPHERE** earth on continents like North and South America or parts of Western and Southern Africa to face the Kaba in Mecca during their prayer. Every Muslim, praying in mentioned continents, NEVER in their life-time scientifically ever faced the Kaba, they actually faced into the direction of space. These Muslims can only face the Kaba figuratively, but never physically.

Surah 2:158 to continue with pagan practice

During pre-Islam, pagans used to go between Safa and Marva to complete their pilgrimage-rites. When some of these pagans accepted Islam, knowing where this idolatry practice of going between Safa and Marva during piigrimage came from, they hesitated to continue doing it, they hesitated to continue with pagan rites, it is then that Allah revealed to Muhammad that this practice is not a sin.

Tafsir al-Jalalayn S. 2:158 "This was revealed when the Muslims were averse to this (circumambulation), because the pagan Arabs used to circumambulate them and there was an idol on top of each mountain, which they used to stroke."
https://quranx.com/Tafsir/Jalal/2.158

Quran Translation by Abdullah Yusuf Ali: "Behold! Safa and Marwa are among the Symbols of Allah. So if those who visit the House in the Season or at other times, should compass them round, it is no sin in them. And if any one obeyeth his own impulse to good, be sure that Allah is He Who recogniseth and knoweth."

Surah 3:161 to clear Muhammad from theft

After a certain war, Muhammad was accussed of stealing clothes from the booty, Muhammad couldn't prove his innocence and Allah conveniently revealed a verse that acquitted Muhammd from theft.

Meaning of Glorious Quran "It is not for **any prophet to embezzle**..."

Quran by Shakir "It's not attributable to **a prophet to act unfaithfully**..."

Muhammad Sarwar "No Prophet can ever be **treacherous**..."

Tafsir - Ibn Al Kathir S. 3:161 "(…a red robe was missing from the spoils of war of Badr. **Some people said that the Messenger of Allah might have taken it.** When this rumor circulated, Allah sent down: It is not for ANY PROPHET TO ILLEGALLY TAKE A PART OF THE BOOTY… This Ayah exonerates the Messenger of Allah…" https://quranx.com/Tafsir/Kathir/3.159 Last accessed 26 April 2021

Tafsir - Al-Jalalayn 3:161 "When some red velvet cloth went missing on the Day of Badr and **some people began to say: Perhaps the Prophet took it** - the following was revealed: It is not for A PROPHET TO BE FRAUDULENT…" https://quranx.com/Tafsir/Jalal/3.161 Last accessed 26 April 2021

This event shows us that Muslims thought of Muhammad as a thief and not as trustworthy, after Muhammad failed to prove his innocence, abra-ka-da-bra and Allah sent a verse and Muhammed recited this verse which made Muslims to drop the charges against Muhammed. When this story was told to a practicing Muslim, he admitted this verse was a cover up and left Islam. See below link for the discussion: https://www.youtube.com/watch?v=J9T5L08bNPw Time line 51:00 Last accessed 26 April 2021

Surah 4:24 allow Muslims to have sex with slave-married-women

T.P. Huges: Dictionary of Islam Pages 596-597 "The term generally used in the Quran for slave is *ma malakat asmanukum:* that which your right hand possesses … MUSLIMS ARE ALLOWED TO COHABIT WITH ANY OF THEIR FEMALE SLAVES … THEY ARE ALLOWED TO TAKE POSSESSION OF MARRIED WOMEN IF THEY ARE SLAVES … On this verse al-Jalalan the commentators say: *it is lawful for them to cohabit with those women whom you have made captive,* **even though their husbands be alive**…"

Quran Translation by Abdullah Yusuf Ali: "Also (prohibited are) women already married, **EXCEPT [ILLA] THOSE WHOM YOUR RIGHT HANDS POSSESS**…"

Sunan Abu Dawud, Vol. 2, Number 2150 "Abu Said al-Khudri said: The apostle of Allah (may peace be upon him) sent a military expedition to Awtas on the occasion of the battle of Hunain. They met their enemy and fought with them. They defeated them and took them captives. **SOME OF THE COMPANIONS OF THE APOSTLE OF ALLAH WERE RELUCTANT TO HAVE INTERCOURSE WITH THE FEMALE CAPTIVES IN THE PRESENCE OF THEIR HUSBANDS WHO WERE UNBELIEVERS**. Allah sent down the Quranic verse: "Married women (are forbidden) unto you, save those (captives) whom your right hands possess…" [Unquote: Imagine, Allah made it legal for Muslims to rape women in the presence of their husbands.]

Surah 4:34 allow Muslims to beat their wives

Tafsir Wahidi – Asbab Al-Nuzul "It happened when Sa'd hit his wife on the face, because she rebelled against him. Then her father went with her to see the Prophet… He said to him: I gave him my daughter in marriage and he slapped her. The Prophet said: Let her retaliate against her husband. As she was leaving with her father to execute retaliation, the Prophet… called them and said: Gabriel has come to me… He, revealed this verse. The Messenger of Allah… said: We wanted something, while Allah wanted something else. What Allah want is good https://quranx.com/Tafsir/Wahidi/4.34 Last accessed 26 April 2021

Quran Translation by Abdullah Yusuf Ali: "Therefore the righteous women are devoutly obedient and guard in the husband's absence what Allah would have them guard, as to <u>those women on whose part you fear disloyalty and ill-conduct</u>: [1] admonish them (first), (next), [2] do not share their beds (and last) [3] **BEAT (TAP) THEM (LIGHTLY)**..." (See heading: Did Allah say beat (tap) them (lightly))

Surah 4:95 to dismiss the disable from partaking in war

Sahih Bukhari: Vol. 6, Page 95, Hadith 118 "Narrated Al-Bara: When the Verse: Not equal are those of the believers who sit (at home) was revealed, the Prophet said: Call so-and-so. That person came to him with an ink-pot and a wooden board or a shoulder scapula bone. The Prophet (ﷺ) said (to him): Write: "Not equal are those believers who sit (at home) and those who strive and fight in the Cause of Allah." Ibn Um Maktum who was sitting behind the Prophet (ﷺ) then said: O Allah's Messenger (ﷺ) I am a blind man. So there was revealed in the place of that Verse, the Verse: Not equal are those of the believers who sit (at home), **except those who are disabled** (by injury, or are blind or lame etc.) and those who strive and fight in the Cause of Allah." (4.95)"

It is strange that Allah had to amend the verse within seconds after Muhammad was reminded of the disabled. Didn't Allah know about them. This proves a finite mind is behind the production of the Quran.

Surah 5:87 to make contractual prostitution legal

Quran Translation by Abdullah Yusuf Ali: "Oh you who believe, **make not unlawful the good things,** which Allah has made lawful to you…"

WHAT ARE THE GOOD THINGS, WHICH ALLAH HAS MADE LAWFUL FOR MUSLIM MEN?

Sahih Bukhari Vol. 7, Page 8, Hadith 13 "Narrated Abdullah: We used to participate in holy battles led by Allah's Messenger and *WE HAD NOTHING (NO WIVES) WITH US*. So we said: Shall we get castrated? He forbade us that and then allowed us to **MARRY**

WOMEN WITH A TEMPORARY CONTRACT and recited to us: *"Oh you who believe, make not unlawful the good things, which Allah has made lawful to you…"*

The Muslim soldiers were willing to castrate themselves to prevent having illegal sex with strange women, but Muhammad introduced a shortterm marriage in order to satisfy the Muslim warriors' sexual lust for the period they were in battle, until they go home and Allah approved it by revealing Surah 5:87.

<u>*Sahih Bukhari Vol. 7, Page 37, Hadith 52*</u> "Allah's messenger said: If a man and a woman agree (to marry temporarily), **their marriage should last for three nights**, if they want to continue, they can do so."

Here Muhammad specified the period for this temporary marriage for at leased 3 nights, while the Muslims are away from their wives. This contract spells *"Islamic legalized prostitution under a new umbrella called temporary marriage"* to satisfy the lust of sexually aroused Muslim warriors.

As per https://www.youtube.com/watch?v=mm5s5lMeuco Time line 14:03 – 25:00

Mut'ah https://www.youtube.com/watch?v=AasZIP2UxwM&t=1441s Time line 17:30

Last accessed 26 April 2021

<u>**Sahih Muslim:**</u> "Ibn Uraij reported: 'Ati' reported that jibir b. Abdullah came to perform 'Umra, and we came to his abode, the people asked him about different things, and mentioned temporary marriage, whereupon he said: Yes, we had been benefiting ourselves by this temporary marriage **DURING THE LIFETIME OF THE PROPHET (ﷺ) AND DURING THE TIME OF ABU BAKR AND UMAR**."

https://quranx.com/hadith/Muslim/USC-MSA/Book-8/Hadith-3248/ Last accessed 26 April 2021

Mut'ah marriage is also mentioned in Surah 4:24 where women received *payment* for services rendered.

Prof. JA Arberry "...Such wives as you enjoy thereby, give them their **WAGES** apportionate..."

Muhammad Sarwar "...If you marry them for **THE APPOINTED TIME** you must pay their dowries..."

Tafsir Ibn 'Abbâs "...It is also said this means: that you should seek with your money marrying women **FOR AN AGREED PERIOD OF TIME** (zawaj al-mut'ah)..." https://quranx.com/Tafsir/Abbas/4.24

Surah 6:108 to stop Muslims from mocking idols

Quran Translation by Abdullah Yusuf Ali: "Revile not ye those whom they call upon besides Allah, **lest they out of spite revile Allah in their ignorance**..."

Tafsir Wahidi - Asbab Al-Nuzul by Al-Wahidi S. 6:108 "Said ibn Abbas, according to the report of al-Walibi: **The idolaters said: O Muhammad, either you stop reviling our idols or we will revile your Lord.** And so Allah, exalted is He, warned against reviling their idols lest they wrongfully revile Allah through ignorance. Qatadah said: The Muslims used to revile the idols of **the unbelievers and the latter used to react against them**. Allah, therefore, warned the Muslims against being the cause which drives ignorant unbelievers... to revile Allah." https://quranx.com/Tafsir/Wahidi/6.108 Last accessed 26 April 2021

Tafsir - Ibn Al Kathir S. 6:108 "**Allah prohibits His Messenger and the believers from insulting the false deities of the idolators**... for the idolators might retaliate by insulting God ... Ali bin Abi Talhah said that Ibn `Abbas commented on this ayah - They (disbelievers) said: O Muhammad! You will stop insulting our gods or we will insult your Lord. Thereafter, Allah prohibited the believers from insulting the disbelievers' idols." https://quranx.com/Tafsir/Kathir/6.108 Last accessed 26 April 2021

Muhammed and his contemporaries were mocking the idols of the Arabian-pagans. Allah never forbid them from mocking these gods, but when these idolaters retaliated by mocking Allah, who couldn't stand being mocked, then only did Allah advise Muslims to stop mocking the idols of these Arabian-pagans.

Surah 22:52 confirms all "Islamic Prophets" had Satanic verses

Tafsir Al-Jalalayn S22:52 "...When he [Muhammad] recited (the scripture) **Satan cast into his [Muhammad's] recitation, what is not from the Qur'ān**, but which those to whom he had been sent would find pleasing. The Prophet had, during an assembly of the Quraysh, after reciting sūrat al-Najm *53:19-20: "Have you considered Lāt and 'Uzzā? And Manāt, the third one?"* **added, as a result of Satan casting onto his tongue without him being aware: "those are the high-flying cranes (al-gharānīq al-'ulā) and indeed their intercession is to be hoped for.** The Quraysh were thereby delighted. **Gabriel, however, later informed the Prophet of this that Satan had cast onto his tongue and he was grieved by it**; but was comforted with this [Surah 22:52] verse that God abrogates (nansakh), nullifies, whatever Satan had cast." https://quranx.com/Tafsir/Jalal/22.52 Last accessed 26 April 2021

Quran Translation by Abdullah Yusuf Ali – Surah 22:52 "Never did We send a messenger or a prophet before thee, but, when he framed a desire, **SATAN THREW SOME (VANITY) INTO HIS DESIRE:** but Allah will cancel anything (vain) that Satan throws in. *Allah will* confirm His Signs..."

Tafsir - Ibn Al Kathir S. 22:52 "How the Shaytan threw some falsehood into the Words of the Messengers and how Allah abolished [it]." https://quranx.com/Tafsir/Kathir/22.52 Last accessed 26 April 2021

PLEASE NOTE: Surah 53 – The Star – in its chronological order is actually the 23RD chapter [see the table presented in Q8], meaning, it's an early Meccan Surah, which dates soon after 610CE. Surah 22 – The Pilgrimage – in its chronological order is actually the 103RD chapter, meaning, it's a late Medinah Surah, which dates before 632CE. The reality is that Muhammad recited the Satanic Verses for about 10-15 years during his 23 years of prophethood. According to Muslim commentaries, Satan made Muhammad recite that which was Satanic Verses. Later, when caught out, to reassure his audience that he is indeed a true prophet, recited Surah 22:52 so that they may know all prophets, somehow, got tricted by Satan.

Since...

- ✓ Muhammad could not discern between Allah's Verses and Satan's Verses, being tricked under Satan's control and ...
- ✓ Muhammad was also bewitched for many months, until he did not know what he was doing in that period (see Q55) ...

How do Muslims know the whole Quran, with its many descrepcies, collected by Uthman into a standardized copy, after Muhammed died and later, edited after Uthman died, is a book *not* from Satan? In fact, since Muslim scholars admit Muhammad was under Satan's control when he uttered the Satanic Verses and being bewitched until he did not know what he was doing for some time-period, is proof that Muhammad was not a true prophet of God according to Surah 15:42 quoted below. Here Allah says Satan only have power over those people who are followers of Satan.

Quran Trans. by Abdullah Yusuf Ali:	Meaning of the glorious Quran	Quran Translation by Shakir
"For over My [Allah's] servants NO authority shalt thou [Satan] have, except such as put themselves in the wrong and follow thee [Satan]."	"As for My [Allah's] slaves, thou [Satan] hast NO power over any of them save such of the froward as follow thee [Satan]"	"As regards My [Allah's] servants, you have NO authority over them, except those who follow you [Satan] of the deviators."

Surah 24:33 slaves, on conditions, may not be forced into prostitution

Quran Translation by Abdullah Yusuf Ali – Surah 24:33 "...But *force not your maids to prostitution* **WHEN THEY DESIRE CHASTITY**, in order that ye may make a gain in the goods of this life. If anyone compels them, yet, after such compulsion, is Allah, Oft-Forgiving, Most Merciful (to them)."

Tafsir Al-Jalalayn "Do not compel your slave-girls, your handmaidens, to prostitution **WHEN THEY DESIRE TO ABSTAIN THEREFROM**... This was revealed regarding 'Abd Allāh b. Ubayy who used to force his slave-girls to earn money through fornication." https://quranx.com/Tafsir/Jalal/24.33

Last accessed 26 April 2021

Tafsir - Ibn Al Kathir "The reason why this Ayah was revealed... Abdullah bin Ubayy bin Salul had slave-girls whom he used to force into prostitution so that he could take their earnings and because he wanted them to have children, which would enhance his status..." https://quranx.com/Tafsir/Kathir/24.32

Last accessed 26 April 2021

Note, Allah did not forbid prostitution in this verse, he only forbids Muslims to force slave-girls into it, **IF THE SLAVES WANTED TO ABSTAIN FROM PROSTITUTION.** The way the verse is formulated gives the impression that if the slave-girls are not forced, prostitution out of free will is allowed. So, whether the slave-girls are forced into prostitution or out of their free will, the earnings made by them went straight to the Muslim-slave-owners. **ALLAH WOULD HAVE DONE BETTER TO SAY: "DO NOT ALLOW PROSTITUTION *UNDER ANY CIRCUMSTANCES.*"**

Surah 33:69 naked Moses to verify no skin defect

Quran Translation by Abdullah Yusuf Ali: "O ye who believe! Be ye not like those who vexed and insulted Moses, but Allah cleared him of the (calumnies) they had uttered: and he was honorable in Allah's sight."

What were the insults against Moses and how did Allah clear his honorable prophet to Bani Israel?

Sahih Bukhari Vol. 4, Page 407, Hadith 616 "Narrated Abu Huraira: **Allah's messenger said**: (The prophet) Moses was a shy person and used to cover his body completely, because of his extensive shyness. **One of the children of Israel hurt him by saying: He covers his body in this way only because of some defect in his skin: either**

leprosy or scrotal hernia or he has some other defect. ALLAH WISHED TO CLEAR MOSES OF WHAT THEY SAID ABOUT HIM, so one day while Moses was in seclusion, he took off his clothes and put them on a stone and took a bath. When he had finished the bath, he moved towards his clothes as to take them, but the stone took his clothes and fled. Moses picked up his stick and ran after the stone saying: O stone! Give me my garment! [He ran] till **he reached a group of bani Israel who saw him naked and found him the best of what Allah had created and Allah cleared him of what they had accused him of.** The stone stopped there and Moses took his clothes and put it on and started hitting the stone with his stick. By Allah the stone still has some traces of the hitting, three, four or five marks. **This was what Allah refers to in his saying:** O you who believe, be ye not like those who annoyed Moses, but Allah proved his innocence of that which they alleged, and he was honorable in Allah's sight. (33:69)"

Sahih Muslim "Hammam b. Munabbih reported that Abu Huraira reported many ahadith from Allah's Messenger (ﷺ) and one, of them speaks that **ALLAH'S MESSENGER (ﷺ) IS REPORTED TO HAVE SAID**: Banu Isra'il used to take bath together, naked and thus saw one anothers' private parts, but Moses (pbuh) used to take a bath alone (in privacy), and they said: By Allah, nothing prevents Moses to take a bath along with us; but scrotal hernia. One day when he (Moses) was taking a bath (alone), he placed his clothes upon a stone, but the stone began to move along with his clothes. Moses raced after it saying: My garment, stone; until (some of the people) of Banu Isra'il looked at the private parts of Moses, and they said: By Allah, there is no trouble with Moses. The stone stopped after he (Moses) had been seen. He took hold of his garments and struck the stone. Abu Huraira said: I swear by Allah that there were six or seven scars on the stone, because of the striking of the stone by Moses (peace be upon him).

https://quranx.com/Hadith/Muslim/USC-MSA/Book-30/Hadith-5849 Last accessed 26 April 2021

Wow, Allah have strange moves to prove to Israel that Moses had no skin disease. Moses seen naked, his private parts exposed and witnessed by Israelites, what a so-called divine vindication of Moses perfect skin.

Allah in Surah 66:5 threatens Muhammad's wives with divorce

<u>*Sahih Bukhari Vol. 1, Page 240, Hadith 395*</u> "Narrated `Umar (bin Al-Khattab): My Lord agreed with me in three things... **(3) Once the wives of the Prophet (ﷺ) made a united front against the Prophet (ﷺ) and I said to them: It may be if he (the Prophet) divorced you, (all) that his Lord (Allah) will give him instead of you, wives better than you.' So this verse (66.5) (the same as I had said) was revealed.**"

Here we see that Allah took Umar's threathening advise to Muhammad's wives that Muhammad might divorce them for their opposing behavior against Muhammad and Allah revealed it as His Word in the pages of the Quran.

SECTION 2

MUSLIMS IS CHANGING THE "MEANING" OF THE QURAN

Whenever I talk to Muslims concerning the Holy Bible, God's Word, not once did any Muslim ever fail to mention that Christians changed the Bible. When this topic arises, Christians should not back out, but continue the dialogue by asking intelligent questions, e.g. ask the Muslim whether he is referring to the Translations of the Holy Bible or the original Hebrew-Greek manuscripts of the Holy Bible. Obviously they are referring to different Translations being produced. In that case, the Christian should easily point out to the Muslim that they also have new Translations. The difference between Christianity and Islam is that Christians never burnt old or partly damaged manuscripts to ensure a universal standardized Hebrew-Greek version of the Bible, like Muslims did with Quranic material to ensure a standardized Quran copy.

LET US NOW INVESTIGATE MORE QURANIC VERSES AND SEE IF MUSLIM TRANSLATORS ARE GUILTY OF WHAT THEY ACCUSE THE CHRISTIANS AND JEWS OFF. IN THIS SECTION, I WILL SHOW THAT MUSLIMS ARE CHANGING THE TRUE MEANING OF THE QURAN AND CONCEAL THE TRUE MEANING OF THE QURAN BY MISTRANSLATING THE ARABIC TEXT INTO ENGLISH TO HIDE SO-CALLED EMBARRASSING MEANINGS OF THE ARABIC CONTEXT OF THE QURANIC MESSAGE.

16 Jesus Christ: begotten son or only son?

Not different Bibles, different Translations

During the debate with Evangelist Jimmy Swaggart, Deedat [and his office, referring to the edited version of the video tape] made an issue of ***John 3:16*** emphasizing that

Christians are now becoming ashamed of the term *"begotten Son"* and are removing it from major Versions of the Holy Bible, e.g.

| *KJV* "God so love the world that He gave His only **BEGOTTEN** Son..." | *New Living Translation* "For God so love the world that He gave His **ONLY** Son..." |

This deceptive poisonous seed of Deedat that the Christians are removing the word *BEGOTTEN* from major versions of the Bible are deeply planted in **many** deceived hearts of Muslims that don't read and study the Bible and Quran for themselves. Even educated Muslims, i.e. attorneys, are being deceived.

Public debate: 13 July 2011 "The way of Salvation in the Bible and Quran" Muslim Speaker, Attorney Mohammed Coovadia [DVD: Quoting Coovadia:] "Christians are changing the Bible, they are now removing the word "begotten" from their Bibles."

What Deedat or his deceived-inmates fail to do, is to inform their audience that the original manuscripts have always been the same. In the original text, the Greek word is *"monogenes"* and there are no variant Greek manuscripts for John 3:16.

The New Strong's Exhaustive Concordance of the Bible - Under Greek Words
"Mono" means: *only, sole, unique, single* and "gene" means *to bring forth, coming from, begotten.*"

Whether the Translators choose "only Son" or "only begotten Son", the original text and its **INTENDED MESSAGE** is not affected, showing the coming of Jesus from the Father to this sinful world and our need for salvation only to be found in Jesus. Honest translators will try to accurately convey the intended meaning of the message as understood by the messenger. They will do this even if it discredits their sectarian beliefs. **Many times, translations are based on word choices** and how best the respective Translators understand the meaning of words, when translating from one language to another.

Even Islam is faced with the same challenges

Quran Translation by Abdullah Yusuf Ali: Preface to First Edition. Page IV, VI "What I wish to present to you is an English interpretation, side by side with the Arabic text. The English shall be, not a mere substitution of one word for another, BUT THE BEST EXPRESSION I CAN GIVE TO THE FULLEST MEANING, WHICH I CAN UNDERSTAND FROM THE ARABIC TEXT… It is my desire that **MY VERSION** should not in any way be deficient in this respect…"

Let's look at the same word "begotten" in Ali's Version and the absence of it in another Version.

Surah 19:88

Quran Translation by Abdullah Yusuf Ali: "They say: (God) Most Gracious has BEGOTTEN a son!"	*Meaning of Glorious Quran* "They say: The Beneficent hath TAKEN unto Himself a son."

- ✓ Ali have "begotten" and Pickthall remove it from his version and added "taken". Which one is right?

- ✓ Ali has the title "Most Gracious", but Pickthall have "Beneficent". Which one is right?

Must we also now conclude that the Quran has been changed and corrupted? The Quran, like the Bible, have different translations. It amazes me how Muslims can so easily discredit the Holy Bible because of word choice during translations since their book has the same difficulties with translation challenges from Arabic to English. To me, that spels out "DISHONESTY"!

According to the Quran, is Jesus Lord?

Quran Translation by Abdullah Yusuf Ali – Surah 9:31 "They take their priests and anchorites [monks] to be their lords beside Allah. And **(THEY TAKE AS THEIR LORD)** Christ the son of Mary; yet they were commanded to worship, but One Allah: there is no god, but He. Praise and glory to Him: (Far is He) from having the partners they associate (with Him)."

What is wrong with the above translation? Ali have splitted the verse into different parts to manupilate its meaning to attack the Christian belief. His first error was to misplace the fullstop (.) after Allah. For his second error, do you see the bold words between round ( ) brackets, its called interpolations. Those bold words are not part of the Arabic text and is Ali's OWN addition to his English Version. That is deceptive, Ali had no right to change the intended Quranic meaning to satisfy his Sunni belief.

Let's look at the transliteration: **Quran Translation by Abdullah Yusuf Ali – Roman Transliteration** "'Itta –khazuuu 'ahbaa-ra-hum wa ruhbaa-nahum 'ar-baabam-min-duunil-**laahi wal-Masii**-habna – Maryam. Wa maaa 'umi-ruuu 'illaa li-ya' – buduuu 'ilaahanw-Waahidaa…"

Notice, the conjunction "and" in Arabic "**wa**" is between "Laahi **wa**l Masii", which should translate as "God and Messiah" or "God and Christ". Also, the first fullstop (.) only appears after the name "Maryam". If we remove Ali's interpolation, the verse when correctly translated reads: "They take their priests and anchorites to be their lords **BESIDE ALLAH AND CHRIST** the son of Mary. Yet they were commanded to worship, but One God: there is no god, but He. Praise and glory to Him: (Far is He) from having the partners they associate (with Him)."

This verse is very specific: The priests and anchorites (monks) are not our lords beside God and Jesus Christ. The priests and monks are not partners to God and Jesus Christ.

17 Is there pornographic language in the Bible?

Deedat, in his booklet: ***"Is the Bible the Word of God?"*** according to *his* self-imposed standards, condemns the language of the Bible (Book of Ezekiel, e.g. firm breasts, etc.) as pornographic language. He boastfully challenges authorities to ban this book [the Bible] as *"it corrupts the minds of its readers"*, he concluded. Even though Muslims, like Deedat, see the Bible's language as pornographic, translators of the Holy Bible, continue to correctly translate its message.

Pornographic language in the Quran

CAN THE SAME BE SAID ABOUT THE QURAN (THAT IT CONTAINS PORNOGRAPHIC LANGUAGE ACCORDING TO DEEDAT'S STANDARDS)?

If you read Ali's Quran translation circulated by Deedat's office, the reader will conclude that such language is not to be found in the pages of the Quran. Let's take an example to prove the point.

<u>Quran Translation by Abdullah Yusuf Ali – Surah 78:33</u> "Verily for the righteous there will be a fulfillment of (the heart's) desires, gardens enclosed and grapevines, **COMPANIONS OF EQUAL AGE** and a cup full (to the brim)."

What is wrong with this translation? Ali is so *embarrassed about the Arabic Text* he simply **IGNORED HALF OF THE VERSE** and left it out as if it doesn't exist. The transliteration reads: "inna li- al- muttaqen mafaaz (an) 32 h.adaa'iq wa- acnaab (an) 33 wa-**KAWAACIB** atraab (an) 34 wa- ka's (an) dihaaq (an)" and should be translated, according to Deedat, with pornographic language.

The Noble Quran	The Koran	Prof. JA Arberry
"...And grape yards; And young FULL BREASTED (mature) maidens of equal age."	"...And vineyards and HIGH BOSOMED..."	"...And vineyards and maidens with SWELLING BREASTS..."

Such dishonesty, with Ali's translation, is not to be found with Bible translators, even if it *"seemingly appears"* according to ignorant Muslims, like Deedat, as pornographic language. If "firm breasts" in the Bible is considered pornographic language, surely *"...full breasted... swelling breasts... and high-bosomed breasts..."* in the Quran and in school-text-books, must also be considered to be pornographic language.

The Quran's language regarding Jesus' conception?

<u>Quran Translation by Abdullah Yusuf Ali – Surah 66:12</u> "And Mary the daughter of 'Imran, **who guarded her chastity** and We breathed into *(her body)* of Our spirit..."

The Noble Quran "Maryam the daughter of Imran, who GUARDED HER CHASTITY. We breathed into (the sleeve of her shirt) through our ruh…"	Meaning of Glorious Quran "Mary, daughter of Imran, WHOSE BODY WAS CHASTE We breath therein *something of our spirit…*"	The Koran "Mary, Imran's daughter, who PRESERVED HER CHASTITY and into whose womb we breathed our spirit…"

Again, what is wrong with these Translations? These Muslim translators of the Quran are so ashamed of the Arabic text, ashamed of Allah's Word, everyone made a somersault when translating this verse. Below, I produced the transliteration and the correct translation that follows from the Arabic word that Muslim Translators so shamefully avoided.

Quran Translation by Abdullah Yusuf Ali: Roman Transliteration – Surah 66:12

"Wallatiii 'ahsanat **FARJAHAA** fananakhnaa fiihaa mir-Ruuhinaa wa ja-'alnaahaa wabnahaaa 'Aayatal-lil- 'aalamiin."

Do you see the Arabic word *"farjahaa"*? What does this word mean?

Message of the Quran: Page 500 Commentary 87 "The description of Mary - *"allati ahsanat* **FARJAHA** idiomatically denoting *"one who guarded her **CHASTITY**"* (**HER PRIVATE PARTS**)."

Mary guarded her private part, e.g. her vagina.

Tafsir - Ibn Al Kathir S. 66:12 "Maryam, the daughter of Imran who guarded her **CHASTITY (PRIVATE PART)** … *we breathed into* **IT (PRIVATE PART)** through Our Ruh…"

https://quranx.com/Tafsir/Kathir/66.11 Last accessed 26 April 2021

Tafsir - Ibn Al Kathir S. 2:223. "As Allah has ordained for you… This refers to Al-**Farj** (the **vagina**), as Ibn `Abbas, Mujahid and other scholars have stated. Therefore, anal sex is prohibited … Ibn Jurayj (one of the reporters of the Hadith) said that Allah's Messenger said: (From the front or from behind, as long as that occurs in the **Farj** (**vagina**)."
https://quranx.com/Tafsir/Kathir/2.222 Last accessed 26 April 2021

Who breathed into Mary's private part, i.e. vagina?

Tafsir - Ibn Al Kathir S. 66:12 "…**WE** breathed into **it (private part)**…"

https://quranx.com/Tafsir/Kathir/66.11 Last accessed 26 April 2021

CAN YOU IMAGINE ALLAH BREATHING INTO MARY'S VAGINA? Talk about pornographic language. Disgusting! According to the Holy Bible, in **Luke 1:35**, the Holy Spirit overshadowed (anointed) Mary and she conceived by a miracle. The language of the Quran is despicable to say Allah breathed into Mary's vagina. If a Biblical scripture read that God breathed into the vagina of Mary, I wonder how Deedat would have rated it? 5 Star pornographic rating! So much for Deedat's hypocracy!

18 Do the Gospels have light or did it once have light?

In *Surah 4:47* below, Ali translated the verse into the past tense "was" to highlight Biblical corruption, but Dr. Asad, Dr. Khalifah and Drs. Khan and Hilali translated it right showing that the Gospels have light, NOT had light.

Quran Translation by Abdullah Yusuf Ali: "Confirming what WAS (already) with you …"	Meaning of Glorious Quran "Confirming That WHICH YOU POSSESS."	Authorized English Version of the Quran "Confirming what you HAVE."	The Noble Quran "Confirming what IS with You."

Surah 5:15

> *Quran Translation by Abdullah Yusuf Ali:* "Revealing to you much that ye used to hide in the Book, passing over much (**that is now unnecessary**): There hath come to you from Allah a (**new**) light…"

The bold words in interpolation (…) brackets are not in the Arabic text of the Quran. Ali placed his sectarian belief into these (…) to emphasize possible Bible corruption. Woe to those who write the book with their own hands, then say: "This is from God.

Surah 5:46

| Quran Translation by Abdullah Yusuf Ali: "Gospel, therein WAS guidance and light" | The Noble Quran "Injeel in which WAS guidance..." | Message of the Quran "Gospel wherein there WAS guidance..." |

The above Translators translated the verse into the past tense *"was"* to promote Bible corruption. It is now easier for Muslims to condemn the Bible as corrupted, since Allah in the Quran seemingly stated that the Holy Bible *once* had guidance. In the Arabic there is **"NO"** indication of past tense, it is timeless and must be translated **"IS"** to be faithful to the intention.

See more accurate translations of the same verse below:

| <u>Meaning of The Glorious Quran:</u> "Gospel wherein IS guidance and a light" | <u>Quran Translation by Prof. JA Arberry:</u> "Gospel wherein IS guidance and light." | <u>The Koran</u> "Gospel in which there IS guidance and light" |

19 Was the Torah given to Moses?

<u>Quran Translation by Abdullah Yusuf Ali: Roman Transliteration Surah 5:44</u>

"...Innaaa 'anzalnat-**TAWRAATA** fiihaa Hudanw-wa Nuur..."

| Quran Translation by Abdullah Yusuf Ali: "It was We who revealed the LAW (TO MOSES)..." | The Noble Quran "Verily, We did send down the TAURAT (Torah: TO MUSA)..." |

The Arabic text only informs us that Allah revealed the Torah (Law). It does **NOT** inform us that it was given to Moses. Ali and Drs. Hilali and Khan are well aware of this fact, hence the interpolation (…) brackets. Pickthall, below, translated it most accurately.

Meaning of Glorious Quran "We did reveal the **TORAH**, wherein is guidance and a light…"

It is crystal clear that the <u>Quran does not indicate</u> who the recipient prophet of the Torah was. Similar observations can be made regarding another verse in the Quran listed below:

Quran Translation by Abdullah Yusuf Ali: Roman Transliteration – Surah 62: 5
"Masalul-laziina hummilut-**TAWRAATA** summa…"

Quran Translation by Shakir – Surah 62:5 "The likeness of those who were charged with the **TAURAT**, then they did not observe it…"

Shakir left the word untranslated, which is not a problem. Notice carefully, the name Moses is not mentioned in both the transliteration and Shakir's translation.

Muslim Translators, this time its Ali and Pickthall who are the guilty parties, who just could not help, but to add the name Moses to their versions without using (…) interpolation brackets to indicate their additions to their English versions.

Quran Translation by Abdullah Yusuf Ali: "The similitude of those who were charged with the (obligation of the) **MOSIAC** Law…"	***Meaning of Glorious Quran*** "The likeness of those who are entrusted with the Law of **MOSES**…"

There are many references in the Quran that speak about a/the book (kitab) given to Moses (2:53,87, 6:91, 154, 11:17, 110, 17:2, 19:51 & 23:49), or even about the "Books of Moses" (53:36 & 87:19), **BUT NONE** of these verses speaks about the Law that was given to Moses.

Authorized English Version of the Quran: Page 790 Footnote "…Nowhere in the Quran do we find that the Torah was given to Moses."

I challenge any Muslim to produce only one verse from the Quran (NOT A MISTRANSLATION) where it stated that the Torah was given to Moses? The only way a Muslim can know the Torah was given to Moses is to turn to God's Holy Word, the Holy Bible.

20 Does Allah pray?

Quran: Roman Transliteration by Abdullah Yusuf Ali – Surah 33:56 "Innallaaha wa Malaaa- i-katahuu yu<u>s</u>alluuna alan-Na-biyy…" [2:157, 33:43]

Let's look at different Muslim Translations.

Surah 33:56 - Translation of Abdullah Yusuf Ali

Quran: Roman Transliteration and Translation by A. Y. Ali: Surah 33:56

Inn	allaaha	wa	malaaa-i-katahuu	yu**salluu**na	alan-Na-biyy...
	God	and	His angels	**send blessing**	on the prophet...

I NEED TO APPLAUSE ALI FOR REFLECTING THE CORRECT STRUCTURE OF THE VERSE. PRESENTING THE TRANSLATION, THE WAY ALI DID, CLEARLY SHOWS THAT BOTH GOD AND HIS ANGELS DO THE SAME ACT, SHARING THE SAME VERB.

What is wrong with his translation? Ali consciously decided to **MIS**translate **salluu** as *"sent blessings"*. The Arabic words "**anzalna**" for "**send**" and "**barakaatu**" for "**blessing**" are not in the Arabic text of this verse. Ali knows this very well as illustrated in the below verses.

Quran Translation by Abdullah Yusuf Ali: Roman Transliteration – Surah 11:73, 15:90, 3:39 "...The mercy of Allah and His **BLESSINGS [BARAKAATU]** on you... We **SENT [ANZALNA]** down on those who divided (Scripture into arbitrary parts) ... While he was standing in **PRAYER [YUSALLII]**..." [2:238]

Considering the above information, the CORRECT TRANSLATION of the verse should read:

Inn	allaaha	wa	malaaa-i-katahuu	yu**salluu**na	alan-Na-biyy...
	God	and	His angels	**pray**	for the prophet...

The reason why Ali mistranslated Surah 33:56 was to hide the fact that the Arabic Quran Text clearly show that Allah and His angels pray. Obviously, that is to much for embarrassed Muslims to swallow. Instead of correctly translating the verse, Ali decided to render a deceptive translation to keep non-Arabic people uninformed that the Quran teach that Allah pray.

Surah 33:56 - Translation of Drs. Hilali and Khan

The Noble Quran "Allah **sends** His **salat** (blessing, mercy, grace and honor) on the prophet (Muhammad) and also **His angels (ask** Allah to bless and forgive him) ..."

Drs. Hilali and Khan decided to *reconstruct the verse* to reflect TWO different things being actioned: (i) Allah **sends** ... and (ii) The angels **ask** ... The Arabic words for *"send and ask"* are not in the Arabic text. The Arabic does not say that Allah sends and His angels ask. As we have seen, the Arabic text says: *"God and His angels salat on the prophet."* They obviously reconstructed it to hide the idea that their God and the angels do the same act, i.e. **salat**, meaning **Allah and His angels pray** for Muhammed. Drs. Hilali and Khan decided to leave the Arabic word "**salat**" untranslated, which is not a problem, but then they gave their *mis*translations of "**salat**" in interpolation (...) brackets to make the non-Arab think the verse says: God sends His blessings, etc. on Muhammad. As already mentioned, the Arabic word for "blessing" is **mubaraka**. The Arabic word for "mercy" is **rahmaan**, "grace" is **rahiim** and for "honor" is **mu'izz**. Muslim Scholars, Drs. Hilali and Khan, as Arabic speakers are aware the correct translation for "*salat*" is "prayer". Let's look at examples where they correctly translated the words **mubarak** and **salat**.

The Noble Quran Surah 19:31 "He [Allah] has made Me [Jesus] **blessed [mubarakan]** wheresoever I be and has enjoined on Me **salat (prayer)** and Zakat, as long as I live ... Page 449 Footnote "The prophet said: Order children for **salat (prayer)** at age 7..." Unquote: Please note that Drs. Hilali and Khan also translated Sahih Bukhari from Arabic into English. Let's see how they translated **salat** in these traditions:

Sahih Bukhari Vol. 7, Page xi, General Contents, Vol. I:8 "The Book of the **Salat (prayers)**."

These Muslim scholars, in Surah 33:56 in their interpolation brackets, dare not even mention **prayer** as a possible translation of the word **salat**. Why? Just like Yusuf Ali, they are embarrassed that their Allah and His angels pray for Muhammad.

Surah 33:56 - Translation of Dr. Rashad Khalifah

Authorized English Version of the Quran "God and His angels **HELP AND SUPPORT** the prophet..."

The Arabic word **nasara** for *"help and support"* is not in this Arabic text. Dr. Khalifah also decided to pervert his English Version to read "help" for **salat**, but based on what he wrote in his book quoted below, we can safely conclude that Dr. Khalifah is also embarrassed and deceptively mistranslated the verse to hide the fact that the Quran show that Allah and His angels pray:

Quran, Hadith and Islam – Page 44 "The word **salat** is very specific and *MEANS ONLY ONE THING*, e.g. the observance of specific practices *INVOLVING* bowing and prostration. *THIS IS TRUE THROUGHOUT THE QURAN*..."

Then why translate it as "help and support" in Surah 33:56? Deception on its highest level! Muslim scholar, Mr. Bashir Vania agrees with Dr. Khalifah's deceitful mistranslation and used it in a public debate dated 10 September 2016:

"Why Christianity? – Why Islam?" [Mr. Vania said:] "In Surah 33:56 yu**salluu**na means **help**."

It is strange that all of these Muslim translators have amnesia about the correct translation for **salat** in this verse. None of them even dare put the correct meaning of **salat**, e.g (**PRAYER**) into interpolations in their versions. Every Muslim seems to be an expert on translating the meaning of this verse contrary to the other Muslims.

Surah 33:56 - Translation of Mustafa Khattab

"Allah showers His blessings upon the Prophet and His angels **PRAY** for him."

http://www.alim.org/library/quran/surah/english/33/MKT#56 Last accessed 26 April 2021

In this Version, the structure of the verse was changed to deceptively show that Allah and the angels do two different things, e.g. God sending blessings and the angels praying. This version clearly shows that the word **salluu** means **pray**. If we look at the Arabic structure of the verse, Allah and His angels do THE SAME THING, **salluu,** the correct translation can only be that Allah and His angels "pray".

Surah 33:56 Tafsir - Ibn Al Kathir

*"**Allah sends His Salah** on the Prophet and also His angels (do so)..."* **The Command to say Salah upon the Prophet:** Al-Bukhari said: "Abu Al-`Aliyah said: "Allah's **Salah** is His **praising** him."

http://www.alim.org/library/quran/AlQuran-tafsir/TIK/33/56 Last accessed 26 April 2021

Again, we clearly see Allah and His Angels **salah** on the prophet. The Arabic word for "**praise**" is **humdo**, which is not in this Arabic text. One thing is clear, Muslim scholars are gifted gymnastic translators, they are very good in presenting summersault translations.

Translation of the word salat by Maulana M. Ali and Hammudah Abdalati

The Holy Qur'an: Part 1, Chapter 1 Al-Fatihah – Page 1 "...Surat al-**Salat**, e.g. the Chapter of **Prayer**...."

Islam in Focus: Chap. 3 The Application of faith: "...**Prayer** (**salah**)."

Muslim scholar Mohammad Hijab and Allah praying

Public debate: 7 November 2018 "Tawheed vs Trinity" Christian Speaker, Dr. David Wood and Muslim Speaker, Mr. Mohammed Hijab [Quoting Wood:] "In Surah 33:56 we read: Surely Allah and His angels pray for the prophet..." https://www.youtube.com/watch?v=ZyhvQ0O4yxI Time line 00:44:26 – 00:45:10 Last accessed 26 April 2021

Wood's argument was that the Quran says: "Allah **PRAY**". In his rebuttal, Hijab ignores the idea that Allah pray and deceived his audience to make them think that *Wood misquoted the Quran as* – Allah and His angels pray **TO** Muhammad, instead of Allah and His angels pray **FOR** Muhammed. [Time line 00:58:25 – 00:58:49, Quoting Hijab] "The translators have Surah 33:56 *FOR* the prophet – **NOT** – *TO* the prophet..." Unquote:

Whether "Allah pray *FOR* the prophet and not *TO* the prophet..." is irrelevant, the point is: "Allah prays" [More examples where the Quran shows that Allah pray: Surahs 2:157, 33:43.]

IN HIS REBUTTAL, HIJAB DIDN'T DARE TO TRY TO EXPLAIN WHAT "SALAH" MEANS.

More examples showing Allah praying and interceding

Tafsir - Ibn Al Kathir S. 11:69 "Say: O **Allah, send prayers** upon Muhammad..."

https://quranx.com/Tafsir/Kathir/11.69 Last accessed 26 April 2021

In a discussion between Christian Apologist Sam Shamoun and a Muslim woman, where she finally, after many attempts to hide the embarrassing truth, confirmed that the Arabic word "yusallii" means "pray".] https://www.youtube.com/watch?v=gkJt2Fu0i_w [Time line 01:39:00 Here is another example of Allah praying: https://www.youtube.com/watch?v=YGionMMWQTA Last accessed 27 April 2021

Quran Translation by Abdullah Yusuf Ali – Surah 6:70 "...Every soul delivers itself to ruin by its own acts: it will find for itself no protector or **INTERCESSOR, EXCEPT ALLAH**..."

Thesaurus Dictionary: "An interceder is someone who uses his influence to persuade someone in authority to forgive another person..."

If Allah intercedes, **TO WHOM DOES ALLAH INTERCEDE TO** on behalf of the souls? Perhaps, in Islam the word "*intercessor*" means: blessings, mercy, grace, honor, help, support, praise, etc.

Most Muslims, unawares, pray daily to Muhammad

Most Muslims are NOT aware that in a certain fragment of their prayers, they stop praying to Allah and pray directly to Muhammad. All Muslims pray in Arabic and most Muslims do not understand what they are reciting in their prayers. They mumble Arabic words without understanding what they are saying.

Quran Trans. by Abdullah Yusuf Ali: Page xii "The ambition of Muslims is to read the sounds of the Arabic Text. I wish their ambition were to understand the Quran, in Arabic or their mother tongue."

If Muslims say they **DO** understand what they are saying in Arabic, then their **salah - prayers** are willful idolatry for what they utter when praying. Let's look at the prayer in question that Muslims recite in the Arabic language five times a day:

SALAH: The Muslim Prayer: Page 23 "*as-salamu (peace) alaika ay-yuhan (be on* **YOU**) *nabiy-yu (o prophet).*"

In this part of their prayer, they are N-O-T asking Allah to bless Muhammad, but they pronounce a blessing **DIRECTLY** to Muhammad. They don't pray to Allah and say: "*O God, bless Muhammad with peace!*" They pray and say to Muhammad: "Peace be on **YOU, OH PROPHET**!"

Youtube presentations: David Wood and Sam Shamoun: Why Muslims pray to Muhammad

https://www.youtube.com/watch?v=c9cvvzJoTeg Last accessed 26 April 2021

A Muslim admits Muslims are praying to Muhammad:

https://www.youtube.com/watch?v=CjsRVkiN-D8 Last accessed 26 April 2021

Do Muslims worship Muhammad and Muslim scholars

The Noble Quran – Appendix II Page 899-900 "They (Jews and Christians) took their rabbis and monks to be their lords besides Allah **(by obeying them in things which they made lawful and unlawful according to their own desires without being ordered by Allah)** [S.9:31] … Adi bin Hatim said: O Allah's Prophet! Thet do not worship them (rabbis and monks). Allah's mrssenger said: Thet certainly do. They (i.e. rabbis and monks) made legal things illegal and illegal things legal and they (i.e. Jews and Christians) follow them and by doing so, they really worshipped them. (Narrated by Ahmad, At-Tirmidhi and Ibn Jarir) …"

So, according to Muhammed, if you obey any other instead of Allah, then you are really worshipping them instead of Allah. To be consistent, this means, not only Christians alone, but also Muslims who obey the statements of Muhammed, their Imams, Maulanas, Muftis, etc. instead of Allah, they (i.e. those Muslims) are really worshipping them (i.e. Muhammed, Imams, Maulanas, Muftis, etc.) instead of Allah. **FOR EXAMPLE:** [1] Allah in the Quran 24:2 says the adulterer must be whipped with 100 lashes, but Muslims, according to Muhammed, stones the adulterer (see heading: Missing Quran verses: Stoning of the adulterer) to death, therefore, they are really worshipping Muhammed instead of Allah. [2] Allah in the Quran 5:5 (see heading: Is food cooked in Christian homes, halaal?) says food prepared by Christians is halaal for Muslims, but Muslim scholars says it is haraam, therefore, they are really worshipping their Muslim scholars instead of Allah.

CONCLUSION: Contemporary Muslim translators of the Quran are not changing the compiled official revised Arabic Uthmanic text, which, was later edited with the adding of diacritical points and vowels and grammatical corrections that was made to it, but they are guilty of mistranslating, misinterpreting and thereby _corrupting the true meaning_ of the revised surviving Uthmanic Quran message to the non-Arab layperson who reads their English Versions set before them. Muslims claim to be pure monotheistic worshippers, yet their prayers and worshipping is also directed to Muhammed and Muslim scholars.

SECTION 3

MUSLIMS DISREGARD THE QURAN

Christians and deadly poison

<u>*Mark 16:17*</u> "And these signs shall follow them that believe; In my name shall they cast out devils; they shall speak with new tongues; 18 They shall take up serpents; **and if they drink any deadly thing, it shall not hurt them;** they shall lay hands on the sick, and they shall recover."

Muslims will read the above verses, especially the bold phrase and challenge Christians to drink deadly poison, saying that if they believe it will not harm them. In responds, the Bible does not expect us to act irresponsible and to tempt the Lord our God. I sincerely believe that if a Christian is on a mission divinely directed by God and if that Christian take deadly poison without knowing what it is, God will protect him, because God is faithful to His promises. Even Jesus Christ Himself, when Satan tempted Him to cast Himself off a cliff (Matt. 4:6), Jesus didn't clown for Satan, He responded by saying to Satan, it is also written (Matt. 4:7).

Let's turn the table on these ignorant, arrogant Muslims, let's take a dive into the Quran Surah 9:51 and Muhammad's advise how to make poison non-affective:

<u>Quran Translation by Abdullah Yusuf Ali:</u> "Say: "Nothing will happen to us, except what Allah has decreed for us: He is our protector: and on Allah let the Believers put their trust."

<u>Sahih Bukhari, Vol. 7, Page 260, Hadith 356</u> "Narrated Sa`d: Allah's Messenger (ﷺ) said: He who eats seven 'Ajwa dates every morning, will not be affected by poison or magic on the day he eats them."

Based on this verse and hadith, I challenge Muslims to drink deadly poison and let's see if Allah will protect them against it, if they don't, based on their self-acclaimed standard, they disbelieve Allah is their protector or let a Muslim take a gun and put it against his head and pull the trigger and let's see if Allah will protect him, remember, the verse says, nothing will happen to you, except what Allah decreed. Of course this is silly and stupid, every day in the world, somewhere a Muslim girl or woman, like any other women are raped, is that Allah's decree? This show the double standards that arrogant Muslims practice in relation to the Bible.

Muslims, the Quran and Ahadith

Muslims claim the Quran is the last revelation or testament from Allah.

Ramadan Annual of the Muslim Digest April/ May Vol. 38, Nos. 9/ 10 Page 312 "...The Holy Quran was revealed over fourteen centuries ago as Allah's **FINAL MESSAGE**..."

Yet they disregard the Quran for Islamic traditions that came about 250 years after the Quran.

Mr. Faruq Sheriff: A guide to the contents of the Quran – Page 60 "One comm. (Kashf al-asrar in commenting on verse ii.100) says: The orthodox view is abrogation applies both to the Quran and to Tradition. Thus the Quran abrogates the Quran; **TRADITION ABROGATES THE QURAN**..."

This can be verified, for example, in the current Hafs Quran ***Surah 24:2*** the punishment for adultery is 100 stripes.

Sunan Abu Dawood: "A man from the Ansar called Basrah said: I married a virgin woman in her veil. When I entered upon her, I found her pregnant. (I mentioned this to the Prophet). The Prophet (ﷺ) said: She will get the dower, for you made her vagina lawful for you. **THE CHILD WILL BE YOUR SLAVE**. When she has begotten (a child), **FLOG HER**..."

https://quranx.com/Hadith/AbuDawud/Hasan/Hadith-2126 Last accessed 27 April 2021

But Muslims ignore this penalty and follow the ruling of the Tradition that the adulterous must be stoned (see heading: Missing Quran verses: Stoning of the adulterer). Tradition abrogates Quran. If the Quran is a final, complete and detailed revelatory book, how can later Islamic traditions abrogate the Quran?

21 According to Quran: what is Halaal and Haraam food?

- **Halaal** food means food that has been made **lawful** by God **for certain people** to eat.

- **Haraam** food means food that is **prohibited** by God **for certain people** to eat.

Not all food, that is lawful or unlawful, for a certain group of people, is automatically lawful or unlawful for another group of people. Sometimes, God can declare a specific diet that is lawful for one group of people to be unlawful for another group of people and vice versa. It depends on **WHAT GOD DECLARED** to be lawful or unlawful and **TO WHOM** these diets have been made lawful or unlawful.

In the Quran, the Author clearly identified what food is lawful and unlawful for Jews, Christians and Muslims to eat or to abstain from. **In other words, when reading the Quran, we must understand which group of people is addressed by Allah and what is made lawful and unlawful by Allah for them.**

Who decides what food is Halaal or Haraam?

Quran Translation by Abdullah Yusuf Ali – Surah 6:119, 16:116 "Why should ye not eat of (meats) on which God's name has been pronounced when he had explained to you in detail what is forbidden to you … **YOU SHALL NOT UTTER LIES WITH YOUR OWN TONGUE STATING: THIS IS LAWFUL AND THIS IS UNLAWFUL…**" (Surah 66:1)

Yet Muslims obey their scholars. The Quran said in detail that Christians' food is lawful, but their scholars knows better than God and forbid Muslims to eat food prepared by Christians!

According to Quran, what's unlawful for Jews to eat?

Quran Translation by Abdullah Yusuf Ali – Surah 6:146 "...**THOSE WHO FOLLOWED THE JEWISH LAW**, we forbade every (animal) with undivided hoof and We forbade them *the fat of the ox and the sheep, except what adheres to their backs or their entrails or is mixed up with a bone*: THIS IN RECOMPENSE FOR THEIR WILLFUL DISOBEDIENCE..."

Here we see that the above stipulated dietary was ONLY forbidden the Jews, **NOT** for the Christians nor Muslims. Also, according to the Quran, it was forbidden, declared unlawful, to the Jews, because of their possible disobedience, **NOT** because it was unclean.

Sahih Bukhari Vol. 3 Page 233-234 Hadiths 424-426 "Narrated Abdullah bin Abbas: Once Allah's messenger passed by a dead sheep and said to the people – Wouldn't you benefit by its skin? The people replied that it was dead. *The prophet said*: **BUT ITS EATING ONLY IS ILLEGAL** ... Allah had forbidden them (Jews) to eat the fat of animals..."

CERTAIN FAT of the ox and sheep were forbidden the Jews to eat, not the ox and sheep as a whole. The verse does NOT forbid the Jews to eat of the flesh of the ox and sheep. Only CERTAIN FAT was pronounced unlawful for them to eat. Notice, in this verse, Muslims and Christians are not forbidden to eat of these certain fat of the ox and the sheep. Only the Jews were forbidden to eat of these parts of the ox and sheep. This verse and the explanation of Muhammad clearly demonstrated that THAT which is forbidden for one group of people, e.g. Jews is not automatically forbidden for all people, e.g. Christians and Muslims to eat. Also notice, according to the Quran and Muhammad, only certain fat as food was prohibited, **not the touching of its skin** and Muhammad explained it likewise. They could use the skin of the sheep and ox for clothing. Nowhere does Allah in the Quran forbid Jews to use the skin of these animals for clothing, nor does Allah forbid Christians and Muslims to eat these fats. According to the Quran, Jesus also came to make certain food that was previously unlawful for Jews to eat, lawful for them to eat. So, according to the Quran, what Allah disallowed, pronounced unlawful in the past, some of it was made lawful in the time of Jesus!

Quran Translation by Abdullah Yusuf Ali – Surah 3:50 "(I have come to you) ... to make lawful to you part of what was (before) forbidden to you..."

According to Quran, what is un/lawful for Muslims?

Quran Translation by Abdullah Yusuf Ali – Surah 6:119 "Why should ye not eat of (meats) on which Allah's name hath been pronounced, when He explained to **you in detail what is forbidden**, except under compulsion of necessity?"

Allah explained in detail what is forbidden for Muslims to eat!

Quran Translation by Abdullah Yusuf Ali – Surah 5:3 [2:173] "**FORBIDDEN TO YOU (FOR FOOD) ARE**:

- dead meat, blood, **FLESH** of swine and that on which hath been invoked the name of other than God,
- that which hath been killed by strangling or by a violet blow or by a headlong fall or
- by being gored to death,
- that which hath been (partly) eaten by a wild animal, unless ye are able to slaughter it (in due form),
- that which is sacrificed on stone (altars),
- (Forbidden) also is the division (of meat) by raffling ...This day have I perfected your religion for you."

Earlier, we have seen Allah forbid the Jews to eat certain fat of sheep and ox, Allah did NOT forbid them the rest of the fat and the flesh (meat) of these animals. Allah's prohibitions in the Quran are specific and detailed. With that in mind, in the Quran, Muslims were forbidden to eat the flesh (meat) of pigs, NOT THE FAT OF PIGS. Nowhere in the Quran is a Muslim forbidden to eat the fat of pigs or to touch pigs. This is not just my interpretation, but also the interpretation of Muslim scholars as demonstrated here:

Authorized English Version of the Quran: Appendix 16 "Dietary Prohibitions" Page 534 "The Quran teaches that God is extremely displeased with those who prohibit anything that was not specifically prohibited in the Quran (16:112-116). The upholding of any prohibitions not specifically mentioned in the Quran is tantamount to idolatry (6:142-152). **IF YOU WORSHIP GOD ALONE, YOU WILL UPHOLD HIS TEACHINGS ALONE** and honor the commands and prohibitions instituted only by Him. The absolute specificity of dietary prohibitions in the Quran is best illustrated in 6:145-146. We learn from these two verses that when God prohibits "meat," he prohibits "meat" and nothing else and when He prohibits "fat" that is what He specifically prohibits. **THESE TWO VERSES INFORMS US THAT "THE MEAT" OF PIGS IS PROHIBITED, NOT "THE FAT." Obviously, God knew that in many countries, lard would be used in baked goods and other food products and that such usage doesn't render the food Haraam.** The Quran prohibits four meats (2:173, 5:3, 6:142-145...)"

Notice, Allah declared the flesh of the pig unlawful for the Muslims to eat, but NOWHERE did Allah forbid the benefit of the fat of the pig as food and its skin for useful products.

FOOD THAT ARE LAWFUL FOR MUSLIMS!

Quran Translation by Abdullah Yusuf Ali – Surah 5:4 "**THEY ASK THEE WHAT IS LAWFUL TO THEM** (as food), Say: Lawful unto you are [1] (all) things good and pure: [2] And what ye have taught your trained hunting animals (to catch) in the manner directed to you by God: Eat what they [animals] catch for you, but pronounce the name of God over it..."

According to the Bible ***Genesis 1:24-25*** when God made the pig and the camel, God saw that it was good.

Yes, later at the time of Prophet Moses, these animals were forbidden to the Jews as food to eat. However, according to the Quran, at the time of Muhammad, the camel was pronounced lawful for the Muslims to eat, again, showing, that which is forbidden one people to eat is not necessarily forbidden to another people to eat. Nowhere in the Bible and Quran are Christians forbidden to eat pork and camel!

Is food cooked in Christian homes Halaal?

The Quran is clear; Muslims are forbidden to eat the flesh of pigs. So, if a Christian offer a Muslim a diet that includes the flesh of pigs, the Muslim must refuse it, not because he is funny, but because he obeys the Quran, but what about other food prepared by Christians?

Quran Translation by Abdullah Yusuf Ali – Surah 5:5 "This day are (all) things good and pure made lawful unto you. **The food of the people of the book is lawful** unto you and yours is lawful unto them."

But guess what? Muslims don't regard this instruction from their Allah. They simply refuse to eat food prepared by Christians. Muslims, in the face of the Quranic instructions, have come up with lots of unquranic reasons to declare food prepared by Christians as unlawful.

Muhammad receive no additional revelations

Quran Translation by Abdullah Yusuf Ali – Surah 6:145 "Say: **I DO NOT FIND IN THE REVELATIONS GIVEN TO ME** any food that is prohibited for any eater, *except:* [1] carrion, [2] running blood, [3] the *MEAT* of pigs [not the whole pig – not the fat of pigs] and [4] the meat of animals blasphemously dedicated to other than God."

ACCORDING TO THE QURAN, there's no revelations given to Muhammad, forbidding Muslims to eat food prepared by Christians or food containing pig-fat. Bring your proof if ye are truthful? Muslims forbidding food, except for that mentioned in the Quran is in direct violation of the Quran.

Quran Translation by Abdullah Yusuf Ali – Surah 6:21 "Who doth more wrong than he who invented a lie against Allah or rejected His signs? But verily the wrong-doers never shall prosper."

According to Quran, when can Muslims eat pork?

Quran Translation by Abdullah Yusuf Ali – Surah 5:3 "Forbidden to you (for food) are: dead meat, blood, the flesh of swine … **BUT IF ANY IS FORCED BY HUNGER**, with no inclination to transgression, Allah is indeed Oft-forgiving, Most Merciful."

Allah says if you are hungry, you can eat pork. Conclusion: if you not hungry, pork is prohibited!

22 Must Muslim women wear scarfs as a religious dress code?

Umar, original messenger of the hijab

Sahih Bukhari Vol. 1, Page 376, Hadith 148 "Narrated `Aisha: The wives of the Prophet (ﷺ) used to go to Al-Manasi, open place to answer the call of nature at night. **UMAR USED TO SAY TO THE PROPHET (ﷺ) "LET YOUR WIVES BE VEILED," BUT ALLAH'S APOSTLE DID NOT DO SO.** One night Sauda bint Zam`a, the wife of the Prophet (ﷺ) went out… Umar addressed her and said: I have recognized you, O Sauda. He said so, as he desired eagerly that the verses of Al-Hijab (the observing of veils by the Muslim women) may be revealed. *So Allah revealed the verses of Al-Hijab (A complete body cover excluding the eyes)*."

Sahih Bukhari Vol. 1, Page 240, Hadith 395 "**NARRATED `UMAR** (bin Al-Khattab): My Lord agreed with me in three things… (2) And as regards the (verse of) the veiling of the women, I said: O Allah's Messenger (ﷺ) **I WISH YOU ORDERED YOUR WIVES TO COVER THEMSELVES FROM THE MEN… SO THE VERSE OF THE VEILING OF THE WOMEN WAS REVEALED.**"

The word "hijab" in the Quran

Women dress code according to Quran: "Hijab in the Quran is the term used by Muslim women to describe their "head cover" that may or may not include covering their face… "Hijab" can be translated into veil… Other meanings for Hijab include: screen, cover, mantle, curtain, drapes, division and divider. Hijab in the Quran, it appears 7 times: 7:46,

33:53, 38:32, 41:5, 42:51, 17:45 & 19:17. **NONE OF THESE "HIJAB" WORDS ARE USED IN THE QURAN IN REFERENCE TO WHAT MUSLIMS CALL TODAY (HIJAB) AS A DRESS CODE FOR THE MUSLIM WOMAN.** Hijab in the Quran has nothing to do with women dress code."

Understanding the word "Jilbab" in Surah 33:59

<u>Tafsir - Tanwîr al-Miqbâs min Tafsîr Ibn 'Abbâs Surah 33:59</u> "(O Prophet! Tell thy wives and thy daughters and the women of the believers to draw their cloaks close round them) *to cover their necks and bosoms*..." https://quranx.com/Tafsir/Abbas/33.59 Last accessed 27 April 2021

Faruq Sheriff agrees: <u>**A guide to the contents of the Quran Page 194**</u> "The Arabic word translated as "outer garment" [in Surah 33:59] is "julbab", a long gown, *which covers the neck and bosom*."

<u>*Sahih Bukhari Vol. 4, Hadith 377, Vol. 6 Page 405 Hadith 435*</u> "Narrated Anas bin Malik: While I was walking with **the Prophet (ﷺ) who was wearing a Najrani outer garment** with a thick hem... Narrated Ibn `Abbas: ... **Umar reported how he at once put on his outer garment** and went to Hafsa and said to her, O my daughter! Do you argue with Allah's Messenger (ﷺ) so that he remains angry the whole day?"

https://quranx.com/Hadith/Bukhari/USC-MSA/Volume-4/Book-53/Hadith-377

Cover your breasts not your heads

<u>*Authorized English Version of the Quran Surah 24:31*</u> "... The believing women... **COVER THEIR CHESTS**..."

<u>*Women dress code according to Quran*</u>: "The Arabic word for chest, **GAYB** is in the verse (24:31), but the Arabic words for head (**RAAS**) or hair (**SHAAR**) are not in the verse. The commandment in the verse is clear: *cover your chest or bosoms,* **but also the fabrication of the scholars and most of the translators is also clear: "cover your head or hair."**

Muslims *might* be able to argue from their traditions 250 years after Muhammad that women's heads must be veiled, but this is an **UNSUBSTANTIATED TOPIC IN THE PAGES OF THE ARABIC QURANS**.

Women abused because of head-covering

Some Muslims still continue to degrade women by punishing them for NOT wearing head-covers:

- *Femina: January 2002 Pages 94-97* "Burka is the only visa required for women to enter Afghanistan.

They will **FLOG WOMEN THAT DON'T HAVE THE VEIL ON**..."

- *Drum: The voice of Africa. March 14 2002 No: 497 Page 20* "While there is little evidence of Taliban-

style Islamic militancy on the streets of Sokoto, in other northern states, churches have been burned

and **CHRISTIAN WOMEN HAVE BEEN ATTACKED FOR NOT COVERING THEIR HEADS.**"

There is not a verse in the Quran that says a woman must veil her head.

Is Purdah Islamic?

The Muslim Digest: June 1966 Vol. 16 No: 11 Page 16 "The purdah system isn't an Islamic institution. It was imported into Islamic countries from Byzantine and Persian Empires. **The present purdah system of completely veiling women is neither Islamic, nor of Arabian origin.**"

23 Does the Quran prohibit Muslims to receive interest?

From: Michael Mahomed, sent 23 July 2012 12:12 **TO: YUSUF ISMAIL'** rehan ali'; 'Brian Marrian', Cc: Mohammed Coovadia'; 'Asad Mohamed', **SUBJECT: INTEREST**: Hi Yusuf Ismail. Perhaps you will be able to share some light on this topic and increase my knowledge. Below, please see a Quranic verse and other quotations. **AYA Surah 2:275** "…Allah hath permitted trade and **FORBIDDEN USURY**. Those who after receiving direction from their Lord, desist, shall be pardoned for the past; … But **THOSE WHO REPEAT** (the offence) are companions of the Fire…" **AYA Page 111 Comm. 324** "Usury is condemned and prohibited in the strongest possible terms. There can be no question about the prohibition." *The Muslim Digest June 1966 Vol. 16 No: 11 Page 4-5* "Dealing in interest is Haram (prohibited) in all places whether in Darul Harb or Darul Islam, whether with Muslims or with non-Muslims. The strong manner in which the Quran and the Ahadith had condemned the taking of interest proves that **NO MUSLIM COULD DARE TO DEAL IN IT**." My understanding, which can be 100% wrong, if a Muslim fast and do good deeds, but **accept interests** on his bank accounts, medical aid savings, properties sold, etc. *after* he or she became aware of the above verse, that Muslim will burn in hell. Please advise if my understanding is right or wrong [if wrong, why?] Kind regards."

FROM: 'YUSUF ISMAIL' Sent: 02 August 2012 03:54 PM, To: Michael Mahomed; Buxson; rehan ali; Brian Marrian, **Subject: Re: Interest**, **YES-U ARE RIGHT**. Sent from my BlackBerry® smartphone.

Muslim Prof. Fazl Ahmad: Muhammad, The Prophet of Islam: Heroes of Islam 1 Page 113 "Allah has forbidden usury…"

Sahih Bukhari Vol. 7, Page 197, Hadith 259 "Narrated Abu Juhaifa: **THE PROPHET (ﷺ) CURSED** the lady who practices tattooing and the one who gets herself tattooed, and **ONE WHO EATS (TAKES) RIBA' (USURY)** and the one who gives it. And he prohibited taking the price of a dog, and the money earned by prostitution, and cursed the makers of pictures."

Yet many Muslims continue to deal with usury. Their love for money is greater than their love for Allah. Dear Muslim friend, reading this passage, do you deal in interest, there is no heaven, BUT hell-fire for you! No, I am not judging you; I am informing you what Islam teach.

SECTION 4

WHAT THE QURAN SAY ABOUT THE BIBLE

As a Bible believing Christian, I continued my investigation to see what the Quran said about the Bible and presented my findings here, hopefully, Muslims will accept the Bible as God's Word and experience its benefits, e.g. salvation, healing, deliverance, etc.

24 Does the Arabic Quran mention the English word "Bible"?

It is **obvious** that one does not find the **English** phrase "Bible" in the **Arabic** Quran. However, since the English word "Bible" is derived from the Greek word "Biblo", instead of looking for the English phrase "Bible" in an Arabic book, one would instead look for the word "Book", the Arabic **equivalent**, namely "Kitab". This is precisely what we find the Quran calling the Judeo-Christian Scriptures, namely "the Book". Interestingly, Muslim scholars and translators of the Quran understood the phrase "Kitab" to be the Arabic equivalent of "Bible".

Message of the Quran – Surahs 3:78, 5:15, 19, 64-65, 68, 4:153 "…There are indeed some among them who distort **THE BIBLE** with their tongues… O followers of **THE BIBLE** … If the followers of **THE BIBLE** would, but attain to [true] faith… The followers of the **OLD TESTAMENT**…"

Message of the Quran: Page 133 Comm. 164 "As is evidence from the sequence, the term *ahl alkitab* (followers of earlier revelation) refers here specifically to the Jews, which justifies its rendering as "followers of the Old Testament"."

Muslim scholar Shabir Ally says: "THE QURAN PRAISES THE BIBLE…"

http://answering-islam.org/Responses/Shabir-Ally/toughquestion.htm Last accessed 27 April 2021

25 Did God reveal the Bible?

<u>Quran Translation by Abdullah Yusuf Ali – Surah 2:136</u> "…**WE BELIEVE IN THE REVELATIONS** given to … Moses and Jesus and that given to (all) prophets from their Lord…"

Both Muslims and Christians agree that "their Lord" refers to the one Supreme God, therefore, we can rest assured God revealed the revelations given to Moses, Jesus and the prophets.

26 Can the Words of God be changed?

<u>Quran Translation by Abdullah Yusuf Ali – Surah 6:34, 10:64 & 18:27</u> "There is **NONE THAT CAN ALTAR** the *"KALIMAA"* WORDS (decree) of God … **NO CHANGE** can there be in the Words of God … **NONE CAN CHANGE** His Words".

Were the revelations given to Moses, the prophets and to Jesus the Word of God, sometime in the past?

❖ If yes! Every Muslim claiming that it got corrupted / changed, belies Allah and does not believe in their Quran that says the Word of God can't be changed – altered.

❖ If no! They belie the validity of Surah 2:136 mentioned above.

27 Did "TODAY'S" Bible exist in Muhammad's day?

<u>The Noble Quran – Surah 46:30</u> "They said: O our people! Verily, we have heard a book (this Quran) sent down after Musa (Moses), confirming what **<u>CAME BEFORE IT</u>**, it guides to the truth and to the straight path (e.g. Islam)." [Allah is also found to be on the straight path – Surah 11:56]

Quran mistranslations can be deceiving

Look at the bold and underlined words "**<u>CAME BEFORE IT</u>**" in Surah 46:30 mentioned above! The verse seems to indicate that the *Revelations given to Moses* only existed before the Quran and it can also indicate that those Bible verses were only valid before the Quran.

Let's look, again, at the bold words and how it must be translated.

Arabic:	Kaloo Ya kawmana Inna Sami'ina Kitaban Unzila Ba'd Musa
English:	They said: O our people! We have heard of a book revealed after Moses
Arabic:	Musadekan Lima **Bayna Yadayede**
English:	Confirming what is **between his hands**

Dr. Muhammad Asad, as an Arabic Muslim Scholar, is well aware of the **MIS**translation done by dishonest Muslims and commented as follow:

Message of the Quran: Page 65 Commentary 3 "...**MA BAYNA YADAYHI – lit. "THAT WHICH IS BETWEEN ITS HANDS"** ... *does not, in itself, mean that which came before it ... but that which lies open ...* THAT IS, SOMETHING THAT WAS *COEXISTENT* IN TIME WITH THE REVELATION OF THE QURAN."

"Between his hands" which Drs. Hilali and Khan replaced with "came before it" was to override the intended meaning that Moses' Revelations still existed in the time of Muhammad in order to give the English reader the impression that the Quran NOW REPLACED the Bible as God's Word and that the Quran is now revealed as the current Word of God to be followed. If the words are translated correctly, the reader, just like Dr. Muhammad Asad, will conclude that **TODAY'S WRIT OF MOSES, JUST LIKE THE QURAN, WAS AVAILABLE TO MUHAMMAD.**

Ali also mistranslated it in his English Version as "before it", but he is very much aware that the Arabic word *"bayna"* means *"between"* and *"yaday"* means *"hands"*.

Quran Translation by Abdullah Yusuf Ali: Roman Transliteration – Surah 5:51 "Wa anih-kum-**bayna**hum-bimaaa ... And this (He commands): Judge thou *"between"* them..."

Quran Translation by Abdullah Yusuf Ali: Roman Transliteration – Surah 38:75 "Qaala Yaaa-Ibliisu maa mana-aka an-tasjuda limaa khalaqtu bi**yadayy** ... (Allah) said: O Iblis! What prevents you from prostrating to one whom I have created with my **hands**..."

Ali knows that if he presents the accurate translation: *"between his hands"* the Quran readers will realize the Holy Bible co-existed with the Quran during Muhammad's day as explained by Dr. Muhammad Asad.

The same Arabic words are used in **Quran Translation by Abdullah Yusuf Ali: Roman Transliteration – Surah 12:111** "…*Maa kaana hadiisany-yuftaraa wa laakin-tasdii-qallazii* **bayna yaday**hi…"

Let's see how Drs. Khan and Hilali translated Surah 12:111 in **The Noble Quran** "It (the Quran) is not a forged statement, but a confirmation of (**ALLAH'S EXISTING BOOKS**) which were before it…" This time Drs. Hilali and Khan agreed with Dr. Asad that *"bayna yadah"* **refers to something in existence**, but sadly placed it between interpolation (…) brackets *as if it is only a translators' opinion*.

Let's see how Muhammad Pickthall translated the same verse:

Meaning of Glorious Quran "It is no invented story, but a confirmation of **EXISTING (SCRIPTURE)**..."

Quran verify today's Bible is uncorrupted

The Noble Quran – Surah 2:89 "And when there came to them (the Jews) a book (this Quran) from Allah, confirming **WHAT IS WITH THEM**…"

Which revelations did the Jews inherit? The Torah, Psalms and that given to the Jewish prophets! These books were in the possession of the Jews. No honest Muslim or Quran believer can deny the Old Testament existed in Muhammad's day according to these Quran verses. This is exactly why Dr. Asad translated the Jewish scripture as Old Testament.

Quran Translation by Abdullah Yusuf Ali – Surah 2:113 "The Jews say: The Christians have naught (to stand) upon and the Christians say: The Jews have naught (to stand) upon. Yet they (profess to) study the (same) BOOK…"

The Noble Quran "…Thought they both **RECITE THE SCRIPTURE**…"

The Bible had to be in existence for the Jews and Christians to study the book or to recite the scriptures during the time of Muhammad.

Quran Translation by Abdullah Yusuf Ali – Surah 2:121 "Those to whom we have sent the book **STUDY IT AS IT SHOULD BE STUDIED**."

Quran Translation by Abdullah Yusuf Ali - Surah 3:23 "They are *invited to* the Book of God..."

Quran Translation by Abdullah Yusuf Ali: Page 128 Comm. 367 "He [Muhammad] appealed to the authority of **THEIR OWN BOOKS**."

The Noble Quran – Surah 5:43 "But how do they come to you for decision, while they **HAVE THE TAURAT**, in which is the decision of Allah..."

Let's see how Ali translated the same verse: **Quran Translation by Abdullah Yusuf Ali:** "...When **THEY HAVE** (their own) LAW before them? Therein **IS** the (plain) command of God..."

28 Did Muhammad have a preserved Biblical text in mind?

The Noble Quran – Surah 4:47 "O you who have been given the scriptures! Believe in what we have revealed (to Muhammad) **CONFIRMING WHAT IS ALREADY WITH YOU**..."

The Quran was seemingly revealed by Allah to CONFIRM the previous scriptures in the possession of the Jews and Christians, not to expose it as false.

Quran Translation by Abdullah Yusuf Ali – Surah 5:50 "Let the people of the Gospel judge by what God hath revealed therein. If any do fail to judge by (the light of) what God hath revealed, they are (no better than) those who had rebelled."

The uncorrupted Gospel had to be in existence at the time this Quranic verse was recited by Muhammad. Here the Christians are reminded to judge by the Gospels, NOT BY THE

QURAN. It is unlikely that Muhammad would have reminded Christians to judge cases with a corrupted scripture.

The Noble Quran Surah 7:157 "Those who follow the Messenger, the prophet who can neither read nor write (e.g. Muhammad) whom they **FIND WRITTEN WITH THEM IN THE TAURAT (TORAH) (DEUT. XVIII 15) AND THE INJEEL (GOSPEL) (JOHN XIV 16)** ..."

Can you see how Drs. Khan and Hilali refer to the current Holy Bible to interpret this Quranic verse? Why would Allah refer Muhammad to corrupted scripture to identify his foretold ministry?

Quran Translation by Abdullah Yusuf Ali – Surah 7:169 "After them succeeded an *(evil)* generation, they inherited the Book... And they study what **IS IN THE BOOK**..."

Ali reveals his racist hatred against the Jews by inserting the word (evil) into this verse, which is not in the Arabic text. There is no reason in the immediate context for Ali to call the next Jewish generation evil. Ali and many Quran translators are corrupting, not the Quranic text, but its meaning to the people, and as we will see later, that is exactly what Muhammad's accusation against the people of the book was, e.g. misinterpretation. This was a golden opportunity for Allah to have revealed to Muhammad that the Jews inherited a corrupted Book or that they study a corrupted Book, *but he didn't.*

The Noble Quran – Surah 10:94 "So if you (O Muhammad) are in doubt concerning that which we have revealed unto you, (e.g. that your name is written in the Taurat (Torah) and the Injeel (Gospel)), then ask those who **ARE READING THE BOOK** (Torah/Gospel) before you."

Please note that the words: **(e.g. that your name is written in the Taurat and the Injeel)** is not in the Arabic text, this is Drs. Khan and Hilali's added interpolations, something we are used to by now. Notice how easily they corrupt the meaning of the Quran and sell the translation for a good sum of money. However, the Bible had to be in existence for people to read from it. Again, why would Allah tell Muhammad to ask confirmation from a people who reads a corrupted Book? That doesn't make sense!

Quran Translation by Abdullah Yusuf Ali – Surah 32:23 "We [Allah] did indeed aforetime give the book to Moses: Be not then in doubt of **IT [THE BOOK GIVEN TO MOSES] REACHING (THEE)**…"

Here the Quran itself acknowledges that the Book given to Moses was in existence during Muhammad's day. It doesn't mention that the Book was corrupted when it reached Muhammad. The next verse demonstrates that Muhammad still regarded the Torah as a guidance from God, not corruption.

The Noble Quran – Surah 28:48-49 "But the truth (e.g. Muhammad with his message) has come to them from Us, they say: Why is he not given the like of what was given to Moses? Did they not disbelieve in that which was given to Moses of old? They say: **TWO KINDS OF MAGIC (THE TORAH AND THE QURAN)** each helping the other! They say: Verily in both we are disbelievers. Say (to them O Muhammad): Then bring a book from Allah, which is a better guide then these two (the Torah and the Quran) that I may follow it, if ye are truthful."

Sunan Abu Dawud "Narrated Abdullah Ibn Umar: A group of Jews came and invited the Messenger of Allah (ﷺ) to Quff. So he visited them in their school. They said: AbulQasim, one of our men has committed fornication with a woman; so pronounce judgment upon them. They placed a cushion for the Messenger of Allah (ﷺ) who sat on it and said: Bring the Torah. It was then brought. He then withdrew the cushion from beneath him and placed the Torah on it saying: I believed in thee and in Him Who revealed thee. He then said: Bring me one who is learned among you. Then a young man was brought. The transmitter then mentioned the rest of the tradition of stoning similar to the one transmitted by Malik from Nafi' (No. 4431)." https://quranx.com/Hadith/AbuDawud/Hasan/Hadith-4434

Last accessed 27 April 2021

It is a proven fact that the uncorrupted Gospel of John also reached Muhammad as per Islamic literature.

Ishaq, "Life of Muhammad" Trans. By Alfred Guillaume, pp. 103-104 "**AMONG THE THINGS WHICH HAVE REACHED ME** [Muhammad] about what Jesus, the Son of Mary, *STATED IN THE GOSPEL, WHICH HE RECEIVED FROM GOD* ... He that hate me, hate the Lord. And if I had not done in the presence works which none other before me did, they had not sin: But from now they are puffed up with pride and think that they will overcome the Lord and also me. But the Word, which is in the Law, must be fulfilled: They hated me without a cause. But when the Comforter has come whom God will send to you from the Lord's presence and the Spirit of truth, which will have gone forth from the Lord's presence, he shall bear witness of me ... **IT IS EXTRACTED FROM WHAT JOHN, THE APOSTLE SET DOWN FOR THEM WHEN HE WROTE THE GOSPEL FOR THEM FROM THE STATEMENT OF JESUS SON OF MARY.**"

The preceding Gospel citation is from John 15:23 to 16:1. Here Islamic tradition admits John's Gospel was written by Apostle John from statements of Jesus (Mary's son) was in existence during Muhammad's day.

29 Does the Quran teach Biblical textual corruption?

Quran Translation by Abdullah Yusuf Ali: Roman Transliteration – Surah 5:50 "Wa anzalnaaa ilay-kal-Kitaaba bil-haqqi musaddiqal-limaa bayna yadayhi minal-Kitaabi WA **MUHAY-MINAN** alay-hi fahkum-baynahum-bimaaa... To thee [Muhammad] we [Allah] sent the scripture [Quran] in truth, confirming the scripture [Bible] that came before it [between your hands] and **GUARDING** it...."

Quran Translation by Abdullah Yusuf Ali: Page 258 Commentary 759 "The Quran comes with a twofold purpose: (1) to confirm the true and original Message, (2) to guard it..."

T.P Huges: Dictionary of Islam Page 368 "al-**MUHAIMIN**: The **PROTECTOR**."

The Pooya / M.A. Ali Commentary on Surah 5:48 "...The Quran, which confirms the earlier revelations and **PRESERVES THEM FROM CHANGE AND CORRUPTION**. The

Rabbis and Priests were the witnesses of Allah's writ, because they had memorized and **KEPT SAFE THE TRUE TEXT OF THE ORIGINAL BOOK.**"

Amazingly, Muslim Quran Commentators admit that the original Book was memorized and kept safe and that the Quran protects it from corruption. Wow!

- ✓ If the Bible was corrupted **BEFORE** the Quran was revealed than it means that Allah gave the Quran to guard and preserve a corrupted Bible.

- ✓ If the Bible was corrupted **AFTER** the Quran was revealed than it means that Allah and the Quran failed to guard and preserve the Bible from corruption. In that case, we can reject all Bible manuscripts dating after the Quran and accept all Biblical manuscripts dating before the Quran.

Meaning of Glorious Quran - Surah 3:84 "Say (O Muhammad): We believe in … **THAT WHICH WAS VOUCHSAFED UNTO MOSES AND JESUS AND THE PROPHETS** from their Lord…"

Message of the Quran - Surah 3:84 "…That which has been **VOUCHSAFED BY THEIR SUSTAINER** unto Moses and Jesus and all the (other) prophets…"

We have seen that the Word of God cannot be changed and that according to Islam the Quran guard the Bible of Muhammad's day from Biblical textual corruption, as it has been vouchsafed from God Himself according to the Quran. Yet some Muslims use misinterpretations of the Quran to *contradict clear Quranic passages that says the Word of God can't be changed,* to attempt to prove that the Bible is now changed – altered – corrupted.

Muslims misquote the Quran to prove Bible corruption

Quran Translation by Abdullah Yusuf Ali – Surah 2:76-79 "Have you then no understanding? Know they not that Allâh know what **they conceal** and what they reveal? And there are among them unlettered people, who know not the book, but they trust upon false desires and **they but guess**. Then woe to those who write the Book with their own hands and then say: This is from Allah, to purchase with it a little price! Woe to them for what their hands have written and woe to them for that they earn thereby."

Quran Translation by Abdullah Yusuf Ali: Page 37 Commentary 83 "The immediate argument applies to the Jews of Medina…"

OBSERVATION:

- The context of the passage is speaking about Jews of Medina, during the period between 610-632AD, who **CONCEALLED** the biblical scriptures, NOT who corrupted the scriptures! We simply ask honest Muslims to consult any English dictionary available to them to tell us the meaning of "conceal".

Cambridge Advanced Learner's Dict: "CONCEAL - To prevent something from being seen."

Thesaurus Dictionary: "CONCEAL - to hide or cover".

To conceal does **NOT** mean to alter OR to corrupt, like some agenda-driven Muslims wished it to mean.

- Among the Jews were unlettered people. They had no knowledge of the scriptures, but **GUESSED** and they wrote down what they guessed and said that their guessed writing was God's Word.

The Quran does not say what Bible hating Muslims want it to say! It does NOT say that Bible scholars or priests, who knew the Book, changed the text and sold it for a price. Nowhere in the Quran does it indicate that the learned Jews corrupted and re-wrote the original manuscripts, burnt the conflicting scripts and sold the new manuscripts for money, like in the case of Islamic history when devoted and loyal Muslims under the leadership of Uthman produced a revised Quran and ordered all conflicting variants to be destroyed and burnt.

- The Quran condemns these local unlettered people who knew NOT the book, wrote down what they guessed and said this is from God.

Furthermore, while there were some that had no idea of what the Bible consisted of, the Quran mentioned others who knew the scriptures and read it in sincerity:

Quran Translation by Abdullah Yusuf Ali – Surahs 3:113-114, 199 "...**SOME OF THE PEOPLE OF THE BOOK ARE AN UPRIGHT PEOPLE**. They recite the verses of God in the night season and they bow down worshiping. They believe in God and the last day. They command what is just and forbid what is wrong. They hastened in good works. They are of the righteous. There are, among the people of the book those who believe in God and in that which has been revealed to you and in that which has been revealed to them, bowing in humility to God. **THEY WILL NOT SELL THE SIGNS OF GOD FOR A MISERABLE GAIN**..."

Quran Translation by Abdullah Yusuf Ali – Surah 7:159, 168-170 "Of the people of Moses [Jews] there is a **group (umma) who guide with truth and judge by it** ... and they diligently study that which is therein ... as to those (Jews) who hold fast by the book..."

Let's look at another verse that Muslims uses to highlight Biblical corruption:

Quran Translation by Abdullah Yusuf Ali – Surah 3:78 "There is among them **[NOT ALL OF THEM]** a section who *distorts the book with their tongues*..." **[NOT WITH THEIR PENS!]**

Meaning of Glorious Quran – Surah 5:14 "...They [Jews] change words from their CONtext..." **[IT DOESN'T SAY THEY CHANGED THE TEXT.]**

Tafsir - Ibn Al Kathir S. 5:14 "(They change the words from their (right) places). Since their **comprehension became corrupt**, they behaved treacherously with Allah's Ayat, **altering His Book from its apparent meanings**, which He sent down, and **distorting its indications**. They attributed to Allah what He did not say, and we seek refuge with Allah from such behavior."

https://quranx.com/Tafsir/Kathir/5.12 Last accessed 27 April 2021

Quran Translation by Abdullah Yusuf Ali – Surah 5:14 Page 245 Comm. 713 & Page 255 Comm. 746 "Israel… They began to misuse Scripture by either taking words **out of their right meaning or applying them to things for which they were never meant … by distorting the meaning.**"

Quran Translation by Abdullah Yusuf Ali – Surah 6:83-90 "Abraham, Isaac, Jacob, Noah, David, Solomon, Job, Joseph, Moses, Aaron, Zakariya, John, Jesus, Elias, Ismail, Elisha, Jonas, Lot… These were the men to whom We [Allah] gave the book, authority and prophethood… Those were the (prophets) who received God's guidance: **COPY THE GUIDANCE THEY RECEIVED**…"

If the Bible was corrupted…

- ✓ **BEFORE** the Quran came to Muhammad, did the Author of the Quran intend for Muslims to follow (COPY) a corrupted book?
- ✓ **AFTER** the Quran came to Muhammad, Muslims will do great to reject Biblical manuscripts dating after 632AD and to follow / copy Biblical manuscripts (guidance) dating before 610AD.

30 Bible tampering before Quran came or after Quran came

We have proven beyond any doubt that the Bible could not be corrupted before the event of the Quran, as it does not make sense for the Author of the Quran to instruct Muhammad to confirm a corrupted book. If the tampering took place after the event of the Quran, then we can easily compare the Biblical manuscripts dated after the Quran (632 C.E.) with Biblical manuscripts dated before the Quran (610 C.E.). In this way we can easily eliminate the corrupted text from the original text. The fact that no tampering took place is established when we realize that the Biblical manuscripts dated before and after the Quran is exactly the same. If the corruption took place before the event of the Quran, why did the author of the Quran not declare in it that the Jews and Christians corrupted the original text? As we have seen, Quranic verses that are misused by Muslim scholars, to show Biblical textual corruption, actual speaks about Biblical verses being misinterpreted.

How was the biblical text seemingly corrupted: universally or locally, publicly or secretly? It is inconceivable to think that Jews and Christians would come together universally, discuss the possibility of changing the original text of the Biblical manuscripts, agree on its corruption and conclude the project in a happy ending. No follower of the Bible will ever condone such sick and illogical arguments. In fact, the reason why Muslim scholars think it is possible, is because that is exactly what happened with the Quran, which resulted in the Uthmanic Revised Quran.

Who did the tampering?

It is true that both Muslims and Christians have at times blamed their respective translators of their holy Books for producing blatant mistranslations from the original text. But to use arguments that mistranslations are evidence that manuscripts are corrupted is totally unacceptable to thinking minds.

What part of the Biblical text was changed?

Muslims today ignore their own scriptures and traditions in order to attempt proving Biblical corruption.

Just like the Quran, the Bible has many translations. In this study alone, I have quoted from over 10 Translations of the Quran, some opposing each other. There is no such a thing as a Protestant Bible and a Catholic Bible, because of the extra seven books (Apocrypha) that Catholics added **in the year 1546** to the Bible Edition circulated by them. The Quran itself, CENTURIES BEFORE 1546, identifies the scriptures in the hands of the Jews and Christians as being **ESSENTIALLY ONE**.

Quran Translation by Abdullah Yusuf Ali – Surah 2:113 "The Jews say: The Christians have naught (to stand) upon and the Christians say: The Jews have naught (to stand) upon. Yet they (profess to) study the **(SAME)** Book."

Let's turn the table on Muslims, not all expert Quran reciters, accept the current canon as accurate.

THREE examples will suffice:

- One of the best shahaba (Quran reciters) deleted three Surahs from his canon as he learned the Quran directly from Muhammad.
- Dr. Rashad Khalifah annihilated Surah 9:128-129 as false insertions from the Authorized English Version of the Quran.
- Muslims scholars admit that over a verse, over 100 times, in the beginning of each Surah, has been added to the Quran.

Tafsir - Ibn Al Kathir S. 1:1 "The scholars agree that the Bismillah is a part of an Ayah in Surat An-Naml (chapter 27). **THEY DISAGREE OVER WHETHER IT IS A SEPARATE AYAH BEFORE EVERY SURAH OR IF IT IS AN AYAH OR A PART OF AN AYAH INCLUDED IN EVERY SURAH WHERE THE BISMILLAH APPEARS**..."

CONCLUSION: Quranic verses affirmed that uncorrupted Biblical scriptures were available at the time of Muhammad by which the Jews and Christians knew truth from falsehood. Some of them concealed the Truth and some were honest. Some unlearned people, who had no access to the Holy Bible, guessed and wrote local false verses for personal gain. The Quran concluded that there were also true believers that hold fast to the book and would not sell false conjectures for gain. The Quran does not state, ANYWHERE in its pages, that the Biblical text was corrupted, but does state that some people misquoted it.

31 Is the message of the Bible universal?

Public Debate: "Is the Bible the Word of God?" Christian Speaker, Evangelist Jimmy Swaggart and Muslim Speaker, Sheik Ahmad Deedat: Q&A Session [Deedat said] "...No, the Quran does not say that the Gospel is guidance for mankind, nor does the Bible say that... Matt. 10:5-6, 15:24 Jesus... saying: Go not into the way of the Gentiles... enter ye not: But go rather to the lost sheep of the house of Israel..."[https://www.youtube.com/watch?v=genex9Bqlml Time line 01:45:40 – 01:47:25

Last accessed 27 April 2021

If we read the **above verses in isolation** from the rest of the teachings of Jesus and Muhammad, we may very well argue that the Gospel **at all times** was only meant for the Jews. Let's look at the context of the Books: Bible and Quran. The Bible clearly stated that the Gospel is **TWO** fold:

Jesus earthly ministry undoubtedly to Jews only

(Bible: Matt. 10:5-6, 15:24).

Quran Translation by Abdullah Yusuf Ali – Surah 3:48-49 "...The Gospel and appoint Him [Jesus Christ] a messenger to the CHILDREN OF ISRAEL..."

Jesus charged His disciples to preach the Gospel to all

(Bible: *Matt. 28:19* "[Jesus said:] Go ye therefore and teach **ALL NATIONS**, baptizing them in the name of the Father, and of the Son, and of the Holy Ghost." (Mark 16:15)

Quran teach that the Gospel is a universal message

The Noble Quran – Surah 3:3 "...Torah and Gospel aforetime as a **GUIDANCE TO MANKIND**..." [6:91]

Quran Translation by Abdullah Yusuf Ali – Surah 3:187 "And remember Allah took a covenant from the People of the Book, **TO MAKE IT KNOWN AND CLEAR TO MANKIND**..."

Quran Translation by Abdullah Yusuf Ali: Page 172 Comm. 494 & Page 771 Comm. 2473: "**TRUTH – GOD'S MESSAGE – COMES TO ANY MAN OR NATION** ... It should be broadcast and published and taught and made clear to **ALL WITHIN REACH**... The *mission* of Jesus is announced in two ways (1) ...His wonderful birth and wonderful life was to turn an ungodly **WORLD** back to God..."

It is obvious Jesus Christ could not reach the whole world in his human form here on earth, hence his **earthly** ministry was only to the Children of Israel. As we have seen, the same Jesus who told His disciples to go to the lost sheep of Israel, at His ascension, also commissioned them to go to all nations.

The same Quran that said Jesus was sent to Israel (Surah 3:48-49), is the same Quran (Surah 3:3, 187) that states His message is for mankind.

According to Allah must Christians uphold the Bible?

<u>Quran Translation by Abdullah Yusuf Ali – Surah 5:46, 50</u> "...**LET THE PEOPLE OF THE GOSPEL JUDGE BY WHAT GOD HATH REVEALED THEREIN...**"

<u>Message of the Quran - Surah 5:68</u> "Say: O followers of the Bible! You have no valid grounds for your believes, **UNLESS YOU (TRULY) OBSERVE THE TORAH AND THE GOSPEL AND ALL THAT HAVE BEEN BESTOWED UPON YOU.**"

According to Quran must Muslims follow the Bible?

Deedat tried to get Muslims to refuse to follow the Biblical Message. In his attempt to do so, he writes…

<u>Is the Bible the Word of God? Page 50</u> "No decent reader can read the seduction of Lot to his mother, sister or daughter, not even to his fiancée if she is a chaste and moral woman. Yet you will come across perverted people who will gorge this filth. Tastes can be cultivated!"

FIRSTLY: Lot did **NOT** have consented sex with his daugthers, in **Genesis 19:32** we read that they made

him drunk and took advantage of him in his drunken state. No court of law will ever pass

judgement against Lot for incest.

SECONDLY: Lot's daughters acted out of their own desire to have sex with their father, not for sexual satisfaction, but for to preserve seed for their father. THIRDLY: God nowhere instructed the daughters to make their father drunk and to have sex with him to preserve seed. God only allowed Moses to record the event in the Bible.

WHEN THE BIBLE REFLECT THE SIN OF PEOPLE, IT DOES NOT MEAN GOD WANT US TO COPY THE SINFUL ACTS, BUT RATHER THAT WE MAY LEARN RIGHT FROM WRONG IN THESE EVENTS.

Just like the Holy Bible, the Quran also reflects the homosexual lusts of the people in Lot's day. Muhammad had no problem to copy this story from the Bible from **_Genesis 19:8_** into the Quran **_Surah 11:78_**. In both Books, Lot is portrayed as a father who offered his daughters to be ravished by homosexual men. Lot should have defended his daughters with his own life. This however, was not necessary because his visitors were not normal men, but angels in human form that came to warn Lot and his family that judgment will fall on the people of that land. The angels were capable of defending themselves, as the story in both Books later reflected. In the Bible, Lot is described as a just man and in the Quran, Lot is described as a prophet. Why don't Muslims speak out about the cowardice behavior of their Allah's prophet, Lot, who instead of being a family protector, rather offered his daughters to be sexually abuse by homosexuals.

WHEN THE QURAN REFLECT THE COWARDICE OF ALLAH'S PROPHET, LOT, TO HAVE HIS DAUGHTERS RAPED BY HOMOSEXUALS, WHY DIDN'T DEEDAT CALL THE QURAN A BOOK OF FILTH? WHY DIDN'T DEEDAT CALL QURAN BELIEVERS A BUNCH OF PERVERTED PEOPLE GORGING THIS FILTH? CAN YOU SEE THE HIGH LEVEL OF DEEDAT'S HYPOCRASY AGAINST THE HOLY BIBLE?

Did Deedat read these Quran passages to his female family members? Perhaps he did in Arabic, which many Muslims doesn't understand.

Amen. Also listen to this clib: **_Mohammed Hijab vs Apostate Prophet Part 1_**

https://www.youtube.com/watch?v=MpBJviHAqh8 [Time line 03:10 – 03:45, 04:37 – 18:25]

Last accessed 27 April 2021

Now for the acid test: Which is the greatest sin: Idolatry or incest? If reading Bible stories that reveal people's sinful nature, e.g. incest, homosexuality, adultery, idolatry, etc., should be censored, how much more should the Quran be censored for reflecting the same, especially after the Quran indicated that idolatry is the unpardonable sin. Not only does Allah record the worse sin in his book, Surah 26:72, Allah also forgives willful idolatry, Surah 4: 153.

Does that mean that the Quran's Author wants Muslims to imitate these sinful deeds (habits)? Of course not! These verses demonstrate the forgiveness of even the worse sin. If the Bible is filth, then the Quran is also filth for reflecting he same types of sin, even worse, Allah instructed people to follow that filth:

<u>Quran Translation by Abdullah Yusuf Ali – Surah 6:90</u> "…Those (prophets) who received God's guidance: **COPY THE GUIDANCE** …"

SECTION 5

MUHAMMAD, A MUSLIM PROPHET

32 Historical background about Muhammad

Muhammad was born in the year 570 C.E., a few months after the death of his father. His mother, Amina died in 576 C.E. The 6 years young Muhammad grew up as an orphan and at the age of 25 years, he married a widow, by the name of Khadijah in 595 C.E. We are told that Muhammad used to go in isolation in a cave of Hira, where he used to worship. In the year 610 C.E. after consultation with his wife and her cousin, Waraqah bin Nawfal (a Christian scholar), he felt convinced that the Angel Gabriel visited him and that Gabriel began to reveal the Quran to him, which continued over a period of 23 years. Khadijah died in 619 C.E. Muhammad, according to Islamic history during 620 C.E., undertook a night journey from Mecca to Jerusalem and to the 7th heaven. Medinah and Mecca, was fully under Muhammed's rule as spiritual and military leader in the year 631 C.E. Muhammad's pilgrimage to Mecca took place in 632 C.E. Muhammad died on 8 June 632 CE.

33 Was Ishmael the progenitor of the Arabs?

Arabs are not the offspring of Abraham through Ishmael. Abraham was a Hebrew, **NOT AN ARAB** and Hagar was an Egyptian, **NOT AN ARAB**. A Hebrew father and an Egyptian mother does not result into an Arab son. Ishmael lived in Abraham's house for 14 years, not as an Arab, but as a Hebrew. Ishmael, in the wilderness, perhaps learnt Egyptian ways from his mother. Ishmael did not speak Arabic, he spoke Hebrew and perhaps later, learnt Egyptian from his mother. According to the hadith, **Ishmael later learnt Arabic from an already existing Arab tribe**, proving he isn't the progenitor of the Arabs.

Sahih Bukhari Vol. 4, Page 376, Hadith 583 "She [Hagar] lived in that way TILL SOME PEOPLE FROM THE TRIBE OF JURHUM PASSED BY HER AND HER CHILD [Ishmael]… **THE CHILD (E.G. ISHMAEL) GREW UP AND LEARNT ARABIC FROM THEM** … and when he reached the age of puberty they made him marry a WOMAN FROM AMONGST THEM [e.g. the Jurhum people] … so Ishmael [later] divorced her and married another woman from among them (e.g. Jurhum)."

In Surah 6:86-89 Ishmael is said to be a prophet and received scripture (a book). This proves, according to the Quran, that the Ishmaelites received admonition from their Lord, but according to **Surah 36:06 (34:44) the Arabs, before Muhammad, received no admonition from their Lord**, proving that the Ishmaelites who received admonition, can't be the pre-Muhammad Arabs, who received no admonition, again, proving they were two different nations or the Quran is contradicting itself.

34 Was Muhammad illiterate?

Quran Translation by Abdullah Yusuf Ali: Roman Transliteration – Surah 7:157
"Those who follow the messenger, the [ummi" **UNLETTERED**] prophet…"

The word *"ummi"* have two meanings: unlettered and gentile. Not all Muslim translators agree on the meaning of *"ummi"*, to be translated as "unlettered" in this verse.

Pickthall's translation read: **Meaning of Glorious Quran** "The prophet who can *neither read nor write*…"

But he admitted it can also mean… **Meaning of Glorious Quran: Page 133 Commentary 1** "… GENTILE."

Below is Imam Rashid Khalifah's and NJ Dawood's translations on the same verse:

Authorized English Version of the Quran "Follow the messenger, the **GENTILE** prophet…"

The Koran: Page 121 Commentary 2 "The word can also mean **GENTILE**."

Also see how Prof. JA Arberry translated the same verse: **Quran Translation by Prof. JA Arberry** "...And those who follow the messenger, the prophet of the **COMMON FOLK**..."

It is obvious that the Arabic word **ummi** also means Gentile. When we study other related verses and the Islamic history of Muhammad, it becomes clear that Muhammad **WAS NOT ILLITERATE AND COULD INDEED READ AND WRITE**. Let's take another verse where the Arabic word **ummi** is used.

Quran Translation by Abdullah Yusuf Ali – Surah h 62:2 "It is He Who has sent amongst the [**UMMI** – unlettered] a messenger from among themselves..."

Ali remained consistent in his translation of the word, but in doing so, it means that the Arabians were **ALL** illiterate people – could not read nor write. Clearly, that can't be true!

"Quran Only" Muslim Scholar Edip Yuksel: 19 Questions for Muslim Scholars – Page 41 (Under the heading: The Quran explains the true meaning of ummy) "Anyone can easily understand that "ummy" does not mean an illiterate person by reflecting on the verse 3:20 below: *"And say to those who received the scripture, as well as* **THOSE WHO DID NOT RECEIVE ANY SCRIPTURE (UMMYYEEN)**... (B) THE QURAN DESCRIBED MECCAN PEOPLE WITH THE WORD "UMMYYEEN = GENTILES (62:2). ACCORDING TO YOUR CLAIM, ALL MECCAN PEOPLE MUST HAVE BEEN ILLITERATE. Who was writing poems in Mecca? Who was reading the poems hanging on the walls of the Kaba? You're imitating Muhammad from his eating to his attire, from his beard to his toothbrush, why do you not imitate his illiteracy?"

Why do you not follow his Sunnah? According to the Quran and hadith, Muhammad's contemporaries knew him as being a literate person.

Surah 25:5

The Noble Quran "And they say: Tales of the ancients, which **HE HAS WRITTEN DOWN**..."

Authorized English Version of the Quran "They also said: Tales from the past that **HE WROTE DOWN**…"

Sahih Bukhari Vol. 5, Page 512, Hadith 717 "Narrated Ubaidullah bin Abdullah: ibn Abbas said: When Allah's messenger was on his deathbed and there were some men in the house, he said: Come near, **I WILL WRITE** for you something after which you will not go astray … Some of them said: **GIVE HIM WRITING MATERIAL SO THAT HE MAY WRITE** for you something…"

Notice, they did not say give his scribes something to write down what Muhammad will dictate to them, they knew he could write and said give him something so that he may write for you.

Sahih Bukhari Vol. 7, Page 65, Hadith 88 "Narrated Urwa: **THE PROPHET WROTE THE (MARRIAGE CONTRACT)** with Aisha while she was six years old and consummated his marriage with her while she was nine years old and she remained with him for nine years (e.g. till his death)."

It is quite clear that Muhammad could write and therefore was not illiterate as some Muslims want us to blindly believe.

Quran Translation by Abdullah Yusuf Ali: Page 7 Introduction C. 23 "But he grew steadfastly in virtue and purity: Untaught by men, **HE LEARNT FROM MEN AND LEARNED TO TEACH THEM**, even as a boy of nine when he went in a trade caravan with Abu Talib to Syria…"

Muslim Prof. Fazl Ahmad: Muhammad, The Prophet of Islam: Heroes of Islam 1 – Page 46 "After their marriage, the Holy Prophet took charge of Khadija's business."

Authorized English Version of the Quran: Page 474 Appendix 28 "…You cannot dictate to an illiterate person… The prophet was a successful merchant. The Muslim scholars who fabricated the illiteracy lie forgot that there were no numbers during the prophet's time; the letters of the alphabet were used as numbers. **AS A MERCHANT**

DEALING WITH NUMBERS EVERY DAY, THE PROPHET HAD TO KNOW THE ALPHABET…" [Unquote: In other words, he could read and write!]

35 Did Muhammad worship idols before he was a prophet?

Some Muslims try to say Muhammed worshipped Allah even before he became a prophet, but Allah in the **Quran Surah 42:52** said Muhammed had no revelation and no faith before his prophethood. If this verse is right, Muhammed had no divine understanding about God, nor did he have faith in that God.

Quran Translation by Abdullah Yusuf Ali – Surah 93:7 & Page 1752 Comm. 6183
"And he [Allah] found thee [Muhammad] wandering and he gave thee guidance … [Unquote: commentary…] The holy prophet was **born in the midst of the idolatry and polytheism of Mecca**, in a family which was the custodian of false worship. He wandered in quest of unity and found it by the guidance of God…"

Let's look at more translations of the above verse:

The Noble Quran "He found **you unaware** (of the Quran… and prophethood) and guided you."

The Koran "Did he not find **you in error** and guided you."

Authorized English Version of the Quran "And he found **you astray** and guided you."

Muhammad grew up in a family of idolatry. It is obvious that Muhammad participate in idolatry. This is why the Quran says in Surah 93:7 that Muhammad was in error when Allah found him. This is why the Quran in **Surah 40:66** below stated that he was forbidden to petition the idols his people petitioned.

Quran Translation by Abdullah Yusuf Ali: "Say, **I HAVE BEEN FORBIDDEN** to invoke those whom ye invoke besides God, seeing the clear signs have come to me from my Lord…"

Message of the Quran "Say, since all evidence of the truth has come to me from my Sustainer, **I AM FORBIDDEN TO WORSHIP** (any of) those beings whom you invoke instead of God…"

Authorized English Version of the Quran "Say, **I HAVE BEEN ENJOINED FROM WORSHIPPING THE IDOLS** you worship besides God…"

Authorized English Version of the Quran: Footnote "The Arabic word **``NAHAA''** used in this verse indicates the **STOPPING OF SOMETHING THAT WAS GOING ON.**"

Muhammad became known for preaching monotheism, yet he continued to reverence the "Black Stone".

Sahih Bukhari Vol. 2, Pages 390-391, Hadith 667 (Pages 394-395, Hadith 675 & Pages 397, Hadith 680) "Narrated Abis bin Rabia: Umar came near the Black Stone and kissed it and said: No doubt I know that you are a stone and can neither benefit anyone nor harm anyone, had I not seen **ALLAH'S APOSTLE KISSING YOU** I would not have kissed you."

Jami` at-Tirmidhi "Ibn Abbas narrated that: The Messenger of Allah said about the (Black) Stone: By Allah! Allah will raise it on the Day of Resurrection with two eyes by which it sees and a tongue that it speaks with, testifying to whoever touched it in truth."

https://quranx.com/Hadith/Tirmidhi/DarusSalam/Volume-2/Book-7/Hadith-961

Last accessed 27 April 2021

36 Did Prophet Muhammad sin during his prophethood?

The Noble Quran Surah 47:19 "…(O Muhammad)… ask forgiveness for **YOUR SIN** and for believing men…"

The Koran Surah 47:19 "…Implore Him to forgive your sins **AND TO FORGIVE THE TRUE BELIEVERS**…"

This verse clearly instructed Muhammad to ask God for forgives for [1] his sins and [2] for his followers.

The Koran Surah 48:2 "...So that God may forgive you **YOUR PAST SINS AND YOUR FUTURE SINS**..."

The Noble Quran Surah 48:2 "...That Allah may forgive you your sins of the past and the future..."

Meaning of Glorious Quran "Allah may forgive thee of thy sin which is past and that which is to come..."

The Noble Quran: Pages 8 Footnote 1 and Pages 127-128 Footnote 2 "Narrated Anas, the prophet said... Jesus will say... go to Muhammad... the slave of Allah whose past and furure sins were forgiven by Allah... *(al-Sahih Bukhari, Vol. 6, Page 3, Hadith 3)* ... (V.4:106) ... Narrated Abu Hurairah: I heard Allah's messenger said: By Allah! I seek Allah's forgiveness and turn to Him in repentance for more than 70 times a day. *(al-Sahih Bukhari, Vol. 8, Page 213, Hadith 319)*."

The Quran and Islamic tradition indicates Muhammad sinned during his prophethood. To understand the seriousness of the word "sin", below are examples of the same word used throughout the Quran? Notice the type of judgment that accompanies this word.

Quran Translation by Abdullah Yusuf Ali – Surahs 3:11-16, 6:6 "...Forgive us then our **SINS** and save us from the agony of the fire... Yet for their **SINS** we destroyed them..."

Does this sound like something God passes over as minor "mistakes"? Of course not! It sounds like Allah is severely punishing people for their "SINS". This is why Muhammad is instructed to also ask forgiveness for his past sins and for his future sins and have done so more than 70 times a day.

37 Did Muhammad know the future?

Quran Transl. by Abdullah Yusuf Ali – Surahs 6:50, 7:188, 10:20, 46:9, 67:26 "…**NOR** do I know what is hidden …**IF** I had knowledge of the unseen…Say: The Unseen is **ONLY** for Allah (to know) …**NOR** do I know what will be done with me or with you … Say: As to the knowledge of the time, it is with God **ALONE**…"

38 Did Muhammad have a perfect memory?

Quran Translation by Abdullah Yusuf Ali – Surah 87:6-7 "By degrees shall we teach thee (Muhammad) to declare (the message), so thou shall not forget, **EXCEPT AS GOD WILLS**."

Sahih Bukhari, Vol. 6, Page 507, Hadith 556 "Narrated 'Aisha: The Prophet heard a man reciting the Qur'an in the mosque and said: "May Allah bestow His Mercy on him as **HE HAS REMINDED ME** of such a Verse of such a Surat."

39 Did Muhammad fear people more than Allah?

Quran Translation by Abdullah Yusuf Ali – Surah 33:37 "Behold! Thou didst say to one who had received the grace of Allah and thy favour: Retain thou (in wedlock) thy wife and fear Allah. But thou didst hide in thy heart that which Allah was about to make manifest: thou didst fear the people, but it is more fitting that thou shouldst fear Allah. Then when Zaid had dissolved (his marriage) with her, with the necessary (formality), We joined her in marriage to thee: in order that (in future) there may be no difficulty to the Believers in (the matter of) marriage with the wives of their adopted sons, when the latter have dissolved with the necessary (formality) (their marriage) with them. And Allah's command must be fulfilled."

Let's look at a Muslim scholars's commentary on this verse: ***Tafsir: Jala – Al Jalalayn S.33:37*** "Zayd b. Hāritha, who had been a prisoner of war BEFORE ISLAM. The Messenger of God (s) purchased him before his call to prophethood and then manumitted him and adopted him as his son. [Muhammad said to Zaid:] Retain your wife for yourself…

[Allah said to Muhammad:] But you had hidden in your heart what God was to disclose. [Allah] **HE WAS TO MANIFEST OF YOUR LOVE FOR HER** and should Zayd part with her you would marry her and **YOU FEARED PEOPLE WOULD SAY: HE MARRIED HIS SON'S WIFE!** Though God is worthier that you fear Him… *SO TAKE HER IN MARRIAGE AND DON'T BE CONCERNED WITH WHAT PEOPLE SAY.* Zayd subsequently divorced her and her waiting period was completed … We joined her in marriage to you. The Prophet consummated his marriage with her [had sexual intercourse with her] … [All this was done] so that there may not be any restriction for the believers in respect of the wives of their adopted sons, when the latter have fulfilled whatever wish they have of them. And God's commandment, that which He has decreed, is bound to be realised."

https://quranx.com/Tafsir/Jalal/33.37 Last accessed 27 April 2021

Why did Muhammad fear what people would say? **HE WAS IN-LOVE WITH THE WIFE OF HIS ADOPTED SON** and he hide his feelings. HE WAS IN-LOVE WITH A MARRIED WOMAN and flirted with her in the absence of his adopted son.

You can listen to renowned Christian Prince here: https://www.youtube.com/watch?v=J9T5L08bNPw [time line 42:09 – 51:00 Last accessed 27 April 2021. In this clib a Muslim found Muhammad's act shameful and left Islam. Also see https://www.youtube.com/watch?v=VcEEdvEBG3I&t=6043s [time line 1:21:00 Last accessed 27 April 2021 where another Muslim left Islam.] Muhammad married Zainab so Muslims may feel no shame to marry the ex-wives of their adopted sons, but funny enough, Allah abolished adoption in Islam just after this marriage. Why then was this verse given for fathers to marry the ex-wives of their adopted sons, if Allah knew he would abolish adoption?

Quran Translation by Abdullah Yusuf Ali – Surah 66:1 "…Thou didst fear the people, but it is more fitting that thou should fear Allah… O Prophet! *Why holdest thou to be forbidden that which Allah has __made__ lawful to thee?* Thou seek to please thy consorts…"

Muhammad had sex with his slave-girl (**GIVEN TO HIM AS A GIFT**) in his wife Hafsah's bed. When she caught them, of course any woman will be angry if you sleep with another woman in her bed. Muhammad after this promised his wives to avoid having sex with Mary the slave-girl and Allah rebuked him for saying he will abstain having sex with his slave-girl in order to please his wives.

Let's look at a few Muslim scholars' commentaries concerning this verse.

Tafsir: Jala – Al Jalalayn S.66:1 "O Prophet! Why do you prohibit what God has made lawful for you, in terms of your Coptic handmaiden Māriya — **WHEN HE LAY WITH HER IN THE HOUSE OF HAFSA**, who had been away, but who upon returning and finding out became upset by the fact that this had taken place in her own house and on her own bed — by saying, 'She is unlawful for me!', seeking, by making her unlawful [for you], to please your wives? And God is Forgiving, Merciful, having forgiven you this prohibition. https://quranx.com/Tafsir/Jalal/66.1 Last accessed 27 April 2021

Tafsir: Maududi - Sayyid Abul Ala Maududi - Tafhim al-Qur'an S.66:1 "One day the Holy Prophet (upon whom be peace) visited the house of Hadrat Hafsah when she was not at home. At that time **Hadrat Mariyah came to him there and stayed with him in seclusion**. *HADRAT HAFSAH TOOK IT VERY ILL AND COMPLAINED OF IT BITTERLY TO HIM*. Thereupon, in order to please her **the Holy Prophet vowed that he would have no conjugal relation with Mariyah in future**. According to some traditions, he forbade Mariyah for himself... **These traditions ... some of these have been reported from Hadrat 'Umar. Hadrat `Abdullah bin 'Abbas and Hadrat Abu Hurairah also**. In view of the plurality of the methods of narration, Hafiz Ibn Hajar in Fath al-Bari has expressed the view that **there is some truth in the story**. But in none of the six authentic collections of the Hadith has this story been narrated. In Nasa'i only this much has been related from Hadrat Anas: "The Prophet had a slave-girl with whom he had conjugal relations. Hadrat Hafsah and Hadrat `A'ishah began to point out this to him repeatedly until he forbade her for himself. Then Allah sent down this verse: 'O Prophet. why do you make unlawful that which Allah has made lawful for you?" https://quranx.com/Tafsir/Maududi/66.1 Last accessed 27 April 2021

Tafsir - Wahidi - Asbab Al-Nuzul by Al-Wahidi S.66:1 "...Umar who said: The Messenger of Allah... entered the house of Hafsah along with the mother of his son, Mariyah. **When Hafsah found him with her in an intimate moment, she said: Why did you bring her in my house?** ... HE SAID TO HER: DO NOT MENTION THIS TO A'ISHAH; SHE IS FORBIDDEN FOR ME (I.E. MARIYAH) ... Hafsah said: How could she be forbidden for you when she is your slave girl? He swore to her that he will not touch her ... The Prophet, Allah bless him and give him peace, decided not to go to his wives for a month ... Allah, exalted is He, revealed (O Prophet! Why bannest thou that which Allah hath made lawful for thee, seeking to please thy wives?)". https://quranx.com/Tafsir/Wahidi/66.1 Last accessed 27 April 2021

Here we see that Muhammad seeked to please his wives by abstaining from sex with a slave-girl after he was caught in bed. Muhammad then abstained from sex with this **slave-girl that was given to him as a gift** and Allah rebuked him saying it was previously made lawfull to him to have sex with a slave-gift. WHEREIN THE QURAN DID ALLAH MAKE SLAVE-GIRLS AS GIFTS SEXUALLY LAWFUL TO MUHAMMAD?

40 Was it Muhammad's duty to explain the Quran?

Quran Translation by Abdullah Yusuf Ali:

Surah 13:40, 42:48 "Thy duty is to make (the message) reach them..."

Surah 24:54 "The apostle's duty is **only** to preach the clear (message)."

Surah 46:9 "...I am, but a Warner open and clear."

Authorized English Version of the Quran – Surah 75:16 Heading "Muhammad forbidden from explaining the Quran." "Move not thy tongue concerning the (Quran) to make haste therewith, it is for us to collect it and to promulgate it: But when we have promulgated it, follow thou its recital (as promulgated): Nay more, it is for **US TO EXPLAIN IT**..."

Quran Translation by Abdullah Yusuf Ali: Surah 55:1-2 "... **GOD IS THE TEACHER** of the Quran."

41 Could Muhammad benefit anyone through guiding them?

Quran Translation by Abdullah Yusuf Ali – Surahs 28:56, 72 21 "You Muhammad **CANNOT GUIDE** even the ones you love… I possess no power to harm you or benefit you through guiding you."

42 Could Muhammad intercede for those he loved?

Authorized English Version of the Quran – Surah 21:25-29 "They possess no power to intercede **EXCEPT ON BEHALF OF THOSE ALREADY APPROVED BY GOD.** The messengers themselves are worried about their own fate…"

43 Is obeying Muhammad conditional?

Quran Translation by Abdullah Yusuf Ali: Surah 60:12 "They will not disobey thee in **any just** matter…"

Authorized English Version of the Quran: Surah 60:12 "Nor disobey you **WHEN YOU ARE RIGHT**…"

44 Did Muhammad cause the moon to split?

Quran Translation by Abdullah Yusuf Ali – Surah 54:1 "The Hour (of Judgment) is nigh *and the moon is cleft asunder.*"

Notice carefully, this verse does **NOT** read:

- "The Hour (of Judgment) is nigh *and **MUHAMMAD CAUSED** the moon to be cleft asunder.*"

The Quran itself does **NOT** attribute the splitting of the moon as a miracle to Muhammad. Although the hadith attributed many fanciful miracles to Muhammed, as we will see, Allah in the Quran does NOT.

Allah deny sending miracles to Muhammad

Surah 54 is actually the 37th Surah in the chronological order of the Quran, as recited by Muhammad, that is, before Muslims re-arranged the order of the Quran as we have it today. Surah 17, which is Surah 50, almost 13 Surahs after Surah 54, Allah clearly states that **he never yet sent a miracle to Muhammad**.

__Quran Translation by Abdullah Yusuf Ali – Surah 17:59__ "**WE REFRAIN FROM SENDING THE SIGNS**, only because the men of former generations treated them as false."

If Surah 54 (37th Surah) was a miracle sent to Muhammed, then Surah 17 (50th Surah) is a lie. In Surah 6, which is the 55th Surah, people inquire from Muhammad why he has no miraculous sign, instead of referring to the splitting of the moon as a miracle, Muhammad recited that Allah does have power to send down a sign, not Allah has sent down a sign already.

__Quran Translation by Abdullah Yusuf Ali – Surah 6:37__ "They say why is not a sign send down to him from his Lord? Say, God hath certainly power **to send down a sign**, but most of them understand not."

Muhammad correctly did not point to a sign and correctly stated that God has power to send a sign. "*__To send__*" refers to the future and "*__sent__*" refers to the past. In Surah 13, which is the 96th Surah, people still asked for a single miracle from Muhammad and this is how Allah responded.

__Quran Translation by Abdullah Yusuf Ali – Surah 13:7__ "The unbelievers say: Why is not a sign sent down to him from his Lord? But thou art truly a warner and to every people a guide."

Muhammad says Quran is given to him as miracle

The Noble Quran: Pages IV and 275 – Footnote "The prophet said: There was no prophet among *the prophets, but was given miracles,* because of which people had security... **BUT I HAVE BEEN GIVEN REVELATION,** which Allah has revealed to me... (Bukhari Vol. 9. Page 282, Hadith 379)."

Muslim scholars admit Muhammad had no miracles

Message of the Quran: Pages 427 Comm. 71 "In many places the Qur'an stresses the fact that Prophet Muhammad, despite him being the last and greatest of God's apostles, **WAS NOT EMPOWERED TO PERFORM MIRACLES**..."

Faruq Sheriff: A guide to the contents of the Quran: Pages 62 "THE QUR'AN DOES NOT ATTRIBUTE ANY MIRACLES TO THE PROPHET..."

The Koran: Page 2 – Introduction: "Muhammad, who disclaimed power to perform miracles."

Quran Translators and their commentaries

Message of the Quran: Page 818 – Commentary 1 "It is practically certain that the above Qur'an-verse ... **REFER TO... A FUTURE EVENT**... to what will happen when the Last Hour approaches. (THE QUR'AN FREQUENTLY EMPLOYS THE PAST TENSE TO DENOTE THE FUTURE, particularly so in passages which speak of the coming of the Last Hour..."

Authorized English Version of the Quran: Page 321 – Footnote "This important sign of the approaching end of the world **CAME TO PASS IN 1969** when humans brought pieces of the moon to earth."

45 Was Muhammad a prophet like unto Moses?

Deuteronomy 18:15-18 "The LORD thy God will raise up unto thee a prophet from the midst of thee, of thy brethren, like unto me; unto him ye shall hearken..."

Muslims believe Deut. 18:15-18 refers to Muhammad

Ahmad Deedat: "What the Bible says about Muhammad? Page 22 "What we say is that Deuteronomy 18:18 does not refer to Jesus, but it is an explicit prophecy about the Holy prophet Muhammad."

They believe it because the Quran stated that Muhammad was foretold in the Law: ***Quran Translation by Abdullah Yusuf Ali – Surah 7:157*** "Those who follow the apostle, the unlettered Prophet, whom they find mentioned in the *Taurat*..."

The Noble Quran "Those who follow the Messenger, the Prophet who can neither read nor write (Muhammad), whom they [Jews/Christians] find written with them in the *Taurat (Deut. Xviii:15)* ..."

Christians do **NOT** believe that Deut. 18:18 referred to Muhammad and that he was a prophet like Moses. No Bible believing Christian accepts Muhammad to be a true Prophet or the Quran to be God's Word. Christians do believe that Deut. 18:15-18 refers to Jesus.

Muslims comparing Moses to Muhammad and Jesus.

Deedat, in his booklet: ***"What the Bible Says about Muhammad"*** quoted similar characteristics shared by Moses and Muhammad to proof that Muhammad is like Moses and Jesus is not. Deedat argued that...

- ❖ Moses and Muhammad were both born naturally of human parents and are buried on earth, whereas Jesus was born of a virgin-woman, had no earthly father and ascended to heaven.

- ❖ Moses and Muhammad became the lawgivers, military leaders and spiritual guides of their peoples and nations.

- ❖ Moses and Muhammad were rejected by their people, fled into exile, returned some years later to become the religious and secular leaders of their nations...

Deedat's examples why Jesus isn't like Moses...

- ❖ Moses was a prophet, but according to Christianity, Jesus is the Son of God.

- Moses died naturally, but Jesus died violently (here Deedat admitted Jesus died.)

- Moses was the national ruler of Israel, but not Jesus during his earthly ministry.

Christians ask

Do these examples attest that Muhammad was like Moses and Jesus not? Those are weak examples. Christians can also produce examples where Jesus is like Moses and Muhammad not. Although the Bible teaches that Jesus was a virgin born child or Son of God, the Bible also teaches He was a prophet, a fact that no true Muslim will deny. Let's look at characteristics where Jesus is like Moses and Muhammad not.

- On both infants (Moses and Jesus) death was plotted by an enemy who wanted them killed – During Muhammad's birth, death was not plotted on boys, but on female infants (Surah 16:58). **Quran Translation by Abdullah Yusuf Ali: Page 671 Comm. 2084** "…Female children used to be buried alive by the Pagan Arabs."

- Both (Moses and Jesus) had miracles, but Muhammad had no miracles according to Quran.

- Moses (*Exodus 32:30-32*) and Jesus offered themselves before God to take the sins of all the people (atonement), Muhammad didn't (*Surah 6:164*).

We have similarities between Moses and Muhammad where Jesus can be contrasted with them and we have similar characteristics between Moses and Jesus where Muhammad can be contrasted with them. Comparing **COMMON** characteristics will not help us to identify the awaited prophet.

The Word of God in all true prophets' mouths

In order to determine, who the prophet was that is prophesied in Deut. 18, let's proceed <u>**AS IF**</u> God did put His Words (Quran) in Muhammad's mouth.

The statement *"I'll put my words in his mouth"* does not help us to identify the prophet to come according to Deut. 18, because God has put His words in every true prophet's mouth.

Jeremiah 1:9 "God said to Jeremiah: Behold I have put my words in your mouth."

John 12.49-50 "For I [Jesus] have not spoken on My own authority, the Father who sent Me has Himself given Me commandment what to say and what to speak and I know that His commandment is eternal life ... I say as the Father has bidden Me."

God placed his words in the mouths of every true prophet. No true Muslim will deny that God has put His words into the mouths of all the true prophets who came before Muhammad. Therefore, the prophet to come cannot be identified, **alone**, by the fact that God will put His Word in his mouth.

A prophet unto WHO?

Deuteronomy 18:15 "The LORD thy God will raise up **UNTO THEE** a prophet from the midst of thee ... 18 I will raise **THEM** up a prophet from among their brethren, like unto you."

The prophet to be raised up will be a prophet **UNTO ISRAEL** – not to the Edomite, Ishmaelite, not a prophet unto the Arabs, but a prophet **UNTO ISRAEL**. Muhammad never preached to the Nation of Israel, the twelve tribes. Muhammad, himself, only preached in Mecca and Medina, according to the Quran, to make the law of God clear to the Arabs.

The Noble Quran - Surah 14:4 "WE SENT **NOT** A MESSENGER, EXCEPT WITH THE LANGUAGE OF HIS PEOPLE, in order that he might make (the message) clear for them..."

Muhammad was send to his people, the Arabs to convey his Message in Arabic to them (see Q10). The prophet in Deut. 18 was promised by God to be raised unto **ISRAEL** – *"I'll raise up unto **THEE** ... I'll raise for **THEM**..."* Muhammad is automatically *disqualified* from being the prophet whose coming was foretold in the Torah. Muhammad hopelessly failed a direct criteria made by God Himself.

ALL MUSLIMS AGREE THAT PROPHET JESUS WAS SENT UNTO ISRAEL! (SURAH 61:6 SEE Q46)

A prophet from among THEIR BRETHREN

Muslims argue that since Ishmael and Isaac are brothers, their descendants are also brethren. We as Christians have no objection to this conclusion. Notice, in the Bible Deut. 23:7, even the tribe of Edomite were considered to be Israel's brother. Even if the tribe of Ishmaelites and the tribe of Edomites may be considered as the brethren of the whole Nation of Israel, **note carefully, in the pages of the Bible, when one tribe of Israel is identified, *"their brethren"* are always the 11 tribes of Israel**, not other tribes.

<u>Numbers 8:21</u> "And the Levites ... 26 minister to their brethren..."

Here the Tribe of Levi is commanded to minister to the remaining tribes of Israel – their brethren here is NOT the Edomites, Ishmaelites, neither the Arabs.

<u>Deuteronomy 17: 15</u> "...one from among your brethren shall you set as king over you..."

Again, *your brethren* here do **NOT** mean Edomites, Ishmaelites, neither Arabs. Never in history, were any man from theses tribes, ever made kings over Israel.

<u>Judges 20:13</u> "The children of Benjamin wouldn't listen to the voice of their brethren, the children of Israel."

The context, again, demands that "their brethren" here *is* the remaining tribes of Israel – NOT the Edomites, Ishmaelites, neither the Arabs.

<u>Acts 3:17-23</u> "...Brethren, I know that you acted in ignorance, as did also your rulers..."

Here the apostle calls his fellow Jews, brethren – he was NOT speaking to the Edomites, Ishmaelites, neither the Arabs, but the remaing tribes of Israel. We must always, CONSISTENTLY, consider the context; we must NOT isolate a phrase from its immediate context to make it says anything we want it to say.

<u>Clearly, we can see that when the whole of the Nation of Israel – the twelve tribes – is considered, then only is their brethren the Edomite or Ishmaelite, but when one tribe of Israelis are considered, then the remaining eleven tribes are being referred to as their brethren, it depends on the context.</u>

How do we know which brethren are being referred to in Deut.18:18? Let's consider the context.

Deuteronomy 18:1-2 "The **LEVITICAL PRIESTS**, that is, all the tribe of Levi, shall have no portion or inheritance with Israel; **THEY** shall eat the offerings by fire to the Lord and His rightful dues. **THEY** shall have no inheritance among **THEIR BRETHREN**…"

The **Levites** shall have no portion or inheritance with Israel. We can clearly see that *"their brethren"* here referred to the *"remaining tribes of Israel"* – e.g. Simeon, Judah, Issachar, Joseph, Benjamin, Reuben, Gad, Asher, Zebulun, Dan and Naphtali – NOT the Edomites, Ishmaelites, nor the Arabs.

Deuteronomy 18:15 "The LORD thy God will raise up unto thee a prophet **FROM THE MIDST OF THEE,** of thy brethren, like unto me… 18 I will raise them up a prophet from among their brethren, like unto you."

The prophet from their brethren will be <u>FROM THE MIDST OF ISRAEL</u>, of thy brethren. He will not be from the midst of the Edomites, Ishmaelites, neither from the midst of the Arabs. This prophet will be from the midst, one of the remaining eleven tribes of Israel, a tribe other than Levi. Again, Muhammad hopelessly failed a direct criteria stated by God Himself. If we isolate the phrase "their brethren" we can erroneously make it say: a prophet from the Edomite or a prophet from the Ishmaelite (remember, Ishmael was not an Arab – see Q33). The context is clear – the prophet to come will be FROM THE MIDST OF THEE – the remaining eleven tribes of Israel, not from Ishmaelites nor Arabs.

God spoke to Moses FACE TO FACE

Deuteronomy 18:15 "The LORD thy God will raise up unto thee [Israel] a prophet from the midst of thee, of thy brethren, like unto me… 16 **According to all that thou desired of the LORD thy God in Horeb**…"

Remember, the prophet to come must be like Moses – the prophetic ministry of Moses was as a mediator between God and Israel. God dealt directly with Moses.

Exodus 33:11 "Thus the Lord used to speak to Moses **FACE TO FACE**." (Deut. 34:10-12)

Quran Translation by Abdullah Yusuf Ali: Surah 4:164 "To Moses, God spoke **DIRECT**."

Again, here Muhammad fails hopelessly, God never spoke directly to him, according to Islam, God sent Gabriel to speak to Muhammad. Therefore, when we consider God's criterion of the prophet to come that will be like Moses, then we see that Muhammad, every time failed and Jesus every time qualified.

John 12.49-50 "For I [Jesus] have not spoken on My own authority, the Father who sent Me has **HIMSELF GIVEN ME COMMANDMENT** what to say…"

Muhammad unrecognized as a prophet like Moses

Quran Translation by Abdullah Yusuf Ali – Surah 28:48 "But (now) when the truth has come to them from Ourselves [God], **THEY SAY: Why are not (signs) sent to him, like those, which was sent to Moses?**"

Considering Jesus as the prophet like unto Moses

Deedat further argues that Jesus cannot be the prophet like unto Moses, because Jesus was the Christ and not the prophet. Note carefully, the Bible does **NOT** teach that the Christ will not be the prophet. In fact, the people confessed that Jesus Christ was that awaited prophet.

John 7:38-40 "…This [Jesus] is indeed **THE PROPHET**."

In Acts 3:14-26 the Apostle Peter specifically connects Jesus Christ with Deut. 18:18. Stephen also connects Jesus Christ in Acts 7:37 with Deut. 18:18. Finally, Jesus connected Himself with the writings of Moses.

John 5:46: "**MOSES WROTE OF ME**."

It is therefore clear that the Bible identified Jesus as the prophet like Moses and NOT Muhammad as a prophet like Moses. Muslims has no problem to conclude that the Bible is not preserved and corrupted, but when they think that certain verses, e.g. Deuteronomy 18:15-18, counts in their favor, again, they conclude that it must be God's Word, preserved, inspired and written by Moses.

Muslims like to say bring us the Gospel of Jesus **NOT** the Gospels of Matthew, Mark, Luke and John, but again, when they think that the Gospel of John counts in their favor, e.g. possible prophecies that refer to Muhammad, they have no problem to use it to confirm verses in the Quran that talks about the Injeel as we will see below.

46 Was Muhammad the promised Comforter?

The Noble Quran - Surah 7:157 "Those who follow the Messenger, the Prophet who can neither read nor write (Muhammad), whom they [Jews and Christians] find written with them in the Taurat (Torah Deut. Xviii:15) **and the Injeel (Gospel of John xiv:16)** ..."

Let's look at the mentioned verse from the Gospel of John to see if it talks about Muhammad!

John 14:16 "I will pray the Father, and he shall give you another **Comforter [*Greek – parakletos*]**, that He may abide with you forever. 17 Even the Spirit of Truth; whom the world cannot receive, because it sees him not, neither know him: but ye know him; for he dwelled with you, and shall be in you."

The Muslim objection that John 14:16 is corrupted

Quran Translation by Abdullah Yusuf Ali: Page 144 Comm. 416 & Page 1540 Comm. 5438 "...The Greek word translated "Comforter" is "Paracletos", which is an *easy corruption from "Periclytos"*, which is almost a literal translation of "Muhammad" or "Ahmad" ... Our doctors contend that Paracletos is a corrupt reading for Periclytos..."

Muslims believe that Christians changed – corrupted the Greek text in order to make the Scripture say that the Comforter is the Holy Spirit and not Muhammed. They believe this, because in their scripture, it says that Jesus prophesied about a coming apostle whose name shall be Ahmad.

Quran Translation by Abdullah Yusuf Ali – Surah 61:6 "...**Jesus, the son of Mary said: O children of Israel! I am the apostle of Allah (sent) to you** ... giving glad tidings of an apostle to come after me, whose name shall be **Ahmad**." [Unquote: Here Jesus Himself confirmed that He is the One sent to Israel, notice, Jesus does NOT confirm that Muhammed will be send to Israel, but ONLY that Muhammed will come.]

Manuscript corruption before or after Muhammad?

The NT manuscripts dates about 5 centuries before Islam. Christians at the time the manuscripts were written, **did not know about a Muhammad or Ahmad** to be born from an Arab family 500 years later, neither did they know he would claim prophethood and preach a Quranic Anti-Bible message. Therefore, they could not have corrupted the manuscripts from Periclytos to Paracletos to turn the attention from an Ahmad to the Holy Spirit. Out of the existing thousands of NT manuscripts dated centuries before Islam, not one manuscript contains the word "periklutos". If the corruption took place after Muhammad came, all that Muslims need to do is compare the manuscripts after 632 AD with those before 610 AD to confirm possible manuscript corruption.

Why the Comforter cannot be Muhammad

Let us read John 14:16 again, carefully and see what it really says:

"...He shall give **YOU** another Comforter..."

Jesus promised His **DISCIPLES** that s standing in front of Him that God would send the Comforter *to them: to Peter, John and to the rest of the disciples*.

Muhammad was never sent to Peter, John, etc. Long after all the immediate disciples of Jesus died, Muhammad came on the scene about 570 years later. Therefore, Muhammad can't be the promised Comforter that would come to Jesus' immediate disciples.

"...He shall give you **ANOTHER COMFORTER**..."

If the word was periclytos, it would mean that Jesus asked the Father to send the disciples ANOTHER AHMAD [Muhammad]. How ridiculous? There was no Ahmad in the 1st century!

"...that He may abide **WITH YOU** forever..."

Jesus promised His disciples that the Comforter would be *with them: with Peter, John and the rest of the disciples*. Muhammad was never with Peter, John, etc. Therefore, Muhammad can't be the promised Comforter.

"17 Even the Spirit of Truth; Whom the world cannot receive, because it sees Him not, neither know Him: **BUT YE KNOW HIM** ..."

The disciples that Jesus spoke to never knew Muhammad. Therefore, Muhammad can't be the promised Comforter.

"...He **DWELLETH WITH** you..."

Muhammad never dwelt with John, Peter, etc. Therefore, Muhammad can't be the promised Comforter.

"...shall be **IN** you..."

When was Muhammad ever inside Peter, John, etc.? They never knew him. Therefore, Muhammad can't be the promised Comforter.

The Comforter that Jesus prophesied would come

John 14:26 "But the Comforter, **which is the Holy Ghost**, whom the Father will send in My Name, He shall teach you all things and bring all things to your remembrance, whatsoever I have said to you."

The Comforter promised to come and to indwell the disciples was the Holy Spirit that was with them in Jesus Christ. This coming of the Spirit was fulfilled on the Day of Pentecost when the great outpouring of the Holy Spirit took place and the Spirit indwelt the disciples, exactly according to the prophecy given by Jesus Christ.

Acts 2.32-33 "...Having received from the Father, **THE PROMISE OF THE HOLY SPIRIT**, He has poured out this which you see and hear."

Advantage of the Comforter sent to Jesus' disciples

John 16:7 "Nevertheless, I tell you the truth, it is to **YOUR** advantage that I go away, for if I do not go away, the Comforter will not come to **YOU**..."

To what advantage was Muhammad (who lived in the 6th century) to John, Peter, etc. (who lived in the 1st century)? Muhammad was of no advantage to the disciples of Jesus Christ. Therefore, Muhammad can't be the promised Comforter. The disciples could not relate to ALL of the teaching of Jesus, because they did not have the Holy Spirit in them, like Jesus did.

The advantage of the coming of the Holy Spirit into the disciples was that they would understand the deeper things of God. Without the Spirit indwelling them, they had no understanding.

1 Corinthians 2.12 "We have received not the spirit of the world, but the Spirit, which is from God that we might understand the gifts bestowed on us by God."

THE HOLY SPIRIT IS THE PARACLETOS-COMFORTER SENT TO THE DISCIPLES, NOT MUHAMMAD WHO IS DEAD!

47 Is Muhammad mentioned in the Old Testament Books?

Deuteronomy 33:1-2 "And this is the blessing, wherewith Moses the man of God blessed the children of Israel before his death. 2 And he said: The LORD came from Sinai and rose up from Seir unto them; He shined forth from mount Paran and he came with ten thousands of saints: from his right hand went a fiery law for them."

Muslims feels this is a prophesy about Moses coming from Sinai – Jesus coming from Seir - Muhammad coming from Paran in Mecca. However, verse 1 is clear that Moses, before his death, is blessing Israel because God led them safely from Sinai, through the wilderness of Seir to Paran.

VERSE 2 SAYS: ...THE LORD [JEHOVAH]...

You have to twist the verse to read a prophesy about Muhammad into it. Muslims, who want to see the unmentioned Muhammad, in these verses have to deceitfully claim that Paran mentioned in verse 2, was actually located in Mecca in Saudi Arabia.

But a study of any good ancient map will show that Paran is located northwards from Mount Sinai.

Quran Translation by Abdullah Yusuf Ali: Page 248 – Commentary 724 "We may suppose that Israel crossed from Egypt into the Peninsula somewhere near the northern extremity of the Gulf of Suez… They went south about 200 miles to **Mount Sinai where the Law was received, then, perhaps a 150 miles north, was the desert of Paran, close to the southern borders of Canaan. From the camp there, twelve men were sent to spy out the land**…"

Numbers 10:12 "*And the children of Israel took their journeys out of the wilderness of Sinai and the cloud rested in the wilderness of Paran ... 33 from the mount of the LORD* ***three days' journey****…13:1 The LORD spoke unto Moses, saying: 2 Send thou men, that they may search the land of Canaan… 3 Moses by the commandment of the LORD sent them from the wilderness of Paran… 25 They returned from searching of the land after forty days. 26 And they went and came to Moses and Aaron, and to all the congregation of the children of Israel, unto the wilderness of Paran, to Kadesh…*"

From Mount Sinai to the Wilderness of Paran at Kadesh Barnea, is about 241km, which resulted in a plausible three-days-journey for Israel. If Paran was in Mecca, it would mean that Israel travelled from Mount Sinai northwards for about 241km and turned eastwards to Midian and then took a detour of about 1600km south to Mecca and travelled the same rout back northward for another 1600km passing Midian to Kadesh Barnea, a total of 3441km, which is impossible for a three-days-journey, considering Israel, as a Nation of millions of people, with all their domestic animals, etc., travelling by foot, through a rough rockey desert area. Such a suggested rout is contradictory to history as Israel never went to Mecca

Song of Solomon 5:16 "His mouth is most sweet: yea, he is altogether **LOVELY** [**machmad**]. This is my beloved and friend…"

Muslims feel that the English word "lovely", which is translated from the Hebrew word "*machmad*" should be rendered as "Muhammad", because, machmad *sounds* like Muhammad.

Again, notice, when Muslims think they have the upper hand, they don't hesitate to accept that Biblical text as being preserved, uncorrupted and inspired, but if the Bible don't say what they want to hear (read) then all of a sudden, its corrupted again. The word [*machmad*] here is a common noun and not a proper noun. It is not a name. Therefore, the name Muhammad is not in the Bible.

The true meaning of any word is **NOT** determined by *how it sounds or by its isolated root meaning*, but must be determined by the context of the respective passage. Other places where the same word appears: 1 Kings 20:6, Lamention 1:19, Ezekiel 24:21 and Hosea 9:16.

I will quote an example from the Quran to expose those Muslims who wants to force their isolated interpretations on the Holy Bible.

Quran Translation by Abdullah Yusuf Ali: Roman Transliteration – Surah 17:13 "Wa kulla 'insaanin 'alzam-naahu **TAAA-'IR**AHUU fii 'unuqih - Every man's **FATE** we have fastened on his own neck…" Here "fate" may be *interpreted* as *"responsibility, burden, sin, etc."* as per the immediate context.

But what does this word literally mean? ***Quran Translation by Abdullah Yusuf Ali: Page 697 Comm. 2187*** "Fate: "TAIR", literally a bird, hence … an evil omen, fate… It depends on our deeds, good or evil and they hang round our necks…"

If we ignore the context and translate it according to its root meaning, the literal translation would read: "Every man's BIRD we have fastened on his own neck…" This proves that the context must be considered.

"In Arabic many words are formed from the same root, but they do not on that account denote Muhammad.

An ignorant Muslim might just as well assert that Muhammad's name occurred in Surah 1:1 Al **HAMDO** lillahi Rabbi 'lalamin (**PRAISE** be to God, the Lord of the worlds) In the same way a Hindu might assert that the name of Ram … was mentioned in the Quran, because in Sura 30:1 we read: **AR-RUM** (The Romans have been overcome) where Arabic dictionaries give **"RUM"** as if derived from the root "ram". This kind of argument is unworthy of men of learning."

http://www.answering-islam.org/BibleCom/songs5-16.html Last accessed 27 April 2021

If you read the Song of Solomon, the context clearly shows the love between a married couple, husband and wife, can be desirable and passionate. Therefore, the translators correctly translated it as "lovely" as demanded by the context. It does not speak about Muhammad.

48 What the "Bible says" about Muhammad?

Muhammad committed adultery

| *Matthew 19:9* "…Who so married her which is put away [divorced] doth **COMMIT ADULTERY**." | *Quran Translation by Abdullah Yusuf Ali – Surah 33:37* "…When Zaid dissolved (his marriage) [divorcement] with her… We joined her in marriage to thee…" |

Muhammad will confess Jesus Christ is Lord

| *Philippians 2:10* "And EVERY TONGUE will confess that Jesus Christ is Lord…" |

Actually, according to the Quran, Muhammed already preached that Jesus Christ is Lord. See Q16 under the heading: According to Quran, is Jesus Lord?

Muhammad was a transgressor of the law

| *James 2:9* "But if ye have respect to persons, ye commit sin and are convinced of the law as TRANSGRESSORS." | *Quran Translation by Abdullah Yusuf Ali – Surah 80:8-10* "But as to him who came to thee striving earnestly and with fear (in his heart), of him was thou Unmindful." |

Whether Muslims agree or disagree with the Bible is irrelevant, the Bible says Muhammad committed adultery and is a transgressor, the Bible says Muhammad will bow the knee and confess Jesus is Lord.

> Muhammad was an anti-Christ

> ***1 John 2:22*** "Who is a liar, but he that denieth that Jesus is the Christ? He is antichrist that denieth the Father and the Son.

49 Was Muhammad a universal or local messenger?

In this section we are not discussing whether Muhammad was a true or false prophet. We only want to understand how the Quran portray his ministry: whether he was only sent to his people, the Quraysh, Arab pagans or as a universal messenger, to ALL NATIONS! The verses discussed below is in its chronological order of recitation as received by Muhammad seemingly from Gabriel.

Quran Translation by Malik – Surahs 73:15 "**O MANKIND**, we have sent towards you a rasool, to bear witness for **YOU** or against **YOU**, as we sent a Rasool towards Fir'on (Pharaoh) before you."

http://www.alim.org/library/quran/surah/english/73/MAL

Please note, the Arabic words for *"O mankind"* are not in this verse. Malik did not even put it between interpolation brackets *(O mankind)* to indicate to the readers of their English Version that it is their desirable interpretation and not what the Arabic text says.

Also, Surah 73 is actually the 3RD Surah in chronological order. It is a Meccan verse. Reading the previous verses, i.e. 73:1-14, none of it indicate that Muhammad was addressing the whole world, in fact, *verse 10 "Bear patiently with what **THEY** say and leave **THEIR** company in a polite manner."* makes it clear that Muhammad addressed the Meccans and that the Meccans rejected Muhammad as a messenger.

Tafsir Al-Jalalayn S. 73 "vs. 10 Bear patiently what they say, that is, **THE DISBELIEVERS OF MECCA**... 15 We have indeed sent to you, **O PEOPLE OF MECCA**, a Messenger, Muhammad..."

https://quranx.com/Tafsir/Jalal/73.10 https://quranx.com/Tafsir/Jalal/73.15

Last accessed 27 April 2021

Tafsir - Sayyid Abul Ala Maududi - Tafhim al-Qur'an 73:15 "The address now turns **TO THE DISBELIEVERS OF MAKKAH**..."

https://quranx.com/Tafsir/Maududi/73.15

Last accessed 27 April 2021

Let's see how other Muslims translated Surah 73:15

Quran Translation by Shakir "We have sent to you a messenger, a witness against you, as We sent a messenger to Firon."

Quran Translation by Mustafa Khattab "We have sent to you a messenger as a witness over you, just as We sent a messenger to Pharaoh."

Muhammad was sent to his people the Arabs **JUST AS** Moses was sent to his people the Israelites.

Surahs 7:158

Quran Translation by Shakir "Say: **O people**! I am the Messenger of Allah to you all..."

Quran Translation by Abdullah Yusuf Ali: "Say: "**O men**! I am sent unto you all, as the Messenger of Allah..."

The people that Muhammad addressed was the Arabs. He did not speak to the Americans, nor the Chinese, nor the Australians, etc. We will see that Quranic verses, hereafter makes it abundantly clear that Muhammad was NOT sent to ALL NATIONS, but to the Arabs ONLY.

Quran Translation by Abdullah Yusuf Ali – Surahs 36:6 "In order that thou [Muhammad] may admonish **A PEOPLE** whose **FATHERS HAD RECEIVED NO ADMONITION** and who therefore remain heedless (of the Signs of Allah)."

This verse shows that Muhammad was sent to the Arabs, he was not sent to admonish the Ishmailites who already received their messenger and a book as per Surahs 3:84, 4:163, 19:54. Muhammad was not sent to the Israelites who already received Moses and a book, etc. Muhammad was sent to admonish a people, THE ARABS, who didn't receive admonition before his prophethood.

Quran Translation by Abdullah Yusuf Ali – Surah 28:59, 10:47 "Nor was thy Lord the one to destroy a population, until He had sent to its centre a messenger … To every people (was sent) a messenger…"

Meaning of the Glorious Quran – Surah 10:47 "For every nation there is a messenger…"

These verses proof that Muhammad is not a messenger to every nation, to every nation there is a messenger. Each nation had a messenger, just like the Ishmaelites had Ishmail, the Israeltes had Moses and the Arabs had Muhammad.

Quran Translation by Abdullah Yusuf Ali – Surahs 6:92, 42:7, 43:44, 16:36&113 "And this is a Book, which We have sent down, bringing blessings and confirming (the revelations), which came before it: that thou mayest warn the mother of cities and all around her … 42:7 Thus have We sent by inspiration to thee an **ARABIC** Qur'an: that thou mayest warn the Mother of Cities and all around her … 43:44 The (Qur'an) is indeed the message for thee [Muhammad] and for **THY PEOPLE [ARABS – NOT FOR THE WORLD]** … 16:36 We assuredly sent **AMONGST EVERY PEOPLE A MESSENGER** … 16:113 **A MESSENGER FROM AMONG THEMSELVES**…"

Surahs 14:4

Quran Translation by Abdullah Yusuf Ali: "We sent **NOT** a messenger, except (to teach) in the language of **HIS**	***Meaning of Glorious Quran*** "We **NEVER** sent a messenger save with the

| (OWN) PEOPLE, in order to make (things) clear TO THEM…". | language of HIS FOLK, that he might make (the message) clear FOR THEM…" |

Muhammad is an Arab messenger to the Arabs, not to Americans, etc. The Quran is in Arabic, the language of his people. I am not an Arab. I am not from Muhammed's people. The Arabic Quran is to make the message clear to his people, not to me. You can NOT read this verse any other way. To say Muhammad was sent to non-Arabs, is to contradict this verse. Allah says: We sent **NOT** a messenger, except to teach in the language of his people, to make things clear to them! Allah did **NOT** say: We sent a messenger, to teach in his language to all the people of the world and to make things clear to the world!

Quran Translation by Abdullah Yusuf Ali: Page 1333 Commentary 4647 "The Quran brings a message of Truth and Guidance to the **APOSTLE AND HIS PEOPLE**…"

Tafsir - Ibn Al Kathir S. 14:4 "Every prophet was sent with the **LANGUAGE OF HIS PEOPLE**… Allah sending messengers to them **FROM AMONG THEM** and speaking their language, so that they are able to understand the Message that the messengers were sent with."

https://quranx.com/Tafsir/Kathir/14.4 Last accessed 27 April 2021

Quran Translation by Abdullah Yusuf Ali – Surahs 23:32 & 44, 32:3, 3:164 "We sent to **them [every nation] a messenger from among themselves** … Then sent We our messengers in succession: every time there came to **a people their messenger** … 32:3 Thou mayest admonish **a people** to whom no warner has come before thee… 3:164 A messenger to people from among the people…"

Muhammad is not a warner to the Ishmailites, Jews and Christians, they had warners, **HE WAS SENT TO A PEOPLE WHO HAD NO WARNERS BEFORE HIM**. Each nation from among them have their messenger who admonishes them in their own language.

Quran Translation by Abdullah Yusuf Ali – Surahs 13:40, 62:2 "… Thus have we sent **THEE [MUHAMMAD] AMONGST A PEOPLE [ARABS]** before whom (long since) have (other) peoples (gone and) passed away; in order that thou might **REHEARSE UNTO**

THEM [A PEOPLE – ARABS]** what We send down unto thee by inspiration ... 62:7 It is He [Allah] who has **SENT AMONG THE UNLETTERED [ARABS]** an apostle amongst themselves, to rehears to them..."

__Quran Translation by Abdullah Yusuf Ali – Surahs 9:120 & 128__ "It was not fitting **FOR THE PEOPLE OF MEDINA AND THE BEDOUIN ARABS OF THE NEIGHBOURHOOD**, to refuse to follow Allah's Messenger ... Now hath come **UNTO YOU A MESSENGER FROM AMONGST YOURSELVES**..."

Muhammad's last duty will be of a local witness

__Quran Translation by Abdullah Yusuf Ali – Surah 16:89__ "One day [on resurrection] we shall raise from all peoples a witness against them, *from amongst themselves* and we shall bring **THEE [MUHAMMAD] AS A WITNESS AGAINST THESE (THY PEOPLE)** ..."

__Quran Translation by Abdullah Yusuf Ali: Page 680 Comm. 2126__ "...The witnesses will be men from amongst the people themselves, men of their own kith and kin, who understood them, explained God's message in their own language. **THE APOSTLE MUHAMMAD WILL BE WITNESS AGAINST ARABS** ..."

This means Muhammad's prophethood was for **ARABIANS, NOT ALL THE WORLD**. Muhammad will **NOT** be a witness against Americans, Ethiopians, etc. but against his people, the Arabs. Any other verses interpreted that Muhammad was a universal messenger is in clear contradictions to the above Quranic verses and Muslim commentaries.

50 Did Muhammad gain personal profit?

Muhammad got paid by Muslims for his prayers to purify them

__Quran Translation by Abdullah Yusuf Ali – Surah 9:103__ "**OF THEIR GOODS TAKE ALMS THAT THOU MIGHT PURIFY AND SANCTIFY THEM** and pray on their behalf. Verily *YOUR* prayers are a source of security for them..."

Tafsir - Ibn Al Kathir S. 9:103 "ALLAH COMMANDED HIS MESSENGER TO TAKE Sadaqah from the **MUSLIMS' MONEY TO PURIFY AND SANCTIFY THEM**..." https://quranx.com/Tafsir/Kathir/9.103

Last accessed 27 April 2021

Tafsir Al-Jalalayn "Take of their wealth some **ALMS TO PURIFY AND CLEANSE THEM** of their sins..."

https://quranx.com/Tafsir/Jalal/9.103 Last accessed 27 April 2021

CAN YOU IMAGINE – Muhammad must be paid with money for Muslims to be purified and sanctified and prayed for. If this was in the Bible, Muslims would call it a money-making-scheme. [64:17, 58:12]

Quran Translation by Abdullah Yusuf Ali – Surah 8:1 "They ask thee concerning (things taken as) spoils of war. Say: (Such) spoils are at the **DISPOSAL OF GOD AND THE APOSTLE**: so fear God..."

We can clearly see how the money went straight to Muhammad, but his followers were not too blind to see how Muhammad pocketed the spoils and they were not too shy to cross question their leader when it came to money: *"...they ask thee?"* meaning they inquired about the profits. Muhammad knew that money can turn a devout follower against a leader and wallah, another convenient revelation saved him out of his dilemma. Allah, forty verses later, changed Muhammad's income-share from 100% to less than 20% at his disposal.

Quran Translation by Abdullah Yusuf Ali – Surah 8:41 "Know that out of all [100%] booty that ye may acquire (in war), a **FIFTH [20%] SHARE IS ASSIGNED TO GOD AND HIS APOSTLE AND TO NEAR RELATIVES, ORPHANS, THE NEEDY AND THE WAYFARER** if ye do believe in God..."

Muhammad became a very rich man through wars that he fought and victories over his enemies.

Sahih Bukhari Vol. 3 Page 280, Hadith 495 "...Allah made the Prophet wealthy through conquests..."

Muhammad became a rich prophet of Arabia owning many houses.

Quran Translation by Abdullah Yusuf Ali – Surah 33:53 "O ye who believe! Enter not the **PROPHET'S HOUSES**..."

51 Did Muhammad show mercy to his enemies?

Sahih Bukhari Vol. 2, Page 337, Hadith 577 "Narrated Anas: Some people from 'Uraina tribe came to Medina and its climate did not suit them, so Allah's Apostle allowed them to go to the herd of camels (given as Zakat) and they drank their milk and urine (as medicine) but they killed the shepherd and drove away all the camels. So Allah's Apostle sent (men) in their pursuit to catch them and they were brought **AND HE HAD THEIR HANDS AND FEET CUT AND THEIR EYES WERE BRANDED WITH HEATED PIECES OF IRON AND THEY WERE LEFT IN THE HARRA** (a stony place at Medina) biting the stones."

Was it necessary for Muhammad to torture the criminals like that? What would the Muslims of today say, if the Israelis or Americans were to torture Islamic terrorists in the same way?

Ishaq, "Life of Muhammad" Trans. By Alfred Guillaume, Page 403 "...Off B. Jumah b. Amr b. Abdullah b. Umayr b. Wahb b. Hudhafa b. Jumah who was Abu Azza **WHOM THE APOSTLE KILLED WHEN A PRISONER** and Ubayy b. Khalaf b. Wahb b. Hudhafa b. Jumah **WHOM THE APOSTLE KILLED WITH HIS OWN HAND** ... Thus God killed on the day of Uhud 22 polytheists."

Would it be right for democrats to execute Muslim prisoners of war as Muhammad killed his prisoners? Jesus taught God's justice, but He didn't teach in-humane torture. The oldest extant biography of Muhammad is called the "Sirat Rasulallah" — "Life of the Prophet of Allah". This book was written 767AD by Ibn Ishaq, a devout Muslim scholar, and later, 833AD, revised by Ibn Hisham. It was written before the major works of Hadith. It is considered an authentic *biography* of Muhammad.

Ishaq, "Life of Muhammad" TRANSLATED by Alfred Guillaume, Page 515: "Kinana al-Rabi, who had the custody of the treasure of Banu Nadir, was brought to the apostle who asked him about it. He denied that he knew where it was. A Jew came, to the apostle and said that he had seen Kinana going round a certain ruin every morning early. When the apostle said to Kinana: Do you know that if we find you have it I shall kill you? He said: Yes! The apostle gave orders that the ruin was to be excavated and some of the treasure was found. When he asked him about the rest he refused to produce it, so the apostle gave orders to al-Zubayr Al-Awwam, **TORTURE HIM UNTIL YOU EXTRACT WHAT HE HAS. SO HE KINDLED A FIRE WITH FLINT AND STEEL ON HIS CHEST, UNTIL HE WAS NEARLY DEAD. THEN THE APOSTLE DELIVERED HIM TO MUHAMMAD B. MASLAMA AND HE STRUCK OFF HIS HEAD, IN REVENGE FOR HIS BROTHER MAHMUD.**"

Think about Muhammad's statement: *"Torture him until you extract what he has."* This is the prophet of Islam in action when he now has the power of the sword. How would you feel if you were watching the news and learned about this happening in your neighborhood? Remember, this episode is all about the love of money.

The Holy Bible declares: **1 Timothy 6:10** "For the *LOVE OF* money is the root of all evil."

Did Muhammad promote lies?

Sahih Bukhari Vol. 5, Page 248-250, Hadith 369 "Narrated Jabir Abdullah: Allah's messenger said: Who is willing to kill Ka'b bin Al-Ashraf *who has hurt Allah and His apostle*? Thereupon Maslama got up saying: O Allah's messenger! Would you like that I kill him? The prophet said: Yes! **MASLAMA SAID: THEN ALLOW ME TO SAY A (FALSE) THING (E.G. TO DECEIVE KA'B). THE PROPHET SAID: "YOU MAY SAY IT** … So they killed him and went to the prophet and informed him."

Muhammad allowed Maslama to lie (deceive) to draw Ka'b out of his home to murder him, because Ka'b has hurt Allah and His Apostle.

Can you imagine?

Ishag, "Life of Muhammad" Trans. By Alfred Guillaume, Pages 675-676 "She was of B. Umayyya b. Zayd. When Abu Afak had been killed she displayed disaffection. Abdullah b. al-Harith b. Al-Fudayl from his father said that she was married to a man of B. Khatma called Yazid b. Zayd. Blaming Islam and its followers she said: I despise B. Malik and al-Nabit and Auf and B. al-Khazraj. You obey a stranger who is none of yours, one not of Murad or Madhhij. Do you expect good from him after the killing of your chiefs? Like a hungry man waiting for a cook's broth? Is there no man of pride who would attack him by surprise? And cut off the hopes of those who expect aught from him? Hassan b. Thabit answered her: Banu Wa'il and B. Waqif and Khatma are inferior to B. al-Khazrahj. When she called for folly woe to her in her weeping, for death is coming. She stirred up a man of origin, Noble in his going out and coming in. Before midnight he dyed her in her blood and incurred no guilt thereby. When the apostle heard what she had said he said: Who will rid me of Marwan's daughter? Umayr b. Adiy al-Khatmi that very night he went to her house and killed her. In the morning he came to the apostle and told him what he had done and he [Muhammad] said, "You have helped God and His apostle, O Umayr! Now there was a great commotion among B. Khatma that day about the affair of bint [girl] Marwaan. She had five sons, and when Umayr went to them from the apostle he said, "I have killed bint Marwaan, O sons of Khatma. Withstand me if you can; don't keep me waiting." That was the first day Islam became powerful among B. Khatma; before that those who were Muslims concealed the fact. The first of them to accept Islam was Umayr b. Adiy who was called the "Reader", and Abdullah b. Aus and Khuzayma b. Thabit. The day after Bint Marwaan was killed the men of B. Khatma became Muslims because they saw the power of Islam."

If Muhammad denied freedom of speech to others, how does that reflect upon Islam and what we see occurring in the Islamic world today?

52 Wine in the Bible and Quran

Does Christendom winks at drunkenness?

Ahmad Deedat: Muhammad, The Natural Successor to Christ (pbuh)! Page 41-43
"CHRISTENDOM WINKS AT DRUNKENNESS on three flimsy pretenses' based on the Holy Bible ... Since this alleged miracle [John 2:7-10] wine continues to flow like water in Christendom ... Islam is the only religion on the face of the earth, which prohibits intoxicants in toto. The Holy Prophet (Spirit) Muhammad (pbuh) had said: WHATEVER INTOXICATES IN GREATER QUANTITY, IS FORBIDDEN EVEN IN SMALLER QUANTITY. There is no excuse in the house of Islam for a nip or a tot."

Firstly, when the Bible mentions wine, it does not refer to Brandy, Black Label, etc., because these alcoholic beverages were only produced more than one thousand years after the Holy Bible was compiled in book form. Wine in the Bible refers to ...

Matthew 26:29, Mark 14:25, Luke 22:18 "I [Jesus] say unto you, I will not drink henceforth of this **FRUIT OF THE VINE**..."

This explains what type of wine Jesus created during the wedding in Cana of Galilee. It is true that some Christians drink themselves to death, but the same can be said of some Muslims. To say Christendom winks at drunkenness is nothing, but a deceptive lie by Deedat, who have no shame to misrepresent other religions, as long as he can, by hook or by crook, promote Islam.

Bible forbid wine as a pleasure beverage

Ephesians 5:18 "**BE NOT DRUNK WITH WINE** wherein is excess, but be filled with the Holy Spirit."

Why did Paul advise Timothy to drink a little wine?

Surprisingly, wine does have some benefits and may be prescribed for certain ailments. This is the reason why Apostle Paul said:

THE AMPLIFIED BIBLE 1 Timothy 5:23 "[Timothy] drink water no longer exclusively, but use a little wine for **THE SAKE OF YOUR STOMACH AND YOUR FREQUENT ILLNESSES**."

The context is clear, Paul never said drink wine during your year-end festivals, etc. wine was prescribed unto Timothy as a medicine for a sickness he had. Many medications prescribed today, by Muslim doctors to patients, including Muslim patients, contain alcohol.

Ahmad Deedat: Muhammad, The Natural Successor to Christ: Page 43 "The Christians accept the Bible quotations on stimulating and intoxicating drinks given above as the infallible Word of God. They believe the Holy Ghost inspired authors to pen such dangerous advices."

Allah say there is benefit in wine

It is strange that Deedat forgot to mention the following Quranic verses, which he forcefully promotes as Allah's (God's) inspired words.

Quran Translation by Abdullah Yusuf Ali – Surah 2:219 "They [Arabs] ask thee [Muhammad] concerning *"khamr"* **WINE** and gambling. Say: In them are great sin and **SOME PROFIT FOR MEN**, but the sin is greater than the profit…"

Quran Translation by Abdullah Yusuf Ali: Page 86 Commentary 240 "Wine: Literally understood as the **FERMENTED JUICE OF THE GRAPE**…"

Message of the Quran "They ask thee about **INTOXICANTS** and games of chance. Say: In both there is great evil and **SOME BENEFITS FOR MEN**…"

Meaning of Glorious Quran "They ask thee about **STRONG DRINK** and games of chance. Say: In both is great sin and *(some) utility for men*…"

Here we see Allah in these occasions inspired Muhammad to say to the Arabs that wine, intoxicants and strong drinks have benefits for men? Does Deedat accept these Quranic quotations on stimulating and intoxicating drinks given above as the infallible words of

Allah? Did Allah give these dangerous advices as inspired words? IF NO, then these verses are not from Allah and the Quran is not God's Word. If yes, can you see how bias, dishonest Muslims are towards the Holy Bible?

Wine not totally forbidden in the Quran

Surah 4:43

The Noble Quran "O ye who believe! **APPROACH NOT *AS-SALAT (THE PRAYER)* WHEN YOU ARE IN A DRUNKEN STATE**…"

Quran Translation by Abdullah Yusuf Ali: "O ye who believe! **APPROACH NOT PRAYERS WITH A MIND BEFOGGED**…"

Meaning of Glorious Quran "O ye who believe! **DRAW NOT NEAR UNTO PRAYER WHEN YE ARE DRUNKEN**…"

These verses demonstrate the following facts:

- ✓ Surah 2 is actually the 87TH Surah and Surah 4 is actually the 92ND Surah in its chronological order.

- ✓ THAT means, after Allah said in Surah 2 there are some benefits in wine, since than, until Surah 4 was revealed, Islam winked their eye at wine and it flew like water in the Arabian streets, until Muslims went drunk to Mosques to pray while being drunk. Deedat biasly overlooked these facts.

- ✓ Secondly, this verse only forbids Muslims "NOT" to pray when they were drunk, PROVING that **WINE WAS STILL NOT TOTALLY FORBIDDEN IN ISLAM**.

Instead of Allah forbidding wine, he only forbids Muslims to draw near prayer when they are drunk. Does Deedat accept this outrageous dangerous advice as Allah's inspired words? Deedat shamelessly made a deceptive statement when he said: "There is no excuse in the house of Islam for a nip or a tot."

Muhammad drank wine

Not only did some Muslims in Muhammad's day turn out to be drunks, Muhammad also drank wine and he even encouraged the butlers to continue to serve wine. Now! Before you scream out: "Blasphemy, Kufir, Enemy of Islam and Christian bigotry, fabricator, here is my evidence. Oh! Yes, it's not taken from Christian or Jewish literature, but from authentic Islamic literature published by devout Muslim Scholars.

Sahih Muslim, Book 7, Number 3018 "Ibn `Abbas said: ... Allah's apostle ... **HE ASKED FOR WATER SO WE GAVE HIM A CUP FULL OF NABIDH AND HE DRANK IT ... HE (THE HOLY PROPHET) SAID: YOU HAVE DONE GOOD. SO CONTINUE IN THE SAME WAY.** So we do not like to change what Allah's Messenger (pbuh) has commanded us to do." https://quranx.com/Hadith/Muslim/USC-MSA/Book-7/Hadith-3018

Last accessed 27 April 2021

TP Hughes: Dictionary of Islam – Page 427 "NABIZ... **A KIND OF WINE MADE FROM DATES, WHICH IS LAWFUL.** (*Hidayah*, Vol. iv, p. 155)"

There you have it, Muhammad drank nabidh and he also gave it to his contemporaries to drink, not only that, Muhammad said, you did good and well. Is serving wine something to be complimented for in Islam? When Muhammad said those who gave him wine, did well and must continue to give people wine, was that good advice from the Muslim prophet or was it bad advice?

Allah and Muhammad only forbid strong drinks

After Muhammad consumed his fair share of wine, then only did he prohibit **STRONG** drinks in Surah 5:93!

Meaning of Glorious Quran "O ye that believe, **STRONG DRINK** ... are an infamy of Satan's handiwork..."

Quran Translation by Abdullah Yusuf Ali – Surah "O ye who believe! **INTOXICANTS** ... are an abomination of Satan's handwork: eschew such that ye may prosper."

This verse **_ONLY PROHIBITS STRONG DRINK_**, not all wine beverages. It is true that some Muslims forbid all kinds of wine, but it is NOT true that Allah, Muhammed and Islam forbid all kinds of wine. True Islam is not the good opinion of Muslims; true Islam is what Allah and Muhammed taught in Islamic literature.

Alcoholic beverages in the Muslim heaven

<u>The Noble Quran – Page 47 Footnote B</u> "Narrated Ibn Umar: Allah's messenger said: Whoever drinks *alcoholic* drinks in this world and doesn't repent (stop drinking alcohol and begs Allah to forgive him before his death) **WILL BE DEPRIVED OF IT IN THE HEREAFTER.** *(Bukhari Vol. 7, Page 338, Hadith 481)*"

Note that this Hadith doesn't say the wine consumer won't enter heaven, it clearly says that he will only be deprived of alcoholic drinks in the hereafter. Alcoholic drinks will be served in the Islamic heaven.

Islam's and Christianity's responds to alcohol users

<u>Sahih Bukhari Vol. 8, Pages 504, Hadith 764 & Page 505, Hadith 765</u> "Narrated Anas bin Malik: The prophet beat a drunk with palm-leaf stalks and shoes. And Abu Bakr gave (such a sinner) forty lashes… Narrated 'Uqba bin Al-Harith: An-Nu'man or the son of An-Nu'man was brought to the prophet on a charge of drunkenness. **SO THE PROPHET ORDERED ALL MEN PRESENT IN THE HOUSE TO BEAT HIM.**"

<u>Sunan Abu Dawud book 38, Number 4467</u>: Narrated Mu'awiyah ibn Abu Sufyan: The prophet (peace be upon him) said: If they (the people) drink wine, **FLOG THEM** and again if they drink it **FLOG THEM**. Again if they drink it, **KILL THEM.**"

<u>Drum Magazine: The voice of Africa. March 14 2002 No: 497 Pages 20</u> "In recent months, several people in northern Nigeria **HAVE BEEN LASHED IN PUBLIC FOR … DRINKING ALCOHOL…**"

Is this the solution Muhammad and his religion offer poor sinful souls that were/are bound by the horrible chains of alcohol?

TRUE BIBLICAL CHRISTIANITY IS A RELIGION OF FAITH.

Hebrews 11:6 "But without faith, it is impossible to please Him: For he that cometh to God must believe that He is and that He is a rewarder of them that diligently seek Him."

Christianity does not practice violence, like Islam, in order to keep its followers from doing wrong. We don't beat or kill those with alcoholic problems. We pray and fast for them, believing God to break the yoke of alcoholism. Listen to the unfailing love-words of the Master:

Luke 4:18-19 "The Spirit of the Lord is upon Me, He had anointed Me to preach the Gospel to the poor, He had sent Me to heal the broken hearted, to preach deliverance to the captives and recovering of the sight to the blind, to set at liberty them that are bruised, to preach the acceptable year of the Lord."

Matthew 11:28-30 "Come unto Me, all ye that labor and are heavy laden and I will give you rest. Take My yoke upon you and learn of Me, for I'm weak and lowly in heart and ye shall find rest unto your souls for My yoke is easy and My burden is light."

O sinner Muslim, come home, softly and tenderly Jesus is calling, calling you to a life of freedom from sin and its worldly pleasures.

53 Did Muhammad believe in superstitions?

The dead are tortured when relatives cry

Sahih Bukhari Vol. 2, Page 210 Hadith 375 "**ALLAH'S MESSENGER SAID:** "The dead person is tortured by the crying of his relative..."

Drinking urine as medicine

Sahih Bukhari Vol. 1, Page 148, Hadith 234 "Narrated Abu Qilaba: **THE PROPHET ORDERED** some people to go to the herd of (Milch) camels and to drink their urine (as a medicine)."

Muhammad believed a black dog is a devil

Sahih Muslim "Abu Dharr reported: The Messenger of 'Allah (ﷺ) said... The black dog is a devil."

https://quranx.com/Hadith/Muslim/USC-MSA/Book-4/Hadith-1032

Last accessed 27 April 2021

Yawning is from Satan

Sahih Bukhari **Vol. 4, Page 325, Hadith 509** "The **PROPHET SAID**: Yawning is from Satan."

Perform wudu because Satan sleeps in your nose

Sahih Bukhari **Vol. 4, Page 328, Hadith 516** "**THE PROPHET SAID**: If anyone of you rousers from sleep and performs the ablution, he should wash his nose by putting water in it and then blowing it out thrice, because Satan has stayed in the upper part of the nose all the night."

Muhammed did wudu with water wherein was excrement, period-blood, dead dogs

Sunan an-Nasa'i "It was narrated that Abu Sa'eed Al-Khudri said: "It was said: 'O Messenger of Allah, you perform Wudu' from the *well* into which dead dogs, menstrual rags and garbage are thrown? ...""

https://quranx.com/Hadith/Nasai/DarusSalam/Volume-1/Book-2/Hadith-327   Last accessed 27 April 2021

Sunan Abu Dawud **Book 1** "Narrated AbuSa'id al-Khudri: I heard the people asked the Prophet of Allah: Water is brought for you from the *well of Buda'ah*. It is a well in which dead dogs, menstrual clothes and excrement of people are thrown. The Messenger of Allah (ﷺ) replied: Verily water is pure and is not defiled by anything. *Abu Dawud said I heard Qutaibah b. Sa'id say: I asked the person in charge of the well of Bud'ah about the depth of the well. He replied: At most the water reaches pubes. Then I asked: Where* *does it reach when its level goes down? He replied: Below the private part of the body. Abu Dawud said: I measured the breadth of the well of Buda'ah with my sheet, which I stretched over it. I measured it with the hand. It measured six cubits in breadth.*" [Unquote: 1 cubit = 0,4572m / 6 cubits = 2.7432m]

https://quranx.com/Hadith/AbuDawud/Hasan/Hadith-67 Last accessed 27 April 2021

Conversion http://extraconversion.com/length/cubits/cubits-to-meters.html Last accessed 27 April 2021

Muhammad said dip the house fly into your drinks

Sahih Bukhari: Vol. 4, Page 338, Hadith 537 "Narrated Abu Huraira: The **PROPHET SAID**: If a house fly falls in the drink of anyone of you, he should dip it (in the drink **again**), for one of its wings has a disease and the other has the cure for the disease." [Unquote: When a fly falls into the drink of a Muslim, how many Muslims will take it out and dip it back again into their drink to follow Muhammad's teaching?]

Did Muhammad allow men to kiss his naked belly?

Sunan Abu Dawud "Narrated Usayd ibn Hudayr… a man of the Ansar, said … You're wearing a shirt, but I am not. The Prophet raised his shirt and the man embraced him and began to kiss his side… and said: This is what I wanted, Messenger of Allah!" https://quranx.com/Hadith/AbuDawud/Hasan/Hadith-5205

Last accessed 27 April 2021

Angels don't enter where there are pictures

Sahih Bukhari Vol. 4, Page 339, Hadith 539 "The **PROPHET SAID**: Angels do not enter a house which has either a dog or a picture in it."

Why a child looks like his father or mother?

Sahih Bukhari Vol. 5, Page 190, Hadith 275 "**MUHAMMAD SAID…** if the man's discharged precedes the woman's discharge, the child attracts the similarity of the man and if the woman's discharge precedes the man's discharge, then the child attracts the similarity of the woman..."

Muhammad vs silk, music, false hair, etc.

The Noble Quran - Page 162 Footnote 4 "...The prophet saying: From among my followers there will be some who will consider illegal sexual intercourse, wearing of silk, drinking of alcoholic drinks and the use of musical instruments as lawful. (*Sahih Bukhari*, Vol. 7, Hadith 494B) ...Vol. 7, Page 101, Hadith 133 "**MUHAMMAD SAID**: Don't wear false hair for Allah sends His curse on such ladies who lengthen their hair artificially." [Unquote: According to Quran 44:51-53 the righteous will wear silk in heaven.]

Tafsir - Ibn Al Kathir "(Dressed in Sundus) means, the finest of silk, such as shirts and the like." https://quranx.com/Tafsir/Kathir/44.51] Last accessed 27 April 2021

Muhammad said, after eating, don't wipe your hands, lick each others' hands

Sahih Bukhari Vol. 7, Page 265, Hadith 366 "Narrated Ibn `Abbas: The Prophet (ﷺ) said, 'When you eat, do not wipe your hands *TILL YOU HAVE LICKED IT, **OR HAD IT LICKED BY SOMEBODY ELSE**.*"

54 Was Muhammad a white man who owned black slaves?

Abdur-Rahman Wright, The Black People of South Africa and The Imported Religions. Page 18 "Why should you become a Muslim? Because it is the religion of **YOUR** ancestor..."

Both Islam and Christianity were born in the east and did not originate in Africa. Muhammad was an Arab and can never be the ancestor of Africans. Islam was born in the Arabian Peninsula, which is part of the continent of Asia. Asia and Africa are different continents, different races and separated by the Red Sea. Islam is not the religion of my African ancestors, but a religion of Arabs. *It is impossible to confuse a "white" Asian-Arab with a "black" African.*

Sahih Bukhari Vol. 1, Page 54, Hadith 63 "...While we were sitting with the Prophet, a man came and said: **WHO AMONGST YOU IS MUHAMMAD? WE REPLIED: THIS WHITE MAN** reclining on his arm..."

More references of Muhammad being a white man can be found here:

Youtube presentation by Dr. David Wood: How Muhammad Ali (Cassius Clay) was deceived by Islam:

https://www.youtube.com/watch?v=sxOM4GrqElw Last accessed 27 April 2021

Sahih Bukhari Vol. 8, Page 117, Hadith 182, Vol.9, Page 275, Hadith 368 "Narrated Anas bin Malik: **ALLAH'S MESSENGER (ﷺ) WAS ON A JOURNEY AND HE HAD A BLACK SLAVE CALLED ANJASHA** ... Narrated `Umar: I came and behold, Allah's Messenger (ﷺ) was staying on a Mashroba (attic room) and **A BLACK SLAVE OF ALLAH'S MESSENGER (ﷺ) WAS AT THE TOP OF ITS STAIRS**..."

Muhammad used slaves for sexual satisfaction

The Koran – Surah 33:50 "O Prophet, we have made lawful for you the wives to whom you have granted dowries **AND THE SLAVE-GIRLS WHOM GOD HAS GIVEN YOU AS BOOTY**..."

Here we see Allah informing Muhammad that sex with his wives AND HIS SLAVE-GIRLS that he captured from their tribes are allowed. Surah 33 is the 90TH revealed Surah in the Quran's chronological order of recited revelations. This is a Medina verse, meaning Muhammad is already a prophet for more than 12 years and still owned slaves, which he misused for sex.

Tafsir: Maududi - Sayyid Abul Ala Maududi - Surah 66:1 "**THE HOLY PROPHET HAD A SLAVE-GIRL** with whom he had conjugal relations" https://quranx.com/Tafsir/Maududi/66.1 Last accessed 27 April 2021

Muslims lie to us when they say Islam eradicated slavery. While "white" Muhammad used "black" slave-girls for his lustful benefit, other Muslims misused the slave-girls to make money through prostitution.

Quran Translation by Abdullah Yusuf Ali – Surah 24:33 "…But **force not your maids to prostitution when they desire chastity**, in order that ye may make a gain in the goods of this life. But if anyone compels them, yet, after such compulsion, is Allah, Oft-Forgiving, Most Merciful (to them)."

Surah 24 is the 102ND revealed Surah in the Quran's chronological order of recited revelations, it was of the last revealed verses in Medinah, meaning Muhammad is already a prophet for at least 20 years and still did not forbid slavery, but only its misuse for making money through forced prostitution.

Bilal, Muhammed's black slave that became Abu Bakr' slave

Sahih Bukhari, Vol. 5, Page 69, Hadith 99 "Narrated Qais: Bilal said to Abu Bakr: If you have bought me for yourself, then keep me (for yourself), but if you have bought me for Allah's sake, then leave me for Allah's Work." [Unquote: Bilal was not a free-man, after Muhammed's death, he was Abu Bakr's slave.]

Muhammad traded with black slaves

Sahih Muslim: "Jabir (Allah be pleased with him) reported: There came a slave and pledged allegiance to Allah's Apostle (ﷺ) on migration; he (the Holy Prophet) did not know that he was a slave. Then came his master and demanded him back, whereupon Allah's Apostle (ﷺ) said: Sell him to me. **And he bought him for two black slaves**…" https://quranx.com/Hadith/Muslim/USC-MSA/Book-10/Hadith-3901

Last accessed 27 April 2021

Black slaves were displayed in mosques

Sahih Bukhari, Vol. 2, Page 56, Hadith 103 "Aisha further said: Once the Prophet (ﷺ) was screening me and I was watching **the display of black slaves in the Mosque** and (`Umar) scolded them."

Islam and the word "kaffir"

The most hated racist word used against black South Africans is "Kaffir". This word comes from the Arabic language of "white" Asian-Arabs. Kaffir, in Arabic, means "*unbeliever*".

Black people will go to hell and white people goes to heaven

On the Day of Judgement, Allah will make all believers (true Muslims) to become white people and then they will enter heaven and all non-Muslims will become black people and they will enter hell.

The Noble Quran – Surah 3:106 "On the Day (i.e. of Resurrection) when some faces **will become white [abyad]** and some faces **will become black [aswad]** as for those whose faces who will become black (to them will be said): Did you reject faith… Then taste (in hell) the torment for rejecting faith. 107 And for those whose faces will become white, they will be in Allah's Mercy (paradise), therein they shall dwell forever."

G.J.O. Moshay - Who is this Allah? Page 164 "[MUHAMMAD SAID] … Allah created Adam… Then He stroke his right shoulder and took out a white race as if they were seeds and He stroke his left shoulder and took out a black race as if they were coals. Then He said to those on his right side [whites]: Towards paradise and I don't care. **HE SAID TO THOSE WHO WERE ON HIS LEFT [BLACKS] TOWARDS HELL AND I DON'T CARE.**"

Allah's worse creation was a black man

Sahih Muslim: "Ubaidullah b. Abu Rafi', the freed slave of the Messenger of Allah (ﷺ) said… **The Messenger of Allah (ﷺ) described their characteristics and I found these characteristics in them.** They state the truth with their tongue, but it doesn't go beyond this part of their bodies (throat). **The most hateful among the creation of Allah is one black man among them (Khawarij)."**

https://quranx.com/Hadith/Muslim/USC-MSA/Book-5/Hadith-2334 Last accessed 27 April 2021

Now compare Muhammad's teaching with Apostle Paul's teaching:

Galatians 3:26 "**FOR YE ARE ALL THE CHILDREN OF GOD** by faith in Christ Jesus… 28 There is neither Jew nor Greek … for ye are all one in Christ Jesus." Thank God I am a Christian who submitted to Paul's teaching of race equality and not Muhammad's racist teaching.

55 Was Muhammad bewitched and possessed?

Sahih Bukhari Vol. 4, Page 267, Hadith 400 "Narrated Aisha: Once the Prophet (ﷺ) was bewitched so that he began to imagine that he had done a thing which in fact he had not done."

Sahih Bukhari, Vol 8, Page 56, Hadith 89 "Narrated `Aisha: The Prophet continued for such-and-such period imagining that he has slept (had sexual relations) with his wives and in fact he didn't. One day he said to me: Aisha! Allah has instructed me regarding a matter about which I had asked Him. There came to me two men, one of them sat near my feet and the other near my head. The one near my feet, asked the one near my head (pointing at me) - What is wrong with him? The latter replied: He is under the effect of magic… [by] Lubaid bin Asam (a man from Bani Zuraiq, an ally of the Jews). The first one asked: What material (did he use)? The other replied: The skin of the pollen of a male date tree with a comb and the hair stuck to it, kept under a stone in the well of Dharwan… The Prophet said: Allah cured me…"

According to these quotations, Muhammad was under the power and control of Satan and according to the Quran, only evil people are under the power and control of Satan.

Quran Translation by Abdullah Yusuf Ali – Surah 15:42 "For over My servants, no authority shalt thou [Satan] have, except such as put themselves in the wrong and follow thee [Satan]."

Muhammad also admitted that he had a devil.

Sahih Muslim: "Abdullah b. Mas'ud reported Allah's Messenger said: There is none amongst you with whom is not an attache from amongst the jinn (devil). The Companions said: Allah's Messenger, with you too? Thereupon he said: Yes, but Allah helps me against him and so I am safe from his hand and *he does not command me, but for good*." https://quranx.com/Hadith/Muslim/USC-MSA/Book-39/Hadith-6757

Last accessed 27 April 2021

56 Does Quran teach Muhammad is the last messenger?

According to the Quran, there is a *distinction* between a messenger and a prophet. It is two different offices. The Quran refer to Muhammad as a messenger and the seal of the prophets.

Quran Translation by Abdullah Yusuf Ali – Surah 19:51, 22:52, 33:40 "…Moses: for he was specially chosen and he was a messenger (**_and_**) a prophet… Never did we send an apostle **or** a prophet before thee… Muhammad the apostle **_and_** the seal of the prophets… Ali's comm. 2503 page 778 Moses was a prophet (received inspiration) _and_ an apostle (had a book of revelation) ..."

Nowhere does the Quran state that Muhammad was the last messenger. The Quran indicated that **a messenger always appears after a prophet.**

Quran Translation by Abdullah Yusuf Ali – Surahs 33:7, 3:81 "…We took from the prophets their covenant: As (We did) from thee… Allah took the covenant of the prophets, saying: "I give you a Book and Wisdom; **_then comes_** to you a messenger, confirming what is with you…"

Islam teach when Jesus returns God's revelation will continue.

The Noble Quran: Page 895 – Appendix II "The Divine revelation has stopped after the death of Prophet Muhammad and it will not resume, **except at the time of the descend of Isa (Jesus)**…"

How did Muhammad die?

Quran Translation by Shakir – Surah 69:45 "And if he had fabricated against Us some of the sayings, We would certainly have seized him by the right hand, Then We would certainly have cut off his aorta."

Tafsîr Ibn 'Abbâs 69:46 "(And then severed his life artery) the life artery of Muhammad (pbuh) https://quranx.com/Tafsir/Abbas/69.46 Last accessed 27 April 2021

Allah said if Muhammad will fabricate lies, Allah will cut off his aorta. Let's see how Muhammad died.

Sahih Bukhari, **Vol. 5, Page 510, Hadith 713** "Narrated `Aisha: The Prophet (ﷺ) in his ailment in which he died, used to say: O `Aisha! I still feel the pain caused by the food I ate at Khaibar and this time, **I feel as if my aorta is being cut from that poison**."

Sunan Abu Dawud: Narrated Abu Hurairah… The Messenger of Allah used to accept presents but not alms (sadaqah). This version adds: So a Jewess presented him at Khaybar with a roasted sheep which she had poisoned. The Messenger of Allah (ﷺ) ate of it and the people also ate. He then said: Take away your hands (from the food), for it has informed me that it is poisoned. Bishr ibn al-Bara' ibn Ma'rur al-Ansari died. So he (the Prophet) sent for the Jewess (and said to her): What motivated you to do the work you have done? She said: If you were a prophet, it would not harm you; but if you were a king, I should rid the people of you. The Messenger of Allah (ﷺ) then ordered regarding her and she was killed. *He then said about the pain of which he died: I continued to feel pain from the morsel which I had eaten at Khaybar. This is the time when it has cut off my aorta.*"

https://quranx.com/Hadith/AbuDawud/Hasan/Hadith-4497 Last accessed 27 April 2021

Muhammad's aorta was cut exactly as Allah said, proving Muhammad was a fabricator of verses of the Quran. When Jesus' death was initiated by the Jews, Jesus prayed for their forgiveness (Luke 23:34) but Muhammad ordered the Jewess to be killed proving that Jesus is merciful.

Muhammad received Quran wearing woman clothes

Sahih Bukhari, **Vol. 3, Page 455, Hadith 755** "Narrated `Urwa from `Aisha... Um Salama said... (the Messenger of Allah) said to her: Do not hurt me regarding Aisha, as the Divine Inspirations *DO NOT* come to me on any of **THE BEDS, EXCEPT THAT OF AISHA**."

Can you imagine Muhammad (54 years) **ONLY** received inspiration when laying in his youngest (9 years) wife's bed? But is the translation above correct? Here is an Arabian Christian's translation for the above.

YouTube: Rob Christian [RC] – Prophet Muhammad a crossdresser! According to RC: "Muhammad said: Divine revelation do not come to me in the **GARMENT OF ANY WOMAN, EXCEPT THAT OF AISHA**." https://www.youtube.com/wratch?v=ddKW_bwe2Vw Clip is 04:47long. Last accessed 27 April 2021

SECTION 6

ALLAH

56 Has the word "Allah" been omitted from the Holy Bible?

Deedat claimed that Christians tampered with the Holy Bible and corrupted it by removing the word "*Allah"* from its text: **Is the Bible the Word of God? Page 22** "The word "Allah" in the Christian Bible. *IN THE LATEST SCOFIELD VERSION, THE WORD "ALLAH" IS NOW OMITTED."*

We have the evidence before us in the **SCOFIELD COMMENTARY** addressed by Deedat. On the same page of his book, a reproduction of a page from *Scofield's First Edition* is provided and on this page a <u>Hebrew</u> word spelled "ALAH" is mentioned in Scofield's commentary. In *Scofield's Second Edition*, this word has been **OMITTED FROM HIS COMMENTARY**.

Only a mentally challenged person, like Deedat, will look at changes made in Scofield's Commentaries as changes made in the Biblical text. No honest Muslim will agree with Deedat's sick idea that biblical textual corruption took place, since the word "alah" is removed from Scofield's Commentary in his second edition. Once more, Deedat's deceptive arguments falls flat to the ground. In fact, in the Bible, in the <u>Hebrew</u> manuscript of our scriptures, there is a <u>Hebrew</u> word "*allah*" and it means: "*oak tree*".

<u>Joshua 24:26</u> "Joshua wrote these words in the book of the law of **God [Elohym]** and took a great stone and set it up there under an **oak [allah]** that was by the sanctuary of the **LORD [Jehovah]**."

YOU CAN PICK UP ANY HEBREW MANUSCRIPT COPY AND YOU, JUST LIKE I DID, YOU WILL FIND THE HEBREW WORD "ALLAH" IN JOSHUA 24:26 UNCHANGED FOR THE PAST THOUSANDS OF YEARS.

57 What is God's name?

Allah is a good Arabic translation for "the God".

<u>Ahmed Deedat: "What is His name?" Pages 10, 25 and 32</u> "God in other languages: "God in English, Got in Afrikaans, Gott in German, Gudd in Danish, Swedish and Norwegian languages ... Elah in Hebrew, Dieus in Portuguese, Dieu in French, Dio in Italian, Dios in Spanish, Dia in Scotland and Irish. Duw in Welsh, **THE ARABIC WORD ALLAH ... IS A UNIQUE WORD FOR GOD.**"

It is already stated by Muslims (see Q11) that Deedat was not a man of Islamic learning. Deedat is wrong again, Allah is **"NOT"** a unique word for "God". The Arabic word Allah = *al + lah*. *"Al"* translates into *"the"* and *"lah"* after the "i" has been dropped, translate into *"God"*. Allah is not a name, but an Arabic translation for the English words: *"The God"*. That is why Christian Arabs use the term *Allah* for "the God".

<u>Muslim Scholar Basheer A. Vania – An Analysis of the Concept of Divinity: Page 7b</u> "Monotheistic: The Islamic Deity is not merely **"god"** (ilah), but **"the God"** (Allah)."

That *ilah* is a good translation for *"God or god"* can easily be confirmed by reading Ali's translation:

<u>Quran Translation by Abdullah Yusuf Ali – Surah 1:1</u> "Bismi**laah**ir-Rahmannir-Rahim... In the name of **G**od, most Gracious, most Merciful ... 16:22 "**ilaah**ukum 'i**laah**unw-waahid... Your **G**od is one **G**od... 2:163 "Wa'**llaah**ukum 'I**laah**unw-Waahid: Laaa '**ilaah**a... And your **G**od is One **G**od: There is no **g**od, but He ... 3:6 ...Laaa '**ilaah**a 'illaa Huwal... there is no **g**od, but He..."

Ali's translation clearly illustrates that **ilah** is a unique word for "**G**od" (Almighty) and also for "**g**od" (idol).

SINCE "ILAAH" HAVE A DUAL MEANING (GOD or god) IT CAN'T BE THE UNIQUE "NAME" FOR THE ALMIGHTY GOD. AS ALREADY ILLUSTRATED, ALLAH ISN'T GOD'S NAME, BUT THE ARABIC TRANSLATION FOR THE ENGLISH WORDS "THE

GOD". NOWHERE IN THE QURAN DOES THE CREATOR SAY: *"MY NAME IS ALLAH"* NOWHERE! I CHALLENGE MUSLIMS TO PROVIDE ONLY ONE QURANIC-VERSE AS PROOF. IF YOU CAN, I WILL ACKNOWLEDGE THAT GOD'S NAME FOR MUSLIMS IS ALLAH, IF YOU CAN'T, STOP FOOLING YOURSELF AND ACKNOWLEDGE THAT GOD'S NAME IS NOT ALLAH.

The Bible and God's Name

To know God's name, the seeker has to turn to the pages of the Holy Bible. In it we read about a prophecy in the Jewish manuscripts, dated hundreds of years before Christianity of how God will come to the earth:

Isaiah 9:5 "For unto us a child is born, unto us a son is given and the government shall be upon his shoulder and his name shall be called Wonderful, Counsellor, **The Mighty God**, The Everlasting Father, The of Peace…"

It won't be hard for both Muslim and Christian to guess what the name is of the person that will be called by the attribute: Mighty God. Note how Isaiah predicted this 700 years, before Jesus came to earth.

Matthew 1:21 "…And thou shall call His name JESUS…"

The reason why the devil and his advocates are against the Holy Name of the Lord Jesus Christ, which is above all other names, is because of the eternal benefit of salvation that mankind derives from the matchless Name as demonstrated in the Bible: **ACTS 4:10-12** "…IT IS BY THE NAME OF JESUS CHRIST … SALVATION IS FOUND IN NO-ONE ELSE, FOR THERE IS NO OTHER NAME UNDER HEAVEN GIVEN TO MEN BY WHICH WE MUST BE SAVED!"

58 Characteristics of Allah in the Quran

Muslims mock the Jewish-Christian Holy Bible, because it gives sharp descriptions, limitations, etc. to God. I truly believe God knows all things, are Perfection beyond

Perfection, and that His Personality, Movements, Thoughts, etc. are Pure Mysterious and what we know about God, is what He revealed to us about Himself in the Holy Bible.

NLT Proverbs 18:17 "Any story seems to be true, until someone sets the record straight."

The questions below are "only" to demonstrate how bias Muslims are towards the Holy Bible.

Does Allah know all things?

Faruq Sheriff informs us: ***A guide to the contents of the Quran. Page 24*** "Several passages in the Quran **IMPLY THAT GOD SEEK KNOWLEDGE,** which he did not possess before: IN ORDER TO OVERCOME THE DIFFICULTY some translators have rendered the phrase *"that he may know (la ya'lam)"* by the words *"that he may test"*, BUT THIS DOES NOT REMOVE THE DIFFICULTY, because *testing also implies an attempt at ascertaining what was in doubt before.* Indeed, in one instance God actually "tests" in order to "know"."

Quran Translation by Abdullah Yusuf Ali – Surahs 2:143, 3:140, 166, 5:94, 11:7, 18:7, 20:43 "…We appointed the Qibla to which thou were used, **ONLY TO TEST THOSE WHO FOLLOWED THE APOSTLE, FROM THOSE WHO WOULD TURN ON THEIR HEELS**. If a wound hath touched you, be sure a similar wound hath touched the others. Such days (of varying fortunes) we give to men and men by turns: that God **MAY KNOW THOSE THAT BELIEVE** … What ye suffered on the day the two armies met was with the leave of God, **IN ORDER THAT HE MIGHT TEST THE BELIEVERS** … O ye who believe! God doth, but make a trial of you in a little matter of game well within reach of game, well within reach of your hands and your lances, that **HE MAY TEST WHO FEAR HIM UNSEEN** … And His Throne was upon the water, that **HE MIGHT TRY YOU, WHICH OF YOU ARE BEST IN CONDUCT**… Then We roused them, **IN ORDER TO TEST WHICH OF THE TWO PARTIES WAS BEST** at calculating the term of years they had tarried … [God said to Moses:] Go both of you [Moses and Aaron] to Pharaoh … speak to him [Pharaoh] mildly, **PERCHANCE HE MAY TAKE WARNING OR FEAR (GOD)**."

It appears that God didn't know whether Pharaoh would take warning. Yes! Pharaoh did not take warning and only at the stage of drowning, as per Quran (Surah 10:90-93), did Pharaoh scream for help.

Quran Translation by Abdullah Yusuf Ali – Surah 29:3, 67:2, 72:26-28 "**WE DID TEST** those before them and God will certainly know those who are true from those who are false ... He who created Death and Life, **THAT HE MAY TRY WHICH OF YOU IS BEST IN DEED**... He (alone) know the unseen, nor does He make any one acquainted with his mysteries, except an apostle whom He has chosen and then He makes a band of watches march before him and behind him, **THAT HE MAY KNOW WHETHER THEY HAVE BROUGHT THE MESSAGES OF THEIR LORD**..."

Quran Translation by Abdullah Yusuf Ali – Surah 12:20 "The (Brethren) sold him for a miserable price, **FOR A FEW DIRHAMS** counted out: in such low estimation did they hold him!"

Allah can only guess Joseph was sold for a few dirhams. Contrast this with the Bible: ***Genesis 37:28*** "So when the Midianite merchants came by, his brothers pulled Joseph up out of the cistern and sold him **FOR TWENTY SHEKELS OF SILVER** to the Ishmaelite, who took him to Egypt."

Allah does not know exact information: ***Quran Translation by Abdullah Yusuf Ali – Surah 53:1-9*** "...Then he approached and came closer, and was at a distance of but two bow-lengths **OR (EVEN) NEARER**."

One Muslim will vanquish 10 unbelievers

Quran Translation by Abdullah Yusuf Ali – Surah 8:65 "O Apostle! Rouse the believers to the fight. If there are twenty [20] amongst you, patient and persevering, they will vanquish two hundred [200], if a hundred [100] they will vanquish a thousand [1000] of the unbelievers..."

Here Allah, promised the Islamic army that one believer will vanquish ten unbelievers. But it is obvious that the unbelievers were not going to stand still for a slaughter amongst them. They were going to fight nail and teeth to the bitter end. And as expected, Muhammad or Allah's military prophecy did not succeed and Muhammad or Allah had to amend their promise to be more realistic.

Quran Translation by Abdullah Yusuf Ali – Surah 8:66 "For the present, God hath lightened your (task) for He knows that there is a weak spot in you. But (even so), if there are a hundred [100] of you, patient and persevering, they will vanquish two hundred [200] …"

Now the odds have been lightened from one against ten, to one against two, because Allah now realizes that there is a weak spot in them. Didn't Allah know this earlier?

Allah prescribing and altering fasting to satisfy Muslim lust

Quran Translation by Abdullah Yusuf Ali – Surah 2:183 "O ye who believe! **FASTING IS PRESCRIBED TO YOU *AS IT WAS PRESCRIBED* TO THOSE BEFORE YOU**…"

But, the Muslims could not practice fasting without sex, like the Jews and Christians, even Muhammed French-kissed his childbride while fasting…

Sunan Abu Dawud "Narrated Aisha, Ummul Mu'minin: The Prophet (ﷺ) used to kiss her and suck her tongue when he was fasting." https://quranx.com/Hadith/AbuDawud/Hasan/Hadith-2380

Last accessed 27 April 2021

So Allah four verses later altered the limits for the Muslims to satisfy their strong sexual desire.

Quran Translation by Abdullah Yusuf Ali – Surah 2:187 "Permitted to you, on the night of the fasts, is the approach [sexual intercourse] to your wives … God know what ye used to do [have sex during the nights of Ramadan] secretly amongst yourselves. But he turned to you and forgave you, **SO NOW ASSOCIATE WITH THEM [HAVE SEX WITH YOUR WIVES DURING RAMADAN NIGHTS]** … until the white thread of dawn appears to you distinct from its black thread; then complete your fast till the night appears; but do not associate with your wives [do not have sexual relations] while ye are in retreat in the mosques. Those are limits (set by) Allah..."

Muslims did not learn self-restrain, but they learnt that if they do opposite to what Allah prescribed, Allah will adjust his laws for their lustful satisfaction. In addition, Muhammad not only suck his wives' tongues while fasting, he also fondled them during menstruation.

Sunan an-Nasa'i "It was narrated that 'Aishah said: The Messenger of Allah (ﷺ) would tell one of us, if she was menstruating, to tie her Izar (waist wrap) tightly then he would fondle her."

https://quranx.com/Hadith/Nasai/DarusSalam/Volume-1/Book-1/Hadith-286   Last accessed 20 June 2021

Allah decree adultery

We understood (see bullet kk) from the Quran (Surah 4:78) that all evil is from Allah. Let's look at a tradition to see, if Muhammad taught that Allah is responsible for evil on the earth.

Sahih Bukhari, Vol. 8, Page 397-398, Hadith 609 "The Prophet said: "**ALLAH HAS WRITTEN FOR THE SON OF ADAM HIS INEVITABLE SHARE OF ADULTERY,** whether he is aware of it or not..."

➢ Allah planned what sin men will commit

Sahih Bukhari, Vol. 8, Page 399, Hadith 611 "The Prophet said... Adam said to Moses ... Do you blame me for **ACTION, WHICH ALLAH HAD WRITTEN IN MY FATE** forty years before my creation?"

Here we see that Adam blames Allah for his disobedience in the garden.

Allah brings misfortune into existence

Quran Translation by Abdullah Yusuf Ali – Surah 57:22 "**NO MISFORTUNE** can happen on earth or in your souls, but is recorded in a decree before **WE BRING IT INTO EXISTENCE**..."

Whatever evil happens on the earth, Allah brings it into existence.

Allah deceives, misleads and sends people astray

CAMBRIDGE ADVANCED LEARNER'S DICT. 4TH EDITION – PAGE 388 "Deceive – to persuade someone that something false is the truth."

The Noble Quran Surah 4:142 "…The hypocrites seek to deceive Allah, but it is **HE WHO DECEIVES** them…"

The Qur'an (Saheeh International) Surah 4:142 "…But **HE IS DECEIVING** them…"

Tafsir - Ibn Al Kathir S. 4:142 "(But it is He Who deceives them) *means: He lures them further into injustice and misguidance. He also prevents them from reaching the truth* in this life and on the Day of Resurrection." https://quranx.com/Tafsir/Kathir/4.142 Last accessed 27 April 2021

Who is the best deceiver: Unbelievers or Satan or Allah? Let the Quran 3:54 speak:

Quran Translation by Abdullah Yusuf Ali – Surah 3:54 "The unbelievers plotted and planned, Allah too planned, the best of **planners** [al**ma**kireena] is Allah."

Tafsir - Ibn Al Kathir S. 3:54 "However, **ALLAH DECEIVED** these people."

https://quranx.com/Tafsir/Kathir/3.52 Last accessed 27 April 2021

"They CHEATED/DECEIVED and GOD CHEATED/DECEIVED. **GOD THE BEST (OF) CHEATERS/DECEIVERS.**"

http://www.alquranenglish.com/quran-surah-ali-imran-54-qs-3-54-in-arabic-and-english-translation

Last accessed 27 April 2021

al**ma**kireena means **cunning**

https://www.google.com/search?q=english+for+almakireena&oq=english+for+almakireena&aqs=chrome..69i57.13921j1j7&sourceid=chrome&ie=UTF-8 Last accessed 27 April 2021

- ✓ Who deceives certain people? Allah! Put the blame where it belongs.
- ✓ Who lures people into injustice? Allah! Put the blame where it belongs.
- ✓ Who prevents people from truth? Allah!
- ✓ Who is the best deceiver? Allah.

CAMBRIDGE ADVANCED LEARNER'S DICT. 4TH EDITION – PAGE 984 "Mislead – to cause someone to believe something that is not true."

The Noble Quran Surah 14:4 "...**ALLAH MISLEADS** whom He wills and guides whom He wills..." (2:26)

Muslims admit that Allah misleads people and they even say it publicly, here is such as example: https://www.youtube.com/watch?v=Cul1CcKf0cU&t=7200s time line 01:57:15 – 02:00:20

Last accessed 27 April 2021

The Noble Quran – Surah 4:88 "...**ALLAH HAS CAST THEM BACK (TO DISBELIEF)**, because of what they have earned. Do you want to guide him whom **ALLAH HAS MADE TO GO ASTRAY**..."

Tafsir - Ibn Al Kathir S. 4:88 "(Allah has cast them back, because of what they earned) **meaning: He made them revert to and fall into error.**" https://quranx.com/Tafsir/Kathir/4.88 Last accessed 27 April 2021

Quran Translation by Abdullah Yusuf Ali: "...**GOD HATH THROWN OUT** of the way..."

The Noble Quran – Surah 6:35, 125 "...Hath Allah willed, He could have gathered them together (all) on true guidance... **WHOMSOEVER HE WILLS TO SEND ASTRAY, HE MAKES HIS BREAST CLOSED**..." (40:33)

- ✓ Who misleads people? Allah! Put the blame where it belongs.
- ✓ Who sends people astray? Allah! Put the blame where it belongs.
- ✓ Who makes people fall into error? Allah! Put the blame where it belongs.

See https://wikiislam.net/wiki/Allah,_the_Best_Deceiver_(Qur%27an_3:54) Last accessed 27 April 2021

If we compare the God of the Christians with the god of the Muslims, we find that the God of Christianity is FAITHFUL at all times. For the Christian God to mislead people is unthinkable based on His Faithfulness! It is blasphemous to say God is a deceiver, misleader and One who takes people from the right way and mercilessly throw them into error. That is the work of Satan. How Allah describes himself with the characteristics of Satan is shocking to a true believer. No Christian will ever believe in such falsehood.

1 Corinthians 10:13 "…God is faithful…" (2 Timothy 2:13)

Allah spreads hatred

Meaning of Glorious Quran – Surah 5:14 "And with those who say: "Lo! we are Christians," We made a covenant, but they forgot a part of that whereof they were admonished. Therefor **We have stirred up enmity and hatred among them till the Day of Resurrection**, when Allah will inform them of their handiwork."

Allah and hate speech towards non-Muslims

Quran Translation by Abdullah Yusuf Ali – Surah 98:6 "Those who reject (Truth), among the People of the Book and among the Polytheists, will be in Hell-Fire, to dwell therein (forever). **They are the worst of creatures**." [Unquote: Are people worst then pigs, worms, insects, etc.?]

Allah's messenger kills the innocent

Quran Translation by Abdullah Yusuf Ali – Surah 18:65-81 "…When they met a young man, he slew him, Moses said: "Hast thou slain an **INNOCENT PERSON** who had slain none? Now will I tell thee the interpretation … As for the youth his parents were people of faith and **WE FEARED THAT HE WOULD GRIEVE THEM**…" Here an innocent person was killed for possible sins he _might_ commit in the future.

Quran Translation by Abdullah Yusuf Ali – Surah 17:16 "When We decide to **DESTROY A POPULATION**, we (first) send a definite order to those among them who are given the good things of this life and yet transgress; so that the word is proved true against them: then (it is) We destroy them utterly." [18:59] When Allah decide to destroy a population (men, women, children and babies), He does it completely.

Sanun Abu Dawud: "Narrated Atiyyah al-Qurazi: I was among the captives of Banu Qurayzah. They (the Companions) examined us, and those who had begun to grow hair (pubes) were killed, and those who had not were not killed. I was among those who had not grown hair.

https://quranx.com/Hadith/AbuDawud/Hasan/Hadith-4390 Last accessed 27 April 2021

According to Quran, Allah was, not, Allah is

The Noble Quran Surah 4:1 "…Allah **IS** ever, an all-watcher over you." [Surahs 33:1-2, 35:45, 76:30]

What is wrong with this verse? In the Arabic, it does not use the present tense, but the past tense "**kan**", which should be translated as "was". Let's see how other Arabic Scholars rendered this verse:

Pickthall translated it as: **_Meaning of Glorious Quran_** "…Lo! Allah **hath been** a watcher over you."

Tafsir - Tanwîr al-Miqbâs min Tafsîr Ibn 'Abbâs Surah 4:1 "…(Lo! Allah **hath been** a Watcher over you)…" https://quranx.com/Tafsir/Abbas/4.1 Last accessed 27 April 2021

Tafsir Al-Jalalayn S. 4:1 "…Surely God **has been** watchful over you…" https://quranx.com/Tafsir/Jalal/4.1 Last accessed 27 April 2021

> ➢ Allah forgets like human-beings

Quran Translation by Abdullah Yusuf Ali – Surah 9:67, 7:51 "They have forgotten Allah, so He had forgotten them … **We forget them, as they forgot**…" (45:34) [Unquote:] Allah forgets like humans.

Allah will inherit the earth

Quran Translation by Abdullah Yusuf Ali – Surah 19:40 "Lo! We, only WE, INHERIT the earth and all who are thereon…"

Allah's image

> ***Genesis 1:26*** "God said: Let us make man in our image, after our likeness…"

Islam also teaches that Allah has an image: **The Noble Quran – Page 123 Footnote 1:** "Narrated Abu Huraira: The prophet said: **ALLAH CREATED ADAM IN HIS IMAGE SIXTY CUBITS IN HEIGHT**…"

Allah is **about** 27,432 metres in height – Allah and Adam qualified to be giants!

Conversion http://extraconversion.com/length/cubits/cubits-to-meters.html Last accessed 27 April 2021

The Noble Quran – Page 777 Footnote 1 C "Narrated Abu-Sa'ld Al-Khudri: We said: Allah's messenger! Shall we see our Lord … He said: **YOU WILL HAVE NO DIFFICULTY IN SEEING YOUR LORD** on that day as you have no difficulty in seeing the sun and the moon. **ALMIGHTY WILL COME TO THEM IN A SHAPE** other than the one which they saw the first time … It will be said to them: Do you know any sign by which **YOU CAN RECOGNIZE HIM? THEY WILL SAY: THE SHIN. SO ALLAH WILL UNCOVER HIS SHIN**… (*Sahih Bukhari Vol. 9 Pages 395-396 Hadith 532B*)" [Unquote: From this Hadith we learn that Allah have at least two different shapes in which He appears.]

Sahih Bukhari Vol. 6, Page 353, Hadith 371 "Narrated Anas: The Prophet said: The people will be thrown into the Hell Fire and it will say: Are there any more (to come)? (50.30) till Allah puts **HIS FOOT** over it…"

The Noble Quran Surah 11:37 "But construct an Ark under Our **EYES**..."

Sahih Bukhari, Vol. 9, Page 369, Hadith 505 "Narrated Anas: The Prophet said: Ad-Dajjal is one-eyed, while your **Lord is not one-eyed**."

The Noble Quran – Pages 892 – Appendix II "There is nothing like unto Him and He is the All-Hearer, the Seer. (V. 42:11) This holy verse proves the quality of **HEARING** and the quality of **SIGHT FOR ALLAH** without likening them to any of the created things. He also says: To one whom I have created with **BOTH MY HANDS**. (V. 38:75)."

The Noble Quran – Page 81 Footnote 1 "All that has been revealed in Allah's Book (the Qur'an) as regards the (Sifat) Qualities of Allah, the Most High, LIKE HIS FACE, EYES, HANDS, SHINS, (LEGS), HIS COMING, HIS ISTAWA (RISING OVER) HIS THRONE AND OTHERS; His Qualities or all that Allah's Messenger qualified Him in the true authentic Prophet's Ahadith (narrations) as regards His Qualities like (Nuzul) HIS DESCENT OR HIS LAUGHING AND OTHERS ETC. **THE RELIGIOUS SCHOLARS OF THE QUR'AN AND THE SUNNA BELIEVE IN THESE QUALITIES OF ALLAH AND THEY CONFIRM THAT THESE ARE REALLY HIS QUALITIES,** without Ta'wil (interpreting their meanings into different things) or Tashbih (giving resemblance or similarity to any of the creatures) or Ta'til (e.g. completely ignoring or denying them e.g. there is no Face, or Eyes or Hands, or Shins etc. for Allah). These Qualities befit or suit only Allah Alone, and He does not resemble any of (His) creatures. As Allah's Statements (in the Qur'an): (1) There is nothing like unto Him, and He is the All-Hearer, the All-Seer (V.42:11). (2) There is none comparable unto Him (V.112:4)."

In light of these preceding factors we are left with two possibilities:

1. Allah has an actual body (30 meters high), making him a giant.

2. Allah assumes a visible shape that will be seen. Muslims should have no problem with God assuming an angelic form [Theophany] in the OT and the Incarnation of God in the Lord Jesus Christ in the NT.

Can Allah write?

The Noble Quran – Surah 7:145 "**We wrote** for him on the tablets..."

Sahih Bukhari, Vol. 9, Page 369, Hadith 501 "Narrated Abu Huraira: The Prophet said: When Allah created the Creation, **HE WROTE IN HIS BOOK ...** it is placed with Him on the Throne: My Mercy overcomes My Anger."

Does Allah promote incest?

Muslims have much to say about the incest recorded in the Holy Bible. What they fail to observe is that incest was not always a horrible sin in the eyes of Almighty God. For example, both the Bible and the Quran teach that the first human beings on earth was Adam and his wife. The Bible mentions her to be Eve. This would only imply that God intended for their children, who obviously was first bloodline brothers and sisters, to have sex in holy matrimony and to bring forth offspring. Therefore, we should determine when God forbid it and then judge it as disobedience after God prohibited it. In Islam, incest even took place six hundred years after the Bible, when Muhammad married his own cousin Zainab, the ex-wife of his adopted son.

Message of the Quran: Page 645 Comm. 42 "The prophet persuaded Zayd to marry his [Muhammed's] **OWN COUSIN, ZAYNAB BINT JAHSH...**"

Message of the Quran – Surah 33:37 "We gave **HER** to thee in marriage."

Allah promote lip services (lies)

Surah 16:106

Quran Translation by Abdullah Yusuf Ali – Surah "Anyone who, after accepting faith in Allah, **UTTERS UNBELIEF - EXCEPT UNDER COMPULSION,** his heart remaining firm in Faith - but such as open their breast to Unbelief, on them is Wrath from Allah and theirs will be a dreadful Penalty."

Authorized English Version of the Quran "Those who disbelieve in God, after having acquired faith and become fully content with disbelief, have incurred wrath from God.

THE ONLY ONES TO BE EXCUSED ARE THOSE WHO ARE FORCED TO PROFESS DISBELIEF, while their hearts are full of faith."

Authorized English Version of the Quran: Footnote on Surah 16:106: God's wisdom decrees that if someone holds a gun by your head and orders you to declare that you disbelief in God, you may grant him his wish. What the heart harbor is what counts."

Message of the Quran: Page 413 Comm. 134 "This relates to believers who, under torture or threat of death, ostensibly "recant" in order to save themselves."

In the Bible we are directed to tell the truth: **THERE'S NO ROOM FOR LIP SERVICE IN CHRISTIANITY, BELIEVING WITH THE HEART AND HYPOCRITICALLY DENY GOD WITH THE MOUTH IS OUT.**

Here are the Master's true words: **_Matthew 10:38-39_** "He that takes not his cross and follows after Me, is not worthy of Me. He that finds his life shall lose it and he that lose his life for My sake shall find it." Here are the inspired words of the Master through His True Apostle Paul: **_Romans 10:9_** "That if thou shalt **CONFESS WITH THY MOUTH** the Lord Jesus and shalt believe in thine heart that God hath raised Him from the dead, thou shalt be saved" **_Romans 8:35_** "Who shall separate us from the love of Christ? Shall tribulation or distress or persecution or famine or nakedness or peril or sword? As it is written, for Thy sake we are killed all the day long, we are accounted as sheep for the slaughter, nay, in all these things we are more than conquerors through Him that love us. For I am persuaded, that neither death, nor life, no angels, nor principalities, nor powers, nor things present, nor things to come, nor height, nor depth, nor any other creature, shall be able to separate us from the love of God, which in Christ Jesus our Lord."

G.J.O. Moshay - Who is this Allah? Page 49 "We are not afraid. We win by losing, we conquer by dying. Augustine, describing the experience of the early Christians, said: The martyrs were bound, jailed, scourged, racked, burned, rent, butchered... and they multiplied."

Allah inspired making of images (images in heaven)

Muslims argue that the Bible is corrupted and not the Word of God, because it teaches men to make images of heavenly beings. I agree that it is **idolatry to bow before graven idols in an act of worship**, as is exactly the case with Muslims that kisses a Black Stone in adoration [see Q35]. The Bible is against idolatry, but not against craftsmanship. Surprisingly, the Quran agrees that Allah's inspiration was the initial channel for the making of images and statues.

Quran Translation by Abdullah Yusuf Ali – Surah 34:12-13 "…Solomon … by the **LEAVE OF HIS LORD** and if any of them [Jinns] turned aside from **OUR COMMAND,** we made him taste of the penalty of the blazing fire. They [jinns] worked for him as desired (making) arches, **IMAGES**…"

Quran Translation by Abdullah Yusuf Ali: Page 1137 Commentary 3806 "Images would be like the images of oxen and *cherubims*."

Jami` at-Tirmidhi "Ali narrated the **MESSENGER OF ALLAH (S.A.W) SAID**: **IN PARADISE THERE IS A MARKET** in which there is no buying nor selling, except for images of men and women. If you desire an image, enter it." https://quranx.com/Hadith/Tirmidhi/DarusSalam/Volume-4/Book-36/Hadith-2550

Last accessed 27 April 2021.

59 "One" God or "three" gods?

Both the Bible and Quran clearly teach that there is only O-N-E God.

- *Malachi 2:10* "…Hath not **ONE** God created us…"
- *Romans 3:30* "…It is **ONE** God, which shall justify the circumcision…"

Quran Translation by Abdullah Yusuf Ali – Surah 22:34 "…Your God is **ONE** God…"

There are not two or three or more TRUE gods. Nowhere in the Biblical scripture will you read about three gods. No true Bible-believing Christian upholds a doctrine of three gods.

That is polytheism. That is Satanic. I agree with the Bible and I agree with Islam that THERE IS ONLY ONE TRUE GOD. The debate between Christians and Muslims should never be around how many true gods there is, since both the Bible and Quran teach that there is only One True God, the differences of belief originates from the interpretations and conclusions between the followers of these respective scriptures and traditions.

If Muslims can show me a verse from the Bible (chapter and verse) [NOT YOUR INTERPRETATION], but a Bible verse that reads: "…there are three gods…" I will renounce Christianity and become an Atheist!

60 Is the word "Trinity" in the Bible text?

THE NEW BIBLE DICTIONARY - PAGE 1298: "The word *"Trinity"* isn't found in the Bible."

Although majority of Christians believe in the "Trinity" doctrine of God, still Bible translators from all denominations stayed honest to the Hebrew-Greek Bible manuscripts and didn't add the terminology "Trinity" to Bible Translations. There is no Bible Translation with the word "Trinity" **found in its verses.**

The word Trinity not found in the Arabic Quran

The word "Trinity" is also not found in the Arabic text of the Quran, but when some Muslim scholars translated the Arabic Quran into their English Versions, they could **NOT RESIST** the temptation to add the word "Trinity" into their versions to create a false idea in the minds of their uninformed readers that Allah in the Quran condemns the "Trinity" that Christians believe in.

Quran mistranslated to reflect the word Trinity

Quran Translation by Abdullah Yusuf Ali – Surah 4:171 "…Say not Trinity…"

The whole premise of Muslims **MIS**translating the Quranic text is to attack Christianity. Ali outrightly provided a wrong translation thinking that non-Arabs would not identify his error.

Christian writer: John Gilchrist: Facing the Muslim challenge – Page 87 "The word used here for **"three"** is **"thalathah"**, a common Quranic word appearing nineteen times in the book. It always means "three" and cannot be translated or rendered "Trinity".

Below are English Quran translations done by Muslims that gave the correct translation of Surah 4:171:

| Meaning of Glorious Quran "...Say not Three..." | The Koran "...Do not say: Three..." |

Let's say for argument sake that the "Trinity" doctrine is false; we would still expect Muslim scholars to be honest when they present us with English Quranic translations. They should not **MIS**translate the Quran to strengthen their misguided view in English Versions. That is blatant deception! **IF** Ali could so easily **MIS**translate the above verse, how many more verses did he mistranslate to make people think Allah in the Quran speaks out against the "Trinity"? Let's look at another deceptive mistranslation of Ali.

Quran Trans. by A. Yusuf Ali Surah 5:73 "They do blaspheme who say: Allah is one of three **in a Trinity**…"

Here again, Ali couldn't help himself, but to **MIS**translate the Quran in order to attack the "Trinity". Below is a more accurate translation from the Arabic into English.

Meaning of Glorious Quran "They surely disbelieve who say: Lo! Allah is the **THIRD OF THREE**…"

The word "Trinity" isn't mentioned at all in the ***Arabic Quranic text***. Ali totally mistranslated these verses by adding the word "Trinity" to his English Version to deceive his readers, to make them think Allah in the Quran speaks out against the "Trinity". Bible translators refrained from adding the word "Trinity" to their translations of the Bible. If only Muslim translators can follow the honest examples set by Christian translators. Muslims who quotes Ali's perverted English Version to discredit the "Trinity" is either ignorant of the Arabic Quranic text or knows that Ali's English Version is false, but uses it deceptively against uninformed Christians to attempt to win arguments on a false basis, that's open deception! That's a shame! The fact that the word "Trinity" is not in the Bible, is not a challenge for Trinitarian Christians, since their belief in the "Trinity" is not based on the much later developed "terminology", but their belief is based on the scriptures itself, from which they derive their understanding of the "Trinity". Their interpretation of scripture! The word "Trinity" is **"NOT"** found in both the Hebrew-Greek Biblical manuscripts with its various English Translations and in the Arabic Quran Text, but it is found in **MISTRANSLATIONS** by some deceiving Muslim Scholars who sells their English Qurans to make a profit.

61 Does the word "Tawhid" appear in the Quran?

Muslims have a hard time proving that Allah is a Unitarian-being. The most often quoted verse, Surah 112:1 "Qul [say:] huwa [He is] Allahu [Allah], **ahad** [one]" to show that Allah is singular, is actually a mistranslation and should be translated as: "Say: He is Allah, **one of [or anyone or none].**" Here are examples where **ahad** in *The Noble Quran* was correctly translated by Muslim Drs Hilali and Khan:

<u>Surah 112:4</u> "… yakun lahu kufuwan **ahad**un… there is **none** co-equal or comparable unto Him…"

<u>Surah 9:6</u> "Wain **ahad**un mina almushrikeena … And if **anyone of [one of]** the Mushrikun…"

<u>Surah 11:81</u> "…wala yaltafit minkum **ahad**un … and let not **any of you [one of you]** look back…"

<u>Surah 2:102</u> "…min **ahad**in illa biithni Allahi… harm **anyone [one of you]** except by Allah's leave"

<u>Surah 2:136</u> "… alnnabiyyoona… bayna **ahad**in … the Prophets … between **any of** them…"

The correct Arabic word for "one" is **wahid**.

The Noble Quran – Surah 37:4 "Inna ilahakum la**wahid**un … Verily your Ilah (God) is indeed **one**…"

The Noble Quran – Surah 2:163 "…ilahun **wahid**un … Ilah (God) is **one**…" (5:73, 16:22, 21:108, 38:5,65)

Sunan Ibn Majah "It was narrated from Abu Hurairah: The Messenger of Allah said: "Allah has ninety-nine names … Whoever learns them will enter Paradise. They are: Allah, Al-**Wahid** (The **One**) … Al-**Ahad** (the **Lone**)…" https://quranx.com/Hadith/IbnMajah/DarusSalam/Volume-5/Book-34/Hadith-3861

Last accessed 26 April 2021

✦ LET US NOW LOOK AT THE ARABIC TERMINOLOGY "TAUHIYD" TRANSLATED AS "ONENESS".

The Concept of Tawhid in Islam "The actual word ***"Tauhiyd"*** **DOES NOT APPEAR IN THE QURAN OR SUNNAH** though the present tense of the verb (from which ***"Tauhiyd"*** is derived) is used in the Sunnah. The division of ***"tauhiyd"*** into the components known to us today **WERE NOT DONE BY THE PROPHET OR HIS COMPANIONS**."

Just like the word "Trinity" that never came from the lips of Biblical characters, likewise the word *"Tawhid",* also never came from the lips of Muhammad, neither from the lips of his Companions until about 250-300 years after Muhammad's death. Both terms *"Trinity - Tawhid"* were first used by respective followers many years after the departure of their leaders. Amazingly, when Christians admit that the word "Trinity" does not appear in the Bible, Muslims often take this as prove that the Christian' belief of the Trinity is false, yet these same Muslims have no problem to accept the Islamic term "Tawhid" that also does not appear in the Quran.

MUSLIMS WHO THINK CHRISTIANS MUST REJECT THE WORD "TRINITY" BECAUSE IT IS NOT FOUND IN THE BIBLE, MUST ALSO REJECT THE WORD "TAWHID" BECAUSE IT IS ALSO NOT FOUND IN THE QURAN.

It is simply dishonest and inconsistent of Muslims to say Christians must reject the word "Trinity" because it isn't found in the Bible, yet they have no problem with the word "Tawhid" that isn't found in the Quran and the authentic Sunnah of Muhammad. This is exactly what brought Muslim scholar, Dr. Nabeel Qureshi to his knees to accept Christianity and to submit his heart to the Lord Jesus Christ, as his Savior, when he decided to approach Islam in the same mindset that he does Christianity, his convictions forced him to reject Islam and to become a Christian.

62 What did Muhammad mean by: "say not three..."?

Meaning of Glorious Quran – Surah 4:171 "...Say not three..." Unquote: **THREE WHAT?**

It is vitally important to note that Muhammad preached against a few misguided *CHRISTIANS IN ARABIA* who SEEMINGLY believed in a false godhead concept of **three distinct gods, namely: Allah being one god, Mary being a goddess and Jesus being a third god**.

Quran Trans. by Abdullah Yusuf Ali Surah 5:116 "...When Allah will say (on Resurrection Day): O Jesus, son of Mary! Did you say unto men: worship me and my mother [Mary] as **TWO GODS BESIDES ALLAH**?"

There is **NOT** one verse in the Holy Bible where Jesus or any apostle ever said that Jesus and Mary are two gods besides God nor that Jesus and His Father are two gods nor that there are three gods. Jesus is not a god besides God. Bible believing Christians reject such evil dogma.

Meaning of Glorious Quran: Surah 5:73 "They surely disbelieve who say: Allah is the **THIRD OF THREE**..."

This concept of three gods is not found in any Hebrew and Greek Biblical manuscripts nor translation. **I agree with Muhammad this concept of three gods: Allah, Mary and Jesus is from Satan out of hell**. Any Bible-believing Christian, together with Muslims, must never get tired to condemn the false teaching that Allah, Mary and Jesus are three gods. I condemn it with my whole heart. It seems that this concept of the godhead of three gods, Allah (Father), Mary (Mother) and Jesus (Son) formed the basis of Muhammad's preaching.

Quran Trans. by Abdullah Yusuf Ali Surah 6:101 "…How can He have a son when He hath no consort? …"

HEREIN LAYS THE WHOLE ISLAMIC-MISCONCEPTION OF JESUS BEING A SEX-BORN SON OF MARY, FOR THIS IS EXACTLY HOW MOST MUSLIMS UNDERSTAND THE QURAN.

Sheikh Abdur-Rahmaan Wright: The Black people of South Africa and the imported religions – Page 3 "So they gave him [God] an invented goddess for wife [Mary]. The next thing, of course, was for these two to have a Son [Jesus] and there you have it, straight away: a set of three gods, a trinity [UNQUOTE: God the Father, Mary the Mother being the second and Jesus the Son the third]."

It's clear that these Muslims look at Jesus' conception in Christianity as a result of a sexual relationship between God and Mary. How disgusting!

Muslim scholar: A.S.K Joommal: The Riddle of the Trinity, Page 27 "The Holy Ghost **had intercourse** with Mary … **committed adultery** with another man's wife (Mary espoused to Joseph Luke 1:27)."

That is blasphemy! That is a demonic Islamic concept, nor found in the Bible or on the lips of Christians.

Quran Translation by Abdullah Yusuf Ali: Page 1806 Comm. 6296 "…We must not think of Him as having a son or a father, for that would be to import animal qualities [sex] into our conception of Him."

When we consider what the Bible teaches, it is very clear that Muhammad **NOWHERE** spoke out against the true Christian concept of the Biblical Godhead of only One God revealed in the Father, Son and Holy Ghost. Muslims are misguided to think Bible-believing Christians believe in Allah, Mary and Jesus as three gods. It seems that it is Muslims who are overwhelmed with the number three:

Sahih Bukhari Vol. 8, Page 172, Hadith 261 "Narrated Anas: Whenever Allah's Messenger (ﷺ) greeted somebody, he used to **greet him three times** and if he spoke a sentence, he used to repeat it thrice."

Sahih Bukhari Vol. 9, Page 136 Hadith 168 "…The Prophet (ﷺ) [said] … if he [you] saw a dream which he [you] disliked, then he [you] should seek refuge with Allah from its evil and Satan and **spit three times**…"

Sunan Ibn Majah "The Messenger of Allah said: 'When anyone of you urinates, **let him squeeze his penis three times**…" https://quranx.com/Hadith/IbnMajah/DarusSalam/Volume-1/Book-1/Hadith-326

63 Does Allah have a Spirit?

Although the Bible and the Quran teaches that there is only one true God, both the Bible and Quran also teaches that this same one God have a Spirit that can manifest apart from God, in other words, God is in one place, e.g. heaven and God's Spirit at the same time can be in many other places, e.g. on earth.

MUSLIMS MAY OBJECT TO THE IDEA THAT ALLAH HAVE A SPIRIT THAT CAN MANIFEST APART FROM ALLAH, BUT IT IS VITAL TO UNDERSTAND WHAT THE QURAN SAY ABOUT ALLAH AND HIS SPIRIT, AND NOT WHAT SUNNI MUSLIMS WANT US TO KNOW ABOUT ALLAH AND HIS SPIRIT.

In the Bible we read:

Genesis 1:1-2 "…And the Spirit of God moved upon the face of the waters."

Ephesians 4:30 "And grieve not the Holy Spirit of God..."

Let's look at the Quranic evidence that Allah have a Spirit that manifests apart from Allah.

Quran Translation by Abdullah Yusuf Ali – Surah 15:29 "When **I [God]** have fashioned him [Adam] (in due proportion) and breathed into him [Adam] of **MY SPIRIT**…"

Below are translations of Surahs 15:29 and 32:9 that reflect the same idea that God who is in heaven, but His Spirit is in Adam, who is on earth.

Meaning of Glorious Quran "When **I** have made him and have breathed into him of **MY SPIRIT** … Then **He** fashioned him and breathed into him [Adam] of **HIS SPIRIT**…"

The Koran "I shaped him and breathed **MY SPIRIT** in him… He shaped him and breathed **HIS SPIRIT** in him…"

Authorized English Version of the Quran "Once I perfect him and blow into him of **MY SPIRIT**… He shaped him and blew into him from **HIS SPIRIT**…"

The Message of the Quran "When I have formed him fully and breathed into him of **MY SPIRIT** … He forms him… and breathes into him of **HIS SPIRIT**…"

The Holy Qur'an "So when I have made him complete and breathed into him of **MY SPIRIT**… Then He made him complete and breathed into him of **HIS SPIRIT**…"

The Holy Qur'an: Page 511 Commentary 1337 – Page 794 Commentary 1960 "This shows that man is made complete *when the **DIVINE SPIRIT** is breathed into him, the **SPIRIT OF ALLAH** that gives him perfection…* This verse shows that the **SPIRIT OF GOD** is breathed into every man."

Here we just witnessed 8 different Muslim Scholars translate the Quran to say that Allah have a Spirit.

Some Muslims object that Allah have a Spirit

Muslims who object to the idea that Allah have a Spirit that can manifest apart from God, quote a different English Quranic Version of Surah 15:29, produced by Muslim Scholars Drs. Hilali and Khan, to substantiate their view that Allah does not have a Spirit that manifests apart from Allah.

The Noble Quran – Surah 15:29 "When I have fashioned him completely and breathed into him (Adam) **the soul which I created for him**, then fall down prostrating yourself unto him."

While the other translations demonstrate that God have a Spirit that was breathed into Adam, here we have a total contradictory version from Drs. Hilali and Khan removing the idea that Allah have a Spirit. The latter version introduced an idea that Allah breathed a created soul into Adam.

That brings us to a possible conclusion: all the above Translations are false or Drs. Hilali and Khan's version is false. Let's look at the transliteration of this verse to see which translations are correct or false!

Quran Translation by Abdullah Yusuf Ali: Roman Transliteration – Surah 15:29 "Fa-'izaa sawway-tuhüü wa nafa<u>kh</u>tu fiihi **MIR-RÜÜHII** faqa-'üü lahüü saa-jidiin."

We immediately notice that Drs. Hilali and Khan **MIS**translated the personal pronoun **MIR** "**MY**" incorrectly as an article "**THE**", which in Arabic is **AL** which is absent in this verse. The correct translation for **MIR-RÜÜH** is "**MY SPIRIT**" and not "**THE SOUL**"! Note, the Arabic word "**KHALAQA**" that translate into "created" is also not in the Arabic text of Surah 15:29. Let's look at verses in the Quran where the word "created" is penned.

Quran Translation by Abdullah Yusuf Ali: Roman Transliteration – Surahs 2:21, 29, 228, 3:59, 4:1 "…Adore your Guardian-Lord who (**created KHALAQA**) you… It is He who hath (**created KHALAQA**) for you… To hide what Allah hath (**created KHALAQA**) in their wombs… He (**created KHALAQA**) him from dust… Who (**created KHALAQA**) you from a single person…"

This further proves that Drs. Hilali and Khan **MIS**translated Surah 15:29 by adding words into their English version that is NOT IN THE ARABIC TEXT. Note, it is true that Adam had a soul, but that isn't what Surah 15:29 says. Here again, it becomes obvious that Drs. Hilali and Khan mistranslated the verse to hide the idea that Allah have a Spirit that manifested apart from Allah. Clearly, both the Biblical Message and the Quranic Message teach that God have a Spirit and of course, it is not an evil spirit, but THE Holy Spirit. God and His Holy Spirit are not two different gods, but one God who manifests His Spirit apart from Him. This is exactly what Christians mean when we say: God the Father and God the Holy Spirit. Not two gods, one God with different manifestations, *e.g. The God (Allah) in heaven and God's Holy Spirit on earth*. Now that we established that Drs. Hilali and Khan's version is inaccurate and that Allah do have a Spirit, let's look at the characteristics of Allah's Spirit as mentioned in the Quran.

Characteristics of Allah's Spirit in the Quran

Quran Translation by Abdullah Yusuf Ali – Surah 15:29 "When I [God] have fashioned him [Adam] (in due proportion) and breathed into him [Adam] of **MY SPIRIT**…"

Allah's Spirit is breathed *OUT FROM WITHIN ALLAH, out of Allah, into Adam.* Allah's Spirit is part of Allah and therefore **uncreated**. Allah created Adam from dust, but it is Allah's Spirit that animated Adam. Muslims have a hard time accepting the Spirit of Allah for who He is. Looking at Surah 19:17 we see that it is Ali who this time **MIS**translated the verse to hide the idea that the Spirit of Allah can assume a human form as a man.

Let's look at Ali's version: **_Quran Translation by Abdullah Yusuf Ali Surah 19:17:_** "…We sent her our **angel** and he appeared before her as a man in all respects."

The Arabic word for "angel" is "**malak**" which is not found in this verse.

Quran Translation by Abdullah Yusuf Ali: Roman Transliteration "…We sent her Our **ruuh** and He appeared before her as a man in all respects."

This time Muhammed Pickthall translated it accurately: **_Meaning of Glorious Quran_** "We sent unto her Our **Spirit** and it assumed for her the likeness of a perfect man." **Here we see Allah's Spirit appearing in a form of a man sent by Allah.** Most Muslims believe that the Spirit of Allah is Gabriel. The fact that Gabriel is a spirit and of course, not an evil spirit, but **A** holy spirit, does *not* mean that Gabriel is **THE** Holy Spirit of Allah. All angels are holy spirits and all fallen angels (demons) are evil spirits. Gabriel, like all other angels, is a spirit **from** God, but he is not **THE** Spirit of Allah. If Gabriel is **THE** Holy Spirit, it would mean that Allah breathed Gabriel into Adam [Surah 15:29] and into Mary [Surah 21:91].

The fact that Gabriel is **not** THE Spirit of God is shown in the Quran:

- ✓ It doesn't say: Allah breathed **Gabriel** into Adam and into Mary.
- ✓ It says: **I** [Allah] breathed **MY** Spirit into Adam and into Mary.

In the Quran, THE Spirit is **DISTINCT** from the angels: **Quran Transl. by Abdullah Yusuf Ali – Surah 2:97** "The day that *the Spirit and the angels* will stand forth in ranks…"

Surahs 70:4, 78:38, 97:4 – Gabriel is among the angels distinct from the Spirit.

When Muhammad was questioned on who THE Spirit is, he had a golden opportunity to inform his inquirers and Quran readers that THE Spirit is Gabriel, but he didn't.

Muhammad knew very little of THE Spirit according to **Quran Transl. by Abdullah Yusuf Ali – Surah 17:85** "They ask thee concerning the Spirit *(of inspiration)*. Say: "The Spirit *(cometh)* by command of my Lord: of knowledge it is only a little that is communicated to you, (O men)".

Here we see the Quranic Spirit of Allah being submissive to Allah, just like the Biblical Spirit of God is submissive to God.

God and His Uncreated Spirit (that is submissive and when sent, can appear visibly in the form of a man) are not two gods, but one God who manifests His Spirit apart from Him. The God and His Spirit is united or a perfect oneness, which is exactly the Muslim concept of *"Tawhid"* – *The Oneness of God. Unity!*

The Concept of Tawhid in Islam *"Tauhiyd"* comes from the verb *"wahhad"* **it literally means to unite**."

The God and His Holy Spirit is not two gods, but two manifestations of God at different places. While God is in heaven, His Spirit is on earth, making God omni-present by virtue of His Spirit in different places!

Allah also moves from one place to another

The Noble Quran Surah 7:143 & Page 220 – Footnote 1 "…So when his [Moses'] Lord [Allah] **APPEARED** unto the mountain… The **APPEARANCE OF ALLAH** to the mountain was very **little of Him**… as explained by the prophet when he recited this verse. (This hadith is quoted by Tirmidhi)."

The Noble Quran Surah 89:22 & Page 777 Footnote 1 C "Your **LORD COMES** with the angels in rows… Narrated Abu-Sa'id Al-Khudri: We said, O Allah's messenger! Shall we see our Lord on the day of Resurrection? He said: …Then **ALMIGHTY WILL COME** to them in a shape other than the one which they saw the first time…" *(Sahih Bukhari Vol. 9 Pages 395 Hadith 532B)."* [Here we see Allah have 2 shapes.]

Sahih Bukhari Vol. 2, Page 136, Hadith 246 "Narrated Abu Huraira: Allah's Apostle said: our Lord, the Blessed, the Superior, **COMES EVERY NIGHT DOWN** on the nearest heaven to us when the last third of the night remains, saying: "Is there anyone to invoke me…"

When Christians say God is HERE, THERE AND EVERYWHERE, it does not mean that this great God is *omnipresent in every nook and corner.* God is omnipresent by virtue of…

[1] being OMNISCIENT [knowing all things],

[2] by breathing (pouring) His Spirit into us makes Him universally present in us.

God and His Spirit is ONE God! That is true Oneness.

64 Does the Quran state that Jesus is created like Adam?

When looking at "WHO" Jesus Christ really is, Muslims quote Surah 3:59 to prove that Jesus was created like Adam. Let's look at this verse and analyze it and see if Jesus was really created like Adam.

Quran Translation by Abdullah Yusuf Ali: "The **SIMILITUDE** of Jesus **BEFORE ALLAH** is as that of Adam: *HE [Allah] created him [Adam] from dust, then said to him: "Be" and he [Adam] was."*

Notice, these are not the words of Allah, but of some third person, if it were the Words of Allah, it would have read: "The similitude [likeness] of Jesus before **ME**, is as that of Adam: I created him from dust..." This verse says that Allah created Adam and then said to the liveless clay man: "be" and Adam "was" – meaning: Adam became a living human-being.

How did Allah create Adam: ***The Noble Quran: Pages 892 – Appendix II*** "He also says: To one whom I have created with **BOTH MY HANDS**. (V. 38:75) ... Page 8 – Commentary 1 "...Allah created you [Adam] with His own hands..." (Sahih Bukhari Vol. 6, Page 5, Hadith 3)." [Unquote: Allah used His left and right hands to form the clay into a shape that would become the first human-being, Adam.]

Quran Translation by Abdullah Yusuf Ali: Page 138 Commentary 398 "If it is said that he [Jesus] was born without a human father, **Adam was also so born**. Indeed, Adam was born without a human father and mother. As far as our physical bodies are concerned they are mere dust. In God's sight Jesus was as dust as Adam was or humanity is. The greatness of Jesus arises from the Divine command "Be" – for after that he [Jesus] was – more than dust – a great spiritual leader and teacher."

Ali erred greatly in his comment. **Adam was not born** without father and mother, Adam was created. If Jesus was great, because of the Divine command: "Be" than Adam was also great, because of the same command: "Be", but then all other prophets were **NOT** great, because Allah never said: "Be" for them to come into existence, all other prophets, *including Muhammad,* were conceived through sex. Untill now, I've entertained the idea that Allah created Adam from dust and then said: Be and Adam was. But, is that what really happened? Ali says: "...The greatness of Jesus arises from the Divine command: *Be...*"

Again Ali erred. There is no evidence in the Quran that Allah said: "Be" and Adam was or Jesus was. For Adam to be created [Surah 30:20] out of dust, would mean Allah first created the earth and from the dust of the earth, Allah with His two hands (Surah 38:75) created Adam's liveless body from the dust. But notice, THEN Allah breathed His Spirit [Surah 15:29] into Adam. Nowhere does it state that Allah said "Be" for Adam to come into existence, which contradicts Surah 3:59 where it is stated that Allah said "be". Again, nowhere did Allah say "Be" and Jesus came into existence, God also followed a process to create the earthly body of Jesus. The Quran Surah 21:91 is clear, Allah breathed His Spirit into Mary's vagina and Jesus was conceived. [see heading: The Quran's language concerning Jesus' conception]. He didn't say: Be and Jesus was! There was a process.

Let us now consider Dr. Asad's comment: **Message of the Quran: Page 76 Comm. 47** "The Quran stresses here… the fact that **Jesus, like Adam… created out of dust,** e.g. out of substances, both organic and inorganic, *which are found in their elementary forms on and in the earth.*"

Now, if the likeness of Jesus is that of Adam – it would mean that Allah took dust from the earth and placed the dust in Mary's womb and from that dust in Mary's womb, transformed it into a fetus and then Allah breathed into the fetus (a developing human-body) [Surah 66:12] and it became a living baby, later to be named Jesus Christ. There is NO Quranic evidence that Allah said: "Be and Jesus was". No evidence.

65 Does the Bible and Quran state Jesus is God's Word?

Jesus was not a created-being that only came into existence from His human conception in Mary'womb. Both the Bible and Quran teaches that Jesus, before His human conception, pre-existed as God's Word and God's Spirit, and what came into existence 2000 years ago, was the created human body of Jesus.

John 1:1 "In the beginning was THE WORD and THE WORD was with God and **THE WORD WAS GOD … 14 AND THE WORD WAS MADE FLESH…**"

Quran Translation by Abdullah Yusuf Ali – Surah 4:171 "O People of the Book! Commit no excesses in your religion: Nor say of Allah aught, but the truth. Christ Jesus the son of Mary was (no more than) a messenger of Allah and His Word, which He bestowed on Mary and a Spirit proceeding from Him: so believe in Allah and His messengers. Say not "Trinity" ..."

Let's look at this verse in fragments, to understand what it is that is being said:

Quran Translation by Abdullah Yusuf Ali: "**O People of the Book**..." [Unquote: This phrase can refer to both Jews and Christians, however, in its context here, it is very important to understand that Muhammad in this verse is not addressing the Jews, neither the whole of Christendom, he is addressing a few local unlettered Arabian Christians who knew not the book - see heading: Muslims misquote the Quran to prove Bible corruption].

Quran Translation by Abdullah Yusuf Ali: "O People of the Book! **Commit no excesses in your religion: Nor say of Allah aught, but the truth**..." [*According to Muhammad*, as discussed above (see Q62), these few Christians in Arabia seemingly believed in 3 gods: Allah – Mary – Jesus. Muhammad is rebuking them to desist such a horrendous belief. If I was standing next to Muhammad, I would also correct those unguided Christians who believed this unbiblical nonsense of 3 gods: Allah – Mary – Jesus]

Quran Trans. by Abdullah Yusuf Ali – Surah 4:171 "O People of the Book! Commit no excesses in your religion: Nor say of Allah aught, but the truth. **Christ Jesus, the son of Mary was (NO MORE THAN)...**" [Please note the interpolation in round brackets (*no more than*) is Ali's own addition to the verse. Those words are not found in the Arabic Text. Here Muhammad proclaimed that Jesus Christ is [1] the son of Mary... showing that Jesus was born of Mary.]

Quran Trans. by Abdullah Yusuf Ali – Surah 4:171 "O People of the Book! Commit no excesses in your religion: Nor say of Allah aught, but the truth. Christ Jesus, the son of Mary was (NO MORE THAN) **a messenger of Allah and His Word, which He bestowed on Mary and a Spirit proceeding from Him**..."

[It is very important to read what is written and not to read the Sunni sectarian beliefs into this verse.

*The verse **DOESN'T** say: "Christ Jesus was created by a Word spoken of God" – it says: "Christ Jesus was His Word, which was bestowed on Mary…"*

Jesus is Allah's uncreated Word that pre-existed Mary. Also, Jesus Christ was a Spirit proceeding from Allah, making Jesus' Spirit uncreated. Jesus' human-body was created in Mary's womb, but Jesus Spirit proceeding from Allah was uncreated. Jesus is NOT biologically part of Mary. God didn't take Mary's egg to fertilize it. There was no sexual sensation involved for the egg to be released. Mary's body was Jesus' mother in the sense that she was the incubator through whom Jesus was born. God breathed His pre-existing Word into Mary and the Word took on flesh and became a fetus – baby. The pre-existence of God's Word and God's Spirit was not known as Jesus, until the incarnation in Mary's womb.

Adam was created from dust (Surah 7:12, 17:61, 18:37, 22:05, 30:20, 32:07, 35:11, 38:71,76, 40:67).

Jesus was **NOT** created from the dust of the earth like Adam, but Jesus was God's original Spoken Word that materialized as a body in Mary's womb, hence Jesus is described as the virgin-borned-Son and grew up to be a man. Jesus in His pre-existence was known as God's Word, but in His human-form, He was known as God's messenger. Jesus Christ therefore has two natures:

- *first* as the uncreated Word of God and
- *second* as a human-being that was conceived in Mary's womb.

According to the Quran, here we have Allah **and** Allah's Spirit **and** Allah's Word, a perfect Trinity. **NOT three different gods**, different attributes.

Muhammad spoke against the false concept of Allah (father) **and** Mary (mother) **and** Jesus (the son) **as three different gods**. That is blasphemy! No Bible-based Christian believes that false concept of the Godhead.

Muhammad was oblivious of the true Christian belief of the Biblical Trinity of ONE GOD revealed in three different manifestations: Father, Son and Holy Spirit.

SECTION 7

FAMILY LIFE IN ISLAM

66 Does Allah promote domestic violence?

Did Muhammed taught wives to retaliate against violent husbands?

Tafsir Wahidi – Asbab Al-Nuzul on 4:34 "It happened Sa'd hit his wife on the face, because she rebelled against him. Then her father went with her to see the Prophet… He [the father] said to him [Muhammad]… he [Sa'd] slapped her [his wife, my daughter]. **THE PROPHET SAID: LET HER HAVE RETALIATION AGAINST HER HUSBAND.**"

https://quranx.com/Tafsir/Wahidi/4.34

Last accessed 27 April 2021

Allah sent Gabriel to Muhammed to support wife beating

Tafsir Wahidi – Asbab Al-Nuzul on 4:34 "It happened Sa'd hit his wife on the face, because she rebelled against him. Then her father went with her to see the Prophet… He [the father] said to him [Muhammad]… he [Sa'd] slapped her [his wife, my daughter]. The Prophet said: Let her have retaliation against her husband. As she was leaving with her father to execute retaliation, **THE PROPHET… CALLED THEM AND SAID: GABRIEL HAS COME TO ME… HE, REVEALED THIS VERSE.**"

https://quranx.com/Tafsir/Wahidi/4.34 Last accessed 27 April 2021

Remember, Muslims believe that the Quran is Allah's Word, not Muhammad's word, therefore, it is not Muhammad ordering wife beating in the Quran Surah 4:34, it is Allah who instructed the Muslim husbands to beat their seemingly disobedient wives. Let's look at Allan's inspiration sent to Muhammed.

Quran Translation by Abdullah Yusuf Ali – Surah 4:34 "Therefore the righteous women are devoutly obedient and guard in the husband's absence what Allah would have them guard, as to those women on whose part *you fear disloyalty and ill-conduct*: admonish them (first), (next), do not share their beds **(AND LAST) BEAT (TAP) THEM (LIGHTLY)**…"

> ### ➤ Muslim scholars agree, Muhammed wanted retaliation, but Allah supported wife beating

Tafsir Wahidi – Asbab Al-Nuzul on 4:34 "It happened Sa'd hit his wife on the face, because she rebelled against him. Then her father went with her to see the Prophet… He [the father] said to him [Muhammad]… he [Sa'd] slapped her [his wife, my daughter]. The Prophet said: Let her have retaliation against her husband. As she was leaving with her father to execute retaliation, the prophet… called them and said: Gabriel has come to me… he, revealed this verse. **THE MESSENGER OF ALLAH… SAID: WE WANTED SOMETHING, WHILE ALLAH WANTED SOMETHING ELSE** and that which Allah wants is good." https://quranx.com/Tafsir/Wahidi/4.34 Last accessed 27 April 2021

Message of the Quran: Page 109-110 Commentary 45 "When the above Quran-verse AUTHORIZING THE BEATING OF A REFRACTORY WIFE WAS REVEALED, **THE PROPHET IS REPORTED TO HAVE SAID: I WANTED ONE THING, BUT GOD HAS WILLED ANOTHER** and what God has willed must be best."

At first, Muhammad ADVISED wives to violently retaliate against their abusing husbands, but after he received Allah's inspiration, he changed his mind and preached that disobedient wives must be beaten.

Did Allah say beat (tap) them (lightly)?

Quran Translation by Abdullah Yusuf Ali – Surah 4:34 "Therefore the righteous women are devoutly obedient and guard in the husband's absence what Allah would have them guard, as to those women on whose part *you fear disloyalty and ill-conduct*: admonish them (first), (next), do not share their beds **(AND LAST) BEAT (TAP) THEM (LIGHTLY)**…"

It is very important to know **WHAT** the Quranic context is saying and **NOT** what Translators of the Quran wants us to think the Arabic Text is saying. We must be careful not to accept the Muslim's emotional sugar-coded interpretation of the Quran, mixed with the direct textual teaching of the Quran. For example, in the above verse, the *interpolations in round (…) brackets are not part of the Arabic Quranic text,* but are **ALI'S PERSONAL ADDITIONS** to his English Quranic Version to soften Allah's harsh punitive steps of bringing supposingly disobedient wives into submission.

Let's read this verse again, **WITHOUT ALI'S ADDITIONS**: "Therefore the righteous women are devoutly obedient and guard in the husband's absence what Allah would have them guard, as to those women on whose part *you fear disloyalty and ill-conduct*: Admonish them, do not share their beds, **BEAT THEM**…"

Below are more Quran Translations on the same verse.

Meaning of Glorious Quran "… Admonish them and banish them to beds apart and SCOURGE THEM."	The Holy Qur'an "…Admonish them and leave them alone in the beds and CHASTISE THEM."

Ali shamefully added the words (tap – lightly) to his English Version, like I said above, to soften-up Allah's harshness towards supposing disobedient wives. Muslims should not be embarrassed about Allah's advice that Muslim husbands may beat or scourge or chastise their wives! **Notice, Allah did not suggest, but instructed husbands to beat their seemingly disobedient wives**. Husbands who are beating their seemingly disobedient wives are good Muslims, submitting to Allah. *"Allah's will is best"* and who dares to disagree with Allah?

PROGRESSIVE NEGATIVE STEPS TO CORRECT SEEMINGLY DISOBEDIENT WIVES:

1. Admonish your disobedient wife (as a Christian, I agree, this is recommendable).
2. Stop sleeping with your wife (this is easy for men with tmultiple wives they can sleep with).

3. BEAT HER.

Abdullah Yusuf Ali's commentary on wife beating

Quran Translation by Abdullah Yusuf Ali: Page 190 Commentary 547 "…If this is not sufficient, **SOME SLIGHT PHYSICAL CORRECTION MAY BE ADMINISTERED**…"

Allah **DIDN'T** say *"slight beating"* – Allah said: "beat them – chastise them – scourge them." Here we see Ali says it is a physical beating, not symbolic.

After Muhammad received Surah 4:34 he gave men permission to beat wives

Sunan Abu-Dawud, Book 11, Marriage (Nikah), Number 2141 & 2142 "Narrated Abdullah ibn Abu Dhubab: Iyas ibn Abdullah ibn Abu Dhubab reported **THE APOSTLE OF ALLAH (PBUH) AS SAYING**: Do not beat Allah's handmaidens, but when Umar came to the apostle of Allah (pbuh) and said: Women have become emboldened towards their husbands, **HE [PROPHET MUHAMMAD] GAVE PERMISSION TO BEAT THEM.**"
https://quranx.com/Hadith/AbuDawud/Hasan/Hadith-2141 Last accessed 27 April 2021

Husbands will not be asked about wife beating

Riyad as-Salihin: "Umar (May Allah be pleased with him) reported that: The Prophet (ﷺ) said: **NO MAN SHALL BE ASKED FOR THE REASON OF BEATING HIS WIFE**". [Abu Dawud]"

https://quranx.com/Hadith/Saliheen/In-Book/Book-1/Hadith-68 Last accessed 27 April 2021

Sunan Ibn Majah: "Umar … said to me: O Ash'ath, learn from me something that **I HEARD FROM THE MESSENGER OF ALLAH. A MAN SHOULD NOT BE ASKED WHY HE BEATS HIS WIFE**…"

https://quranx.com/Hadith/IbnMajah/DarusSalam/Volume-3/Book-9/Hadith-1986

https://www.youtube.com/watch?v=2uy2xoP_EOs Time line 2:40 – 8:55 Last accessed 27 April 2021

Even Muhammad, also, beat his wife

Sahih Muslim, book 4, Hadith 2127 "Aisha said: When it was my turn for Allah's messenger (PBUH) to spent the night with me, he turned his side, put on his mantle and took off his shoes and placed them near his feet and spread the corner of his shawl on his bed and then lay down till *HE THOUGHT THAT I HAD GONE TO SLEEP*. He took hold of his mantle slowly and put on his shoes slowly and opened the door and went out and then closed it lightly. I covered my head, put on my veil and tightened my waist wrapper and then went out following his steps till he reached Baqi. He stood there for a long time. He then returned and I also returned. He came to the house and I also came to the house and as I lay down in the bed the holy prophet entered the house and said: Why are you out of breath? Then I told him. He said: Was it the darkness (of your shadow) that I saw in front of me? I said: Yes. **HE STRUCK ME ON THE CHEST, WHICH CAUSED ME PAIN**…"

http://hadithcollection.com/sahihmuslim/Sahih%20Muslim%20Book%2004.%20Prayer/sahih-muslim-book-004-hadith-number-2127.html Last accessed 27 April 2021

Here's a Youtube clib, dated 5 July 2013, of a Muslim scholar explaining the above hadith, saying Aishas of today must be hurt like Muhammad hurt her: https://www.youtube.com/watch?v=rvByv4bmRoY

Last accessed 27 April 2021

Umar also beat his wife and daughter

Sunan Ibn Majah: "It was narrated that Ash'ath bin Qais said: I was a guest of 'Umar and in the middle of the night, he went and **HIT HIS WIFE AND I SEPARATED THEM**…"

https://quranx.com/Hadith/IbnMajah/DarusSalam/Volume-3/Book-9/Hadith-1986

Last accessed 27 April 2021

Sahih Bukhari Vol. 6, Page 105, Hadith 132: "Narrated Aisha [daughter of Abu Bakr and wife of Muhammad]: A necklace of mine was lost at Al-Baida and we were on our way to Medinah. The prophet made his camel kneel down and dismounted and laid his head on my lap and slept. **ABU BAKR CAME TO ME AND HIT ME VIOLENTLY ON MY CHEST**... I kept as motionless as a dead person, because of the position of Allah's messenger (on my lap) **ALTHOUGH ABU BAKR HAD HURT ME**..."

Muslim women in the 7TH century suffered much abuse

Sahih Bukhari Vol. 7, Page 479, Hadith 715: "Aisha said the lady came wearing a green veil and complained to her and showed her *A GREEN SPOT ON HER SKIN CAUSED BY BEATING*. It was the habit of ladies to support each other, so when Allah's messenger came, Aisha said: **I HAVE NOT SEEN ANY WOMAN SUFFERING AS MUCH AS THE BELIEVING WOMEN**. Her skin is greener than her clothes..."

Arabian Muslim wives suffered under Allah's inspiration. Even atheists know it's wrong to hit women.

Muhammad disapproved severely beating your wives before sex

Sahih Bukhari Vol. 7, Pages 100-101, Hadith 132: "Narrated Zam'a: The prophet said: None of you should flog his wife **AS HE FLOGS A SLAVE AND THEN HAVE SEXUAL INTERCOURSE WITH HER**..."

Muhammed would have sone better to totally prohibit wife and slave beating, but that would make Muhammed a Quran disobeying Muslim.

Did Job, famous for his patience, also beat his wife?

Quran Translation by Abdullah Yusuf Ali – Surah 38:41-44 "Job ... And take in thy hand a little grass and strike therewith: and break not (thy oath) ... Commentary 4202 Page 1227 Job ... **HE MUST HAVE** said in his haste to the woman that he would beat her: he is asked now to correct her with only a wisp of grass, to show that he was gentle and humble as well as patient and constant."

DOES BEATING YOUR WIFE INDICATE HOW HUMBLE YOU ARE? Hahaha Christians won't believe such a horrendous version of a wife beating Job.

Muhammed said beat your non-praying teen-ager

The Noble Quran – Page 449 Footnote "…The prophet has said: Order your children for salat at the age of 7 and **BEAT THEM** at the age of 10."

67 Are women allowed to attend mosques?

The Muslim Digest Vol. 31 Nos. 2 to 5 Sept. to Dec. 1980 Page 95 "Mr. Deedat is absolutely confused by claiming: there is no prohibition against women attending mosque and this is not traditionally done - It is not necessary for us to expound the Islamic prohibition on women attending the Musjid, for all Muslims who accept the Sunnah of our Nabi (S.A.W) are fully aware that the practice of the Shariah, which has come to us authoritatively down the long corridor of 14 centuries, is the Haqq"

> Where must Muslim women pray

The Noble Quran – Page 449 Footnote "Every Muslim, male and female, is obliged to offer Salat (prayers) regular five times a day… The male in the mosque in congregation and **THE FEMALE AT HOME**."

Awake to the call of Islam: Vol. 2, No: 12, Page 23, March 1976, Rabi-ul-Awwal 1396, Published by: The Young Men's Muslim Association P.O. Box 5036 Benoni South African "**HOMES – BEST MOSQUES FOR WOMEN. RASOOLULLAH'S (S.A.W.) PREFERENCE FOR WOMEN TO PERFORM THEIR PRAYERS AT HOME**, yet we still have people who are clamoring for female attendance at the Mosques for the purpose of congregational prayers. HAZRAT AYESHA (R.A.) SAID: THE SALAAT OF A WOMAN IN HER ROOM IS BETTER THAN HER SALAAT IN HER HOUSE. **HER SALAAT IN THE DARKEST CORNER OF HER ROOM, IS BETTER THAN HER SALAAT IN HER ROOM**… Quran [Surah 33:33]"

68 Were Muhammad's wives' examples to the community?

Sahih Bukhari Vol. 6, Page 406, Hadith 435: "She [the wife of Umar] said: How strange you are, O son of al-Khattab! You don't want to be argued with whereas your daughter, **HAFSAH SURELY, ARGUES WITH ALLAH'S APOSTLE SO MUCH THAT HE REMAINS ANGRY FOR A FULL DAY!** Umar then reported how he at once put on his outer garment and went to Hafsah and said to her: O my daughter, do you argue with Allah's apostle so that he remains angry the whole day? *Hafsah answered: by Allah, we argue with him. Umar said: Know that I warn you of Allah's punishment and the anger of Allah's apostle."*

The tension was so great that Allah of the Quran had to once again conveniently reveal verses to Muhammad's comfort:

Quran Translation by Abdullah Yusuf Ali – Surah 66:5 "It may be, if he [Muhammad] divorced you (all) [Aisha and Hafsah] that God will give him in exchange consorts [other wives] *BETTER THAN YOU*:

(a) **WHO SUBMIT (THEIR WILLS)** [his 2 wives were not submissive,]

(b) **WHO BELIEVE,** [insinuating his 2 wives were not believers,]

(c) **WHO ARE DEVOUT,** [insinuating his 2 wives were not devout,]

(d) **WHO TURN TO GOD IN REPENTANCE** [his 2 wives didn't repent,]

(e) **WHO WORSHIP (IN HUMILITY),** [his 2 wives didn't worship?]

(f) **WHO TRAVEL (FOR FAITH) AND FAST** [his 2 wives didn't travel/fast].

Previously married or virgins."

If God wanted to give Muhammad BETTER wives as mentioned above, it could only mean his wives lacked character. Hafsah and Aisha had such bad attitude, Allah had to threaten them with a revelation that if they don't chance their attitude, Muhammad may exchange them for better wives.

69 Marriage, divorce and remarriage in Islam

When can a divorced couple remarry?

If Muslim couples who divorced, realized that they were foolish and want to reconcile in marriage, they may **NOT,** according to Allah, reconcile in marriage, she is unlawful to him, **UNTIL** after she married another man and the second husband had sex with her and divorced her, then **ONLY** may she be reconciled to her first ex-husband for their union to be blameless in the sight of Allah.

Let's see if this is what Islam teaches: **_Quran Translation by Abdullah Yusuf Ali – Surah 2:230_** "If a husband divorces his wife (irrevocably), he can **NOT** after that, remarry her, **UNTIL AFTER SHE HAS MARRIED ANOTHER HUSBAND AND HE HAS DIVORCED HER**. In that case there is no blame on either of them if they reunite..."

Can you imagine the love of your life whom you divorced, because of problems you thought can't be resolved and later realized how stupid you were and want to reconcile with her in marriage, *but Allah says she is HARAAM until she first married another man and after he (the second husband) divorced her, then only is she HALAAL to be re-joined to you (first husband) in re-marriage!* Notice, when this second man marries her, it depends on when he divorces her, before she can reunite with her former ex-husband. Also, they can only divorce after the second husband had sex with her and then only, if the second husband divorced her, may she be re-joined in marriage to her former husband. **No sex with the second husband – no remarriage to her former husband.**

Tafsir - Ibn Al Kathir S. 2:230 "(...until she has married another husband) meaning, until she legally marries another man. For instance, if she has sexual intercourse with any man, even her master (if she was a servant), she would still be ineligible for marriage for her ex-husband (who divorced her thrice), because whomever she had sexual relations with was not her legal husband. If she marries a man without consummating the marriage, she will not be eligible for her ex-husband... Allah's Messenger was asked about a woman who marries a man who thereafter divorces her (thrice). She then marries another man and he divorces her before he has sexual relations with her, would she be allowed for her first husband, Allah's Messenger said: (No, until he enjoys her `Usaylah (sexual relation)."

https://quranx.com/Tafsir/Kathir/2.229 Last accessed 27 April 2021

Sahih Bukhari Vol. 7, Pages 139, Hadith 190: "Narrated Aisha: ... [A woman] came to the prophet and said – O Allah's messenger, my first husband divorced me and then I married another man who entered upon me to consummate his marriage, but he proved to be impotent... Can I re-marry my first husband in this case? **ALLAH'S MESSENGER SAID: IT IS UNLAWFUL TO MARRY YOUR FIRST HUSBAND, TILL THE OTHER HUSBAND CONSUMMATED HIS MARRIAGE [HAD SEX] WITH YOU.**"

No reconciliation with your ex-wife, until another husband married her, had sex with her and divorced her. Allah says than *only* may you reunite with your ex-wife, which is now another man's ex-wife. I am so glad I am a Christian and not a Muslim! Imagine your loved-one in the arms of another man, and you waiting on that man to have sex with her and to divorce her so you can reunite again with your flower!

Conditions for divorce in Islam

Sahih Bukhari Vol. 7, Pages 6-7 "A man may say to his brother (in Islam): Have a look at either of my wives (and if you wish), I will divorce her for you."

Abdurraghiem Hasan Sallie: The Decree of the Murtad (Apostate) According to the Islamic Law Page 29 "If the Apostate is a male and married, his marriage would terminate with immediate effect. The wife would then have to annul – *fasakh* the marriage and observe her *iddah* - period of waiting of three menstrual cycles."

Sodomized boy's mother is unlawful to sodomizer

Sahih Bukhari Vol. 7, Pages 30 "Narrated Abu Ja'far: If a person commits homosexuality with a boy, then the mother of that boy is unlawful for him to marry."

70 Monogamy in Christianity

God's original pattern of marriage was one husband and one wife. Both the Bible and Quran teach that the first married couple was Adam and his wife. The Bible identifies her as Eve, not Adam and Steve, nor Ann and Eve. Judaism, Christianity and Islam disapprove of same sex marriages (homosexuality and lesbianism).

Although God's pattern was monogamy from the beginning of time, God also in the Bible, in later generations in the OT permitted marriages of one husband and many wives. The fact that God allowed it in the OT, does **NOT** substantiate the claim that God is approving it today. God previously allowed many things, which He forbids today. For example, God approved incestuous marriages between the children of Adam and Eve, but He doesn't approve it today.

As Christians, we need to study the Bible to see what God approved for today. God in the NT promotes monogamy, hence Christianity promotes monogamous marriages and teach that other forms of marriages are wrong.

__Matthew 19:4-6__ "[Jesus] answered ... Have ye not read that He which made them at the beginning made them male and female and said: For this cause shall a man leave his father and mother and shall cleave to his **WIFE [NOT WIVES] AND THEY TWAIN [NOT THREE OR MORE]** shall be one flesh... 9 I say unto you: Whosoever shall put away his wife, except it be for fornication [she committed sex before marriage and kept it silent from her husband] and shall marry another, committed adultery and whoso married her which is put away doth commit adultery."

Another place where Jesus was also challenged on marriage is *__Matthew 22:23-30__*. Notice, this passage does not deal with polygyny. It is a clear-cut monogamy case where brothers *at different times* were married to the same woman. Both Jesus and Paul preached monogamy.

Apostle Paul said:

__1 Corinthians 7:2__ "...Let **EVERY MAN** have his own **WIFE**..."

2 Timothy 3:2 "A bishop... **the husband of one wife**... 12 the deacons be **the husbands of one wife**..."

71 Polygamy (definition)

THE NEW STANDARD ENCYCLOPEDIA – PAGE 1009

- ✓ Monogamy – one husband, one wife.
- ✓ Polygamy – plurality of consorts (includes: polygyny and polyandry)
- ✓ Polygyny – one husband, many wives.
- ✓ Polyandry – one wife, many husbands.

CAMBRIDGE ADVANCED LEARNER'S DICT. 4TH EDITION – PAGE 1183 "Polygamy: the custom of being married to more than one person at the same time."

72 Polygamy in Islam

Does the Quran allow for polygamy relationships?

The Quran did **not** allow polygamy in the **strict sense** of the word. Polygamy *includes* polygyny and polyandry. The Quran **DID** allow for polygyny relationships in early Islam, for about a few days or months and then prohibited it, the Quran, however **DOES** allow captured slave-women (slave - wives) to be raped in the presence of their husbands by Muslim warriors (see heading: Surah 4:24 allow Muslims to have sex with slave-married women).

Quran Translation by Abdullah Yusuf Ali – Surah 4:3 "If ye fear that ye shall not be able to deal justly with the orphans, **marry women of your choice, 2 or 3 or 4**..."

Here the Quran introduced polygyny. Notice, the Quran does **NOT** teach that every Muslim man must marry more than one wife, but here the Quran states **IF** he wants to and predetermine that he can be fair and just to more than one wife, he may. Polygyny was therefore conditional.

The Holy Qur'an: Page 187 Commentary 535 "This passage permits polygyny under CERTAIN CIRCUMSTANCES, *it does not enjoin it* …"

What was the first Quranic condition for polygyny?

Quran Translation by Abdullah Yusuf Ali Surah 4:3 "…Marry **women [nisaa]** of your choice, 2 or 3 or 4…"

Here the Quranic Message is absolutely clear for Muslims to marry a WOMAN OR WOMEN, yet 50 year old Muhammad violated this condition and got married to a little girl of 6 years young. Muhammad at the age of 53 consummated his marriage (had sex) with his childbride when she was 9.

Sahih Bukhari Vol. 5, Pages 152, Hadith 234 "Narrated Aisha: The prophet engaged me, when I was **A GIRL [NOT A WOMAN]** of six (years) … Allah's messenger came to me in the forenoon and my mother handed me over to him and at that time I was a **GIRL [NOT A WOMAN] OF 9 YEARS OF AGE** …"

Sahih Bukhari Vol. 5, Pages 152, Hadith 236 "Narrated Hisham's father: **[MUHAMMAD] CONSUMED THE MARRIAGE WHEN SHE WAS 9 YEARS**."

Without presenting verifiable Islamic evidence, embarrassed Muslim Scholars tell us these authentic ahadith are NOT authentic and that Aisha was NOT 9, but 19 years old when Muhammad consummated his marriage with her.

Dr. Zakir Naik confirmed that these ahadiths are authentic and that Aisha was 9 years young when Muhammad consummated his marriage with her. https://www.youtube.com/watch?v=avrog9uG5Z4

Last accessed 27 April 2021

Other embarrassed Muslims, like Dr. Rashid Khalifah, wants us to understand that Muhammad was not in favor of this marriage and that the girl's father forced Muhammad to marry Aisha.

Authorized English Version of the Quran: Appendix 30 "Polygamy" – Page 477
"There were 3 political marriages in the prophet's life. His close friends **Abu Bakr and Omar INSISTED** that he marries their daughters, Aisha and Hafsah, to establish traditional family ties among them…"

Did you notice that Dr. Khalifah gave no reference for the source he may be quoting? Actually, it is Muhammed who *INSISTED* to marry Aisha at 6. Here is the evidence:

Sahih Bukhari Vol. 7, Page 12, Hadith 18 "Narrated Urwa: **THE PROPHET ASK ABU BAKR FOR AISHA'S HAND IN MARRIAGE**…"

Note, it is not the father insisting Muhammad must marry his daughter, but it was Muhammad who asked for her hand in marriage. Notice, in the quote below, how Abu Bakr tries to persuade Muhammad that they are brothers, in oder to get Muhammed to backoff from marrying his 6-year young daughter.

Sahih Bukhari Vol. 7, Page 12, Hadith 18 "Narrated Urwa: The prophet ask Abu Bakr for Aisha's hand in marriage. **ABU BAKR SAID: BUT I AM YOUR BROTHER**…"

Abu Bakr neither insist Muhammed must marry Aisha nor did he approved Muhammed's request. Do you know what the word "but" implies? It cancels out what Muhammed requested. Finally, look at Muhammad's persisting conclusion that silenced the subjected Abu Bakr.

Sahih Bukhari Vol. 7, Page 12, Hadith 18 "Narrated Urwa: The prophet ask Abu Bakr for Aisha's hand in marriage. Abu Bakr said: but I am your brother. **THE PROPHET SAID: YOU ARE MY BROTHER IN ALLAH'S RELIGION AND HIS BOOK, BUT SHE IS LAWFUL FOR ME TO MARRY**."

It is clear that Abu Bakr didn't insist to give his baby in marriage to his 50-year-old military state leader. It is not Abu Bakr that insisted, but Muhammed who insisted for the marriage to happen.

In fact, modern day Muslims are now codemning Muhammad's action: ***Youtube Debate Topic: Islam is a religion of peace: Muslim penal: Zeba Khan – Muslim American***

Advocate and Maajid Nawaz – Director: The Quilliam Foundation – Non Muslim penal: Douglas Murray: Author of Neoconservatism (Why we need it?) and Ayaan Hirsi Ali – Women's Rights Advocate: **MUSLIM SPEAKER MAAJID SAYS**] "The fact that Douglas referred to the fact that he [Muhammad] had a bride that was under-age is something that **WE CAN NOW LOOK BACK AT AND SAY THAT WAS AN AWFUL PRACTICE**." https://www.youtube.com/watch?v=rh34Xsq7D_A [Time line 01:02:32 Last accessed 27 April 2021

Abu Bakr had no choice, because Muhammad had a liking in little girls and how he can fondle them.

Sahih Bukhari Vol. 7, Page 11, Hadith 17: "Narrated Jabir bin Abdullah: When I got married, Allah's messenger said to me: What type of lady have you married? I replied: I married a matron. He said why don't you have a liking for the virgins and fondling them? Jabir also said: **ALLAH'S MESSENGER SAID: WHY DIDN'T YOU MARRY A YOUNG GIRL, SO THAT YOU MIGHT PLAY WITH HER AND SHE WITH YOU**."

In fact, little **pre**puberty girls were given in marriage and if their husbands wanted to divorce their **pre**puberty wives, they had to wait a three months' period according to:

Quran Translation by Abdullah Yusuf Ali – Surah 65:4 "Such of your women as have passed the age of monthly courses, for them the prescribed period, if ye have any doubts, is **three months and for those who have no courses (it is the same)** ..."

Tafsir - Ibn Al Kathir S. 65:4 "...The waiting period of the woman in menopause whose menstruation has stopped due to her older age is three months ... The same for **THE YOUNG, WHO HAVE NOT REACHED THE YEARS OF MENSTRUATION IS 3 MONTHS** like those in menopause. This is the meaning of His saying: (for those who have no courses)" https://quranx.com/Tafsir/Kathir/65.4 Last accessed 27 April 2021

Tafsir Al-Jalalayn S. 65:4 "...Those who have **NOT YET MENSTRUATED, BECAUSE OF THEIR YOUNG AGE**, their period shall be three months..." https://quranx.com/Tafsir/Jalal/65.4 Last accessed 27 April 2021

Sahih Bukhari Vol. 7, Page 49-50, Chapter 39: "Giving one's young children in marriage (is permissible) by virtue of the statement of Allah in S.65:4 – For those who have **NO COURSES (I.E. THEY ARE STILL IMMATURE)** – and **THE IDDA FOR THE GIRL BEFORE PUBERTY IS THREE MONTHS** (in the above verse). Hadith 64 "Narrated Aisha: that the prophet wrote the marriage contract with her when she was **6 YEARS OLD AND HE CONSUMMATED HIS MARRIAGE WHEN SHE WAS 9 YEARS OLD** and she remained with him for nine years (e.g. till his death)."

Sahih Bukhari Vol. 8, Page 95, Hadith 151: "Narrated `Aisha: I used to play with the dolls in the presence of the Prophet, and my girl friends also used to play with me. When Allah's Messenger (ﷺ) used to enter (my dwelling place) they used to hide themselves, but the Prophet would call them to join and play with me. (**THE PLAYING WITH THE DOLLS AND SIMILAR IMAGES IS FORBIDDEN, BUT IT WAS ALLOWED FOR `AISHA AT THAT TIME, AS SHE WAS A LITTLE GIRL, NOT YET REACHED THE AGE OF PUBERTY.**)"

Why are modern-day Muslim men aged 50 years and older, not following the Sunnah of Muhammad [Surah 33:21] by marrying and consummating their marriages (having sex) with little girls aged at 9 years young?

The first condition is *"marry women"*, but Muhammad, like Aisha said, he married a LITTLE girl.

Limited number of women Muslims could marry

Quran Trans. by Abdullah Yusuf Ali – Surah 4:3 "…Marry women of your choice, **two or three or four** …"

The Quran *restricted the number of wives up to four wives*, but Muhammad **contradicted** his own message and was married to **MORE THAN FOUR** wives at the same time.

Sahih Bukhari, Vol. 3, Pages 454, Hadith 755 & Vol. 7, Page 5, Hadith 6 "Narrated Urwa from Aishah: "The wives of Allah's Apostle were in two groups. One group consisted of ***[1] Aisha, [2] Hafsa, [3] Safiyya and [4] Sauda and the other group consisted of***

[5] Um Salama and the other wives [at least two more wives – increasing the wives to 7] … Narrated Anas: The prophet used to go round (have sexual relations with) all his wives in one night. **HE HAD NINE WIVES.**"

Sahih Muslim: "Anas reported: The Messenger of Allah (ﷺ) used to have sexual intercourse with his wives with a single bath." https://quranx.com/Hadith/Muslim/USC-MSA/Book-3/Hadith-606

Last accessed 27 April 2021

Muhammad had 5 wives in excess of the Quranic limit stated for Muslim men. It seems Muhammed preached laws unto Muslims that he himself was not subjected too. Even his wife said that Allah hurries to satisfy his desire.

Sahih Bukhari, Vol. 7, Pages 35, Hadith 48 "Narrated Hisham's father: Khaula bint Hakim was one of those ladies who presented themselves to the Prophet (ﷺ) for marriage [Surah 33:50]. `Aisha said: Doesn't a lady feel ashamed for presenting herself to a man? But when the Verse: (O Muhammad) You may postpone (the turn of) any of them (your wives) that you please,' (33.51) was revealed, Aisha said: O Allah's Messenger (ﷺ) I do not see, but, that your Lord hurries in pleasing you."

What was the next Quranic condition for polygyny?

Quran Translation by Abdullah Yusuf Ali – Surah 4:3 "…Marry women of your choice, two or three or four; **but if ye fear that ye shall not be able to deal justly (with them), then only one**…"

How did Quran Translator, Abdullah Yusuf Ali understood this verse? **Quran Translation by Abdullah Yusuf Ali: Page 179 Commentary 509** "Provided you could **TREAT THEM WITH PERFECT EQUALITY, IN MATERIAL THINGS AS WELL AS IN AFFECTION AND IMMATERIAL THINGS.**"

In Quranic days, if a Muslim husband wanted to marry a second wife, the Quranic condition was that he must evaluate his emotional, financial, etc. position to determine whether he **WOULD BE** able to treat all his wives fair and just.

If, after his evaluation, he honestly concluded that his budget *would not* allow him to equally provide for his second wife, just like he currently provided for his first wife, then polygyny was out for him. He must have been able to strategically confirm that he would be able to support both wives equally and not provide more for a favorite wife and neglect one of the other wives.

Quran Translation by Abdullah Yusuf Ali: Page 1122 Commentary 3749 "In the Muslim household there is *NO ROOM FOR A FAVORITE WIFE.*"

Polygyny was subjected to **prior confirmation of definite** equality treatment towards all the wives. If a man envisioned no equality treatment towards all of his wives, Surah 4:3 says: No polygyny.

Did Allah say no-man can treat his wives equal?

I'm still to find a Muslim that treats his wives fair and just in material ***and immaterial things***. No matter how sincere a Muslim vow that he will treat all his wives the same, or are treating them all the same, Allah in the Quran says it is impossible for him to treat all his wives with perfect equality.

Quran Translation by Abdullah Yusuf Ali – Surah 4:129 "Ye are **NEVER** able to be just and fair as between women, **EVEN** if it is your ardent [devout] desire…"

Any Muslim who says he will be able to treat his wives fair and just or he is treating all his wives fair and just, he is either a liar or Allah in Surah 4:129 is a liar that says men can never be fair (just) even if they try

How do Muslim Translators understand Surah 4:129?

Quran Translation by Abdullah Yusuf Ali: Page 179 Commentary 509: "I understand the recommendation to be towards **MONOGAMY**."

Authorized English Version of the Quran – Surah 4:129 Heading: "Polygyny **DISCOURAGED**".

Since the Quranic condition in Surah 4:3 for polygyny is based on the condition that you must be able to treat your wives just (fair) and the confirmation from Allah in the Quran Surah 4:129 is that no-man can treat his wives fair and just, that means polygyny is out for **ALL** Muslims.

If Surah 4:129 is correct than polygyny is banned in Islam.

Did Muhammad treat his wives fair and equal?

__Sahih Bukhari, Vol. 3, Pages 454-455, Hadith 755__ "Narrated Urwa from Aishah: ...Um Salama [from the second group of Muhammed's wives] called Fatima [Muhammed's] daughter and sent her to Allah's Apostle and said to him: **YOUR WIVES REQUEST YOU TO TREAT THEM AND THE DAUGHTER OF ABU BAKR ON EQUAL TERMS...**"

Why do Muslims continue to practice polygyny?

Some are unaware of the Quranic polygyny conditions in Surah 4:3 and the Quranic confirmation in Surah 4:129 that no-man can fulfill these conditions. In other words, they are not practicing polygyny based on the Quran, but based on their ignorance of what they think Islam teach.

Some are aware of the **im**possibility to fulfill the polygyny condition, but they throw a blind-eye to this criterion, because one wife cannot fulfill their sexual – lustful desires.

__Malise Ruthven: Islam: A very short introduction: Page 98__ "If polygyny is prohibited **men who can't remain satisfied with only one wife** will look outside the bounds of matrimonial life and create sexual anarchy and corruption. (Maududi, Tafhim al-Quran, ii, 7-8: Comm. on S.4:3)"

__Authorized English Version of the Quran: Page 478 – Appendix 30 – "Polygamy"__ "Unless we are sure God's Law [Surah 4:3 treat them fair] will not be abused [which we now know can't be uphold – Surah 4:129], **WE HAD BETTER RESIST OUR LUST** and stay away from polygamy."

Are there more women than men in the world?

The Encyc. Britannica 15TH Edition Vol. 7 p. 998 "Reliably, human populations studied at birth, **there is an excess of males, about 106 boys are born for 100 girls**. Throughout life, however, there is greater mortality of males; this slowly alters the sex ratio until **beyond the age of 50 years there is an excess of females**."

Gender Ratio by Hannah Ritchie & Max Roser "Natural sex ration at birth is **around 105 boys to 100 girls**... **For 50-year-olds the ratio is close to 1-to-1; for 70-year-olds there are 89 males per 100 females**... https://ourworldindata.org/gender-ratio Last accessed 27 April 2021

Those who use the more women than men ratio argument as a basis of polygyny must therefore marry available grannies from the age of 70 years or older, not young girls. Remember, the first condition is marrying women not children or young girls – *marry women (nisaa)* and if you use the more women than men argument, then you must marry women of 50 years or older. Some Muslims argue that polygyny is justifiable, because there are many men who are becoming homosexuals, meaning there are lesser men to marry women. What these Muslims don't tell their audience, is that many women are also lesbians.

73 Does Allah allow Muslim-men to have pre-marital sex with captured women (slaves)?

Quran Trans. by Abdullah Yusuf Ali – Surah 4:24, Page 187 Comm. 537 "(Prohibited are) women already married, **except those whom your right hands possess**... Whom your right hands possess: e.g. captives..."

T.P. Huges: Dictionary of Islam Pages 596-597 "The term generally used in the Quran for slave is *ma malakat asmanukum:* **that which your right hand possesses** ... MUSLIMS ARE ALLOWED TO COHABIT WITH ANY OF THEIR FEMALE SLAVES ... THEY ARE ALLOWED TO TAKE POSSESSION OF MARRIED WOMEN IF THEY ARE SLAVES ... On this verse al-Jalalan the commentators say: *it is lawful for them to cohabit with those women whom you have made captive,* **even though their husbands**

***be alive*...** Slaves ... are the lawful property of their master [who] has the power to take to himself any female slave, the position of slaves are as helpless as the stone idols of Arabia..."

Here we see that Allah prohibited sex with women who are not your wives, but Allah does allow Muslim men to also have sex with women (single or married to other men), if those women are their slaves, worst still, Allah revealed that Muslim men can have sex with captured women in the presence of their captured, helpless husbands, if that is not rape, I don't know what rape is.

If America is in war with Afganistan and America wins and takes Muslims captive, will it be morally acceptable for the America soldiers to rape the Muslim women in the presence of their husbands, fathers, brothers, etc.? Will you condemn such action? If yes, do you condemn Allah who gave Muhammed the go ahead for Muslims to rape their captives?

Surah 23:1-6

Quran Translation by Abdullah Yusuf Ali: "...Those who humble themselves in their prayers ... **WHO ABSTAIN FROM SEX, EXCEPT WITH [1]** those joined to them in the marriage bond *or* **[2] (THE CAPTIVES)** whom their right hands possess..."	*The Koran* "...Who are humble in their prayers... **WHO RESTRAIN THEIR CARNAL DESIRES (EXCEPT WITH** [1] their wives *and* [2] slave girls, for these are lawful to them: transgressors are those who lust after others then these) ..." [Surah 70:29-30]

The Koran – Surah 33:50 "O Prophet, we have made lawful for you the wives to whom you have granted dowries **AND THE SLAVE-GIRLS WHOM GOD HAS GIVEN YOU AS BOOTY**..."

Here we see that Allah revealed unto the Muslims that they could have sex with two groups of women, their wives (which is obvious) **AND WITH CAPTIVE WOMEN (SINGLE OR MARRIED)**.

In the Bible, the OT, sex outside of marriage, even with captives of war were forbidden.

Deuteronomy 21:10-14 "When thou goest forth to war against thine enemies, and the LORD thy God hath delivered them into thine hands, and thou hast taken them captive, 11 And seest among the captives a beautiful woman, and hast a desire unto her, that thou wouldest have her to **THY WIFE**; 12 Then thou shalt bring her home to thine house; and she shall shave her head, and pare her nails; 13 And she shall put the raiment of her captivity from off her, and shall remain in thine house, and bewail her father and her mother a full month: and after that thou shalt go in unto her, **AND BE HER HUSBAND, AND SHE SHALL BE THY WIFE**."

Looking at above passage, there is not even a hint of rape or lust being dump upon the women taken in war. In fact, just the opposite is given. When a woman who is not a Jew is made a captive and the Israelite falls in love with her, he is not allowed to touch her for 30 days so that she may mourn the loss of her family and country. The intention of this law is to protect her against any lust (rape). Sex is not to be simply a thing of lust, but of true love and care. Gentile woman was protected under this covenant, just like Jewish women.

Muhammad said men's penis will be erected 24/7 in heaven

Sunan Ibn Majah **Volume 5, Book 37, Hadith 4337** "It was narrated from Abu Umamah that **THE MESSENGER OF ALLAH (ﷺ) SAID**: There is no one whom Allah will admit to Paradise, but Allah will marry him to seventy-two wives, two from houris and seventy from his inheritance from the people of Hell, all of whom will have desirable front passages. **HE WILL HAVE A MALE MEMBER THAT NEVER BECOMES FLACCID (SOFT).** https://quranx.com/Hadith/IbnMajah/DarusSalam/Volume-5/Book-37/Hadith-4337

Last accessed 27 April 2021

Quran Translation by Abdullah Yusuf Ali – Surah 36:55 "Verily the Companions of the Garden shall that Day **HAVE JOY** in all that they do."

Jalal - Al-Jalalayn S. 36:55 "Indeed today the inhabitants of Paradise are busy ... **delighting in pleasures such as deflowering virgins**..." https://quranx.com/Tafsir/Jalal/36.55 Last accessed 27 April 2021

74 Islam and the status of women?

One male witness equals two female witnesses

Quran Translation by Abdullah Yusuf Ali – Surah 2:282 "Get two witnesses out of your own men and if there are not two men, then a man and two women…"

Women's minds are deficient

Sahih Bukhari Vol. 3, Page 502, Hadith 826 "The prophet said: Isn't the witness of a woman equal to half of a man? The women said: Yes! He said: This is because of the **DEFICIENCY OF THE WOMAN'S MIND.**"

Women made from a man's rib

Sahih Bukhari Vol. 4, Page 346, Hadith 548 "Allah's Messenger said: Treat women nicely, for a woman is created from a rib, and the most curved portion of the rib is the upper portion, so if you should try to straighten it, it will break, but if you leave it as it is, it will remain crooked. So treat women nicely."

Women are most harmful affliction

Sahih Bukhari Vol. 7, Page 22, Hadith 33 "The prophet said: After me I **have not left any affliction more harmful to men than women.**"

Angels curse women who desert their husbands' beds

Sahih Bukhari, Vol. 7, Page 93, Hadith 122 "Narrated Abu Huraira: The Prophet said: If a woman spends the night deserting her husband's bed (does not sleep with him), then the angels send their curses on her till she comes back (to her husband)."

Women are the majority in hell

Sahih Bukhari Vol. 7, Page 94, Hadith 124 "Narrated Usama: The Prophet said... I stood at the gate of the fire and saw the MAJORITY OF THOSE WHO ENTERED IT WERE WOMEN."

75 Are Muslims who have Christian friends, true Muslims?

The Noble Quran – Surah 5:51 "*O you who believe!* **TAKE NOT** the Jews and Christians as **auliya** (friends, protectors) they are but **auliya** (friends, protectors) to each other. And he amongst *YOU THAT TURNS TO THEM (FOR FRIENDSHIP) IS OF THEM*. Verily Allah guideth not a people unjust."

Tafsir - Ibn Al Kathir S5:51 "The **PROHIBITION** of taking the Jews, Christians and Enemies of Islam as Friends: **ALLAH FORBIDS HIS BELIEVING SERVANTS FROM HAVING JEWS AND CHRISTIANS AS FRIENDS, BECAUSE THEY ARE THE ENEMIES OF ISLAM AND ITS PEOPLE,** *MAY ALLAH CURSE THEM*."

Wow, Muslims who have Christians as friends are in direct violation of Allah's instruction. Does that mean Muslims, who have Christians, are disobeying Allah's instruction? Allah says these Muslims are of them, they are actually Christians, since they disobey Allah. This is not about the feelings of a good Muslim; this is what Allah declared in the Quran.

Every Muslim that reads this and still have Christian friends, in their hearts, they don't believe Allah, but outwardly, they pretend to be Muslims. You are not guided by Allah if you have Christians as friends.

"Islam is an Arabic word meaning *submission*. In the religious context it means: *submission to God's will*." https://www.google.com/search?q=what+does+submit+in+Islam+means%3F&oq=what+does+submit+in+Islam+means%3F&aqs=chrome..69i57j0.18236j1j7&sourceid=chrome&ie=UTF-8

Last accessed 27 April 2021

Muslims with Christian friends have not yet submitted to Allah's Will! What about a Muslim who have Christian families?

Muslims with Christian parents as friends are wrong

The Noble Quran – Surah 9:23 *"O YE WHO BELIEVE!* **TAKE NOT** as **auliya** (supporters and helpers) your fathers and your brothers if they prefer disbelief to belief. And whoever of you does so than ye is one of the zaliman (wrong doers)."

Wow, if you are a Muslim and your family reject Islam, you should not turn to them for support, help or friendship, if you do turn to your disbelieving family, Allah says you are a wrong doer.

The Noble Quran – Surah 3:57, 11:18 "…Allah does not like the zalimun (wrong-doers) … The curse of Allah is upon the zalimun (wrong-doers)."

Muslims are instructed not to greet Christians first

Sahih Muslim: "Abu Huraira reported Allah's Messenger as saying: Do not greet the Jews and Christians before they greet you and when you meet one on the roads force him to go to the narrowest part of it." https://quranx.com/Hadith/Muslim/USC-MSA/Book-26/Hadith-5389

Last accessed 27 April 2021

SECTION 8

ISLAM AND THE SWORD

76 How is Christianity and Islam spread: peace or violence?

When the need arises to discuss freedom of belief, Muslims almost never fails to mention the "Crusaders" and the song: "On with Christian Soldiers matching as to war – with the Cross of Jesus going on before…"

The questions before us are…

1. *Where in the Gospel* are Christians called to go to a physical war with pagans?

2. *Did Jesus Christ or his true followers in the Gospel* lead any war to spread Christianity?

3. *Did Jesus Christ or His disciples in the Gospel* order the physical death of those who left Christianity?

NOWHERE IN THE GOSPELS are Christians instructed to fight a physical war against non-believers. NEVER in history did Christ and the early church in the Gospel lead a physical war to spread Christianity. Neither did Jesus or His disciples ordered for backsliders from Christianity to be killed. True Christians who believe in the Gospels will not consciously go against Christ's teaching of peace to take up physicsl arms to spread Christianity. Any Christian who spreads Christianity through violence, suppression, any type of force, *left Christianity*. True Christians <u>are subjected</u> to the teachings of the Gospel. Hear the words of the Prince of Peace, Jesus Christ our Lord and Saviour.

<u>*Matthew 7:21*</u> "Not everyone that said unto me, Lord-Lord, shall enter into the Kingdom of heaven **BUT HE THAT DOETH THE WILL OF MY FATHER** which is in heaven."

Even Apostle Paul gave us divine advice who our real enemy is and he also gave us instructions how we ought to fight our enemy: <u>*Ephesians 6:11-18*</u> "Put on the whole armor of God that ye may be able to stand against the **WILES OF THE DEVIL. FOR WE WRESTLE NOT AGAINST FLESH AND BLOOD** but against principalities, against powers, against the rulers of the darkness of this world, against spiritual wickedness in high places. Wherefore take unto you the whole armor of God that ye may be able to withstand in the evil day... having your *loins girt about with Truth*, having on the *breastplate of righteousness*, your feet shod with the preparation of the Gospel of peace... Taking the *shield of faith*, wherewith ye shall be able to quench all the fiery darts of the wicked. Take the *helmet of salvation* and the **SWORD OF THE SPIRIT, WHICH IS THE WORD OF GOD**: Praying always with all prayer and supplication in the Spirit and watching thereunto with all perseverance and supplication for the Saints."

The Christian is inspired to go to war, not against men, but against the devil, even our armor is spiritual. You cannot fight a physical war with spiritual weapons. If the Crusaders fought wars to spread Christianity, they were unchristian in their behavior. Now, let us turn to Islam and investigate whether its fundamental teachings uphold compulsion of religion or not. To be fair in our evaluation, we need to use the same set of measures used for Christianity, above, against Islam:

1. ***Where in the Quran*** are Muslims called to go to a physical war with pagans?
2. ***Did Muhammad or his followers*** lead any war to spread Islam?
3. ***Did Muhammad or his companions*** order the physical death of those who left Islam?

Quran Translation by Abdullah Yusuf Ali – Surahs 16:125: "Invite (all) to the Way of thy Lord with wisdom and beautiful preaching and argue with them in ways that are best and most gracious: for thy Lord knoweth best, who have strayed from His Path and who receive guidance."

My responds: We understand that Muhammad and Muslims were persecuted by the Meccans, because of the Islamic message condemning idolatry. At this stage Muhammad preached no violence for Islam to be spread. In fact, Muhammad did not have the military power to withstand the Meccans and fled to Medina to practice Islam where Muhammad, at first, continued to preach peace.

Quran Translation by Abdullah Yusuf Ali – Surahs 2:190 "Fight in the cause of Allah **THOSE WHO FIGHT YOU**, but do not transgress limits; for Allah loveth not transgressors. 191 And slay them wherever ye catch them and **TURN THEM OUT FROM WHERE THEY HAVE TURNED YOU OUT**; for tumult and oppression are worse than slaughter; but fight them not at the Sacred Mosque, **UNLESS THEY (FIRST) FIGHT YOU THERE**; but if they fight you, slay them. Such is the reward of those who suppress faith. 2:256 **LET THERE BE NO COMPULSION IN RELIGION: TRUTH STANDS OUT CLEAR FROM ERROR**: whoever rejects evil and believes in Allah hath grasped the most trustworthy hand-hold, that never breaks. Allah heareth and knoweth all things. 4:75 And why should ye not fight in the cause of Allah and of those who, being weak, are ill-treated (and oppressed)? Men, women, and children, whose cry is: "Our Lord! Rescue us from this town, whose people are oppressors; and raise for us from thee one who will protect; and raise for us from thee one who will help!"

Notice, in Mecca, Muhammad did not have military power to defend Muslims from being persecuted and there he preached absolute peace. When the persecution became heavy, he fled to Medina where Muhammad's military power grew. Muhammad continued to preach peace during the Medina stage, but with increased military power he began to **preach self-defense from oppressors, which is good**. But as Muhammad's military power increased, so violent sermons became prevalent.

Muslims can fight against fraudulant Muslims

Quran Translation by Abdullah Yusuf Ali – Surah 49:9 "If two parties among the Believers fall into a quarrel, make ye peace between them: but if one of them transgresses beyond bounds against the other, then fight ye (all) against the one that transgresses, until it complies with the command of Allah; but if it complies, then make peace between them with justice, and be fair: for Allah loves those who are fair…"

Islam teach apostates must be killed

Public debate 17 Oct. 2017: Why Muslim? Why Christian? Christian Speaker, Dr. John Azumah, Muslim Speaker, Attorney Yusuf Ismail "[DVD: Time line 00:00:00 – 00:00:00 Yusuf:] **NOWHERE,** is there indication in the Quran or in the Prophetic Traditions, where apostasy is punishable by death."

Yusuf, being the intelligent giant and well research person that he is and well versed in the Quran and Ahadith, here obviously, as Dr. Azumah in his rebuttal mentioned, Attorney Yusuf deceptively choose not to admit Muhammad did preach violence and killing of the apostate, nevertheless, I will provide those examples here.

The Noble Quran – Surah 4:89 "They wish that you REJECT FAITH, AS THEY HAVE REJECTED (FAITH) and thus that you all become equal. So take not auliya (protectors or friends) from them, till they emigrate in the way of Allah. **BUT IF THEY TURN BACK (FROM ISLAM) TAKE (HOLD OF THEM) AND KILL THEM,** wherever you find them."

Please note, the above translation was done by dedicated Arabic speaking Muslim doctors and scholars. Notice, the verse does not say, if they attack you, fight them, no, the verse is very clear: If they leave Islam, Muhammad didn't say: "Smile with them" – **NO**, he said: …Kill them…"

Instead of reinforcing the above Surahs dealing with peace, Muhammad now being military strong, preached violence. He is no more preaching peace – the orders are clear – you leave Islam, death follows. Not only did Muhammad preach it in the Quran, but also in the Ahadith.

The Noble Quran: Page 151 – Footnote 2 "ALLAH'S MESSENGER SAID: The blood of a Muslim … cannot be shed, **EXCEPT … THE ONE WHO REVERTS FROM ISLAM (APOSTATES) AND LEAVE THE GROUP OF MUSLIMS** … (Sahih Bukhari Vol. 9, Page 11, Hadith 17)"

Sahih Bukhari Vol. 9, Page 50, Hadith 64 "Narrated `Ali: I heard the Prophet (ﷺ) saying: In the last days… young people… will go out of Islam … **WHEREVER YOU FIND THEM,**

KILL THEM, FOR THERE WILL BE A REWARD FOR THEIR KILLERS ON THE DAY OF RESURRECTION."

Clearly, Yusuf Ismail, when he said, nowhere is there indication in the Quran or Prophetic Traditions where apostasy is punishable by death, he either lied with open eyes and a smile or he was genuinely ignorant of Islamic dogma calling for the death of apostates. Let's hope he was ignorant.

Sunan an-Nasa'i: "Narrated from 'Ikrimah: "Some people **APOSTATIZED** after accepting Islam. Ali burned them with fire. Ibn 'Abbas said: … I wouldn't burn them; the Messenger of Allah [SAW] said: No one should be punished with Allah's punishment. If it was me, I would have killed them; **THE MESSENGER OF ALLAH [SAW] SAID: 'WHOEVER CHANGES HIS RELIGION, KILL HIM.**"

https://quranx.com/Hadith/Nasai/DarusSalam/Volume-5/Book-37/Hadith-4065

Last accessed 27 April 2021

Sahih Bukhari "Narrated `Ikrima: Ali burnt some people and this news reached Ibn `Abbas, who said: Had I been in his place I would not have burnt them, as the Prophet (ﷺ) said: Don't punish (anybody) with Allah's Punishment. No doubt, I would have killed them, for **THE PROPHET (ﷺ) SAID: IF SOMEBODY (A MUSLIM) DISCARDS HIS RELIGION, KILL HIM.**"

https://quranx.com/Hadith/Bukhari/USC-MSA/Volume-4/Book-52/Hadith-260

Last accessed 27 April 2021

Prof. Masudul Hasan: History of Islam, Vol. 1, Page 98 "Commanders were instructed before taking action against an apostate tribe, **IT SHOULD BE CALLED UPON TO RETURN TO ISLAM AND PUNITIVE ACTION SHOULD BE TAKEN <u>ONLY</u> ON THE EVENT OF THE REFUSAL OF THE TRIBE TO OFFER ALLEGIANCE TO ISLAM**. If the call of Adhan rose from the tribe that was *indicative of their return to Islam*."

We can clearly see from these examples that the fighting and killing, was no more about people oppressing the Muslims, but about Muslims forcing apostates to return to Islam or be killed. The Medina verses revealed the true Islam, what Islam is like, when Islam is military strong.

Modern-day Muslim scholars agree, kill apostates

<u>Abdurraghiem Hasan Sallie: "The Decree of the Murtad (Apostate) according to the Islamic law": Pages 3,7,23,24,25,26 & 30 [Available from: A. Sallie, 2 Nerina Street, Parow North, 7500 Cape Town, Phone no: 021 930 3403]</u> "Apostacy (also spelt apostasy) is the act of abandoning one's religion [leaving Islam] for another ... The Arabic word for apostasy is *riddah* ... **IBN KATHIR, VOLUME 4, PAGES 296-299: THE LEARNED JURISTS, IMAMS. MALIKIY, SHAFI-IY AND HAMBALIY AGREE THAT APOSTASY CARRIED THE DEATH PENALTY IRRESPECTIVE OF GENDER ... THE HOLY PROPHET (PBUH) HAD SAID: WHOEVER CHANGES HIS [ISLAMIC] RELIGION, THEN KILL HIM. THE HOLY PROPHET HAD SAID TO HIM [SAYDUNA MU-ADTH BIN JABAL]: CALL BACK ANY MAN WHO TURNS AWAY FROM ISLAM (THROUGH RIDDAH).**

IF HE RETURNS (THEN ALL IS WELL), BUT IF HE REFUSES, THEN HE MUST BE BEHEADED. The punishment in a Muslim country for apostasy is the death penalty. Before execution the apostate is incarcerated, but granted respite for three days. He must be fed daily with a spare diet of one loaf of bread. During the respite, knowledgeable scholars – Ulama, must try and convince and encourage him to repent and to revert to Islam. If, he fails, the **APOSTATE IS EXECUTED ... THE ABOVE ACCOUNT CONTAINS USEFUL GUIDANCE FOR MUSLIMS IN THE REPUBLIC OF SOUTH AFRICA. WHILE ISLAMIC LAW CANNOT BE IMPLEMENTED IN THIS COUNTRY, MUSLIMS CAN HOWEVER, REGISTER THEIR DISGUST BY EXCOMMUNICATING APOSTATES FROM THE MUSLIM SOCIETY – UMMAH** ... Those who duck and dive in such situations… who associate with apostates are traitors, hypocrites (and a danger to Islam)."

The latter quote also shows that Islam seems to be peaceful in South Africa, it's not, the South African Law stops Islam's violence to murder people who leaves Islam to embrace Christianity. Praise the Lord, Muslims are coming with tears in their eyes to Jesus Christ, accepting Him as their Lord and Savior. Halleluiah!

NOT ONLY ARE MUSLIM BACKSLIDERS KILLED, BUT ALSO PAGANS (NON-BELIEVERS) AND JEWS ARE SAID BY MUHAMMAD TO BE KILLED - CHRISTIANS ARE FIRST GIVEN THE OPTION TO PAY A TAX FOR PROTECTION AGAINST THE MUSLIM SWORD, BUT IF THEY DON'T PAY, THEIR END IS THE SAME LIKE THE OTHERS, DEATH IF YOU REJECT ISLAM.

Islam teach that disbelievers must be killed

Let's look at more Quranic verse where Allah inspire Muslims to fight non-Muslims if they reject Islam.

The Noble Quran – Surah 8:38-39 "Say to those who have **DISBELIEVED**, if they cease (from disbelieve) there past will be forgiven, but if they return (thereto) then the examples of those (punished) before them have already preceded (as a warning). **FIGHT THEM UNTIL THERE IS NO MORE "FITNAH" (DISBELIEVE AND POLYTHEISM, E.G. WORSHIPPING OTHERS BESIDES GOD) AND THE RELIGION [DIIN] (WORSHIP) WILL BE ALL FOR ALLAH ALONE (IN THE WHOLE OF THE WORLD), BUT IF THEY CEASE (WORSHIPPING OTHERS BESIDES ALLAH)** then certainly Allah is All-Seer of what they do."

Here Muhammad preached Muslims must fight unbelievers **UNTIL** certain outcomes are established:

[1] Fight them until there is no more unbelieve – polytheism;

[2] Fight them until there is no more idolatry and

[3] Fight them until faith in Allah remains (no other religions exists).

This is a clear contradiction to Surahs 16:125 and 2:256 when Muhammad was still military weak.

Muslims not to live in peace with non-Muslims?

Every time a Muslim says that Islam teach "peace" – that Muslim is either a cold liar or they are blatantly ignorant about their own dogma. The Quran clearly states that while Islam is weak, Muslims should call for peace, this is exactly the strategy Muhammad followed in Mecca and at his entry into Medina, but when his military power was established, he marched against Mecca and subdued the overpowered Meccans. Again, this is exactly the Islamic strategy (see heading: Modern-day Muslim scholars agree, kill apostates), but as soon as Islam takes over, death is on the horizon.

Quran Translation by Abdullah Yusuf Ali – Surah 47:35 "Do not display cowardice and **DO NOT CALL THE INFIDELS TO PEACE WHEN YOU ARE SUPERIOR TO THEM**."

The above verse is another Medina sermon after Muhammad gained military power. Muslim Scholar interpretations agree that there should be no peace, where Islam is superior.

Tafsir - Ibn Al Kathir S. 47:35 "(**SO DO NOT LOSE HEART** *AND BEG FOR PEACE WHILE YOU ARE SUPERIOR*) *meaning, in the condition of your superiority over your enemy. If, on the other hand, the disbelievers are considered more powerful and numerous than the Muslims, then the Imam (general commander) may decide to hold a treaty, if he judges that it entails a benefit for the Muslims.* **This is like what Allah's Messenger did when the disbelievers obstructed him from entering Makkah and offered him treaty in which all fighting would stop between them for ten years**."

https://quranx.com/Tafsir/Kathir/47.32

Last accessed 27 April 2021

When Muhammad was persecuted in Mecca, he preached peace, later in 622AD he fled to Medinah. There, when Muhammad's military power was established, he preached apostates and non-believers must be fought, until they become Muslims or be killed, at this stage, he no more enforced Surah 2:256 *"There's no compulsion in religion."* His message was clear: Fight **un**believers – not fight those who robbed your caravans – BUT FIGHT THOSE WHO DOES **NOT** BELIEVE IN ISLAM – clearly, Muslims are instructed to use physical war against non-Muslims, UNTIL THE NON-MUSLIMS BECOME MUSLIMS.

<u>Quran Translation by Abdullah Yusuf Ali – Surah 9:3, 5</u> "…And proclaim a **GRIEVOUS PENALTY TO THOSE WHO REJECT FAITH** … **SLAY THE IDOLATERS** wherever you find them **… IF THEY REPENT AND TAKE TO PRAYER** and pay the alms-tax *let them go* their way…"

Why must the idolaters be slain? Because they rejected faith. Why must the idolaters be spared? They repent, take to prayer and pay tax.

Muslims ordered to fight Christians until they join Islam or pay jizyah

<u>The Noble Quran – Surah 9:29</u> "**FIGHT AGAINST THOSE** who (1) believe not in Allah, (2) nor in the Last Day, (3) nor forbid that which had been forbidden by Allah and his messenger (Muhammad pbuh) (4) **AND THOSE WHO ACKNOWLEDGE NOT THE RELIGION OF TRUTH (ISLAM) AMONG THE PEOPLE OF THE SCRIPTURE (JEWS/CHRISTIANS),** until they pay the Jizyah with willing submission…"

Who must be fought? Those who believe not …

Muslim scholar Nadir Ahmed: *<u>"Does Islam promote violence against non-Muslims?"</u>* *<u>Dated 15 Sept 2011</u>* - was shocked to learn what Surah 9:29 says and asked the moderator if they could change the topic. His best defends was that Surah 9:29 have a typo. https://www.youtube.com/watch?v=g3f_pC0-Oys

Time line 00:00 – 02:40 Last accessed 27 April 2021

Muslims might recite the Quran in Arabic, but majority of them have no clue to what it means. Nadir lost the debate in the first three minutes, even before the Christian, Dr. David Wood took the podium to present his case. Hahahahaha. What a joke!

Here Muhammad and Muslims are influenced to fight pagans, Jews and Christians. Why? Because we believe not in the Islamic god, nor do we forbid what Muhammad forbid and we don't recognize Islam. Clearly, the reason to fight us, is not self-defense, but to spread Islam. Not only did Muhammad preach it as Allah's inspiration, but it was also his daily conversation.

The Noble Quran: Page 808 – Footnote A "Narrated Anas bin Malik (Arabic words) ALLAH'S MESSENGER (Arabic words) SAID: I HAVE BEEN ORDERED TO FIGHT THE PEOPLE TILL THEY SAY: [1] **LA ILAHA ILLALLAH (NONE HAS THE RIGHT TO BE WORSHIPPED, BUT ALLAH)** and if they say so, [2] perform As-Salat (the prayer) like our Salat (prayer), [3] face our Qiblah and [4] slaughter as we slaughter, then their blood and property will be sacred to us and we will not interfere with them, except legally … (*Sahih Bukhari Vol. 1, Page 234, Hadith 387*)."

Dr. Muhammad M. Khan, below, spoke out loud and clear – fight those who reject Islam.

Sahih Bukhari Vol. 1 Page xxvi "Allah revealed in Sura IX the order to discard (all) the obligations (covenants, etc.) and commanded the Muslims to **FIGHT AGAINST ALL THE PAGANS AND AGAINST THE PEOPLE OF THE SCRIPTURES (JEWS AND CHRISTIANS), IF THEY DO NOT EMBRACE ISLAM**…"

Why must Muslims fight us? We do not embrace Islam.

Faruq Sheriff: A guide to the contents of the Quran Page 59 "Several INCONSISTENCIES EXIST IN THE VERSES OF THE QURAN. One important incompatibility is that which exists between the statements in ii.256 to the effect that there shall be no compulsion in religion and that in ix.29 which commands Moslems to fight non-Moslems, including Jews-Christians."

Tafsir - Ibn Al Kathir S. 9:28-29 "Idolators are no longer allowed into Al-Masjid Al-Haram. Allah commands His believing servants, who are pure in religion and person, to expel the idolators who are filthy in the religious sense, from Al-Masjid Al-Haram. After the revelation of this Ayah, idolators were no longer allowed to go near the Masjid. This Ayah was revealed in the ninth year of Hijrah. The Messenger of Allah sent `Ali in the company of Abu Bakr that year to publicize to the idolators that no Mushrik will be allowed to perform Hajj after that year, nor a naked person allowed to perform Tawaf around the House. Allah completed this decree, made it a legislative ruling, as well as, a fact of reality. `Abdur-Razzaq recorded that Jabir bin `Abdullah commented on the Ayah, (O you who believe! Verily, the Mushrikin are impure. So let them not come near Al-Masjid Al-Haram after this year) "Unless it was a servant or one of the people of Dhimmah." Imam Abu `Amr Al-Awza'i said: Umar bin `Abdul-`Aziz wrote (to his governors) to prevent Jews and Christians from entering the Masjids of Muslims and he followed his order with Allah's statement: Verily, the Mushrikin are impure. Ata' said: All of the Sacred Area the Haram is considered a Masjid, for Allah said: So let them not come near Al-Masjid Al-Haram (at Makkah) after this year. This Ayah indicates that idolators are impure and that the believers are pure. In the Sahih is the following, (The believer does not become impure.) **Allah said: and if you fear poverty, Allah will enrich you, out of His bounty. Muhammad bin Ishaq commented: The people said: Our markets will be closed, our commerce disrupted and what we earned will vanish. So Allah revealed this verse and if you fear poverty, Allah will enrich you, out of His bounty from other resources, (if He wills), until, (...and feel themselves subdued.) This Ayah means, `this will be your compensation for the closed markets that you feared would result. Therefore, Allah compensated them for the losses they incurred because they severed ties with idolators, by the Jizyah they earned from the People of the Book**. Similar statements were reported from Ibn `Abbas, Mujahid, `Ikrimah, Sa`id bin Jubayr, Qatadah and Ad-Dahhak and others. Allah said: Surely, Allah is All-Knowing in what benefits you, All-Wise in His orders and prohibitions, for He is All-Perfect in His actions and statements, All-Just in His creations and decisions, Blessed and Hallowed be He. **This is why Allah compensated Muslims for their losses by the amount of Jizyah that they took from the people of Dhimmah. The Order to fight People of the Scriptures until They give the Jizyah ...** Therefore, when People of the Scriptures disbelieved in Muhammad, they had no beneficial faith in any Messenger or what the

Messengers brought ... Had they been true believers in their religions, that faith would have directed them to believe in Muhammad, because all Prophets gave the good news of Muhammad's advent and commanded them to obey and follow him. Yet when he was sent, they disbelieved in him, even though he is the mightiest of all Messengers. Therefore, they do not follow the religion of earlier Prophets. because these religions came from Allah, but because these suit their desires and lusts. Therefore, their claimed faith in an earlier Prophet will not benefit them because they disbelieved in the master, the mightiest, the last and most perfect of all Prophets. Hence Allah's statement: Fight against those who believe not in Allah... This honorable Ayah was revealed with the order to fight the People of the Book, AFTER THE PAGANS WERE DEFEATED, the people entered Allah's religion in large numbers, and THE ARABIAN PENINSULA WAS SECURED UNDER THE MUSLIMS' CONTROL. Allah commanded His Messenger to fight the People of the Scriptures, Jews and Christians, on the ninth year of Hijrah, and he prepared his army to fight the Romans and called the people to Jihad announcing his intent and destination. The Messenger sent his intent to various Arab areas around Al-Madinah to gather forces, and he collected an army of thirty thousand... The Messenger of Allah marched, heading towards Ash-Sham to fight the Romans until he reached Tabuk, where he set camp for about twenty days next to its water resources. He then prayed to Allah for a decision and went back to Al-Madinah because it was a hard year and the people were weak, as we will mention, Allah willing. Paying Jizyah is a Sign of Kufr and Disgrace Allah said, (until they pay the Jizyah), if they do not choose to embrace Islam." https://quranx.com/Tafsir/Kathir/9.28 Last accessed 27 April 2021

Muslims admit Islam threatens with the sword

See bullet X – how early Muslims used the sword to conquer the Middle East, parts of Africa, etc.

Presented by **_Dr. D. Wood: Zaakir Naik's plot to silence critics of Islam._** Famous Muslim scholar, Dr. Zaakir Naik, informed Muslims to repel with good against those voicing their opinion about Islam, but he also said that Muslims must keep a list of those who speaks against Islam and when they travel to Muslim country they need to be reported to the country officials to make an arrest where you will be punished, imprisoned and, or killed under Islamic capital punishment. Look here:

https://www.youtube.com/watch?v=p8e_T7v0H5c&t=595s Last accessed 27 April 2021

A contemporary scholar in Egypt, Sheikh Muhammad Mutawilli al-Sha'rawi, wrote: **_"You Ask and Islam Answers" Page 52_** "Some ask: HOW DOES ISLAM SAY THAT THERE IS NO COMPULSION IN FAITH AND YET IT COMMANDS THE KILLING OF THE APOSTATE? We say to them... once you embraced the faith you are not free... **you should be bound to Islam otherwise you will suffer punishment**..." [As cited in "Behind the Veil"]

Offensive War to Spread Islam: "It may be said, what is the value of a faith in Islam, which is a result of a threat? Abu Sufyan was not a believer and then he **BELIEVED AFTER HE WAS THREATENED BY DEATH**. We say to those who question: What is required of an infidel ... is to have its tongue surrendered to the religion of God ... *HIS HEARTFELT FAITH ... IT WILL COME LATER.*" [As cited in "Behind the Veil]

While Islam is satisfied with the false testimony of the tongue of a person under the threat of death, Christianity **CALLS** for the satisfaction of **BOTH** a heartfelt and honest confession of faith from believers.

When the Ethiopian expressed his desire to convert to Christianity, the evangelist told him: **_Acts 8:37_** "If you **BELIEVE WITH ALL YOUR HEART**, you may."

The Apostle Paul put it this way: **_Romans 10:9_** "That if thou shalt confess with thy mouth the Lord Jesus and shalt believe in thine heart that God hath raised Him from the dead, thou shalt be saved."

SECTION 9

ISLAM AND THE CROSS

77 Crucifixion and resurrection of Jesus Christ: fact or fiction?

Christian view: crucifixion and resurrection is a fact

OVER A BILLION CHRISTIANS BELIEVE, ACCORDING TO THE HOLY BIBLE, Jesus Christ was nailed to the cross, died on the cross, His corpse was taken from the cross, buried and He resurrected on the third day.

The crucifixion and resurrection of Jesus Christ is the heart of the Christian faith. Everything a Christian believes in and hopes for revolves around Jesus' death on the cross and His resurrection on the third day. The resurrection is the divine vindication that Jesus didn't die for any crime He committed, but died in place of sinners, reconciling us back to an infinitely holy and just God.

Faith in "THE GOSPEL MESSAGE" of Jesus Christ' death on the cross and His resurrection from the dead, is the **"ONLY"** way to experience salvation. If there is "no" crucifixion and "no" actual resurrection of Jesus Christ – there is "no" Biblical salvation – "no" redemption – "no" heaven – "no" hell – "no" true Christianity and the Bible is false.

1 Corinthians 1:23 "…But we preach Christ crucified…"

1 Corinthians 15:17 "If Christ be not raised, your faith is vain…"

1 Corinthians 15:20 "But now is Christ risen from the dead…"

Muslim view: crucifixion and resurrection is a fiction

Over one billion Muslims believe that Jesus Christ, the son of Mary, did **NOT** die on the cross and by default, was **NOT** resurrected. Muslims are divided into two schools of thought:

✓ **THE MAJORITY OF SUNNI MUSLIMS** *believe* that Allah changed the figures of someone-else to look like Jesus Christ and THAT person was arrested, put on the cross and died, while the real Jesus ascended into heaven alive without tasting death. This is known as *"The Substitution Theory".*

✓ **THE MINORITY OF SUNNIS AND OTHER ISLAMIC SECTS**, believes that Jesus Christ, the son of Mary, was put on the cross, but contrary to the Bible, they believe He **NEVER** died on the cross, but only fainted on the cross and therefore, He was taken alive from the cross and placed in a tomb where **HE RESUSCITATED** and later ascended into heaven without tasting death. This is known as *"The Swoon Theory".*

The Christian belief (*Christ DIED on the cross and was RESURRECTED*) and the Muslim belief (*Christ did NOT die on the cross and was NOT resurrected*) can't both be right, either both faiths are wrong or one of them is wrong and the other is right!

78 Did Jesus Christ know about his betrayal and crucifixion?

In order to discredit the Biblical crucifixion event, Mr. Deedat wrote: **<u>Crucifixion or Crucifiction? Page 16</u>** "It *appears* that **Jesus knew nothing** about the contract for his crucifixion."

After reading the above, the uninformed reader would think Deedat did a thorough research on the topic in the Bible, Quran and other reliable (historical) literature.

Reading Deedat's booklet, right from the start, it becomes notable that Deedat don't have reliable evidence to support his hypothesis. Deedat failed miserably to provide any Biblical, Quranic or historical references to substantiate his guess that Jesus knew nothing about the contract for His crucifixion. The uninformed readers of Deedat's booklet, is left with only Deedat's unverified 21st century misguided view, 2000 years later after this historic event. If Deedat could at least have read the Bible, not necessarily to believe in it, but just to know and understand what is recorded in the Bible, he would have come to the biblical knowledge that Jesus, not only knew about the contract of His crucifixion that awaited Him, but *that Jesus actually prophesied about His crucifixion, His death and His resurrection.*

Matthew 20:18 "[Jesus said:] The Son of man *shall be betrayed and be condemned to death*. 19 They shall deliver Him to the Gentiles to mock and to scourge and to **CRUCIFY HIM AND THE THIRD DAY HE SHALL RISE AGAIN** … (26:20) Now when the even was come, He sat down with the twelve. 21 And as they did eat, He said: Verily **I SAY UNTO YOU THAT ONE OF YOU SHALL BETRAY ME** … 45 Then came He [Jesus] to His disciples and saith unto them: Sleep on now and take your rest: **BEHOLD, THE HOUR IS AT HAND AND THE SON OF MAN IS BETRAYED INTO THE HANDS OF SINNERS. 46 RISE, LET US BE GOING, HE IS AT HAND THAT DOTH BETRAY ME**. 47 … Judas, one of the twelve, came and with a great multitude with swords and staves, from the chief priests and elders of the people… 56 They that laid hold on Jesus led Him away to Caiaphas…" (Mark 14:18, Luke 22:21, John 13:21).

For Deedat to have made the claim that Jesus knew nothing about the contract of His crucifixion shows that Deedat either failed to read the Gospels with understanding or he read it, but consciously suppressed the evidence at hand and blatantly lied to his audience (deceived them) that Jesus knew nothing about His crucifixion.

It is sad that *many* people blindly accepted Deedat's unverified suggestions as divine truth, as if Deedat received revelation after the Bible and Quran. It's also sad that these Muslims accepted Deedat's claims as historical truth, as if Deedat quoted from reliable sources. Deedat was either ignorant or deceptive about the fact that Jesus knew nothing about the contract (betrayal and crucifixion).

79 Were the disciples' witnesses of the crucifixion of Jesus?

Many Muslims **mis**quote the Bible at large that the disciples were not eye-witnesses of the events of the crucifixion of Jesus, because the Bible in one place indicated that the disciples forsook Jesus in the Garden of Gethsemane when the Jews and Romans came to arrest Him.

Ahmad Deedat: "Resurrection or Resuscitation?" Page 10 "You see, the disciples of Jesus were **NOT EYE OR EAR-WITNESSES** to the actual happenings of the previous three days, as vouched for by St. Mark who says that at the most critical juncture in the life of Jesus "THEY ALL FORSOOK HIM AND FLED..."

If Deedat carefully studied our scriptures, he would have noticed **THE DISCIPLES "FIRST" EYE-WITNESSED THE ARREST OF JESUS CHRIST AND "THEREAFTER" FLED AND FORSOOK HIM**.

Mark 14:48 "Jesus answered... Are ye come out, as against a thief, with swords and with staves to take Me? 49 I was daily with you in the temple teaching and ye took Me not, but the scriptures must be fulfilled. 50 *They all forsook Him and fled*." (Matthew 26:55-56).

See, they first eye-witnessed the arrest of Jesus Christ, then they fled. To stop your reading at this point and conclude the disciples were not eye or ear witnesses, is just lazy and evidently not scholarly.

Carefully notice, if you read on to get a whole picture, some of the disciples **RETURNED** individually to witness the illegal trial of Jesus Christ that was held by the Jewish Elders in the palace of the high priest.

Mark 14:53 "Peter followed Him afar off, **even into the palace** of the high priest..."

John 18:15 "Simon Peter followed Jesus and **so did another disciple, that disciple was known unto the high priest and went in with Jesus** into the palace of the high priest. 16 But Peter stood at the door without, then went out that other disciple, which was known unto the high priest and spoke unto her that kept the door and ***brought in Peter***."

Peter, when he denied knowing Jesus, he stood near to where Jesus could see him in the palace, proving Peter was an eye-witness to the trial.

Luke 22:60 "Peter said: I know not what thou say and immediately, while he yet spoke the cock crew. 61 **The Lord turned and looked to Peter**..."

After the Jews and Romans arrested Jesus Christ, then only did His disciples flee and forsook Him in the Garden of Gethsemane (Mark 14:50), but the Bible is very clear, Peter and another disciple returned to witness what happened to Jesus during his illegal hearing (Mark 14:53 – John 18:15-16 – Luke 22:60-62). It is not strange that Deedat forgot and most Muslims conveniently forget to mention these verses that attest that the disciples were eye-and-ear-witnesses of the arrest and illegal trial the Jewish leaders held with Jesus. As we have seen and will see, it is evident that Deedat constantly suppressed Biblical evidence that testified against his hypothesis.

Notice, it was only **after the trial** that Peter again denied knowing Jesus and fled. Deedat failed to provide substantiated evidence that no disciple was present at these events and therefore his claim that no disciple was an eye-ear-witness, again, falls flat to the ground.

It's noted that Muslims don't accept ALL of the Bible as inspired from God, but it's dishonest of any Muslim to say that the Bible teach that ALL the disciples were not eye-ear-witnesses to these events. It was deception for Deedat or any Muslim to suppress the Biblical evidence and then argue it is not there. But the truth will always be victorious. Even a child can read these verses and confirm that the Bible teach that SOME of Jesus' disciples were eye-ear-witnesses.

Luke 23:49 "And **all his acquaintance and the women that followed him** from Galilee stood afar off, BEHOLDING THESE THINGS."

John 19:26 "When Jesus therefore **saw His mother and the disciple standing by** whom He loved, He said unto His mother: Woman, behold thy son!"

As we have seen, after Jesus' disciples eye-ear-witnessed His arrest, then only did they left Him. We have seen that some of them returned and were witnesses of His illegal trial and finally, **all His acquaintance beholds His crucifixion**. Muslims might reject the Bible as inspired, but no honest Muslim can read the Bible and conclude from the Bible that none of His disciples were eye-ear-witnesses to these events.

Public Debate: Did Jesus Rise from The Dead? Muslim Speaker, Dr. Shabir Ally & Christian Speaker, Dr. Michael Licona [Quoting Ally:] "It is quite possible that **the disciples of Jesus witnessing the crucifixion event**, later on came to the conclusion for whatever reason that God raised Jesus from the dead."

https://www.youtube.com/watch?v=kgUjaXHyBsw&feature=youtu.behttps%3A%2F%2Fwww.youtube.com%2Fwatch%3Fv%3D5-9-vWtTcU8 [Time line – 00:47:00 – 00:47:13 Last accessed 27 April 2021

Deedat obviously misrepresented the Biblical evidents and all those uninformed Christians who believed Deedat's lie that the disciples were not witnesses and the Muslims who still spread this lie, is deceived.

80 Why do most Sunni Muslims believe Jesus was not on a cross and was not killed?

Most Muslims and non-Muslims, do **NOT READ, NOR UNDERSTAND ARABIC**, hence there is a total dependency on translations, either in the Quran-reader's mother-tongue or English. Unfortunately, most Quran translations are based on Muslim sectarian interpretations, rather than an honest translation from the Arabic text into English. Therefore, most of the time, the non-Arabs' understanding of the Quran, is based on **WHAT** they read in the *translated text*, **RATHER** than what is written in the *original text*.

MOST MUSLIMS BELIEVE JESUS WAS NOT CRUCIFIED AND NOT KILLED, BECAUSE SOME MUSLIM SCHOLARS TRANSLATED THE QURAN OR INTREPETED THE QURAN TO SAY:

- **"SOMEONE-ELSE WHOM GOD MADE TO LOOK LIKE JESUS WAS CRUCIFIED AND KILLED" – THIS IS REFERRED TO AS THE SUNNI SUBSTITUTION THEORY – MEANING, THE REAL JESUS WAS NOT CRUCIFIED, NOR KILLED, BUT TAKEN ALIVE TO HEAVEN BY ALLAH.**

- **"A CERTAIN RACE DID NOT CRUCIFY JESUS, NOR KILLED JESUS" – HE WAS CRUCIFIED BY ANOTHER RACE, BUT HE DID NOT DIE ON THE CROSS, HE**

ONLY FAINTED, WHILE HANGING ON THE CROSS – THIS IS KNOWN AS THE AHMADIYYAH SWOON THEORY.

ALL THREE OPPOSING VIEWS CAN'T BE RIGHT AT THE SAME TIME, BUT AS WE WILL LATER SEE, ALL THREE OPPOSING VIEWS ARE WRONG AND THE REAL JESUS WAS ACTUALLY CRUCIFIED AND KILLED.

Quran mistranslated to support *"The Substitution Theory"*

IA Ibrahim: A Brief illustrated guide to understanding Islam – Page 58 "Muslims believe that Jesus was "NOT" crucified. It was the plan of Jesus' enemies to crucify Him, but God saved Him and raised Him up to Him. **BUT THE LIKENESS OF JESUS WAS PUT OVER ANOTHER MAN. JESUS' ENEMIES TOOK THIS MAN AND CRUCIFIED HIM, THINKING HE WAS JESUS.**"

How did Muslims arrive at this **un**biblical idea that another man was made to look like Jesus and that this other man, who looked like Jesus, was crucified? BECAUSE OF THE BLATANT ENGLISH QURAN MISTRANSLATIONS, PEOPLE THINK THAT IS WHAT ALLAH SAID IN THE ARABIC QURAN.

The Noble Quran - Surah 4:157 "And because of their saying (in boast): We killed Messiah Jesus, son of Mary, the Messenger of Allah, **BUT THE RESEMBLANCE OF JESUS WAS PUT OVER ANOTHER MAN (AND THEY KILLED THAT MAN)** and those who differ therein are full of doubts. They have no (certain) knowledge. They follow nothing, but conjecture. For surely they killed Him [the real Jesus Christ] not."

Do you see the bold words: "**BUT THE RESEMBLANCE OF JESUS WAS PUT OVER ANOTHER MAN (AND THEY KILLED THAT MAN)**"? *These words are **NOT** found in the Arabic text of the Quran, but are additions and interpolations added into the English text by Muslim scholars, Drs. Hilali and Khan to establish "The Substitution Theory" in the minds of ignorant people who read their version thinking it is what the Arabic say.* They are writing their own Quran saying this is what Allah said, while Allah did not say it, then they sell their mistranslated books for a profit.

Some Muslims who both read and understand Arabic, spoke out against the above CORRUPTED ENGLISH *MIS*TRANSLATION of Surah 4:157 by Sunni Muslim scholars, Drs. Hilali and Khan.

Muslim scholar, Dr. Muhammed Asad confirmed: **_Message of the Quran: Page 134 – Commentary 171:_** "There exist among Muslims **FANCIFUL LEGENDS** telling us God substituted for Jesus a person resembling Him, whom was subsequently crucified in His place. **NONE OF THESE LEGENDS FINDS THE SLIGHTEST SUPPORT IN THE QURAN OR IN AUTHENTIC TRADITIONS.**"

Muslim scholar, Maulana Muhammed Ali also confirmed: **_The Holy Qur'an: Page 223 – Commentary 646_** "The story, that someone else was made to resemble Jesus, **IS NOT BORNE OUT BY THE WORDS OF THE QURAN.**"

Public Debate: Did Jesus Rise from The Dead? Muslim Speaker, Dr. Shabir Ally and Christian Speaker, Dr. William Lane Craig [Quoting Ally:] I find that almost universally that Muslim commentators have said that Jesus was not put on a cross, but someone-else was made to resemble Jesus and THAT someone-else was put on the cross ... **HOWEVER, IN MINE OWN STUDY OF THIS, AFTER CAREFULLY READING THE CLASSICAL COMMENTATORS, I FIND THERE IS NO REASON FOR HOLDING THAT PARTICULAR BELIEF ... FROM THAT BRIEF NARRATIVE IN THE QURAN ONE COULD "NOT" BUILD SUCH AN ELABORATE THEORY THAT SOMEONE-ELSE WAS MADE TO LOOK LIKE JESUS AND PUT ON THE CROSS INSTEAD."** https://www.youtube.com/watch?v=5-9-vWtTcU8 Time line 28:28 – 30:10 – Last accessed 27 April 2021

Public Debate: 27 October 2018 – Was Christ crucified? (Christian Speaker, Reverent Samuel Green and Muslim Speaker and Historian, Mr. Adnan Rashid: [Quoting Rashid:] **"SUBSTITUTION THEORY, I AGREE WITH SAMUEL THAT IT IS NOT A QURANIC POSITION** ... there is nothing whatsoever from the prophet on this issue..." https://www.youtube.com/watch?v=K24xIPcl1H4 Time line 43:23 – 43:39

Last accessed 27 April 2021

It is obvious that the corrupted English mistranslation – The Noble Quran – was produced by Muslim scholars, Drs. Hilali & Khan, to promote their FICTION: *"The Substitution Theory"*. It would have been better for these dishonest Muslim scholars to remove their opinions from their English Quranic Text Version and to place their opinions into their commentaries, to ensure that the casual readers of their Version don't mistake their [Drs. Hilali and Khan's] opinions to be part of the Quranic text.

It is, therefore, clear that the Arabic Quran does NOT support *"The Substitution Theory"* and Muslims who believe in it does so blindly. Their faith is built on fiction or in the words of Muslim scholar, Dr. Muhammad Asad, they follow *"fanciful legends"*. They believe the opinions of Drs Hilali and Khan thinking it is Allah's Word.

"The Substitution Theory" reveals the two-face hypocrisy of Sunni Muslims

It is deceptive that **Sunni Muslims argue** that God will be unfair to let Jesus die for the sins of another person, yet these same Sunni Muslims, unashamedly, have no problem to argue that someone-else died in Jesus' place, for the accusations that was brought against Jesus.

"The Substitution Theory" portrays the Islamic Jesus as a coward

The Biblical view of Jesus portrays Him as a self-sacrificing redeemer who willing laid down His life for those who believes in Him – the corrupted Quranic view of Jesus being substituted with someone who looked like him, portrays Jesus as a coward who allowed an innocent person to be mistakenly arrested, crucified and killed.

"The Substitution Theory" shows Allah allowed the innocent to die for another

If Allah made another man to look like Jesus and allowed that man to die in the place of Jesus, is strong evidence that Allah is comfortable for an innocent person (man with Jesus' resemblance and not guilty of the accusations that was made against Jesus) to die for another person (the real Jesus).

"The Substitution Theory" confirms the Quranic view that Allah is a deceiver

Public Debate: Did Jesus Rise from The Dead? Muslim Speaker, Dr. Shabir Ally and Christian Speaker, Dr. William Lane Craig "[Ally:] I find that almost universally that Muslim commentators have said that Jesus was not put on a cross, but someone-else was made to resemble Jesus and that someone-else was put on the cross and **IN THIS WAY GOD FOOLED THE ENEMIES OF JESUS** who wanted to crucify Him..." https://www.youtube.com/watch?v=5-9-vWtTcU8 Time line 28:28 – 28:45 – Last accessed 27 April 2021

To believe in the *"Substitution Theory"* would mean that **Allah not only fooled (deceived)** the enemies (accusers) of Jesus Christ, but Allah also deceived the Romans who arrested and crucified another man who seemingly looked like Jesus Christ, Allah also deceived the followers of Jesus Christ who then thought the actual Jesus Christ was arrested and crucified, whilst it was another man that looked like Jesus and Allah also deceived every Christian that ever lived, all historians and the rest of the world to make them think and believe that the real Jesus was crucified, while it was another man that looked like Jesus who was crucified.

Maybe it is easy for Sunni Muslims who believe in *"The Substitution Theory"* to accept that Allah fools people, since the **QURAN ITSELF DESCRIBED ALLAH AS A DECEIVER AND MISLEADER**.

The Noble Quran Surah 4:142 "... It is ALLAH WHO DECEIVES them."

Tafsir - Ibn Al Kathir S. 4:142 "(But it is HE WHO DECEIVES them) means, He lures them further INTO INJUSTICE AND MISGUIDANCE. *He also prevents them from reaching the truth in this life and on the Day of Resurrection.*" https://quranx.com/Tafsir/Kathir/4.142 Last accessed 27 April 2021

Tafsir Al-Jalalayn S. 4:142 "The hypocrites seek to trick God ... but He is tricking them." https://quranx.com/Tafsir/Jalal/4.142 Last accessed 27 April 2021

The Noble Quran Surah 14:4 "Then ALLAH MISLEADS whom He wills..."

Can you imagine, over one billion Muslims believe, not Satan, but "Allah" deceives, misleads and fools people, (i.e. crucifixion of Jesus Christ where another man was crucified)? The idea that an infinitely holy God, not only allow us to be deceived, but that He Himself actually deceives us, is blasphemous to God-fearing Christians. Far be it from God to be a deceiver (misleader). Here the Quran is obvious in gross error. No thinking person will agree with the Quran that our Holy God is a deceiver (misleader) and one who fools people!

According to Apostle Paul in the Holy Bible: **_1 Corinthians 1:9_** "God is faithful."

Although Muslims reject the writ of Paul as being inspired, they should, if honest, at least admit that Paul's Message is a more honorable description of God being faithful, than Muhammad's Message describing God as a deceiver and misleader. So happy I am a Christian.

"The Substitution Theory" contradicts Jesus life events

Substitution Theory	Birth – Childhood – Manhood – **ASCENSION – RETURN –** Death – Resurrection.
Quranic Life Events	Birth – Childhood – Manhood – Death – Resurrection – **ASCENSION.**

Quran Translation by Abdullah Yusuf Ali – Surah 19:33 "So peace is on me [Jesus] the day I was **born**, the day I **die** and the day I shall be **raised up to life** (again)."

Notice that Jesus in the Quran, in the above verse, does **NOT** teach that He will ascend to heaven **before His death**. He clearly stated that He was born, will die and resurrect. If Jesus Christ ascended to heaven before His death, then Jesus Christ in the Quran, misinformed us about His chronological life events. If Sunni Muslims want to argue that Jesus forgot to mention about His ascension before His death, it would mean that we can **NOT** trust Jesus' words _as recorded in the Quran_ or His words were accurately recorded in Surah 19:33, but Muslims are adding incorrect chronological events to His life.

Muslim writer, A.H. Obaray: Miraculous Conception, Death, Resurrection & Ascension of Jesus as Taught in the Kuran – Page 45 "**NO ONE CAN NOW SHIFT**

THE DEATH OF JESUS TO THE FUTURE. The parallel statement with John who died shows that Jesus also died. IN FACT, THERE IS NOT EVEN ONE SINGLE PASSAGE THROUGHOUT THE KURAN SHOWING JESUS WILL RETURN TO DIE."

If you believe that Jesus has been raised up alive and He has yet to die in the future, **THEN YOU HAVE CHANGED THE ORDER OF THE SEQUENCES IN SURAH 19:33.**

<u>*Quran Translation by Abdullah Yusuf Ali: Page 774 Commentary 2485*</u> "Those who believe Jesus never died should ponder over Surah 19:33."

Carefully note, Ali never said: *"**We** who believe Jesus never died should ponder over Surah 19:33".* In other words, Ali tells you that according to Surah 19:33 Jesus died. The fact that Jesus died is becoming common amongst Muslim scholars.

<u>*Ramadan Muslim Readers Digest Vol. 29 No's 3 & 4 Oct. Nov. 1978 Page 19:*</u> "Minority of the Muslim scholars believe that **JESUS IS DEAD**."

The sequential order of Jesus' life events as taught in the Bible and Quran is clear: birth-childhood-manhood-death-resurrection-ascension, which invalidates the chronological order of the Sunni Muslims: *"Substitution Theory":* birth – childhood – manhood – **ascension – return** – death.

"The Substitution Theory" contradicts secular history

<u>*Encyclopedia Britannica, 1993, Vol. 3, Page 762*</u> "**JESUS CHRIST, THE MOST FAMOUS VICTIM OF CRUCIFIXION.**"

<u>*Debate: 02 April 2009 – Can historians prove Jesus was raised from the dead? Christian Speaker, Dr. Michael Licona and Dr. Bart Ehrman (Historian and atheist)*</u> [Quoting Ehrman:] I agree that historians will tell you that Jesus was crucified. This, I believe is as certain historical as what you will get **from the ancient world that Jesus Christ was crucified under Pontius Pilate**, but the historians cannot tell you that Jesus was crucified *for your sins, that is theological*." [https://www.youtube.com/watch?v=-iE6YX9O5tE Time line 01:05:00 - 01:05:45 – Last accessed 27 April 2021

Even, if Muslims reject the Bible as inspired, to reject the crucifixion of Jesus Christ, paramount to rejecting history. If Muslims want to hold onto their misguided interpretation that the Quran deny that Jesus Christ was crucified, they subject the Quran to also contradict a historical event. No wonder we now see that Muslim scholars also now historically report that Jesus Christ was crucified.

Public debate: 25 June 2009: Crucifixion & Resurrection of Jesus: Fact or Fiction? Christian Speaker, Attorney John Gilchrist and Muslim Speaker, Doctor Shabir Ally [Ally says] His crucifixion is historically verified. Historians will agree that Jesus died by crucifixion."

https://www.youtube.com/watch?v=PHdrnjnAnq4 Time line 02:03:38– 2:03:46 Last accessed 27 April 2021

Prof. Masudul Hasan: History of Islam, ISBN 81-7435-016-0, Vol. 1, Page 29 "Jesus Christ was betrayed by the Jews and **CRUCIFIED**."

Muslim historians know that the Jews betrayed Jesus and confirm that Jesus Christ was crucified, but they (majority of Muslims) are too proud to accept history, hence they turn to fables (legends – fiction) of a substituted Jesus who died, so much so that Drs. Hilali and Khan even corrupted their English Version of the Quran in Surah 4:157 to support their Sunni sectarian view. They write the Quran with their hands and say this is from Allah, selling their corrupted English Version making a profit of millions of dollars.

Quran negate that the Jews crucified and killed Jesus Christ

Quran Translation by Abdullah Yusuf Ali – Surah 4:157 "*They* said (in boast): *We* killed Christ Jesus the son of Mary, the Apostle of God, **BUT THEY KILLED HIM NOT, NOR CRUCIFIED HIM**, but so it was made to appear to *them* … But for a surety *they* killed Him not."

Authorized English Version of the Quran "…**THEY** never killed him, **THEY** never crucified him…"

Sahih International and Shakir "…**THEY** did not kill him, nor did **THEY** crucify him"

Meaning of the Glorious Quran "...**THEY** slew him not, nor crucified him..."

The Horizon August / September 2011 – Page 13 "Quran 4:157: **THEY (JEWS)** said boasting: We killed Christ Jesus, the son of Mary, the messenger of Allah, but **THEY (JEWS)** killed him not..."

Clearly, the Quran **NEGATE THAT THE JEWS CRUCIFY AND KILLED CHRIST JESUS**. The Quran doesn't say **CHRIST JESUS WAS NOT CRUCIFIED AND KILLED AT ALL**. This is not just a Christian interpretation, but also Muslim scholars' interpretation.

Quran Translation by Abdullah Yusuf Ali: Page 137 – Commentary 394, Page 230 – Commentary 663/4 "...iv: 157 where it's said **THE JEWS** neither crucified, nor killed Jesus... The Quranic teaching is that Christ was not killed, nor crucified **BY THE JEWS**... The words are: **THE JEWS** did not kill Jesus..."

The Noble Quran: Appendix II – Page 911 "Muslims believe that Jesus was not crucified **BY THE JEWS** as revealed in the Holy Quran by Allah..."

THE QURAN STATES **THE JEWS DIDN'T** CRUCIFY, NOR KILLED JESUS.

THE QURAN NOWHERE STATE **THAT NO ONE** CRUCIFIED, NOR KILLED JESUS.

The Holy Qur'an: Page 223 Commentary 645 "The words *ma salabu-hu* **DO NOT NEGATE** Jesus being nailed to the cross..." [Unquote: it negate that the Jews did it.]

Public Debate: Did Jesus Rise from The Dead? Between Muslim Speaker, Dr. Shabir Ally and Christian Speaker, Dr. William Lane Craig "[Quoting Ally:] In brief, it seems to me that the Quran does not necessitate the belief that someone-else was put on the cross and **DOES NOT DENY AS A FACT THAT JESUS WAS PUT ON THE CROSS, IT JUST DENIES THAT THE ENEMIES OF JESUS WHO BOASTED DID NOT REALLY HAD THE UPPER-HAND**." https://www.youtube.com/watch?v=5-9-vWtTcU8 Time line 30:22 – 30:37 – Last accessed 27 April 2021

Who then crucified and killed Jesus Christ?

If the Jews didn't crucify and kill Jesus Christ, who did it? Here the Quran is silent and we need to turn to the Holy Bible to determine scripturally who crucified and killed Jesus Christ.

Matthew 20:18 "[Jesus said] …The Jews shall deliver the Son of man to **THE GENTILES TO MOCK, TO SCOURGE AND TO CRUCIFY HIM**… 27:1 When the morning was come, all the chief priests and elders of the people took counsel against Jesus to put Him to death. 2 When they had bound Him, they led Him away and **DELIVERED HIM TO PONTIUS PILATE THE GOVERNOR** … 26 Then released he [Pilate unto them] Barabbas and **WHEN HE [PILATE] HAD SCOURGED JESUS, HE [PILATE] DELIVERED HIM [JESUS] TO BE CRUCIFIED**."

Mark 15:1 "…The elders and scribes and the whole council bound Jesus and carried Him away and **DELIVERED HIM TO PILATE**."

Luke 23:1 "The whole multitude of them arose and **LED HIM UNTO PILATE**."

John 18:31 "Then said Pilate unto them: Take ye Him and judge Him according to your Law. The Jews, therefore, said unto him: *IT IS NOT LAWFUL FOR US TO PUT ANY MAN TO DEATH… 35 PILATE ANSWERED: AM I A JEW? THINE OWN NATION AND THE CHIEF PRIESTS HAVE DELIVERED THEE TO ME…*"

The Quran and Bible are clear that the Jews didn't crucify nor kill Jesus. The Bible further informed us that *the Law did not allow the Jews to put Jesus to death during the Passover.* They, the Jews handed Jesus Christ over to the Gentiles, the Romans, to Pontius Pilate the Roman governor who gave the order to crucify and kill Jesus Christ.

The Noble Quran: Appendix II – Page 912 "[Drs. Hilali and Khan confirms] … (11) Who finally decided to pass the death sentence against him? Matthew says: Pontius Pilate…"

Muslim Scholars, who now believe that **THE REAL** Jesus was arrested and placed on the cross, do so because they *realized* that the Quran does not deny the crucifixion of

Jesus Christ, the Quran only denied that the Jews did it and the Bible confirmed that the Romans did it.

81 Does the Bible teach that Jesus was put on the cross?

Matthew 26:47 "While [Jesus] yet spoke, Judas, one of the twelve, came and with him, a great multitude with swords and staves from the Chief Priests and Elders of the people. 48 Now [Judas] that betrayed Him [Jesus] gave them a sign, saying: Who I shall kiss that same is He: hold Him fast. 49 He came to Jesus and said: Hail, master and kissed Him. 50 Jesus said unto him: Friend, wherefore art thou come? Then came they and laid hands on Jesus and took Him."

These verses clearly suggest that it is the actual Jesus, the son of Mary, that was arrested and not another man who seemingly looked like Jesus. There are no historical records to support *"The Substitution Theory"* (the Sunni fiction that the man who was arrested, was not Jesus, but only looked like Jesus.) If it was another man, the man with the new image would have tried to escape or explain to the Romans and Jews that he was not Jesus of Nazareth. The answers Jesus gave proved He was the actual Jesus, the son of Mary, that was arrested and not another man that seemingly looked like Him.

Mark 14:48 "**Jesus answered** and said unto them: Are ye come out, as against a thief, with swords and with staves to take Me? 49 **I was daily with you in the temple** teaching and ye took Me not, but the scriptures must be fulfilled." (John 18:12)

NOWHERE in the Bible and in the **Arabic** Quran will you ever read that someone who looked like Jesus Christ was arrested! *"The Substitution Theory"* is a myth – a legend – a fiction.

Matthew 28:5-6 "The angel answered and said unto the women: Fear not ye, for I know that ye seek **Jesus, which was crucified**."

Mark 16:5 "Entering into the sepulcher they saw a young man sitting... 6 He saith: Be not affrighted: **Ye seek Jesus of Nazareth, which was crucified**..." (John 19:41)

It's **impossible** to read the Bible and to conclude from it, Jesus was substituted and not crucified. It requires a good deal of Bible-twisting to reach such an unfounded conclusion.

FROM: ABU BAKR AKOO [email addresses removed] **SENT: 26 JULY 2012 09:59 PM TO: MICHAEL MAHOMED**; Brian Marrian, Ahmed Pandor, Yusuf Ismail, Ayoob Karim, Mohammed Coovadia. **SUBJECT: CRUCIFIXION OR CRUCI-FICTION?** BISMILLAHIR RAHMAANI RRAHEEM IN THE NAME OF THE ONE TRUE GOD WHO (JESUS AND MUHAMMAD PBUT WORSHIPED) THE MOST GRACIOUS THE MOST MERCIFUL. Thanks for the questions... 1) Was Jesus on the cross? 2) Who was on the cross? ... I cannot assert whether he was actually on a cross or not, because the only authentic source of information we [Muslims] have to prove this is the Qur'an ... ***HOWEVER, I AS A STUDENT OF THE BIBLE MAY ARGUE FROM A BIBLICAL PERSPECTIVE THAT HE WAS PUT ON THE CROSS...***"

Public Debate: 27 October 2018 – Was Christ crucified? (Christian Speaker, Reverent Samuel Green and Muslim Speaker and Historian, Mr. Adnan Rashid https://www.youtube.com/watch?v=K24xIPcl1H4 Time line 03:25 – 03:36 Quoting Rashid:] "The four Gospels are unanimous on the matter of the crucifixion – Matthew, Mark, Luke and John are unanimous that Jesus was crucified."

Muslims who changed their invented legendary-fictional belief from *"The Substitution Theory"* to Jesus was put on the cross, but contrary to Biblical evidence, continue to still believe Jesus NEVER died on the cross, but He only fainted on the cross, they believe it with**OUT** support from the Bible, Quran, Authentic Islamic Traditions and Historical evidence. You can't use the Bible to prove Jesus never died on a cross.

Muslim scholars admit Jesus Christ, son of Mary, was put on the cross

Ahmad Deedat: Crucifixion or Cruci-fiction" – Pages 31 "Contrary to common believe, **Jesus was not nailed to the cross, but was bound.**"

DID YOU NOTICE, again, Sunni Muslim, Deedat provided no Biblical- or Quranic-, neither historical evidence to support his new found faith that Jesus was not nailed, but bound to the cross? Authentic Islamic sources are silent on this issue that Jesus was not substituted or nailed to the cross.

Nowhere in these sources and in historical material will you read: "Jesus Christ was not nailed, but bound to a cross," meaning that Deedat doesn't have any, whatsoever proof, but blind guessing. Although Deedat denied that Jesus was nailed to the cross, **DEEDAT PUBLICLY ADMITTED JESUS CHRIST WAS PUT ON THE CROSS**. Praise the Lord! Deedat abandoned the traditional Sunni Muslim *"Substitution Theory"* and came a step closer to the Christian Belief. Halleuia!

If Deedat would only have read the Bible to learn from it, he would have seen in the Bible, in the OT in the Messianic Psalms, it was prophesied that Christ would be nailed (pierced) and wasn't simply just to be bound to the cross as Deedat blindly propagated.

Psalms 22:16 "...The wicked have enclosed Me: **THEY PIERCED MY HANDS AND MY FEET**."

In fact, the Bible in the NT is VERY clear that Jesus Christ was nailed to the cross.

John 20:25 "...[Thomas] said unto them: **Except I shall see in His hands the print of the nails and put my finger into the print of the nails** ... I will not believe. 26 ... Then came Jesus ... and said... 27 ...to Thomas: Reach hither thy finger and behold My hands..."

Deedat would have done better to state in his booklet that the Bible does teach that Jesus was nailed to the cross, but that he doesn't believe in the Bible and therefore, rather believe in his imagination that Jesus was bound to the cross. It is very sad that Muslim scholars think they have the right to give their own emotional misinterpretations of how the crucifixion happened, without providing verifiable evidence, thinking that Christians don't know their own scriptures. The point, however, is to illustrate here that Muslim scholars who does not accept the Gospels as the inspired Word of God, after reading the Gospels as we have it today, publicly admits that Jesus Christ, according to the Gospels, was placed on the cross and even promote it in their booklets. Halleluiah! More Muslim scholars who understand Arabic and read the Quran, as well as the Bible with understanding, came to the realization that these books (Bible and Quran) **DOESN'T** teach Jesus was substituted (fiction), but that the real Jesus was actually placed on the cross (fact). Amen!

Public Debate: 11 April 2003 "The Crucifixion of Jesus Christ: Fact or Fiction?" Christian Speaker, Mr. Michael Mahomed (myself) and Muslim Speaker, Mr. Ayoob Karim [DVD available: Mr. Karim in his 45 minutes presentation, argued that Jesus was substituted and the other man who looked like Jesus was crucified, but after I presented my case, Mr. Karim, in his first 15 minutes rebuttal, switched positions and said:] "… **Jesus hung on the cross for at least 3 hours.**"

Authorized English Version of the Quran [Heading for Surah 4:157] "**CRUCIFYING THE BODY OF JESUS.**"

I find Muslims to be very misleading or deceptive to argue, from no Biblical and no Quranic support, neither from historical sources, that Jesus Christ was not put on the cross and that some Muslims argue that Jesus was put on the cross, but not nailed to the cross.

82 Do the Quran and Bible teach that Jesus fainted on the cross?

Muslims who now reject the Sunni fiction that Jesus was not on the cross and now accepts a historical position that Jesus was on the cross (which is what the Bible teach), continues to **DENY WITHOUT** Quranic evidence that Jesus Christ died on the cross, but while being on the cross, Jesus seemingly went in a coma and was taken alive from the cross and layed in a room-like tomb where He later resuscitated, this is known as *"The Swoon Theory"*. The Ahmaddiyah Islamic sect (a minority Muslim movement) was the first Muslims to propagate this theory.

Nowhere in the Bible, Quran and Authentic Islamic Traditions does it state that Jesus Christ fainted or swooned or went into a coma on the cross. Nowhere!

Public Debate: Did Jesus Rise from The Dead? Muslim Speaker, Dr. Shabir Ally and Christian Speaker, Dr. Michael Licona [Quoting Ally:] "I think a tenable position is to say, and **THIS IS BASED ON FAITH, IT IS NOT A HISTORICAL FACT, WE CANNOT PROVE THAT IT HAPPENED, IS TO SAY THAT: "JESUS WAS TAKEN DOWN PREMARTUALLY FROM THE CROSS AS WE KNOW HE WAS AND THAT HE WAS STILL ALIVE IN THE TOMB**..."

https://www.youtube.com/watch?v=kgUjaXHyBsw&feature=youtu.behttps%3A%2F%2Fwww.youtube.com%2Fwatch%3Fv%3D5-9-vWtTcU8 [Time line – 02:18:00 – 02:18:15 – Last accessed 27 April 2021

Clearly, Dr. Ally believes Jesus was on the cross and that Jesus fainted on the cross, but he also clearly confirmed it can't be proven from the Quran, Ahadith and historically that Jesus was taken alive from the cross while being in a coma. Dr. Ally surely depended on a lot of Bible-denying, Islamic-blind-faith. Deedat also used a lot of Bible-twisting faith to deceive non-Bible readers to make them think Jesus fainted on the cross. But as we'll see, the Bible clearly stated that Jesus died on the cross. Muslims who now rejected their fabricated Sunni fiction that Jesus was substituted, and accept the Ahmaddiyah fiction that Jesus swooned on the cross, who read the Bible with an open-mind, agree that *according to the Bible, Jesus was put on the cross and died on the cross*.

Public debate: 25 June 2009: Crucifixion & Resurrection of Jesus: Fact or Fiction? Christian Speaker, John Gilchrist and Muslim Speaker, Shabir Ally [Time line 05:30 – 05:44 Quoting Ally:] *"The Gospels says that Jesus died on the cross and a couple of days later, He began to appeared alive to His disciples. So two points the Gospels tells us: First - Jesus died. Second - He was raised back to life...* **09:27 – 09:38 The stories in the Gospels have it that Jesus was crucified on the cross, that He died and then He was taken down. His corps was put, not in a shallow grave, but in a tomb**..."

https://www.youtube.com/watch?v=PHdrnjnAnq4 Last accessed 27 April 2021

A Muslim might not believe in ALL the Bible as inspired and true, but it is **impossible** for honest Muslims to read the Bible and to conclude from the Bible that Jesus Christ was never, at any time, put on the cross and that Jesus never died on the cross.

<u>Muslim writer, M.O. Seepye: "Is the Crucifixion a fact or fiction?" – Page 8</u> "According to the four Gospels, Jesus died on the cross."

<u>Public Debate: 23 Feb. 2013 Christian Trinity or Islamic Tawheed: Which is the True Nature of God? (Christian Speaker, Elder Brian Marrian and Muslim Speaker, Mr. Yusuf Buxson) Q&A Session:</u> [DVD: Unquote: 2ND Question – A Muslim in laying a platform for his question, made this confirming statement – quote:] "According to the Bible that I have personally read, Jesus had died for 3 days. This is not proven through Quran; this is proven through Bible that Jesus has died for 3 days."

Muslims might deny that ALL the Bible is an inspired record of the death and resurrection of Jesus Christ, but they have to admit that according to what is written in the Gospels, Jesus died on the cross. You can't read the Bible and declare that it teaches differently. You have to twist the Bible to conclude that according to it, Jesus NEVER died on the cross. Muslims have no Biblical, Quranic or historical proof, but confessed blind faith that Jesus Christ swooned on the cross. They have to twist the Bible passages to make their uninformed-crowds that don't read the Bible themselves, to think that Jesus according to the Bible did not die on the cross, but He swooned on the cross. The words: fainted, swooned and a coma is not mentioned in the related crucifixion texts of the Bible, Quran, Authentic Islamic Traditions and Historical records.

83 Does the Quran and Bible teach Christ would not die?

In his mission, at all cost, to prove that Jesus never died on the cross, Deedat argued that…

<u>Crucifixion or Cruci-fiction? – Page 15</u> "God will never allow His Christ to be killed."

Again, as we are used to by now, Deedat didn't produce any Biblical or Quranic evidence that God would not allow Christ to be killed. Since the Bible, Quran and Ahadith does not teach that God would not let the Christ be killed, we may ask, did God reveal to Deedat that God would not allow His Christ to be killed? Is Deedat the last Islamic prophet? In fact, as we will later understand (see Q86), both the Bible and Quran are clear that God not only allowed it, but God actually caused the death of Christ.

The Noble Quran - Surah 2:91 "When it is said to **THEM (THE JEWS):** Believe in what Allah has sent down – THEY say: We believe in what was sent down to us – and THEY disbelieve in that which came after it, while it is the truth confirming what is with them. **SAY (O MUHAMMAD TO THEM):** Why then have you **KILLED THE PROPHETS OF ALLAH** aforetime, if you indeed have been believers?"

Here we read that Allah told Muhammad to ask the Jews standing before him, why they killed the prophets of God. This is another gross error, in the Quran, since Islam explicitly teach that Jesus was the second last true prophet and Muhammad was the seal (last) of the true prophets, if so, what prophets in between Jesus and Muhammad was killed by these Medinah Jews standing in front of Muhammad? Or did Allah tried to tell Muhammad to ask those Jews why their ancestors killed the prophets? If so, it means Allah got his question wrong. See below Biblical verse to demonstrate how the Quranic verse should have been constructed.

Matthew 23:31 "[Jesus said:] Wherefore ye be witnesses to yourselves that **YE ARE THE CHILDREN OF THEM** which killed the prophets."

The fact that OTHER prophets, now including Muhammad, were killed, would substantiate the fact that God would allowed for Jesus to be killed. For Deedat to say that God would never allow the Christ to be killed is a bogus statement, not supported in both the Bible and Quran. *In fact, Christ's death was prophesied in both the Biblical OT Messianic verses, the Gospels and Quran.*

Daniel 9:26 "...Gabriel informed me [Daniel that] **CHRIST SHOULD BE CUT OFF**..."

Isaiah 53:3 "He was despised, rejected of men and was wounded for our transgressions. He was bruised and by His stripes we are healed … **HE WAS CUT OFF OUT OF THE LAND OF THE LIVING**…"

NOT ONLY WAS IT PROPHESIED ABOUT 700-YEARS BEFORE JESUS WAS KILLED, BUT IT TRULY HAPPENED.

Matthew 27:50 "Jesus, when He had cried again with a loud voice, **YIELDED UP THE GHOST**. 62 Now the next day… the chief priests and Pharisees came unto Pilate, 63 Saying: Sir, we remember that, **WHILE HE WAS YET ALIVE**, said after three days I'll rise…"

Mark 15:37 and ***Luke 23:46*** also agrees, Jesus Christ gave up His Spirit, which means, Jesus died.

Two facts are illustrated: (1) Jesus gave up His Spirit – He died and (2) The Jews referring to Jesus as a deceiver, while He was alive, emphasize that they believed Jesus died! In fact, allfour Gospels is unanimous that Jesus gave up the Spirit.

John 19:30 "…He said: It's finished and He bowed His head and **GAVE UP THE GHOST** … 32 Then came the soldiers and broke the legs of [those] … which were crucified with Him. 33 But when they came to Jesus and **SAW THAT HE WAS DEAD ALREADY** THEY BRAKE NOT HIS LEGS."

Public debate 22 September 2011: Did Jesus die by crucifixion - Christian Scholar, Dr. Mike Licona and Muslim Speaker, Attorney Yusuf Ismail: Q&A session [Quoting a Muslim man laying a platform for his question said:] "The Gospel of John, Jesus died and the Roman soldier pierced Him. According to the Bible, He was already dead." https://www.youtube.com/watch?v=nw0T5KM6tGw

Time line 00:15 – 00:27 – Last accessed 27 April 2021

The Bible is clear – Jesus yielded up the Ghost – He died. There is no other interpretation. You can't read the Gospels and from it argue that Jesus NEVER died. Let me repeat myself again, it will take a lot of Biblical-twisting to argue from the Bible that Jesus never died on the cross.

Jesus' bones, while on the cross, was not broken

Deedat tried to respond and like usual, got it wrong again. "[Deedat said:] And the bones were not broken, says the Bible. The bones of a **DEAD PERSON**, whether you break it or not, is of the least consequence. http://answering-islam.org/Debates/Deedat_McDowell.html

https://www.youtube.com/watch?v=05jOZAo9u6g

Last accessed 27 April 2021

Deedat hopelessly missed it like always. **Nowhere does the Bible or history indicate that dead people's bones must be broken or was broken**. Why did they break the legs of the impaled LIVING victims? A person who was crucified, would hang and struggle to breath, to avoid suffocation, the impaled would push up on his legs to let the air out and then relax it to exhale. When the Romans wanted to bring about a quick death, they would break the LIVING victims' legs to prevent them the exercise of pushing on their legs and to be able to breath, in breaking the LIVING victims' legs, the victims would suffocate and die. When the Romans came to the crucified Jesus to break His legs, they saw that He was already dead and **did not break His legs**. Jesus was so exhausted of all the beatings, blood lost, excruciating pain, dehydration, He could not even carry His own cross to the end and when crucified, He had no strength to continue to push up on His legs to repeat the exercise to be able to breath and therefore in no time suffocated and died a quick death on the cross.

84 Does the Quran teach Jesus survived the cross?

Public Debate: Did Jesus Rise from The Dead? Between Muslim Speaker, Dr. Shabir Ally and Christian Speaker, Dr. Michael Licona "[Quoting Ally:] ... THIS IS BASED ON FAITH, it is not a historical fact, we cannot prove that it happened, is to say that *Jesus was taken down premartually from the cross* as we know he was and that he was still alive in the tomb, but in the tomb he met his final end – **THERE IN THE TOMB SOME MUSLIM SCHOLARS SAY THAT GOD CAUSED HIM TO DIE**…"

https://www.youtube.com/watch?v=kgUjaXHyBsw&feature=youtu.behttps%3A%2F%2F www.youtube.com%2Fwatch%3Fv%3D5-9-vWtTcU8 Time line – 02:18:00 – 02:18:23 Last accessed 27 April 2021

Since Dr. Ally with no Biblical, no Quranic, no Ahadith nor historical evidence, believe Jesus swooned on the cross, I can only conclude his position is based on blind-faith. How Muslim scholars can propagate, WITHOUT BIBLICAL, QURANIC AND HISTORICAL EVIDENCE that Jesus survived death on the cross and cling to blind-faith is beyond my understanding. They continue to invent new unverified theories – fanciful legends – fiction – simply, because they are doctrinated from childhood not to believe the Bible.

Quranic verses show that Jesus Christ died

Quran Translation by Abdullah Yusuf Ali – Surah 3:144 "Muhammad is no more than a **messenger** [ra̱suul]: *many were* **the messengers** [ru̱suul] that passed away before him…"

Many Muslims uses this translation to prove that Jesus didn't yet die; they say, "many, but not all", yet as we have already seen, Ali believed according to Surah 19:33 that Jesus already died. It is therefore strange to see him rendering this verse like this, especially since it's not what the **ARABIC TEXT** says. In above verse, do you see the words *"many were"*?

These words are **NOT** in the Arabic Text of the Quran and Ali didn't even use interpolation brackets (…) to let his readers know that the words *"many were"* is his own additions. They write the Quran with their own hands and say this is from Allah.

This time, it is Shakir who got it right. ***Quran Translation by Shakir – Surah 3:144*** "Muhammad is no more than a messenger. **THE MESSENGERS** have already passed away before him…"

When this verse is translated correctly as Shakir have it, everyone can immediately see that according to the Quran the messengers before Muhammad **DIED**. Nowhere in the Quran will you read that Jesus ascended into heaven without tasting death.

The Holy Qur'an: Pages 168-169 – Footnote 496 "…Some of the companions thought that the Prophet was not dead. Abu Bakr went in and seeing that life had departed, ascended the pulpit and read this verse, which had a magical effect upon his hearers, all of them being convinced that the prophet had passed away, **AS ALL PROPHETS HAD PASSED AWAY BEFORE HIM**… **THIS VERSE AFFORDS A CONCLUSIVE PROOF THAT JESUS CHRIST WAS ALSO DEAD** otherwise Abu Bakr's argument could not have silenced the doubters of the prophet's death."

Prof. Masudul Hasan: History of Islam, Vol.1 – Page 76 "The holy prophet said: **has any prophet before me lived forever** that might make you think that I will live with you forever."

This is conclusive evidence that Muhammad didn't believe that Jesus never died yet. The Quran also confirmed Jesus died since Allah has not granted any man immortality.

The Noble Quran – Surah 21:34 "And we [God] granted not to **ANY HUMAN BEING IMMORTALITY BEFORE YOU (O MUHAMMAD),** then if you die, would they live forever?"

To follow the *"Substitution and Swoon Theories"* that Jesus never died **yet**, is to doubt the chronological life events of Jesus given in the Quran. It is to doubt the above verses. It is also to belie the Muslim scholars who said Jesus died in the tomb.

85 Does Surah 4:157 have historical errors?

Quran Translation by Abdullah Yusuf Ali: "They said (in boast): **We killed Christ Jesus, the son of Mary, the Apostle of God**, but they killed him not nor crucified him, but so it was made to appear to them and those who differ therein are full of doubts with no certain knowledge…"

The first historical error

The Quran says that the Jews boasted in killing Christ. The Jews awaited the Christ and **NEVER** accepted Jesus as the Christ, therefore, they never did and never will boast that they killed the Christ.

In ***John 1:11*** "He came unto His own, and His own received Him not."

In ***John 9:22*** the Jewish leaders agreed to excommunicate anyone who confessed Jesus to be the Christ.

Ahmad Deedat: Crucifixion or Cruci-fiction" – Page 15 "They held a queer logic that if they succeeded in killing any **WOULD-BE** Messiah (Christ), it would be a sure proof of his **IMPOSTURE**. Hence the insistence of the Jews, *as a people, rejecting Jesus as their promised Messiah.*"

The Quran would have been historically correct, if it stated that the <u>Jews boasted in that they initiated the crucifixion and death of a would-be Christ.</u> Clearly, the Quran is mistaken to say the Jews boasted in killing Christ. Muslims, like Deedat, are aware that the Jews rejected Jesus as the Christ, therefore the Quran's error remains.

The second historical error

The Jews accepted that Jesus was not the true expected Christ. In fact, in the Bible ***John 18:31*** (see heading: Who then crucified and killed Jesus Christ?) Pontius Pilate told the Jewish leaders to judge Jesus according to their Law AND THE JEWISH LEADERS ADMITTED that they were forbidden to put any man to death, therefore, they **NEVER** boasted in killing Jesus.

The third historical error

The Quran says that the Jews boasted in killing God's Messenger. They **NEVER** accepted Jesus as the Messenger of God.

In **John 18:30-35** they labeled Jesus as a malefactor (an evildoer) and as a Nation, they rejected Jesus before Pilate. Even after Jesus was crucified and died, in **Matthew 27:63** they continued to call Jesus a deceiver.

Muslim Scholar, Dr. Muhammad Asad, identified these historical errors and tried to cover it up in his English Quran Translation by adding words to it, that are not found in the Arabic text. Let's see how Dr. Asad rendered this verse in question:

The Message of the Quran "And their boast: Behold, we have slain Christ Jesus, son of Mary (**WHO CLAIMED TO BE**) an apostle of God…"

Do you see the bold words? Those words are not part of the Arabic Text of the Quran. Any attorney will tell you that if your source, as a witness, is wrong, that source will be kicked out of any state court of law. Here we see the Quran, in one verse, is contaminated with at least three historical errors and therefore, the Quran is not a credible source of what happened to Jesus.

86 What does "…so it was made to appear to them…" mean?

Quran Translation by Abdullah Yusuf Ali – Surah 4:157 "They said (in boast): We killed Christ Jesus the son of Mary, the Apostle of God, but they killed him not nor crucified him, **but so it was made to appear to them** and those who differ therein are full of doubts with no certain knowledge…"

Since their plan succeeded to get the Romans to put Jesus Christ to death, they may have boasted that they initiated the death of Jesus, even so, *according to the Bible and Quran it was actually God who caused Jesus to die, therefore, it only appeared to the Jews that they caused the death of Jesus Christ.*

Below are Biblical and Quranic evidence where it is stated that God caused the death of Jesus Christ:

Matthew 26:31 "Jesus said unto them: All ye shall be offended because of Me this night: as it is written: *I will smite the shepherd* and the sheep of the flock shall be scattered abroad. 32 After I am risen again I'll go before you into Galilee." (John 19:10, Matt. 20:28, John 10:11).

John 19:10 "Then said Pilate unto Him: Speak Thou not unto me? Know Thou not that I have power to crucify … and to release Thee? 11 Jesus answered: Thou have no power against Me, *except it was given thee from above*."

In the Quran, although the Jews boasted that they crucified and killed Jesus, the author of the Quran is very clear that they, the Jews, didn't do it. Since their initiation to kill Jesus succeeded, it so appeared to them that they killed Jesus through the filthy hands of the Gentiles.

According to the Quran, regardless who does the literal killing, it is Allah who actually kills:

Quran Translation by Abdullah Yusuf Ali – Surah 3:145, 8:17, 9:51, 22:66 "Nor can a soul die, except by Allah's leave … It is not ye who slew them; it was Allah … Say: Nothing will happen to us, except what Allah has decreed for us … It is He Who gave you life, will cause you to die, and will again give you life…"

In the Quran Surah 5:116-7 below, Jesus acknowledged that God caused His death.

Quran Translation by Shakir "Allah will say: O Isa … Did you say to men: Take me and my mother for two gods besides Allah! He'll say: I didn't… aught save what Thou didst enjoin me with: That serve Allah, my Lord and your Lord and I was a witness of them so long as I was among them, but when *THOU DID CAUSED ME TO DIE*…"

The Holy Qur'an "… [Jesus said:] Thou [God] didst cause me to die…"

While the two above translations make it clear that God caused Jesus to die, Ali, in his translation below, try to make it look like Jesus was not killed, but that God took him up into heaven.

Quran Translation by Abdullah Yusuf Ali: "…I was a witness over them whilst I dwelt amongst them; when Thou didst take me up…"

Despite Ali's deliberate false Translation; the Quran is clear that God took Jesus up into heaven sometime **AFTER** the death of Jesus.

Quran Translation by Abdullah Yusuf Ali – Surah 3:55 "Allah said: O Jesus! I will take thee **AND** raise thee to Myself…"

Notice, Allah predicted **TWO DISTINCT EVENTS** in this verse:

[1] Allah will take Jesus and

[2] Allah will raise Jesus to Himself.

The taking is different from the raising. What does it mean that Allah took Jesus? Here is Dr. Muhammad Asad's translation:

Message of the Quran – Surah 3:55 "God said: O Jesus! Verily, **I SHALL CAUSE YOU TO DIE** and exalt you unto myself."

Faruq Sheriff, in his book: **_A guide to the contents of the Quran, Page 94_** wrote: "Surah 3:55 … clearly makes his **ASCENSION FOLLOW DEATH**."

God caused Jesus to die and after His resurrection, took Jesus up into heaven (Surahs 19:33, 3:55).

87 Who differ in the crucifixion and death of Jesus Christ?

Quran Translation by Abdullah Yusuf Ali – Surah 4:157 "They said (in boast): We killed Christ Jesus the son of Mary, the Apostle of God, but they killed him not nor crucified him, but so it was made to appear to them and **those who differ therein are full of doubts with no certain knowledge. But for a surety they killed him not**."

Notice, Bible-believing Christians are not full of doubts concerning the crucifixion, death and resurrection of Jesus Christ. All Bible believing Christians believe that Jesus Christ was crucified, died on the cross and was resurrected on the third day, according to the Bible (**_1 Corinthians 1:23, 15:20_**), a fact which Muslim commentators admit.

Quran Translation by Abdullah Yusuf Ali – Page 230 Comm. 663: "The Orthodox Christian Churches make it a **CARDINAL POINT** of their doctrine that his life was taken on the cross."

WHO DIFFER ABOUT THE CRUCIFIXION OF JESUS WITHOUT BIBLICAL AND QURANIC KNOWLEDGE?

- ✓ *MOST MUSLIMS...* Believe Jesus ascended to heaven before He tasted death, a FICTION.
- ✓ *MAJORITY OF SUNNI MUSLIMS...* Believe Jesus was substituted and not put on the cross, a FICTION.
- ✓ *MINORITY OF SUNNI MUSLIMS...* Believe Jesus was put on the cross, fainted on the cross, a FICTION.
- ✓ *AHMADDIYAHS...* Believe Jesus was put on the cross and fainted on the cross, a FICTION.
- ✓ *FEW MUSLIM SCHOLARS...* Believe Jesus fainted on the cross, but died in the tomb, a FICTION.
- ✓ *QURAN ONLY MUSLIMS...* Believe Jesus was dead on the cross, a Fact.

Muslim writer A. Obaray: Miraculous Conception, Death, Resurrection and Ascension of Jesus as Taught in the Kuran Page 3 "Coming to the Muslims one finds no unanimity. **THEY ARE DIVIDED AMONG THEMSELVES ON THE MATTER OF JESUS**, so much so, that there is mudslinging one against the other."

Quran Translation by Abdullah Yusuf Ali: Page 230 Comm. 664: "There is difference of opinion as to the exact interpretation of this verse... **ONE SCHOOL** holds that Jesus did not die the usual human death, but still lives in the body in heaven – **ANOTHER** holds that he did die (v. 120) but not when he was supposed to be crucified..."

Public Debate: Did Jesus Rise from The Dead? Muslim Speaker, Dr. Shabir Ally / Christian Speaker, Dr. William Lane Craig "[Quoting Ally] "What does the Quran actually says about the crucifixion of Jesus, **ACTUALLY MUSLIM SCHOLARS ARE NOT REALLY SURE**. That is not something unique with reference to this topic concerning Jesus, the Quran is a book consisting of 6000 and more verses… when it comes to the verse dealing with the crucifixion of Jesus (S.4:157) **WE HAVE A VARIETY OF MUSLIM INTERPRETATIONS**…" https://www.youtube.com/watch?v=5-9-vWtTcU8 Time line 00:27:04 – 00:27:27

Last accessed 27 April 2021

88 Did Jesus rise from the dead and ascended into heaven?

Matthew 28:5 "The angel answered and said unto the women: Fear not ye, for I know that ye seek **JESUS, WHICH WAS CRUCIFIED. 6 HE IS NOT HERE: FOR HE IS RISEN**…" (Mark 16:6, Luke 24:6-7)

It is Gospel clear: Jesus Christ was born and grew up performing many miracles during His Prophethood. Israel as a nation rejected Jesus as the Christ and handed Him over to the Roman Gentiles who mocked, scourged and crucified Jesus. This was caused by the will of God. But the story does not end there. Jesus rose victoriously from the dead and ascended into heaven.

Mark 16:19 "…After the Lord had spoken unto them, He was received up into heaven…"

NOWHERE IN THE QURAN does it state that *Jesus will be raised to heaven alive "BEFORE" his death.* Muslims who says Jesus ascended to heaven before death obviously argues from silence. According to Surah 19:33 and 3:55 quoted above, Allah caused Jesus to die, resurrected Him and then took Him to heaven.

89 What was the sign of Jonah?

Ahmad Deedat: What was the sign of Jonah? Pages 1-2 "Over a thousand million Christians today **BLINDLY** accept that Jesus of Nazareth is the Christ. The name that was given to Mary, for her yet unborn son, was Jesus not Christ. It was only after His baptism at the hands of John the Baptist that He, claimed to be the Christ."

Deedat's double hypocrisy standards

Deedat accusers Christians of blindly accepting Jesus is the Christ before His water-baptism, yet he doesn't hesitate to inform his audience in his 50 minutes opening argument during his public debate with Josh McDowell:

Was Christ Crucified? "The Muslim believes this authoritative statement as the veritable Word of God and as such, **HE ASKS NO QUESTIONS AND DEMANDS NO PROOF**. He says: There are the Words of my Lord, I believe and I affirm."

It is obvious that Deedat was never interested in Biblical Truth, but rather exercised his double standards against the Bible to discredit its Message. Let's see if the Bible and Quran teach that *Jesus was the Christ since His birth.*

Luke 2:11 "…Born this day in the City of David a Savior, which **IS CHRIST**…"

Jesus WAS BORN CHRIST! Not only did Deedat misrepresent and misinterpret the Bible, but also the Quran. The Quran agrees with the Bible that Jesus was the Christ since birth. Deedat is aware of this fact as he mentioned it in his below booklet:

Ahmad Deedat: Desert Storm – Has it ended? Christ in Islam – Page 4 "[Before Jesus was born an angel appeared unto Mary and said:] …O Mary! God giveth thee glad tidings of a Word from Him: **HIS NAME SHALL BE CALLED CHRIST JESUS**…"

Did Jesus believe he would be alive in the tomb?

Matthew 12:40 "For as Jonas was three days and three nights in the whale's belly so shall the Son of man be three days and three nights in the heart of the earth."

The Muslim's argument is that since Jonah was alive in the whale's belly for three days and three nights, so must Jesus be alive in the tomb for three days and three nights.

So they have two arguments:

1. because Jonah was alive in the whale's belly - Jesus must have been alive in the tomb …

2. because Jonah was for 3 days and 3 nights in the whale's belly, therefore Jesus should have been in the tomb for 3 days & 3 nights.

They say, if Jesus died on the cross, then He was not like Jonah and since Jesus was only Friday (day and night), Saturday (day and night) plus Sunday in the tomb (but not a third night), He failed to be like Jonah. When reading Matthew 12:40 we need to understand that Jesus never said: "...AS JONAH **WAS ALIVE** IN THE FISH'S BELLY SO SHALL **THE SON OF MAN BE ALIVE** IN THE TOMB..." and therefore we should not misread this misinterpretation into the passage.

Muslim writer: A. Obaray - "Miraculous Conception, Death, Resurrection and Ascension of Jesus as taught in the Kuran" Pages 25-29 "The event of Jonah who was swallowed by the fish has been time and again used by the Ahmadiyya's as an argument to prove Jesus did not die on the cross, but later died a natural death. They use the words of the Bible and from what has been observed *THEY SPLIT UP THE WORDS OF JESUS AND ISOLATE A PHRASE OR A CLAUSE OF HIS STATEMENT SO AS TO GIVE IT A DISTORTED MEANING IN SUPPORT OF THEIR ARGUMENT.*"

Everyone reading the Gospels knows Jesus spoke in parables (Matthew 13:34). He never intended for His audience to think He will be alive in the tomb since He clearly, after stating the Jonah parable in Matthew 12 without explaining it, taught explicitly that He will die and resurrect.

Matthew 16:21 "From that time forth began Jesus to shew unto His disciples, how that He must go unto Jerusalem and suffer many things of the elders and chief priests and scribes and **be killed and be raised again the third day**... 17:9 As they came down from the mountain, Jesus charged them, saying: Tell the vision to no man, **until the Son of man be risen again from the dead**... 17:22 "Jesus said unto them: The Son of man shall be betrayed into the hands of men. 23 And **they shall kill Him and the third day He shall be raised again** ... 20:28 Even as the Son of man came not to be ministered unto, but to minister and to **give his life a ransom** for many... 26:32 But **after I am risen again**, I will go before you into Galilee."

If Matt. 12:40 is taken into context with all of the Gospel, one can see that Jesus never intended for His audience to think He will be alive, but that He'll surely be in the tomb as Jonah was in the fish belly.

Did Jesus say he would be dead for literal 72 hours?

Jesus spoke in a figurative style, a fact, to which even Islam's late giant had to admit.

Ahmad Deedat: Crucifixion or Cruci-fiction Page 69 "Maybe, he [Jesus] was speaking figuratively."

That's exactly how the Jews understood Jesus.

Matthew 27: 63 "[The Jews said to Pilate] ... that deceiver said: After three days I am to rise again… Command therefore that the sepulcher be made secure **UNTIL THE THIRD DAY**."

The Jews heard what Jesus said and yet never asked Pilate to secure the tomb until AFTER the third day. They knew that the prediction wasn't literal and that the resurrection of Jesus was to take place **WITHIN** three days, hence their request for the tomb to be secured until the third day, not until after the third day.

John 2:19 "Jesus answered and said unto them: Destroy this temple, and **IN [NOT AFTER]** three days I will raise it up. 20 Then said the Jews: Forty and six years was this temple in building, and wilt thou rear it up **IN** three days? 21 *BUT HE SPAKE OF THE TEMPLE OF HIS BODY.*" (Matthew 26:61, Mark 14:58).

When Jesus disciples in ***Acts 10:40*** said that Jesus raised from the dead ON THE THIRD DAY, the people **DID NOT** attempt to disprove the disciples that Jesus referred to literal three days and three nights of 72 hours. They knew what Jesus meant.

Even in the OT ***Ester 4:16*** where the Jews are asked to fast for 3 days and then will Ester go into the king to intercede for the lives of the Jews, but in ***Ester 5:1*** we read that ON THE THIRD DAY she went to the king. It is important that any text be read in the environmental background of the Jewish culture and not in isolation.

Jonah 1:17 "Jonah was in the belly of the fish three days and three nights."

WHEN WAS JONAH VOMIT OUT OF THE FISH? THE BOOK OF JONAH DOES NOT INFORM US WHEN THE FISH VOMITED JONAH OUT OF ITS BELLY. Let's hear from Islam's late champion, Deedat: When he thinks Jonah was vomited out of the fish?

Ahmad Deedat: "What was the sign of Jonah?" page 7 "For three days and three nights the fish takes him around the ocean… **ON THE THIRD DAY** it vomits him on the seashore."

Deedat never said the fish vomited Jonah out on the fourth day, that would have been after literal 3 days and 3 nights, but Deedat, as providence would have it, clearly stated that the fish vomited Jonah out <u>ON THE THIRD DAY</u>. Here Deedat clearly indicated what Jesus meant, but he obviously in other places tried to just **MIS**present the time factor to be literal. Jesus, of course, understood His own figurative language, He never intended for us to believe He will be dead for literal 72 hours (3 days and 3 nights). Jesus in all four Gospels unanimously informed us that He will resurrect **WITHIN** 3 days:

Matt. 17:22 "Jesus said… 23 They shall kill Him and the THIRD DAY He shall raise again."

Mark 9:31 "He [Jesus] taught His disciples and said: …He shall rise the THIRD DAY."

Luke 9:22 "[Jesus told them:] …the Son of man …will be slain and be raised the THIRD DAY."

John 2:19 "Jesus said: Destroy this temple and IN THREE DAYS I will raise it."

Let's turn the table onto Muslims and show what a real contradiction looks like in the Quran. When Zachariah was in the temple praying and an angel came to him and told him that he would not be able to speak to no man for three **[WHAT?]**

Quran Translation by Abdullah Yusuf Ali:

Surah 19:10 "(Zachariah) said: O my Lord! Give me	***Surah 3:41*** "He [Zachariah] said: O my Lord! Give

a Sign. Thy sign, was the answer, shall be that thou shall speak to no man for three **NIGHTS, ALTHOUGH THOU ART NOT DUMB.**"	me a Sign. Thy Sign, was the answer, shall be that thou shall speak to no man for three **DAYS, BUT WITH SIGNALS.**"

Although the two chapters were seemingly revealed over different periods, they refer to the same event. The words in Surah 19 were initially uttered, followed by a repeat in Surah 3, but only this time a variant time-factor was introduced.

- ✓ DID ALLAH, GABRIEL AND MUHAMMED SAY: THREE NIGHTS OR THREE DAYS?
- ✓ OR DID THE UTHMANIC SCRIBES MAKE A SCRIBAL ERROR IN THE QURAN?

90 Who moved the tombstone?

Ahmad Deedat: "Who Moved the Stone?" Pages 1, 12 "Is a question which has worried theologians for the past two thousand years. **IF AT ALL**, it was Nicodemus and Joseph who removed the stone!"

On the cover of the above booklet: Dr. GM Karim says: "To this question, Mr. Deedat has very simplistically and convincingly resolved the problem besetting the minds of all thinking Christians..."

Again, we asked: Where did Deedat get his answer from that it was Nicodemus and Joseph who removed the tomb-stone? Did Allah reveal that information to him? Deedat, in his attempt to answer a Biblical question: *"Who moved the stone?"* once more ignored the Biblical evidence before him.

Matt. 28:2 "...**THE ANGEL OF THE LORD** descended from heaven and came and **ROLLED BACK THE STONE** from the door and sat upon it..."

Deedat managed to deceive Dr. Karim and billions of Muslims to make them think that Nicodemus and Joseph removed the stone. This is not a problematic question besetting the minds of thinking Christians. We know who moved the stone. Any Sunday school child who reads the Bible can answer this question. In fact, any atheist who reads the Bible can answer this question. In fact, any honest Muslim who reads the Bible can answer this question. It is clear that Deedat never read the Bible to understand it, but rather to suppress Biblical evidence for his Islamic agenda. That is sad!

91 Why did the apostles think they saw a spirit?

Ahmad Deedat: Resurrection or Resuscitation? – Pages 9-10 "Why did they get terrified? Did Jesus look like a ghost?"

If only Deedat took time to study, at least the Quran, he would have discovered that a spirit can appear in the form of a man and would have understood that in the Bible when the disciples saw Jesus **they thought** they saw a spirit who looked like Jesus. The Quran and Bible readers know that spirits can appear in human form.

Meaning of the Glorious Quran – Surah 19:17 "...Then We sent unto her Our Spirit and it assumed for her the likeness of a perfect man."

Deedat should have realized a Spirit can appear in the form of a man and since the disciples knew Jesus died (was dead) and _slow to believe_ that Jesus resurrected, they thought they saw a spirit that took the form of Jesus. Who said so? The same Bible that Deedat failed to read with understanding: **Luke 24:37** "They were terrified and affrighted and **SUPPOSE THEY HAD SEEN A SPIRIT**." If Deedat would have read the Bible to understand it, he would have noticed this verse which answered his question before he asked it, or perhaps Deedat did see it, but as his usual habit was, he suppressed Biblical evidence in his hope to bring doubt to uninformed Christians and to establish disbelief of what the Bible teach in the hearts of Muslims who are too lazy to read the Bible for themselves.

92 Did Jesus teach all resurrections results into immortality?

Deedat misunderstood the resurrection

Ahmad Deedat: Resurrection or Resuscitation? – Pages 11 "Jesus had himself pronounced that the resurrected bodies get spiritualized by saying at the resurrection, neither shall they die any more - meaning that the resurrected persons will be immortalized."

Let's see what Jesus was asked and what Jesus answered:

Matthew 22:23 "The same day came to Him the Sadducees, which say that there is no resurrection and asked Him: 24 Saying, Master, Moses said: If a man die, having no children, his brother shall marry his wife and raise up seed unto his brother. 25 Now there were with us seven brethren and the first, when he had married a wife, deceased and having no issue, left his wife unto his brother. 26 Likewise the second also and the third, unto the seventh. 27 Last of all, the woman died also. 28 Therefore, **IN THE RESURRECTION** whose wife shall she be of the seven for they had her. 29 Jesus answered and said unto them: Ye do err, not knowing the scriptures, nor the power of God. 30 For **IN THE RESURRECTION** they neither marry, nor are given in marriage, but are as angels of God…"

See how easily Deedat misread the scripture. Jesus never said **ALL RESURRECTIONS** are angelized (spiritualized). Jesus spoke about "**THE LAST DAY RESURRECTION**".

Lazarus resurrected, but not immortalized

In ***John 11:32-44*** Jesus resurrected Lazarus who was dead for four days, of course, Lazarus was not immortalized, not spiritualized, not angelized and sometime later Lazarus died again.

In ***Surah 5:110*** Jesus also resurrected people. If Deedat is right that all resurrected people are immortalized than it means that those raised by Islamic Jesus 2000 years ago, were all immortalized and must still be alive today, walking around somewhere on earth,

A FICTION, not supported by the Quran and Bible. The people resurrected by Jesus died again, but the resurrected Jesus Christ ascended into heaven and is alive forevermore, a truth to which both the Bible and Quran testifies too.

Revelation 1:18 "[Jesus said:] I'm He that live and **was dead and behold, I'm alive**..."

It was the above verse quoted by Josh McDowell that ended Ahmad Deedat's deceptive flourishing debates over Christians. Look here: https://www.youtube.com/watch?v=hr2U_8PDfwI to witness the Deedat public embarrassing moment. Nowhere in the Bible did the disciples preach Jesus was resurrected from the dead as a spiritualized-being.

CONCLUSION: The Quran deny that the Jews crucified Jesus Christ, BUT DO NOT DENY that the crucifixion took place. Most Muslims know that the crucifixion event is historical, but tried to produce it as a fiction, that someone else died in Jesus place. Some Muslims who reject the substitution theory believes that Jesus was placed on the cross. The Bible gives conclusive evidence that Jesus died on the cross. Both the Bible and Quran declared Jesus Christ died, victoriously resurrected from the dead and ascended into heaven where He now is resident since 2000 years ago. No Bible-reader will mistake resurrected people as immortalized beings, unless they, like Deedat, twist the scripture to achieve their agenda that Jesus never resurrected.

SECTION 10

SALVATION

93 Did Allah, before people were born and sinned, ordained them to burn in hell-fire?

Adam, Abrahan, Moses, Jesus, Muhammad, we will all end up in hell-fire

Quran Trans. by Abdullah Yusuf Ali Surah 7:179 "Many are the jinn and **MEN WE HAVE MADE FOR HELL**. They have hearts wherewith they understand not, eyes wherewith they see not and ears wherewith they hear not. They are like cattle - nay more misguided: for they are heedless (of warning)."

THIS VERSE DOESN'T SAY ALLAH MADE ALL JINNS FOR HELL – IT SAYS ALLAH MADE MANY JINNS FOR HELL. THEREFORE, MANY JINNS WERE MADE FOR HELL AND FEW JINNS WERE NOT MADE FOR HELL.

THE SAME VERSE SAYS ALLAH MADE MEN FOR HELL – IT DOES NOT SAY ALLAH MADE MANY MEN FOR HELL OR ALLAH MADE FEW MEN FOR HELL, IT SAYS MEN WERE MADE FOR HELL, ITS ALL INCLUSIVE.

Let's see how other Muslim Scholars translated the above verse:

Sahih International "And We have certainly created for Hell many of the jinn and **MANKIND**."

The Noble Quran "We have created many of the jinn and **MANKIND** for hell..."

Let's look at a few tafsirs (Muslim scholar commentaries):

Tafsir - Ibn Al Kathir "(And surely, We have created for Hell) We made a share in the Fire for (many of the Jinn and **MANKIND**)..." https://quranx.com/Tafsir/Kathir/7.179 Last accessed 19 June 2021

Tafsir Al-Jalalayn "We have indeed urged unto Hell many of the jinn and **MANKIND**."

https://quranx.com/Tafsir/Jalal/7.179 Last accessed 19 June 2021

Tafsir - Ibn 'Abbâs "We created for (hell many of the jinn and **HUMANKIND**...)"

https://quranx.com/Tafsir/Abbas/7.179 Last accessed 19 June 2021

Clearly, Allah created mankind (humans) to burn in hell. They will not burn because they sinned. They will burn because that is the reason or purpose of Allah for mankind. Allah does not offer mankind any salvation, as we will see, until **AFTER** mankind have burned in hell for some undisclosed period.

The Quran does teach that men will enter paradise, but of course, that can only be after some burning experience in hell-fire. Notice, it says "mankind", this include prophets, unless they not part of mankind.

Even sinless Jesus, who is in heaven now, is promised hell-fire

According to the Bible **_Mark 16:19_** "So then after the Lord [Jesus] had spoken unto them, He was received up into heaven and sat on the right hand of God." **_Luke 24:51_** "And it came to pass, while He [Jesus] blessed them, He was parted from them and carried up into heaven."

The Quran, about 577 years later agree that Jesus ascended into heaven and is with Allah in heaven:

Quran Translation by Abdullah Yusuf Ali – Surahs 3:55 and 4:158 "Behold! Allah said: "O Jesus! I will take Thee and **raise Thee to Myself** ... Nay, Allah **raised Him up unto Himself**..."

Clearly, Jesus is not in the first, second, third, fourth, fifth, sixth, nor seventh Islamic heavens, but Jesus is with Allah above the seven Islamic heavens. Sad to say, just like innocent babies who died before committing a sin, likewise, the sinless Jesus who is now, according to both the Bible and Quran, in heaven, Allah will let Jesus leave his presence to go burn in hell-fire as promised in Surah 7:179. Let's look at another Quranic verse, Surah 21:98, where Jesus Christ is again promised hell-fire.

Meaning of Glorious Quran "Ye (idolaters) and **THAT, WHICH YE WORSHIP** beside Allah are fuel of hell…"

Quran Translation by Shakir "You and **WHAT YOU WORSHIP**, besides Allah, are the firewood of hell…"

The Noble Quran "You and **THAT WHICH YOU ARE WORSHIPPING** besides Allah, are (but) fuel for Hell…"

Tafsir - Ibn 'Abbâs "O people of Mecca and your idols will come i.e. Gehenna."

https://quranx.com/Tafsir/Abbas/21.98 Last accessed 19 June 2021

The Noble Quran: Page 440 – Footnote 1 "The Quraish pagans were delighted and said – We are pleased to be with our gods in the hell-fire, as the idols will be with the idolaters (in the hell fire) and therefore **JESUS WILL BE WITH HIS WORSHIPPERS**…"

Tafsir - Ibn Al Kathir "The Idolators and **THEIR GODS ARE FUEL FOR HELL**… (Hasab for Hell): means firewood … Ad-Dahhak said: The fuel of Hell means **THAT WHICH IS THROWN INTO IT** … (Surely, you will enter it): means, you will go into it … (and all of them will abide therein *forever*) means, the worshippers and **THE OBJECTS OF THEIR WORSHIP WILL ALL ABIDE THEREIN FOREVER**."

https://quranx.com/Tafsir/Kathir/21.98 Last accessed 27 April 2021

Here we see that some Muslim scholars believe Jesus will abide in hell-fire **FOREVER**. Notice, the Arabians from the Quraish tribe perfectly understood Muhammad when he said Jesus and His worshippers, BOTH will be in hell-fire. Far be it that Jesus will burn in hell. Rubbish! No Christian will ever believe such hog-wash that Jesus will burn and remain in hell-fire forever. I don't! Do you?

> Innocent babies who committed no sin and died, will burn in hell

Sahih Muslim "A'isha, the mother of the believers, said that Allah's Messenger (ﷺ) was called to lead the funeral prayer of a child of the Ansar. I [Aisha] said: Allah's Messenger, there is happiness for this child who is a bird from the birds of Paradise for *it committed* *no sin nor has he reached the age when one can commit sin*. HE [MUHAMMAD] SAID: 'A'ISHA, PER ADVENTURE, IT MAY BE OTHERWISE, because God created for Paradise those who are fit for it, while they were yet in their father's loins and **created for Hell those who are to go to Hell. He created them for Hell, while they were yet in their father's loins**."

https://quranx.com/Hadith/Muslim/USC-MSA/Book-33/Hadith-6436 Last accessed 27 April 2021

https://www.youtube.com/watch?v=_nn56hEF_5Y Last accessed 27 April 2021

Notice, the child has committed no sin YET, NOR HAS IT REACHED THE AGE TO SIN, the age of accountability, worse of all, they have no COMMITTED sin that Allah can point to, for Allah to be fair in His judgement to send them to hell, proving Allah is NOT just and Quran is wrong to say Allah is merciful.

Men will burn in hell and some will later be rescued from hell to enter heaven

Let's look at Quranic verses where Allah says some men will be rescued from hell-fire to enter paradise:

Quran Translation by Prof. Arthur J. Arberry – Surah 19:70 "We shall know very well those most deserving to burn there, 71 **Not one of you there is, but he shall go down to it**; that for thy Lord is a thing decreed, determined. 72 Then **We shall deliver those that were godfearing**; and the evildoers We shall leave there, hobbling on their knees."

Here again we see Allah confirmed that the godfearing will first burn in hell-fire and then be rescued. Muhammed also explained it like that to his audience.

Sahih Bukhari, Vol. 1, Page 428, Hadith 770 "Narrated Abu Huraira... *[Muhammad] said*: ... till when Allah intends mercy on whomever he likes amongst the people of Hell, **He will order the angels to take out of Hell those who worshipped none, but Him alone**. The angels will take them out by recognizing them from the traces of prostrations, Allah has forbidden the fire to eat away those traces."

Here Muhammed says that the black-mark (traces of prostration during salah) on Muslims brow, caused by putting their heads on the carpet during prayer, it will not be burned away by the hell-fire and that the angels will recognize those Muslims who used to worship Allah alone and rescue them from the hell-fire.

The Noble Quran: Page 8 Commentary 1 "Narrated Anas: **The prophet said**: On the day of the resurrection *THE BELIEVERS* will assemble and say – Let us ask somebody to intercede for us with our Lord. So they will go to Adam and say: You are the father of all the people and Allah created you with His hands and ordered the angels to prostrate themselves to you and taught you the names of all things, **intercede for us with your Lord so that he may relieve us from this place** … [unquote: All prophets will refuse to intercede, but finally Muhammad will accept the challenge – quote:] … So they will come to me and I will proceed till I ask my Lord's permission and I will be given permission. When I see my Lord, I will fall down in prostration and he will let me remain in that state as long as he wishes … I will raise my head … and then I will intercede … and will say: **none remains in hell than those whom the Quran imprisoned and who have been destined to an eternal stay in hell**. (Sahih Bukhari Vol. 6, Page 5, Hadith 3)."

Muslim scholars agree, humans will be brought to hell-fire and then only will the godfearing be saved.

Tafsir - Ibn Al Kathir "**Everyone will be brought to Hell**, then the Righteous will be saved." https://quranx.com/Tafsir/Kathir/19.71 Last accessed 27 April 2021

Tafsir Al-Jalalayn "**There is not one of you but shall come to it, that is, [but] shall enter Hell**. That is an inevitability [already] decreed by your Lord, [something which] He made inevitable and [which] He decreed; He will not waive it." https://quranx.com/Tafsir/Jalal/19.71 Last accessed 27 April 2021

It is verses like these that brought Sultan Muhammad to his knees and made him to reject Islam that offered *no salvation, without the bad news that he first has to taste hell-fire* and after considering these horrendous verses, he accepted Christianity that offered him heaven, without first having to burn in hell.

Sultan Muhammad Paul: Why I became a Christian? – Page 10: "…After a long search I found the following tradition in the Mishkat: "Ibn Masud said that the prophet of Islam said: **ALL PEOPLE SHALL ENTER HELL.** Then they will come out of it according to their works … The meaning of the Quran (Surah 19:71-72) was plain…"

Muhammad was clear that Muslims, sincere Muslims with the traces of prostration on their brow, who worshipped none but Allah, will burn in hell for a period before they are saved. Modern Muslim Scholars admit that PEOPLE will first burn in hell for a period and that some will later be saved from out of hell-fire.

Debate: 27 October 2018 Was Christ crucified? (Christian Speaker, Reverent Samuel Green and Muslim Speaker (Historian) Mr. Adnan Rashid: [Rashid:] "Muslims have a guarantee of salvation. As long as we die Muslims. We die in a state of imaan. **We will eventually be taken out of hell-fire and we will have salvation.**" https://allanruhl.com/adnan-rashid-vs-samuel-green-on-salvation-in-christianity-and-islam/

Time line 10:28 - 10:50 Last accessed 27 April 2021

I thank the God of the Bible for promising me a heaven, without, first having to taste hell-fire. Even so, come Lord Jesus Christ, come quickly. So Allah first decreed that mankind will burn in hell and later get salvation to enter heaven.

Quranic Abraham worshipped idols, perhaps the reason he will be hell-fire

No Jew, nor Christian will ever entertain the Quranic fabrication that Abraham, the father of faith, will burn in hell-fire, even for just a short while. Perhaps, this is easy for Muslims to believe, because according to the Quran, Abraham is guilty of at least three occasions of idolatry.

Quran Translation by Abdullah Yusuf Ali – Surah 6:75 "So also did We show **ABRAHAM** the power and the laws of the heavens and the earth, that he might (with understanding) have certitude. 76 When the night covered him over, **HE SAW A STAR: HE SAID: THIS IS MY LORD.** But when it set, he said: I love not those that set. 77 When

HE SAW THE MOON RISING IN SPLENDOUR, HE SAID: THIS IS MY LORD. But when the moon set, he said: Unless my Lord guide me, I shall surely be among those who go astray. *78* **WHEN HE SAW THE SUN RISING IN SPLENDOUR, HE SAID: THIS IS MY LORD; THIS IS THE GREATEST (OF ALL).** When the sun set, he said: O my people! I'm free from your (guilt) of giving partners to Allah"

These verses don't make sense at all, must we assume that Abraham NEVER saw the sun, stars and moon before. According to the Quran, Abraham who lived thousands of years ago, died with the hope that Allah might forgive his sins on the Day of Judgement:

Quran Translation by Abdullah Yusuf Ali – Surah 26:69 "Rehearse to them (something of) Abraham's story... 77 the Lord and Cherisher of the Worlds ... 82 Who, I hope, **WILL** forgive me my faults **ON THE DAY OF JUDGMENT**".

According to the Quran, Abraham died without the assurance that his sins were forgiven and that he died hoping his sins will be forgiven on the Day of Judgement.

Not only Abraham, but according to Islam, all prophets died unsure of their destiny.

Quran Translation by Abdullah Yusuf Ali – Surah 46:9 "...**NOR DO I [MUHAMMAD] KNOW WHAT WILL BE DONE WITH ME** or with you [my followers] ..."

Authorized English Version of the Quran – Surah 21:28 "They do not intercede, except for those already accepted by Him and **THEY [THE PROPHETS] ARE WORRIED ABOUT THEIR OWN NECKS**."

The prophets died worried about salvation. We now know they will all burn in hell-fire (7:179, 21:98) and will later be rescued (19:71).

Muhammed even believed that his own father is in hell-fire

Sunan Abu Dawud "Anas said: A man asked, where is my father, Messenger of Allah? He replied! Your father is in Hell. When he turned his back, he said: My father and your father are in Hell."

https://quranx.com/Hadith/AbuDawud/Hasan/Hadith-4700

https://quranx.com/Hadith/Muslim/USC-MSA/Book-1/Hadith-398

Last accessed 27 April 2021

94 Does Allah prefer people to sin instead of being sinless?

Sahih Muslim: "Abu Huraira reported Allah's Messenger having said: By Him in Whose Hand is my life, **IF YOU WERE NOT TO COMMIT SIN, ALLAH WOULD SWEEP YOU OUT OF EXISTENCE** and He would replace (you by) those people who *would commit sin* and seek forgiveness from Allah, and He would have pardoned them."
https://quranx.com/Hadith/Muslim/USC-MSA/Book-37/Hadith-6622

Last accessed 27 April 2021

Thus, Allah prefer sinners above sinless people. Why? Because Allah will feel justified when he sends people to a burning hell, since he ordained mankind to first burn in hell and then, perhaps later, allow certain people to be rescued from hell to enter heaven.

Allah predetermined for people to sin and do evil

Sahih Bukhari, Vol. 8, Page 397-399, Hadiths "609 The Prophet said: "**ALLAH HAS WRITTEN FOR THE SON OF ADAM HIS INEVITABLE SHARE OF ADULTERY,** whether he is aware of it or not… 611 The Prophet said… Adam said to Moses … Do you blame me for **ACTION, WHICH ALLAH HAD WRITTEN IN MY FATE** forty years before my creation?"

Sahih Muslim: "Abdullah (b. Mas'ud) reported that Allah's Messenger (ﷺ) who is the most truthful (of the human beings) and his being truthful (is a fact) said: Verily, your creation is on this wise. The *constituents* of one of you are collected for forty days in his mother's womb in the form of blood, after which it becomes a clot of blood in another period of forty days. Then it becomes a lump of flesh and forty days later Allah sends His angel to it with instructions concerning four things, so the angel writes down his livelihood, his death, his deeds, his fortune and misfortune. By Him, besides Whom there is no god, that one amongst you acts like the people deserving Paradise, until between him and

Paradise there remains but the distance of a cubit, when suddenly **THE WRITING OF DESTINY OVERCOMES HIM AND HE BEGINS TO ACT LIKE THE DENIZENS OF HELL AND THUS ENTERS HELL**…" [Unquote: 1 cubit = 0,4572m]

https://quranx.com/Hadith/Muslim/USC-MSA/Book-33/Hadith-6390 Last accessed 27 April 2021

Conversion http://extraconversion.com/length/cubits/cubits-to-meters.html Last accessed 27 April 2021

Allah's will, is for some people to disbelieve

__Quran Transl. by Abdullah Yusuf Ali Surah 10:100__ "No soul can believe, **EXCEPT BY THE WILL OF ALLAH**."

__The Noble Quran – Surah 6:35, 125__ "…And hath Allah willed, He could have gathered them together (all) on true guidance … Whomsoever **HE WILLS TO SEND ASTRAY, HE MAKES HIS BREAST CLOSED**…"

95 Do Christianity offer salvation without first going to hell?

Christianity teaches that **TRUE** Christians are **ALREADY** saved from the judgements of God and need not hope for forgiveness at the White Throne Judgement in the near future, we now enjoy forgiveness of sins and are guaranteed salvation without having to burn in hell.

__Mark 16:16__ "He that believed and is baptized **shall be saved**; but he that believed not, shall be damned."

__Romans 10:9__ "That if thou shalt confess with thy mouth the Lord Jesus and shalt believe in thine heart that God hath raised Him from the dead, **thou shalt be saved** … [8:1] *There is* therefore **NOW** no condemnation to them, which are in Christ Jesus…"

Christianity offers you no hell, but a promise from God that eternal life is yours, if you believe. Obviously, if you reject His promised, Eternal Life, damnation awaits you by your own decision.

96 Are Christians free to sin, since Jesus paid for their sins?

<u>Romans 6:1-2</u> "What shall we say then? **SHALL WE CONTINUE IN SIN** that grace may abound? **GOD FORBID!** How shall we, that are dead to sin, live any longer therein…"

Muslims, without scriptural evidence, like to say that Christians can sin if they like, because Jesus already paid for our future sins. Once again, their argument can be used against them, for if that is the case, Christians can argue that Muhammad was free to sin as he like, because Allah forgave Muhammad's past sins as well as his future sins (see Q36). The Bible does NOT teach nor do Christians believe that we can sin as we please, no, we believe that if we sin and we repent, He is faithful to keep His promise to forgive us and to allow us to enter heaven.

97 What is righteousness?

There are two types of righteousness: man's self-righteousness and God's righteousness. In this study we will look at God's righteousness from an Islamic and Christian point of view.

<u>Quran Translation by Abdullah Yusuf Ali – Surah 2:177</u> "It is not righteousness that ye turn your faces towards east or west, **BUT IT IS RIGHTEOUSNESS: TO BELIEVE** in God and the last day and the angels and the book and the messengers…"

Righteousness before Allah is to believe and therefore practice that which Allah prescribed as ordinances. Surah 2:177 reflects five of the <u>SIX BASIC PRINCIPLES OF ISLAM</u>: Believe in (i) God, (ii) angels, (iii) holy books, (iv) prophets, (v) predestination and (vi) Day of Judgement.

Romans 4:3 "For what said the scripture? Abraham **BELIEVED GOD AND IT [HIS FAITH] WAS COUNTED UNTO HIM FOR RIGHTEOUSNESS**."

We are not righteous, because of what we do, but we are righteous, because we believe God. It is obvious that our faith, which is our righteousness, it inspires us to do good works.

98 Will our good works save us from hell?

Deceived Muslim scholars says: "YES!"

Attorney Mohammed Coovadia: Basic Islamic Principles... Page 8 "It is our actions and inactions that determine our destiny."

As we have seen, it is not our deeds that determines our destiny, but it is Allah who predetermined and created mankind to burn in hell and later to be rescued out of the fire to enter paradise. Mr. Coovadia, here obviously contradicted nultiple Quranic verses (7:179, 19:70-72).

Public debate: Why Christianity? Why Islam? Dated 10 September 2016 – Christian speaker, Pastor Michael Mahomed and Muslim speaker, Apologist Mr. Bashir Vania [Mr. Vania said:] "**THIS CONCEPT OF GOOD WORKS IS SO IMPORTANT IN ISLAM** that the Quran tells us that god will not punish a people even if they are idol-worshippers, as long as their behavior is good, they still have a chance for salvation because of their good behavior..."

Mr. Vania's understanding of how to obtain salvation with regard to good works in Islam is contradicted by the Quran, which stated in one place [Surah 4:48] that Allah does not forgive idol-worshipping and in the below verse that those who die in unbelief, Allah will not recognize their good works.

Quran Translation by Abdullah Yusuf Ali – Surah 2:217 "...And if any of **you turn back from their faith and die in unbelief, their works will bear no fruit** IN THIS LIFE

AND IN THE HEREAFTER; THEY WILL BE COMPANIONS OF THE FIRE AND WILL ABIDE THEREIN."

According to Muhammed, we are not saved by our good works:

The Noble Quran: Page 28 – Footnote 1 "Narrated Aishah, the prophet said: Do good deeds properly, sincerely and moderately and receive good news, **BUT ONE'S GOOD DEEDS WILL NOT MAKE HIM ENTER PARADISE.** They asked: Even you, O Allah's messenger? He said: Even I, unless or until ALLAH PROTECTS OR COVERS ME WITH HIS PARDON AND MERCY" (Sahih Bukhari Vol. 8, Page 315, Hadith 474)."

But as we have seen, the mercy of Allah will only be considered after you toasted in hell for a period. According to the Quran, those who will enter paradise are those who believe and do good works.

Quran Translation by Abdullah Yusuf Ali – Surah 2:225 "But give glad tidings to those **who believe and work righteousness**, that their portion is Gardens…"

Notice, in this verse, Allah did not say you won't go to hell-fire at all and straight away go to heaven, he only promised that you will enter paradise. When? In this verse, Allah didn't stipulate EXACTLY when you will enter heaven, but from other verses, we know he predestined mankind to first burn for an undisclosed period. Will we enter paradise because of our good works? Islam says: "NO!" Christianity agrees, no good works will save you from hell-fire.

Ephesians 2:8 "For by grace are ye saved through faith and that not of yourselves: it is the gift of God: 9 Not of works, lest any man should boast."

Four facts are clear: (1) We are saved by grace through faith in God; (2) not of ourselves; (3) it is a gift (not something we earned) and (4) not of any good deeds we have done or will do! Salvation is a big done by God through Jesus Christ! That doesn't mean we must not have good works, it only means our good works don't save us. Now that we are ALREADY saved, as a token of our appreciation of our salvation, we do good works.

1 Timothy 6:18 "That they do good [and] that they **be rich in good works**…"

Romans **12:21** "Overcome evil **with good**…"

Even the Quran emphasized that true Christians haste in doing good works:

Quran Translation by Abdullah Yusuf Ali – Surah 3:113-114, 199 "… Some of the People of the Book are an upright people… They command what is just and forbid what is wrong and **THEY HASTENED IN GOOD WORKS AND THEY ARE OF THE RIGHTEOUS**…"

Muslims like to bring up the case of Hitler and ask if he, at his death-bed accepted Jesus Christ's work of Salvation on the cross, will Hitler go to heaven, REGARDLESS all the murders he committed? Well, if Hitler sincerely repented, God knows, if he did, God would not treat him different from any other who sinned. God is Most Merciful and Most Gracious. Salvation is the matter of the heart and confession of the tongue and if you have an opportunity to live after your convertion your changed life will be evident. What if Hitler at his death-bed would have sincerely accepted Islam?

Attorney Mohammed Coovadia: Basic Islamic Principles… Page 16 "The prophet said: Didn't you know that **CONVERTING TO ISLAM ERASES ALL PREVIOUS SINS**?"

Sahih Bukhari *Vol. 3, Page 69-70, Hadith 125* "Narrated Abu Huraira: The Prophet (ﷺ) said: Whoever established prayers on the night of Qadr out of sincere faith and hoping for a reward from Allah, then all his previous sins will be forgiven…"

This simply means that Allah would have forgiven Hitler all his previous sins! This also means that if a non-Muslim man who raped women and sodomized boys and was a serial killer, who later in life realized that his deeds were wrong and he converted to Islam, that all that man's previous sins is forgiven. This proves Muslims are bias towards Islam as reasonably just opposed to Christianity for the same thing. But even if you convert to Islam and all your previous sins are erased, remember, regardless your good or evil works, in the Quran, Allah, before creation or before your birth, already decreed that mankind was created for hell and only after some have toasted for a while, according to the above Surahs and Ahadith, will Allah rescue believers from hell.

Allah could not get the shahadah – testimony right

The shahadah (testimony) is the first of <u>FIVE PILLARS OF ISLAM</u>, followed by the salat (prayers), zakat (alms), sawm (fasting) and hajj (pilgrimage). The shahadah is important for Muslim conversion.

Quran Translation by Abdullah Yusuf Ali: 16:2 "…(Saying:) Warn (man) that - there is no god, but I, so do your duty unto **ME**" [Unquote: Here Allah speaks in the first person: "I … Me".]

Quran Translation by Abdullah Yusuf Ali: Roman Transliteration – Surah 3:18 "Shahi-dallaahu 'anna-**Huu** laaa 'ilaaha… There is no god, but **He**: That is the witness of Allah…"

That is not the witness of Allah, this is the witness of a third person speaking about Allah, if this was Allah, it should have been in the first person like in Surah 16:2 "There is no god, but **I**" or "There is no god, but **Me**" – That would have been the witness of Allah. That would have been Allah speaking. **HE** denotes a third person. Also, for Allah to say there are **no gods** [ilaah] is a false statement – there are billions of gods (idols), perhaps, Allah meant to say: "There is no <u>G</u>od, but Me." And Allah knows best!

99 What is the original sin?

Did Satan really disobey Allah or was Allah unjust against Satan?

In the Quran, the first sin was **APPARENTLY** committed by Satan. Notice, I said: "apparently". Let me explain: If I have five boys and five girls and **I SAY: BOYS PLEASE WASH MY CAR** and they did, but my girls did not help them to wash my car, is it fair and just of me to say my girls are disobedient for not washing my car when I commanded my boys to wash my car? No! I never commanded the girls in the first place. Since I gave them no command, they did not disobey me. If I say the girls are disobedient, that would make me unfair and unjust.

ACCORDING TO THE QURAN, ALLAH INSTRUCTED THE ANGELS TO BOW BEFORE ADAM.

Quran Translation by Abdullah Yusuf Ali: 15:28-30 "Behold! thy Lord said **TO THE ANGELS**: I am about to create man … When I have fashioned him … fall ye down in obeisance unto him. **SO THE ANGELS** prostrated themselves, **ALL OF THEM TOGETHER**." (38:71-73).

Notice, here Allah said A-L-L the angels obeyed Allah's order and prostrated themselves before Adam. If Satan is an angel, then Allah lied in the above verses when he said A-L-L the angels prostrated. As we can see, there's no disobedience from the angels whom Allah told to bow before Adam.

God did NOT instruct the animals or anyother creatures to bow themselves before Adam, therefore, no other creatures disobeyed Allah's commandment. The Quran is clear – Allah only commanded the angels (Surah 2:34, 7:11, 17:61, 20:116)

Tafsir - Ibn Al Kathir S. 18:50 "The angels were created from light…"

What creature was Iblees (Satan)?

Tafsir - Ibn Al Kathir S. 2:34 "…Iblis was **NOT** an angel…"

https://quranx.com/Tafsir/Kathir/2.34

Last accessed 27 April 2021

Quran Translation by Abdullah Yusuf Ali: 18:50 "…Iblis. He was one of the Jinns…"

Quran Translation by Abdullah Yusuf Ali: 55:15 "He created Jinns from fire free of smoke."

In Islam, Angels and Jinns are two different creatures and they are made from different elements.

ALLAH IN THE QURAN, NEVER INSTRUCTED THE JINNS TO BOW BEFORE ADAM!

When Allah instructed the angels to bow before Adam, Satan didn't bow and was not disobedient, because Allah did not instruct the jinns to bow. For Allah to accuse Satan in Quran 18:50 of being disobedient, simply makes Allah unjust, since Allah never instructed him to bow. Also, why did Allah not accuse ALL the jinns of disobedience, since none of them bowed, why is Allah victimizing Iblis (Satan)? You cannot disobey an order, if an order is not given to you. In the Quran, Allah said that Satan became one of the disbelievers (Surah 38:74), this is another error on Allah's side. How can Satan become one of the disbelievers, if he is the first disbeliever? Allah should have said that Satan became a disbeliever or Satan became the first disbeliever. To say that Satan became one of the disbelievers, assumes that there were disbelievers before Satan.

Adam was the first to disobey Allah and caused his offspring to fall into sin

In the Quran, Allah informed Adam that Satan is his enemy (Surah 20:116-117) and that they (Adam and his wife) may eat of all the trees in the Garden, but to stay away from a certain tree in the Garden.

Quran Translation by Abdullah Yusuf Ali – Surah 7:19-22, 20:121 "[God said:] O Adam, dwell thou and thy wife in the Garden and enjoy (its good things) as ye wish: but approach not this tree or ye run into harm and transgression. *Then began Satan to whisper suggestions to them, bringing openly before their minds all their shame that was hidden from them (before): He [Satan] said: Your Lord only forbade you this tree, lest ye should become angels or such beings that live forever.* And he swore to them both that he was their sincere adviser. So by the deceit he brought about their fall: when they taste of the tree, their shame became manifest to them … Then did Satan make them slip from the (Garden) and get them out of the state (of felicity) in which they had been … **ADAM DISOBEYED HIS LORD**…"

NOTE: Satan reminded Adam of his Lord's directive, but Adam accepted Satan's advice and disbelieved (disobeyed) God's directive.

The first sin committed by Adam and Eve that caused them to be put out of paradise was disobedience to God's Word! After Adam and Eve sinned; God put both of them out of the Garden.

Quran Translation by Abdullah Yusuf Ali – Surah 2:38 "We [Allah] said: Get ye down, ALL (YE PEOPLE) …"

In the above Quranic verse, it was Adam and his wife who sinned, they were the ONLY two people at that time in existence, yet when God put them out of the Garden, the verse reveals that, not a dual couple (pair of two), but a plural (more than two people) audience was addressed and put out of the Garden.

Quran Translation by Abdullah Yusuf Ali: Page 712 – Commentary 2251 "[Surah] ii:30-38 deals with the **COLLECTIVE RACE THROUGH ADAM**…"

The Quran and Bible agree that all humans, today, **BECAUSE OF THE ORIGINAL (FIRST) SIN COMMITTED BY ADAM AND HIS WIFE**, we are living outside of the Garden of bliss. When Adam sinned, *we in Adam* fell with him. We are out of the state (of felicity), because of Adam and Eve's sin. When they were put out of the Garden, because of their sin, all of mankind in Adam's loins was put out of the Garden.

Sahih Bukhari, Vol. 6, Page 234, Hadith 262 "Narrated Abu Huraira: The Prophet (ﷺ) said: Moses argued with Adam and said to him (Adam) - **YOU ARE THE ONE WHO GOT THE PEOPLE OUT OF PARADISE BY YOUR SIN** and thus made them miserable."

Clearly, according to the above, Prophet Moses had the understanding that we are out of the Garden, not because of our sin, but because of Adam and Eve's original sin of disobedience. Adam and Eve were created sinless, but after they sinned and fell, their offspring were born as a fallen race.

Quran Translation by Abdullah Yusuf Ali: Page 744 – Commentary 2392 "… Cf. ii:34, where the story is told of the **FALL OF MANKIND THROUGH ADAM**."

WE ARE BORN IN A FALLEN STATE, BECAUSE OF THE ORIGINAL SIN OF ADAM AND EVE. WE ARE NOT BORN WITH SIN, WE ARE BORN IN A FALLEN STATE,

SUBJECT TO SIN. OUR NATURE IS SINFUL, HENCE, IT IS INEVITABLE THAT ALL OF ADAM'S OFFSPRING, WITHOUT DOUBT, WILL SIN AND ARE SINNERS.

Jami' at-Tirmihi "Anas narrated **THE PROPHET ( ) SAID**: *Every son of Adam sins*. The best of the sinners are the repentant." https://quranx.com/Hadith/Tirmidhi/DarusSalam/Volume-4/Book-35/Hadith-2499

Last accessed 27 April 2021

Bulugh al-Maram "Anas narrated that **ALLAH'S MESSENGER SAID**: *All the sons of Adam are sinners…*" https://quranx.com/Hadith/Maram/English/Book-16/Hadith-1520
Last accessed 27 April 2021

Public debate: "Salvation in Islam and Christianity" – Christian speaker, Dr. John LeMond and Muslim speaker, Dr. Bilal Philips [quoting Philips:] "As **THE PROPHET SAID**: *ALL of Adam's descendants constantly commit sins.*" https://www.youtube.com/watch?v=nqBQzfy7yyg Time line 46:15 – 46:20:

Last accessed 19 June 2021

Sahih Bukhari, Vol. 4, Page 400, Hadith 611 "Narrated Abu Huraira: **THE PROPHET ( ) SAID**: Were it not for Bani Israel, meat would not decay and *were it not for Eve, no woman would ever betray her husband*."

So, because of the original sin of Adam and Eve, all of Adam's offspring are in a fallen state and are sinners and according to Muhammed, that's why wives betray their husbands. It is for this reason that we, as sinners, cannot bear one anothers sin, because as sinners, we need a savior, hence no offspring of Adam can be my savior, can bear my sins. The Quran agrees.

Quran Translation by Abdullah Yusuf Ali: Surah 53:38 (17:13-15) "Namely, that **NO BEARER OF BURDENS** can bear the burden of another…"

Let's read and understand what is actually written and not read our own idea into the verse. What does the phrase: *"No bearer of burdens"* mean? It means: *"no sinner"*.

Understanding the verse in its proper context means: *"No sinner can bear the sin of another sinner."* This would include every progeny of Adam, whether TRUE prophets of God or priests, **EXCEPT JESUS CHRIST**, He is not of the seed (offspring) of Adam.

The Noble Quran – Surah 3:47 "She said: O my Lord! How shall I have a son when no man has touched me." [Luke 1:34]

Jesus is not of Adam's sperm reproduced, but God's Word (Surah 4:171) bestowed on Mary. All of us are from this world, but Jesus Christ is from above (John 8:32 quote below), from heaven, a Spirit proceeding from God (Surah 4:171).

100 Jesus saves

John 8:23 "He [Jesus] said unto them: Ye are from beneath; **I am from above**: ye are of this world; **I'm not**

of this world."

We can't bear one another's sin, because we are all sinners from this world, but Jesus was not a sinner. Jesus is not from the seed of Adam, when Adam fell, we all in Adam fell, except for Jesus, He is not from Adam's seed. He was a virgin born Son. He is from above (see Q65). Jesus Christ, therefore, is the only man that was not contaminated with the fall of Adam. The Quran 19:19 and Bible Luke 1:35 describes Jesus as a holy, pure, faultless son. Even during His lifespan, He remained sinless.

John 8:46 "Which of you convinceth Me of sin? And if I say the truth, why do ye not believe Me?"

1 Peter 2:22 "Who did no sin, neither was guile found in His mouth."

1 John 3:5 "And ye know that He was manifested to take away our sins; and in Him is no sin."

Jesus Christ, He is the only one who is sinless and therefore, could and did bear our sins on the cross of Calvary. REMEMBER, the Quran did not say no one can bear the sins of another, it says no bearer of burdens – no sinner can bear another's burden - sin. It is not a Pauline idea, as Muslim Scholars inaccurately argues, that Jesus Christ must borne our sins, it was God's idea, as we now know, 700 years before Paul was born. Let's look at an OT prophet's Messiahic prophesy:

Isaiah 53:5 "But he was wounded for our transgressions, he was bruised for our iniquities: the chastisement of our peace was upon him; and with his stripes we are healed... 11 for he shall bear their iniquities. 12 he hath poured out his soul unto death: and he was numbered with the transgressors; and **HE BARE THE SIN OF MANY**, and made intercession for the transgressors."

As Adam disobeyed God and took us out of paradise, so Jesus obeyed God and takes us back to paradise. In fact, **JESUS** Himself preached that He is our ransom and if any man comes to Him, will be saved!

Matthew 20:28 "Even as the Son of man came not to be ministered unto, but to minister, and **TO GIVE HIS LIFE A RANSOM FOR MANY**... [11:28] Come unto Me, all ye that labor and are heavy laden, and I will give you rest." (Acts 15:11 and Romans 3:24)

John 10:9 "I'm the door: by Me if any man enters in, **HE SHALL BE SAVED**..."

BIBLIOGRAPHY

QURAN TRANSLATIONS:

- Ali A.Y. (1934) English Quran Translation and Commentary, Published by Islamic Propagation Centre International

- Ali, Abdullah Yusuf - Roman Transliteration of the Holy Quran Revised Edition - Adam Publishers & Distributors, Shandar Market, Chitli Qabar, Delhi 110006 (ISBN 81-7435)

- Ali, Muhammad (Maulana) – The Holy Qur'an, Arabic Text, English Translation and Commentary - Revised Edition – Seventh Edition Published in the United States by Specialty Promotions CO. INC. Chicago, Illinois through special arrangement with Ahmadiyyah Anjuman Isha'at Islam Lahore, Pakistan 1985

- Arberry, AJ (Professor) - The Koran, Oxford Paperbacks, Oxford University Press (ISBN 0-19-281628-4)

- Asad, Muhammad (Dr.) - The Message of THE QURAN Translated and Explained

- Baker, MA (Imam) - Die Heilige Quran (The Holy Quran Translated into Afrikaans) Published by IDM Publications a division of Islamic Dawah Movement of Southern Africa: P.O. Box 48009, Qualbert, 4078, Durban, South Africa Tel: 031-304 6883 – Fax 031-305 1292, E-mail: idm@ion.co.za

- Dawood, NJ - The Koran: Revised Translation, (ISBN 0-14-044558-7)

- Hilâlî, Muhammad (Dr.) and Khân, Muhammad (Dr.) The Noble Quran, English Translation of the meanings and commentary

- Khalifah, Rashad (Dr.) - The Authorized English Version of the Quran (ISBN 0-9623622-2-0)

- Pickthall, Muhammad - The Meaning of the Glorious Qur'an

- Pooya/ M.A. Ali Comm. on Surah 5:48, http://www.al-islam.org/quran/

- ❖ (Last accessed 27 April 2021)
- ❖ SAHEEH INTERNATIONAL – The Qur'an: English meanings Revised and Edited.
- ❖ Published by AL-MUNTADA AL-ISLAMI TRUST (ISBN 9960-792-63-3)
- ❖ Shakir - Quran Translation

TAFSIR IBN AL KATHIR

- (Abridged) Vol. 1 – Comment on Surah 2:223 Al-farj (the vagina).
- (Abridged) Vol. 10 – Comm. on Surah 66:12 Chastity (private parts)
- http://answering-islam.org/Quran/Science/semenproduction.htm
- Surah 4:34 Wife beating http://www.bible.ca/islam/islam-wife-beating-hadith.htm
- Surah 5:13-15 misinterpreted https://www.answering-islam.org/Shamoun/bible_authentic1.htm
- Surah 33:56 Allah pray www.answering-islam.org/authors/shamoun/allah_worships.html

(Last accessed 27 April 2021)

SAHIH BUKHARI

Khan, Muhammad Mushin (Dr.) - It's Trans. and Meanings (Arabic – English): Islamic University, Medina Al-Munawwara, Published by: Nusrat Ali Nasri for Kitab Bhavan – 1784 Kalan Mahal, Darya Ganj, New Delhi 110002 (India)

- Volume 1 ISBN 81-7151-014-0
- Volume 2 ISBN 81-7151-015-9
- Volume 3 ISBN 81-7151-016-7
- Volume 4 ISBN 81-7151-017-5
- Volume 5 ISBN 81-7151-018-3
- Volume 6 ISBN 81-7151-019-1

- Volume 7 ISBN 81-7151-020-5
- Volume 8 ISBN 81-7151-021-3
- Volume 9 ISBN 81-7151-022-1

SAHIH MUSLIM

- Volume 2

  http://answering-islam.org/Gilchrist/Jam/chap4.html

- Book 7, Number 3018 – Wine Nabidh

  https://sunnah.com/search/?q=FULL+OF+NABIDH

- Book 7, Number 3018, Book 4, Hadith 2127

  https://muflihun.com/muslim/4/2127

  (Last accessed 27 April 2021)

SUNAN OF ABU DAWUD

- Vol. 2, No: 2150 "Intercourse with captives
  https://www.muslimhope.com/RightHand.htm
- Book 11, No: 2126 Vagina http://answering-islam.org/Quran/Science/semenproduction.htm
- Book 11, Marriage https://quranx.com/Hadith/AbuDawud/USC-MSA/Book-11/Hadith-2141/
- Book 38, Wine drinkers https://quranx.com/Hadith/AbuDawud/USC-MSA/Book-38/Hadith 4467
- (Last accessed 27 April 2021)

MALIK'S MUWATTA: https://quranx.com/Hadith/Malik/USC-MSA/Book-3/Hadith-39

(Last accessed 27 April 2021)

ENCYCLOPEDIA

- Glassé, Cyril - The Concise Encyclopedia of Islam, 1989

  Samuel Green: *The Different Arabic Versions of the Quran*

  http://answering-islam.org/Green/seven.htm

  (Last accessed 27 April 2021)

- Encyclopedia Britannica, 1993, Vol. 3

- Encyclopedia Britannica 15TH Edition Vol. 7

  http://answering-islam.org/Women/birthrate.html

  (Last accessed 27 April 2021)

- The World Book Encyclopedia – Volume 15 - Page 102-103 "P"

- The New Standard Encyclopedia: Odhams Press Limited, Copyright 1936

DICTIONARIES:

Oxford Dictionary:

https://www.google.com/search?q=what+does+recension+mean%3F&oq=what+does+recension+mean%3F&aqs=chrome..69i57j0l7.8304j0j7&sourceid=chrome&ie=UTF-8
Last accessed 27 April 2021

- Hughes, Thomas Patrick, Dictionary of Islam (Revised by Eminent Scholars)

  The BOOK House Publishers and Booksellers, Trust Bldg., Urdu Bazar,

  Post Box 734, LAHORE-2 (Pakistan)

- The New Bible Dictionary: © The Inter-Varsity Fellowship 1962 (London)

  ISBN 0 85110 608 0 (IVP) / 0 85110 820 2 (International Christian Handbooks.

  Cambridge Advanced Learner's Dictionary 4TH Edition Edited by Colin McIntosh, [ISBN 978-1-107-65313-9]

- Thesaurus (Computer)

THE MUSLIM DIGEST: (Registered at the G.P.O. as a newspaper)

- June 1966, Vol. 16 - No: 11 Page 16
- Oct. / Nov., 1978, Vol. 29 - Nos. 3 & 4
- Sept. to Dec. 1980, Vol. 31 - Nos. 2 – 5

RAMADAN ANNUAL OF THE MUSLIM DIGEST: (Registered at the G.P.O. as a newspaper)

- Oct. Nov. 1978, No's 3 & 4Vol. 29
- April/ May, Nos. 9/ 10, Vol. 38 Page 312

NEWS PAPERS:

- The Horizon August / September 2011 horizon@vodamail.co.za
- The Star … Friday, Nov. 29 2002

MAGAZINES:

- Drum The voice of Africa. 14 March 2002 No: 497
- Femina: January 2002 (Magazine)

BOOKS:

- Abdalati, Hammudah - Islam in Focus
- https://www.muslim-library.com/dl/books/English_Islam_In_Focus.pdf

  (Last accessed 27 April 2021)

  Abdul Azziz bin Abdullah bin Baaz (Sheikh) It is compulsory to act on the Sunnat and its rejection is Kufr (Translated by Mufi A. H. Elias.) Printed by: Jet Printers. 141 Anderson Street, JHB 2000 - Tel: 331-2371 /2 /3

- Ahmad, Fazl (Prof.) - Muhammad, The Prophet of Islam: Heroes of Islam 1
- Arthur, Jeffrey: Islam, Muhammad and His Religion (New York: The Liberal Arts Press, 1958)

- Bucaille, Maurice (Dr.): The Bible, The Quran & Science – Page 238, (ISBN 81-7435-337-2)

- Campbell, William (Dr.) - The Quran & the Bible in the light of history and science

    https://answering-islam.org/Campbell/s1c2.html

    https://answering-islam.org/Campbell/s4c2b.html

    http://www.bible.ca/islam/islam-myths-embryology.htm

    (Last accessed 27 April 2021)

- Coovadia, Mohammed (Attorney) - Basic Islamic Principles for Christians and those of other Faiths

Deedat, Ahmed [Islamic Propagation Centre International]

- Al-Quran: The Miracle of Miracles!
- Is all of the Bible God's Word?
- What the Bible says about Muhammad?
- Muhammad, The Natural Successor to Christ (pbuh)!
- What is His name?
- Crucifixion or Cruci-fiction?
- Resurrection or Resuscitation?
- What was the sign of Jonah?
- Desert Storm – Has it ended? Christ in Islam
- Who Moved the Stone?

Gilchrist, John

- Jam Al-Quran: The Codification of the Quran Text

    https://answering-islam.org/Gilchrist/Jam/index.html

(Last accessed 27 April 2021)

- Facing the Muslim Challenge (ISBN 0-9583905-5-1) [MERSA P.O. Box 1804 Benoni]

Guillaume, Alfred

- (Translator) - Ishag, "Life of Muhammad"

  https://www.thereligionofpeace.com/pages/muhammad/Guillaume--Life%20of%20Muhammad.pdf

- IA Ibrahim: A Brief illustrated guide to understanding Islam

  Published by Darussalam, Publishers and Distributors, Houston, Texas, USA – ISBN 9960-34-011-2

- Islam [ISBN 0140203117]

  http://answering-islam.org/Shamoun/idolatry.htm Last accessed 27 April 2021

- Hasan, Masudul (Prof.)

  History of Islam: Revised Edition, Vol. 1, Adam Publishers & Distributors:

  16 Shandar Market, Chitli Qabar, DELHI-110006 INDIA (ISBN 81-7435-016-0)

- Jaffer I.E. (Prof.) and Rafudeen MA (Dr.) (2021) A History of Islam, Department of Religious Studies and Arabic. University of South Africa

- Jhazbhay MID (Prof) and Rafudeen MA (Prof), (2021) An Introduction to Islam, Department of Religious Studies and Arabic. University of South Africa

- Joommal, ASK - The Riddle of the Trinity

- Khalifah, Rashad (Dr.) Quran, Hadith and Islam – Page 44

  https://www.masjidtucson.org/publications/books/qhi/qhi.html Last accessed 27 April 2021

- Moshay, GJO - Who is this Allah? (ISBN 095183861)

Win by losing – Page 49

Blacks towards hell – Page 164

https://books.google.co.za/books?id=VxAvAgAAQBAJ&pg=PA164&lpg=PA164&dq=Then+He+stroke+his+right+shoulder+and+took+out+a+white+race&source=bl&ots=VrQJLBSGec&sig=ACfU3U1T6Lwi4u0zApLOzh6J79MfMfIHeA&hl=en&sa=X&ved=2ahUKEwjl_dXHuKDjAhUmTBUIHaMkCUwQ6AEwCnoECAcQAQ#v=onepage&q=Then%20He%20stroke%20his%20right%20shoulder%20and%20took%20out%20a%20white%20race&f=false

(Last accessed 27 April 2021)

- Obaray, AH

    Miraculous Conception, Death, Resurrection & Ascension of Jesus as Taught in the Kuran

    Kimberley S Africa; Pub. By Author, 1962

- Ruthven, Malise - Islam: A very short introduction (ISBN 0 19 285334 1)
- Sallie, Abdurraghiem Hasan - The Decree of the Murtad According to the Islamic law
- Seepye, MO - Is the Crucifixion a fact or fiction?

    The Crescent Islamic Defense and Dissemination Service Organization

- Sherif, Faruq - A Guide to the Contents of the Quran

    Published by Garnet Publishing Ltd. 8 Southern Court, Suth Street, Reading, RGI 4QS, UK

    [ISBN 1 85964 045 1]

- Vania, Basheer A. - An Analysis of the Concept of Divinity - Published by Institute for Islamic Services
- Von Denffer, Ahmed - Ulum al Quran: Introduction to the Science of the Quran.

http://www.islamicbulletin.org/free_downloads/quran/ul_umal_quran.pdf

(Last accessed 27 April 2021)

- Wright, Abdur-Rahman (Sheikh)

    The Black People of South Africa and The Imported Religions

    Published by Islamic Dawa Society - PO Box 42622 Fordsburg 2033

- Awake to the call of Islam: Vol. 2, No: 12, Page 23, March 1976, Rabi-ul-Awwal 1396 Published by: The Young Men's Muslim Association P.O. Box 5036 Benoni South African

- It is compulsory to act on the Sunnat and its rejection is Kufr

Behind the Veil

- Dr. Mosa El Mosawy: El-Sheaa and Correction https://answering-islam.org/BehindVeil/btv12.html

- You Ask and Islam Answers https://answering-islam.org/BehindVeil/btv1.html

- Offensive War to Spread Islam https://answering-islam.org/BehindVeil/btv2.html

    Last accessed 27 April 2021

SALAH, the Muslim Prayer – Published by Islamic Propagation Centre International

WEBSITES: (Last online confirm dated 5 July 2019

Women dress code according to Quran:

http://www.submission.org/Dress_Code_1.html

Ibn Kathir, Edition published by Maktabat Masr

http://groups.google.com/groups?oi=djq&ic=1&selm=an_390704909

Mufti Muhammad Taqi Usmani – The Preservation of the Quran.

https://www.ilmgate.org/the-preservation-of-the-quran/

Brief History of the Compilation of the Quran:

www.alseraj.net/maktaba/kotob/english/quran/TheNobleQuran/dept/MSA/quran/compilationbrief.html

Email discussion: Dr. MSM Saifullah

http://www.answering-islam.org/Quran/Text/hajjaj.r.html

Islamic Awareness, Versions of the Quran?"

https://www.google.com/search?q=islamic+awareness+-+versions+of+the+quran&oq=islamic+awareness+-+versions+of+the+quran&aqs=chrome..69i57j33.19130j1j4&sourceid=chrome&ie=UTF-8

Sultan Muhammad Paul: Why I became a Christian?

https://www.ijfm.org/PDFs_IJFM/13_4_PDFs/06_Sultan%20M%20%20Paul.pdf

Shabir Ally:

Noah's Flood http://answering-islam.org/Responses/Shabir-Ally/q16_copied.htm

Quran praise Bible http://answering-islam.org/Responses/Shabir-Ally/toughquestion.htm

The estimated distance from the earth to the sun

http://hypertextbook.com/facts/KathrynTam.shtml.

http://dcmusgrove.blogspot.com/2011/06/how-big-is-universe.html.

The estimated distance from earth to moon

http://askville.amazon.com/distance-earth-moon/AnswerViewer.do?requestId=2346608.

The Concept of Tawhid in Islam

https://www.bismikaallahuma.org/islam/tawhid-in-islam/

How Muhammad Ali (Cassius Clay) was deceived by Islam: Youtube presentation by Dr. David Wood:

https://www.youtube.com/watch?v=sxOM4GrqElw

A Muslim admits that Muslims are praying to Muhammad

Youtube: Discussion with David Wood and Sam Shamoun:

https://www.youtube.com/watch?v=CjsRVkiN-D8

Dr. Zakir Naik - The earth is egg-shaped

https://www.youtube.com/watch?v=NosGnATJE7A Time line 00:02:20

Youtube presentation by Dr. Jay Smit: Why dates of the different Qurans are so damaging? https://www.youtube.com/watch?v=X4vC4rDI8UU [Last viewed 28 July 2020]

PUBLIC DEBATES

- Was Christ Crucified?

    August 1981 - Christian Speaker, Mr. Josh McDowell and Muslim Speaker, Mr. Ahmad Deedat

    Transcript: http://answering-islam.org/Debates/Deedat_McDowell.html

    Video: https://www.youtube.com/watch?v=05jOZAo9u6g

- Is the Bible the Word of God?" 1986 - Christian Speaker, Evangelist Jimmy Swaggart and Muslim Speaker, Sheik Ahmad Deedat

    https://www.youtube.com/watch?v=genex9BqlmI

    Q&A "Was original Quran burnt?" - Time line 01:32:10 – 01:36:14

    Q&A "Is the Injeel guidance for all mankind? Time line 01:45:35 – 01:47:25

    (Last online confirm dated 5 July 2019)

- The Crucifixion of Jesus Christ: Fact or Fiction?

11 April 2003: Christian speaker, Br. Michael Mahomed and Muslim Speaker, Mr. Ayoob Karim propagated Substitution Theory – First 45 minutes' presentation (DVD copies available)

- Can historians prove Jesus was raised from the dead?

  02 April 2009: Christian Speaker, Dr. Michael Licona and anti-Christian Speaker and Dr. Bart Ehrman (Professor and Historian, also an agnostic and atheist)

  https://www.youtube.com/watch?v=-iE6YX9O5tE

  Historians agree Jesus was crucified - Time line 01:05:00 - 01:05:45

- The Crucifixion & Resurrection of Jesus Christ: Fact or Fiction

  25 June 2009: Christian Speaker, Mr. John Gilchrist and Muslim Speaker, Dr. Shabir Ally and

  https://www.youtube.com/watch?v=PHdrnjnAnq4

  Two points: One, Jesus died and two, He was raised back to life – time line 00:05:30 – 00:05:44

- The Bible and the Quran in relation to Science:

  31 January 2011: Christian speaker, Mr. Piet Strydom & Muslim speaker, Mr. Ayoob Karim https://www.youtube.com/watch?v=lMd5ynlY52I

  Earth is ostrich egg-shaped: Time line 00:11:45 – 00:12:20

- The way of Salvation in the Bible and Quran

  13 July 2011: Christian Speakers, Dr. Mark Harlan - Elder Brian Marrian (PACT) and Muslim Speakers, Attorney Mohammed Coovadia - Bashir Vania (Islamic Info Centre) - DVD copies available

- Christian Trinity or Islamic Tawheed: Which is the True Nature of God?

  23 February 2013 Muslim Speaker, Mr. Yusuf Buxson and Christian Speaker, Elder Brian Marrian - DVD copies available

- Has the Quran been accurately transmitted?

    01 October 2013: Christian speaker, Dr. James White and Muslim speaker, Yusuf Ismail https://youtu.be/RNB7GHmk7uE [3 of 3 timeline 00:06:00 00:07:00]

    (Last online confirmed dated 5 July 2019)

- Which is the Word of God: Bible or Quran?

    27 September 2014: Christian speaker, Apologist Jay Smith and Muslim speaker, Dr. Shabir Ally

    https://www.youtube.com/watch?v=fWHV9VnOJtc

    Ten variant readings of the Quran: Time line 00:59:14 – 00:59:40

    (Last online confirm dated 5 July 2019)

- Why Christianity? – Why Islam?

    10 September 2016: Christian speaker, Ps. Michael Mahomed and Muslim speaker, Mr. Bashir Vania

    DVD copies available

- Why Muslim? Why Christian?

    17 October 2017: Christian Speaker, Dr. John Azumah and Muslim Speaker, Yusuf Ismail

    DVD copies available

- Was Christ crucified?

    27 October 2018: Christian Speaker, Br. Samuel Green and Muslim Speaker, Historian Adnan Rashid

https://www.youtube.com/watch?v=K24xIPcI1H4

- Matthew, Mark, Luke and John are unanimous that Jesus was crucified - Time line 00:03:25 – 00:03:36

- Tawheed vs Trinity

  7 November 2018: Christian Speaker, Dr. David Wood and Muslim Speaker, Mr. Mohammed Hijab

  https://www.youtube.com/watch?v=ZyhvQ0O4yxl

  (Last online confirmed dated 5 July 2019)

- Did Jesus rise from the dead?

  Christian Speaker, Dr. William Lane Craig and Muslim Speaker,

  Dr. Shabir Ally https://www.youtube.com/watch?v=5-9-vWtTcU8

  God fooled the enemies – Time line 00:28:28 – 00:28:45

  Comm said Jesus wasn't put on a cross: Time line 00:28:28 - 00:30:10

  Quran doesn't deny Jesus was on a cross: Time line 00:30:22

- Did Jesus rise from the dead?

  Christian Speaker, Dr. Michael (Mike) Licona and Muslim Speaker, Dr. Shabir Ally

  https://www.youtube.com/watch?v=kgUjaXHyBsw&feature=youtu.behttps%3A%2F%2Fwww.youtube.com%2Fwatch%3Fv%3D5-9-vWtTcU8

  Disciples of Jesus witnessing the crucifixion: Time line 00:47:00.

  Faith (no history) Jesus didn't die on the cross Time line 02:18:00

  God caused Him to die in the tomb: Timeline 00:18:00

BIBLES

- The Holy Bible, King James Version [KJV]

  Copyright © 2002 by Zondervan www.zondervan.com

- The New Strong's Exhaustive Concordance of the Bible

  Copyright © 1995, 1996 by Thomas Nelson Publishers

ISBN 0 7852 1155 1

- *The Interlinear Bible: Hebrew-Greek-English* - Jay P. Green, Sr. - General Editor and Translator – Hendrickson Publishers

    One Volume Edition Copyright © 1976/7/8/9/80/81/84

    Second Edition © 1986 - ISBN 0 913573 25 6

- *The Amplified Bible* - Copyright © 1987 by The Zondervan Corporation and the Lockman Foundation - Published by Zondervan Publishing House http://www.zondervan.com

- *New Living Translation (NLT)* - Tyndale House Publishers, Inc.

    Holy Bible, New Living Translation, copyright © 1996 by Tyndale Charitable Trust - 03 04 05 06 – 5432, 118M / 617M

RECOMMENDED WEBPAGES

- Christian Prince

    https://www.youtube.com/channel/UCRYDyW5rWLgGl1qJCYr5wWQ/feed

    https://www.google.com/search?sxsrf=ALeKk0044UaT_NQUepNRNGgZocf-7-1cLg:1599365522298&source=univ&tbm=isch&q=Christian+Prince:+Muslim+left+Islam+sizzling+debate&sa=X&ved=2ahUKEwjt7cnu1NPrAhW9SRUIHWVLBfQQsAR6BAgKEAE&biw=1280&bih=610

- Dr. David Wood https://www.youtube.com/user/Acts17Apologetics

- Dr. Jay Smith https://www.youtube.com/c/pfanderfilms/videos

- Rob Christian https://www.youtube.com/c/RobChristian/videos

- Answering Islam https://www.answering-islam.org/

- Versions of the Quran http://www.faithbrowser.com/versions-of-the-quran/

- Muslims admit Arabic Quran Versions exist

    https://submission.org/verify_are_all_Arabic_versions_of_Quran_the_same.html

GOD BLESS YOU. EVEN SO, COME LORD JESUS CHRIST!

www.ingramcontent.com/pod-product-compliance
Lightning Source LLC
Chambersburg PA
CBHW080237170426
43192CB00014BA/2473